دوست گرامی خانم آویر

سلامتی و خوشی شما جانی را همیشه
خواستیم - با سلام فراوان

ابوالقاسم خامنه در

July - 5 - 2018

ZARATHUSTRA

MYTH | MESSAGE | HISTORY

ABOLGHASSEM KHAMNEIPUR

 FriesenPress

Suite 300 - 990 Fort St
Victoria, BC, Canada, V8V 3K2
www.friesenpress.com

Copyright © 2015 by Abolghassem Khamneipur
First Edition — 2015

ISBN
978-1-4602-6881-0 (Hardcover)
978-1-4602-6882-7 (Paperback)
978-1-4602-6883-4 (eBook)

1. History / Middle East / Iran

Distributed to the trade by The Ingram Book Company

TABLE OF CONTENTS

For my father, Rahim Khamneipur (1910–1999)
He was a formidable struggler for survival,
and his only enemy was time.

———————————

INTRODUCTION

The life and message of the Prophet Zarathustra are shrouded in the fog of ancient history. The historical Zarathustra is, for the most part, unknown to the general public. What is known of his life and message are topics shared amongst scholars, linguists, and historians whose interest in the man is primarily academic. This book examines the importance of this ancient personality in history as well as various factors that have led to the diminishment of his popularity in the modern era.

According to recent scholarship, *Zarathustra* [in Greek: Zoroaster—from which we get Zoroastrianism] lived between 2000 and 1400 BC. Zarathustra was known to the ancient Greeks; Aristotle, for instance, believed that Zarathustra had been born 6,000 years before Alexander's time. This highlights the fact that, in the time of Aristotle and Plato, Zarathustra as a historical personality was shrouded in ancient mystery. As many events and historical facts were practically unrecordable in the ancient times, the main source of information was limited to oral narratives passed from one generation to the next. Many of these verbal accounts from early antiquity were often distorted. Often the meaning of events would change as each narrator would add, alter, or embellish something to the original story. For this reason, often mythological accounts of real events are unrecognizable as real histories.

Fortunately, we have scriptures and documents that are believed to have been composed by Zarathustra himself, namely the Gathas. The Gathas help us to shed some light into the real events surrounding Zarathustra, including the approximate date of his message and the historical consequences thereof. Furthermore, at a later date, as the *Zoroastrian* [Zarathustrian] Iranian religion became closely connected to the dynasty of the Sassanian rulers and the leadership of the Iranian society—and underwent serious challenges when the Sassanian dynasty fell apart at the invasion of the Arab Muslim conquerors in 640s. This event is believed to have engendered further loss and erasure (at Arab hands) of historical or cultural accounts, especially physical or textual evidence of the ancient religion and its founder. In other words, much of the evidence of Zarathustra's religion, his message, and the data pertaining to his personality were probably lost.

The result was the gradual alteration of the once-dominant Zoroastrian culture and religion, not to mention the memory of the person of Zarathustra in ancient Iran. According to the Roman historian Plutarch, Aristotle supposedly mentioned to the young Alexander, before his invasion of the Achaemenian Empire: "The Persians are one of the two pillars of civilization, if you destroy them, then we will rule the world alone."

Even after the fall of the Sassanian Empire and the subsequent conversion of the Iranian population to the new Islamic religion, not *all* Zoroastrians converted to Islam. After centuries of pressure by the Islamic majority, some communities still continue to adhere to the Zoroastrian religion in Iran; though many left the country between 800 and 1000 AD and emigrated to India, where they settled as farmers in the province of Gujarat. This diasporic Zoroastrian community in India, and a much smaller and ancient community of their coreligionists in Iran, are all that remains of the Zoroastrian civilization of pre-modern times. It is not uncommon for many Zoroastrians today to believe that the most glorious era in the history of Zoroastrianism was the time when their religion was the most dominant within the Iranian society. It was through the Zoroastrian community in India— which came in to contact with the western scholars, specifically the British—that the European historians of the mid-1850s rediscovered this ancient religion and its history, and with this, the personality of its founder, Zarathustra.

In writing this book, my main purpose is not to present a rehash of the existing collection of academic and specialized publications concerning Zoroastrianism, but rather to attempt the difficult task of introducing him to a wider audience. With the exception of those actually belonging to the Zoroastrian faith, only two small groups of people are familiar with events surrounding Zarathustra. The first is the small community of academics, historians and linguists who are occupying themselves professionally with Zarathustra. The second group comprise those well-acquainted with the writing of the German philosopher Friedrich Nietzsche, more specifically his book, *Thus Spoke Zarathustra* [in German: *Also Sprach Zarathustra*], which was published in four parts between 1883 and 1891.

It is understood that Zoroastrianism has influenced many world religions in general, and Judeo-Christianity in particular. It is my contention that beliefs matter, for they are the wellspring of our actions. Even if an individual is a non-believer, they will still be conscious of their actions if they are not in accordance with the mainstream religious traditions of their the society.

It is a simple yet inescapable truth that most works by academic—be they historians, religious scholars or linguists—are aimed at other academics. My goal is to write a comprehensive work intended instead for the general public. It is not the aim of this book to promote religion in general, or Zoroastrianism in particular, but simply to look at some noteworthy events of the past from a historical perspective.

Despite what some people think of as the dawn of an atheistic era in history, religion in one form or another will always have a future with humankind. Atheism was—and will always remain—the domain of a small minority of intellectuals. The question of the existence of God is not connected to our knowledge of the reality in which we live, but the belief in the supernatural is firmly a part of our own psychopathological nature and rooted deep in the human subconsciousness.

I am especially grateful to Professor Ehsan Yarshater from Columbia University, who helped and encouraged me; Mahnaz Moazami Yeshiva University and Parvaneh Pourshariati from Ohio State University; and Dr. Rastin Mehri from Douglas College for his great advice.

ZARATHUSTRA

MYTH | MESSAGE | HISTORY

1. THE HISTORICAL ZARATHUSTRA

In deciding to distinguish between history and Mythology, I prefer Mythology. History is what we were always taught to be the truth, but turned out to be all lies, written later by the winners. But mythology, which they always told us are all lies, at the end turned out to be the truth.

Jean Cocteau (1889–1963)

A myth is going through the fabric of history: Zarathustra, is either portrayed as a *magus* [Wiseman], a great philosopher, or a prophet. Most of the well-known personalities of Western literature have mentioned his name with respect, but they scarcely present any historical context for him. Until recently, no person has offered any detail or explanation about who he really was. It is true that the details of his personal life are shrouded in the mists of ancient history, but to many modern-day Zoroastrians, the clarity of his mind and his teachings are not. Many modern Zoroastrians claim that his teachings mark a new phase in the history of the Western world and that he had started the new consciousness of civility and morality in human history. Georg Wilhelm Friedrich Hegel (1770–1831) the celebrated German philosopher of Enlightenment—and the teacher of Karl Marx—writes about him:

> Zarathustra was like a hinge between the ancient, archaic world of the stone age, later early bronze age, and perhaps the start of human history and civilization itself. We could say reasonably that the events surrounding the humans before him and his time are shrouded in darkness, whereas after him human society has really entered into civilization and recorded history. [...] In Persia first arises that light, which shines itself and illuminates what is around it.... The principle of development begins with the history of Persia, this constitutes therefore the beginning of human history.[1]

Thus, for many, Zarathustra stands at the dawn of human spiritual history as one of its founding figures and great thinkers. He initiated this history with his teaching, which interpreted the history of Being in moralistic terms. To the noted philosophers, the historical Zarathustra is credited with originating the first known moral and ethical religion in human history—where human salvation was dependant only moral behaviour, and not on ritualized sacrifices to the gods.

> Zarathustra is the most important person in the recorded history of religion, bar none, and above all the others. The first man to promulgate a divinely revealed religion. He influenced the religions of Judaism, Christianity, Mithraism, Islam, Northern

Buddhism (Mahayana), Manichaeism and also the Pagan Norse myths of the Nordic World. Over half the world and the western civilization has accepted a significant portion of his teachings under the guise of one or another of the aforementioned faiths.[2]

Before discussing Zarathustra's life and his teachings in more detail, the followings outline may present the core of his message:

- The one creator God Ahura Mazdâ created everything. He represents light, enlightenment, goodness and truth.

- The Wicked Spirit or *Ahriman* is the cosmic source of all evil powers—the equivalent to the Devil—and represents darkness, lies, and falsehood.

- Angels or lesser sacred beings assist the creator God. They include Mithra the deity associated with loyalty, contracts and representing the sun; also Varuna, Anahita and others.

- The sacredness of the three basic natural elements: Water and Earth and Fire. The absolute necessity and the strict instruction to keep these three elements clean and pure at all times, for all future human existence depends on their pureness and health.

- The respect for the world of beneficent animals and the environment at large, for humans and nature are interconnected.

- The immortality of the soul. Every human being has an immortal soul, the spirit or the soul of human beings existed before their birth and will continue to exist after their death. The spirit itself is immortal.

- All humans are born free of sin, i.e., there is no original sin.

- The resurrection [in old Persian: *Frashigird*; in Avestan: *frasho-kereti*] wherein after death, human beings will be resurrected and undergo judgment for their moral or amoral behaviour during their lifetime.

- Heaven and Hell. After death and resurrection, every person will be judged. In the other world they will cross the Chinvat Bridge [in Avestan: *Cinvatô Peretûm*, meaning *Bridge of Judgement*], and if approved they will continue up to Paradise [from Old Persian: pairi daeza, meaning *enclosed garden*]. Otherwise they will fall over the bridge down into hell, or the place of worst existence.

- Every person is responsible for their own moral behaviour. They are free to choose the way they lives in this life.

- The *Saoshyant* [Messiah or Savior] shall appear at the End of Time to save the world from the powers of evil. According to later traditions, the Saoshyant will be born from the seed of Zarathustra himself.

- The Saoshyant will be born to a virgin girl who has bathed in the holy lake of Kansaoya (modern-day Lake Hamoun), wherein Zarathustra's seeds are preserved.

- The final victory of the forces of goodness and light and truth. The coming of the Saoshyant will make the world perfect and immortal. Evil and falsehood will disappear, and Ahura Mazdâ will triumph. At that point the dead will be resurrected, and the world will be restored to its original perfection.

- According to the Zoroastrian belief and tradition, all forms of asceticism (fasting, celibacy, self-mortification and all forms of abstinence) as well as overindulgence are forbidden and regarded as sin. Life, which is regarded as sacred, ought to be lived in full, and any form of abuse of the physical body is highly discouraged.

- Men and women have to cover their heads at all times when in places of worship (such as temples) during religious ceremonies and at religious places, to show their obedience to the almighty creator God.

- The end of time for humankind and the other living species will be the moment when a celestial object will hit the world, at which time rivers of molten metal will flow down the mountains like rivers.

Zarathustra saw in the workings of the world a clear sign that evil is an independent force in and of itself, and that it has to be combatted at all times. The Prophet Zarathustra is traditionally viewed as a human being, and his teachings have been regarded as universal and for all mankind. This differs from prophets of Judeo-Christian and Islamic traditions who were generally connected to, or representing, a certain group of people. They were often associated with a certain tribe or spoke for the interests and requirements of specific people or a certain religious community.

Furthermore, all men who have been called prophets—save for Zarathustra—have claimed that they were in communication, either directly or indirectly (through a vision) with the supernatural with God or with an unexplained deity. Zarathustra, however, never pretended to be in communication with God or to be a messenger of the supernatural. Rather he claimed merely that "good thoughts came to him in his mind" after having wandered in solitude for ten years in the wilderness of nature.

Of course, any kind of communication or contact with the supernatural or divine is viewed as highly subjective, mythological, or irrational by the scientific community. However it is important to distinguish that in the Gathas [holy Zoroastrian scriptures] Zarathustra, never claimed to have had any communication with the supernatural or any direct visitation by a deity.

What Zarathustra suggests is that, while fetching pure water from a lake, he had what he described as an *internal vision*, which perhaps developed like an idea from his own mind and his consciousness. He did not suggest that he had been bestowed with the only true knowledge of the reality of the world. This internal vision had developed in his own mind; as such he *recognized* the realities which he then decided to convey—they weren't shown to him. Some have questioned whether Zarathustra's religion was indeed a monotheistic religion, highlighting its dualistic character as is exemplified by the existence of Ahura Mazdâ (the creator God) vis-à-vis the wholly independent, Ahriman (bad and destructive spirit). It is clear that, for Zarathustra, worship focused only upon Ahura Mazdâ [in Middle Persian: Ohrmazd]. According to Prof. Almut Hintze:

> There is a general agreement among scholars that there is one supreme God in Zoroastrianism, Ahura Mazdâ. From the oldest sources, the Gathas and Yasna Haptanghaiti, to present day religious practice, all worship, both ritual and devotional, is focused on him only. One of the difficulties arises from the fact that the notions monotheism, polytheism and dualism are defined not on the basis of Zoroastrianism but on that of other religions, in particular the Judeo-Christian tradition. Denoting the worship of false gods in contrast to that of the one true God of the Jews and the Christians, the term polytheism has had negative meanings from its

earliest attestations onwards. The expression monotheism was subsequently coined as its antonym to
denote belief in one single god, and is first attested
in 1660 in the writings of the English philosopher
Henry More. In relation only to his own religion
namely Christianity.

Having been defined from the scholarly perspective of the Judeo-Christian faith since the period of
the enlightenment, the two terms came to constitute a dichotomy of mutually exclusive opposites.
Consequently monotheism was claimed as the label
of the Judeo-Christian tradition only, and endowed
with greater prestige than the polytheism attributed
to non-Judeo-Christian religions.[3]

Clearly, the word Monotheism here refers to the religion articu-
lated within the Judeo-Christian faiths, rather than a categorization
of religions in a broader sense. As in the Hebraic and the Christian
holy books, the notion of Light is of particular importance in the
Zoroastrian ideology. Professor Jenny Rose from Claremont
Graduate University in California writes:

Physical fire is an emblem of the "endless Light"
that are the visible manifestation of "Ahura
Mazdâ" and of which the sun is the most beautiful (YH 36.6).... The notion of Ahura Mazdâ is
a combination of both physical light and concep-
tual order (order and or truth).... Porphyry, the
Neoplatonist philosopher of the third century AD
wrote that Pythagoras had learned from the Magi
(Zoroastrian priests) that God himself, whom they
call Oromazes (Ahura Mazdâ), resembles light with

{ 7 }

regard to his body, and truth with regard to his soul. (Life of Pythagoras 41)[4]

Furthermore, we can see here that the worldview of Zarathustra—who deals with the fate of mankind in this world and the next—has a finite scope in terms of time. Time will end for humanity and all other living things at a certain point, which is the end of time.

Also an integral part of the ideology and the doctrine of Zoroastrianism is the concept of nature as a whole, which, apart from all the living species as humans and animals, includes the elements such as water, earth and fire, forming one unity. Throughout their existence, both humans and animals have souls, and furthermore, humankind is responsible for the well-being of animals. As for example in the prayer "Geush Urvana", whose author is believed to be Zarathustra himself, the soul of the animal speaks to the creator Ahura Mazdâ, saying:

> To you immortals, the soul of the animal lamented
> For whom did you create me, who made me?
> The cruelty of fury and violence, of wantonness and
> brutality [of men], holds me in bondage.
> I have no other pastor but you.
> Where are Truth [asha] and Good Thought [vohu
> manah] and their Rule.
> Let them come to me now
> Acknowledge me now, O Mazdâ,
> as fit for the great Task.[5]

Additionally, the explicit requirements of his teachings are to keep the primal elements of this world, namely water and the earth clean and unpolluted at all times. According to Zarathustra, the ultimate fate of humankind will depend on the health of the environment, as both the humans and the environment are connected to each other as one unit. One of the great sins is to pollute the environment.

The end of time has been projected, according to the Zoroastrian worldview, as an event comparable to a galactic catastrophe of cataclysmic proportions. Similar to a natural-geological catastrophe, he speaks in the Gathas of "rivers of molten metal will flow down the mountains ..." There are no Horseman who spread pestilence, but his apocalyptic view of the end of the world for both human and animal-kind is seen more as a natural and physical and possibly cataclysmic catastrophe on this planet. More details about these points in following chapters. Furthermore, Zarathustra envisages a universal worldview for all humans and their final destiny, irrespective of where and when they live.

Those personalities known to us, from the various religious scriptures, as prophets often highlight historical events. This is exemplified in chapters of the Old Testament, which refer to the Achaemenid Empire, the Egyptian Pharaonic world, the Babylonian Empire, the Greek civilization, the Roman Empire, and finally the events highlighted in Koranic passages pertaining to the Islam. These prophets were only answering to the great historical events which had happened before or during their time. These prophets' actions and statements were all a reaction to historical events unfolding in their lifetime. They were personally involved in those historical realities, and they could look back at past important historical events, such as empire forming and fading away and so on.

In the case of Zarathustra, it is different, for he lived in a pastoral environment with an oral but non-literary environment and during a time that bordered on pre-history. No important historical events on which Zarathustra could look back were recorded from the time before he lived. Based on the proclamations in his Gathas, it can be construed that his environment was a small and simple community somewhere in the steppes of south-central Asia, reliant on herding of domesticated animals as pastoralists. His vision and his teachings are not a reaction to past or present historical events from his perspective, but purely based on reasonable and logical thinking.

{ 9 }

As already suggested Zarathustra's life and times bordered on prehistory, for he lived, according to the latest academic estimation, between 2000 and 1400 BC and therefore could not look back at important historical events as later literary cultures could. We should not forget that Aristotle and Plato estimated him to have lived 6,000 years before their time, which would put him approximately 8,500 years before our time.

His teachings can be said to reflect the nature of the workings of this world from a purely philosophical–ethical point of view. He perceives the life of humans ruled by goodness and ethical behaviour in a constant battle against the forces of evil, falsehood and darkness. His vision for humankind and religious teachings are still being used today by all monotheistic religions of the world, without them having added any new component to it. Zarathustra is not a prophet in the traditional Judeo-Christian sense, but rather a man whom the prophets themselves have imitated. He was, in that sense, the Prophet of the Prophets—indeed, if ever a human lived who might qualify as divine, then surely it was Zarathustra.

Here we are citing a short passage from one of Zarathustra's prayers, namely the Ahunavaiti Gatha:

> Hear with your ears the Best, look upon it with clear thought. When deciding between the two beliefs, each for himself before the great consummation, think that it be accomplished to our pleasure.

> The two primal Spirits, who reveal themselves in vision as twins, are the Better and the Bad, the Right and Wrong, in Thought and in Word and in Action. And between these two the wise choose the right the foolish not so.

> In the beginning, when those two Spirits came together, they created Life and Not Life, and at the

end, the followers of the Lie and the Wrong shall inherit the Worst Existence, but Best Existence shall be for those who follow the right.

Of the two Spirits, he that followed the Lie chose the Worst. The Holier Spirit, he that clothes himself with the massy heavens as with a garment, chose the Right. So should do likewise they that would please Lord Mazdâ by beautiful action.

The Daivas also chose wrongly between the two. Infatuation came upon them as they took counsel together, so that they chose Worst Thoughts. Then together they rushed to Violence that they might weaken the world of man.

If, O mortals, you shall abide diligently unto those commandments which Ahura Mazdâ has commanded you, of happiness and pain, long punishment for the followers of the lie, darkness and falsehood, and blessings for the followers of the right truth and light, then hereafter all shall be well.[6]

1.1 A BRIEF LOOK AT THE HISTORY OF ANCIENT IRAN

Before we can enter into any kind of discussion of Zarathustra's life, time, and influence on Middle Eastern history in general—and monotheism in particular—it will be necessary to give a short introduction into the history of greater Iran up until the time of the Islamic conquest and the emergence of Zoroastrianism as a world religion in 644 AD.

Modern Iran is not a political entity whose existence sprung from the calculation and oil-based strategies of world powers. Nor is it the result of the long-term planning and obscure political machinations of colonial powers such as the British Empire. Nor were its borders artificially construed and then drafted upon a map of the Middle East after the First World War as is the case with other countries in the region.

The Iranians were one branch of the extended Indo-European family of peoples who moved out of what is today the central Russian steppes and settled in Europe, Iran and northern India, in a series of invasions and migrations circa 2500–2000 BC. The name Iran itself means the land of the Aryans. This explains the close relationship between the Persian language and some of the main European languages of antiquity and today. Languages like Latin, old German, and even English—being itself a mixture of German, Latin and other tongues. The Indian language- Sanskrit too [Indian liturgical language of Hinduism] is also directly related to that ancient language of the Indo-Europeans. We can trace many familiar words roots through these languages.

For instance the English word *daughter* relates to the Persian *dochtar* and the German *tochter*. Likewise, *father* relates the Persian *pedar*, the German *vater*, and Latin *pater*. *Mother*, in Persian, is *mader* and in German *mutter*. In French we have the verb *mourir* [to die], which shares roots with the Persian *mordan* and the Latin *mortuus*. A *kiss* in English shares roots with *buss* in Persian and *kuss* in German. The root of *door* informs the German *tur* and the Persian *dar*. Indeed even the word *name* in Persian is *nam* and in Latin is *nomen*.

Consider the Persian feminine name Turandocht. *Turan*, in Persian, means *people of the east* [i.e., China] while *docht* stems from the contraction of *dochtar* [daughter]. Therefore Turandocht (a popular woman's name in Iran) means *daughter of the east*; the European form, as exemplified in Pucci's opera of that name is Turandot.

There is also one special word about which we will speak in more detail later; in Latin it is *Deus*, in French *Dieu*, in Persian *Dives,* in

Sanskrit *Dives*. It is a word that means *God*, and in English, of course, it forms the root of the word divine.

This word shows—as so many other do—that the Iranian people and the Persian language has no connection to any Semitic race or language. All Arabic words that have entered Persian can be dated back to the Islamic intrusion into Persia, circa 700 AD and onwards.

Long before the Aryan-speaking migrants arrived from the north into the Iranian plateau, there were other people who had settled and were living in that area. Indeed humans have dwelt there as early as 100,000 BC, in what historians call the Old Stone Age. There is evidence that by approximately 5000 BC agricultural settlements were flourishing west of the Zagros Mountains, in what would later called the Sumerian and the Mesopotamian civilizations. Interestingly, excavations in that region, in a settlement called Hajji Firouz Tappeh, has unearthed the remains of the world's first known wine jar, complete with traces of wine, and remains of various resins used for the flavouring and preservation of wine. Before and during the period of the Aryan–Iranian migration, the Empire of Elam flourished in that area—which later was called the provinces of Khuzestan and Fars in southern Iran, with the cities of Susa and Anshan. The Elamite people spoke a language not related to either Mesopotamian or ancient Iranian, and transmitted both their heritage and culture to later Iranian ruling dynasties. South of the modern-day city of Kashan, in a place called Tepe Sialk, a vast ziggurat[7] has been discovered, once part of an ancient Elamite settlement dated to circa 3000–2900 BC.

The Persians of greater Iran, descendants of the Aryan tribes who populated the country from the north—as opposed to the Arabic-speaking population of the Middle East, who were of Semitic descent—represented an ancient civilization and a political and military power that existed from the beginnings of history itself, and it remained so until at least 644 AD, when the Islamists conquered the Sassanian Empire, one of the main players in the arena of world history. The greater Roman Empire—and later East Rome or the

Byzantine Empire—had from its beginnings until the fall of the Sassanians in 644 AD, only one real major rival and formidable enemy, namely the Persians.

The Roman Empire, whose power and influence extended almost to the furthest reaches of the known Roman world, had to share that world with the Persian Empire in a rivalry that lasted several centuries. The only western power, who succeeded in invading Persia, was not Rome, but the Macedonian Alexander, who in a weak moment of the Achaemenid rulers, entered the Empire from the west in 328 BC. It was Alexander, it is believed, who ordered the original scriptures of the Gathas—written on cow skin and kept in a secure fortification in the city of Estakhre Babakan—to be burned. According to historians, the Gathas are the most sacred scriptures in the Zoroastrian faith, and believed to have been written by Zarathustra himself.

The history of Iran begins with the Proto-Elamite people of circa 3200 BC. It was much later that a new ruling family of leaders emerged from the tribe of the Parthians, with the first emergence of a smaller local ruler named Achaemenes [in Persian: Hakhamanesh] who established the ruling house of the Achaemenid Dynasty. The rule of the Achaemenid Dynasty started circa 700 BC with Achaemenes, a minor local ruler in a small kingdom called the Kingdom of Anshan in southwestern Iran and ended with the conquest of greater Persia by Alexander of Macedonia in the year 330 BC.[8] Alexander of Macedonia, after having defeated Darius III, the last Achaemenid ruler in 330 BC, burned down the Persian capital Persepolis and gave orders to destroy and to burn the Avestan records and the ancient Zoroastrian holy scriptures. These were kept in a Tower in the Fortification of the city of Estakhre Babakan, which was in antiquity a military garrison city in western Iran, this city does no longer exists. This fact has been also reported among others by a Zoroastrian priest by the name of Arda Wiraz.

It is known by historians that, during the Achaemenid Dynasty—and probably throughout the Iranian history—slavery was forbidden by law. Persia was the only great empire of antiquity, where no records of slavery have been recorded in its entire history. Furthermore, total religious freedom was used as an political strategy to unite people of different races and religions, who lived under the rule of the greater Persian empire.

It is significant to mention here that, at no time in the Iranian history, did any king, emperor or ruler pretend or declare themselves to be of divine origin, or to be related to divinities as in ancient Greece and Egypt. Nor did any Persian ruler ever elevated himself or any other person so as to become *deified* as the roman Emperors. After the downfall of the Achaemenian Dynasty in the year 334 BC, a new group of rulers came to power in the country. They established the Parthian Empire, also known as the Arsacid Empire, which lasted from 227 BC until 224 AD. It was in this period that a fierce rivalry and hostilities was recorded in history between the Parthians and the Republican (and the later Imperial) Rome.

The Arsacid [in Persian: Ashkanian] empire fell when the forces of king Arthabanus IV were defeated in battle on April 28, 224 AD, by Ardeshir I of the house of Sassan. Here the new Sassanian Dynasty started their rule of the Empire, which they called Eranshahr (or Iranshahr). The first Sassanian King being Ardeshir I [in Greek: Artaxerxes I], who was from the city of Estakhre in the province of Fars, started his rule in the year 224 AD. The rule of the Sassanian Dynasty ended tragically 644 AD during the reign of Yazdegerd III with the final Arabic–Islamic victory in the Battle of Qadisiyah. Yazdegerd III, the twenty-ninth and final Sassanian King, was the grandson of Khosrow II [in Persian: Khosrow Parviz] and died tragically in 651 AD in the city of Merv. The end of the Sassanian rule over Iran, in 644 AD, marked the end of Zoroastrian religion (and culture) as the national religion of the Iranian people.

It was in the time of the Sassanian Iran that woman could also become rulers of the nation and ruled as Queens. In the Zoroastrian ideology, men and women were considered equal and had the same rights. There was Queen Pourandokht and later Queen Azarmidokht, who ruled the nation, and according to historians, were capable rulers of great integrity. Furthermore, the famous Roman chronicler and historian Plutarch reports that, during the Parthian period of the Iranian history, woman were also fighting as soldiers in the army, some Greek amphoras show pictures of Persian woman as soldiers.

1.2 AHURA MAZDÂ AND THE ROCK INSCRIPTIONS IN ANCIENT IRAN

Before entering into the details of the Zoroastrian religion, and the life of the Prophet himself, it is necessary to mention here some historical context of Ahura Mazdâ, the god whom Zarathustra introduced to mankind.

Looking at the Iranian history, we have the kings of the Achaemenid Dynasty, who ruled the greater Iranian plateau, and were one of the great historical players of the Middle East and the eastern Mediterranean in antiquity. The last king of the Achaemenid Dynasty was Darius III, who was defeated by Alexander of Macedonia, after he invaded Persia in 334 BC. Among the achievements of the Achaemenid Kings, who ruled greater Persia from 550–330 BC, are the invasion and conquest of the Babylonian Empire and the liberation of the Israelites, who previously had been imprisoned and deported to Babylon by their king Nebuchadnezzar.

It was, in antiquity, a tradition for great rulers to glorify their achievements in stone, for no other solid and reliable long term means of communications to future generations existed. We know that Egyptian rulers have glorified themselves and entered history by leaving behind various statues, obelisks and palaces with inscriptions, all in stone. The Persian kings, however, believed in monuments and inscriptions carved in the stone cliffs of steep and inaccessible mountains. This tradition, started by some local Iranian rulers in antiquity, and was adapted by the kings of the Achaemenid Dynasty and then continued later by the Sassanian kings from 224 AD until the Islamic conquest of Iran in the year 644 AD.

Thus we have carvings on mountain rocks and inscriptions as historical documentation from as far back as 521 BC. Over eleven hundred years of stone carvings, bearing witness to the veneration of Ahura Mazdâ, by the kings and rulers—Ahura Mazdâ the supreme creator God, introduced to mankind by the Prophet Zarathustra. What is surprising, however, (and a great puzzle for historians) is that none of these records so carefully set in stone contain the name of the Prophet Zarathustra himself.

One of the important of these sites is the monumental relief carvings on the rocks of Mount Bisotun in western Iran. The Bisotun Inscription was done on the orders of the King Darius I of the Achaemenid Dynasty, who ruled the Persian empire from 522 BC until his death 486 BC. King Darius [in Old Persian: Darayavaush] extended the borders of the empire in the west to Thracia and Macedonia (west of the Istanbul of today) and in the east to the Indus river. The Persian Empire reached, under Darius I, its maximum extent. He was succeeded by his son Xerxes.

The Bisotun monument features the image of the king himself, surrounded by a great trilingual inscription set in the mountain rock. Because it is written in Old Persian, Elamite, and Babylonian, this inscription is regarded by historians to be the most important document of the entire ancient near east, and an important key to the understanding of its languages. The Middle Eastern equivalent of the Rosetta stone, the Bisotun Inscription made it possible to decipher cuneiform writing, and thus open the door to previous totally unknown historical details of ancient civilizations.

Perhaps most remarkable is the fact that, after the monument completion, King Darius gave orders for the stairway leading to the monument to be demolished and the path to the cliff to be destroyed. In so doing he cut off any access to the monument itself, which remained undisturbed for over 2,500 years. Work on the Bisotun relief carvings started, according to historians, on the December 28, 521 BC. This monument and the inscriptions were known in antiquity and have been mentioned by several chroniclers—the Greek historian Ctesias of Cnidus, who noted its existence some time around 400 BC, believed it to be dedicated by Queen Semiramis of Babylon to the god Zeus. Furthermore, Tacitus, the Roman chronicler and the Greek historian Diodorus both mention it, believing it to be an inscription made by Semiramis and calling it Bagistanon.

In 1598 the Englishman Robert Shirley saw the monument during his travels to Persia—he and his brother Sir Anthony Shirley were on a diplomatic and military mission on behalf of the Austrian Habsburg emperor, to reinforce the Persian military with artillery and cannons, in order to engage the Ottoman empire on their eastern borders. It was Shirley who brought the monument to the attention of western European scholars though he incorrectly attributed the inscriptions to be of Christian origin.

Coming to the content of the inscriptions, Darius I declares, in some detail, all his deeds as King of Kings and counts the battles he fought. We will mention here just those lines, which contains the name Ahura Mazdâ. What is of greatest importance here is the fact that as much as Ahura Mazdâ is recognized here as the supreme creator god and venerated, there is no mention of the prophet who first recognized him—Zarathustra—anywhere in the rock inscriptions.

Carved into Mount Bisotun, we see the image of King Darius, with his right hand raised to the great god Ahura Mazdâ, and the inscriptions say:

> I am Darius, the great King, King of Kings, the King
> of Persia, the King of countries, the son of Hystaspes,
> the grandson of Arsames, the Achaemenid. [...]

> King Darius says, by the grace of Ahura Mazdâ I am
> King; Ahura Mazdâ has granted me this kingdom....[9]

Furthermore, we have a monumental inscription ordered by King Darius for his own mausoleum at Naqsh-e Rustam, not far from the modern-day city of Shiraz. The double inscription carved in the rock on his tomb reads as follows:

> A great God is Ahura Mazdâ, who created this earth, who created yonder sky, who created man, who created happiness for man, who made Darius King, one king of many, one lord over many.

> I am king Darius, the great king of kings, king of countries containing all kinds of man, king in this great earth far and wide, son of Hystaspes, an Achaemenid, a Persian, an Aryan and having Aryan lineage.

> King Darius says, by the favour of Ahura Mazdâ, these are the countries which I seized outside of Persia, I ruled over them, they bore tribute to me and they did what was said to them by me, my laws was held firmly....

> King Darius says, Ahura Mazdâ, when he saw this earth in commotion, he thereafter bestowed it upon me.... By the favour of Ahura Mazdâ I put it down in its place.... Darius the King says.... May Ahura Mazdâ protect me from harm, and my royal house, and this land, this I pray to Ahura Mazdâ, this may Ahura Mazdâ give to me. O man, this which is the command of Ahura Mazdâ, let this not seem

repugnant to you, do not leave the right path, do not rise in rebellion. A great god is Ahura Mazdâ, who created this excellent thing which is seen, who created happiness for man....

King Darius says, For this reason Ahura Mazdâ bore me aid, ...because I was not disloyal, I was not a Follower of the Lie†, I did not do wrong, neither I nor my family. I walked in justice, neither to the weak nor to the mighty did I do wrong... You who shall be king hereafter, remember the man who follows the Lie, or who shall do wrong, be not a friend of them, but punish them.

---

† *Follower of the Lie* [*drauga*, from Avestan word for lie *Drugh*]

Furthermore, later King Artaxerxes III (358–338 BC) of the same dynasty, has in his inscriptions in the palace of Persepolis:

Says Artaxerxes the King, This stone staircase was built by me in time... May Ahura Mazdâ and Mithra protect this country, and what has been built by me...[10]

After having considered the above, it is still a matter of discussion between historians, to which extent the rulers of the Achaemenid dynasty were committed Zoroastrians, or if other gods were also worshipped next to Ahura Mazdâ by the general population of the Empire.

1.3 ZARATHUSTRA—HIS LIFE IN HISTORY AND LEGEND

Before entering into the details of the life and times of the Prophet who founded the Zoroastrian religion, we have to investigate his proper name. The name Zarathustra is, according to latest linguists, such as Prof. Almut Hintze, the correct name of Zoroaster, the founder of Zoroastrianism and the writer of the Zoroastrian scriptures, the Avesta. It is worth noting at this point that Nietzsche's *Thus Spoke Zarathustra* has in reality nothing to do with the real prophet Zarathustra—Nietzsche has just used the Prophet's name for the propagation of his own philosophical agenda.

The name Zoroaster is derived from the writings of the Greek chronicler Xanthus of Lydia,[11] who-lived mid fifth century BC and that name was taken up later by Plato (429–347 BC).[12] It was Xanthus of Lydia, who introduced Zarathustra to the Greek cultural world, and he accorded him great respect, calling him "the greatest religious legislator of ancient times," without however going into the details of his teachings. The influence of Xanthus of Lydia has shaped the views of philosophers from Pythagoras to Plato. From the Greek cultural world, the name *Zoroaster* enters the western culture in various forms, such as Sarastro[13] Zoroastris, Zaratos, Zoroastres and others.

In the old Greek Alphabet there is no Sh sound but only S; therefore, the Sh sound from the name of ZarathuSHtra was omitted in Greek. Take for instance the Greek historian Diodorus Siculus, who lived in the first century BC, during the reign of the Emperor Augustus. Diodorus Siculus[14] uses the name *Zathraustes*—a name closer to the original name of the Prophet Zarathustra, than Zoroastres. Diodorus Siculus states in his work that Zarathustra was an Aryan, and a native of east Iran. As most Greek chronicles writings has been taken over by the western European culture, the name Zoroaster has entered the European, and with that in the English vocabulary.

A tradition preserved in a few late sources—no later than second or third century AD—set Zarathustra's date of death at 228 years before Alexander, meaning in the sixth century BC, but this dating has been now rejected. Present day historians and linguists believe that he lived actually during the Aryan–Iranian pastoral period on the central Asian steppes (2000–1400 BC), shortly after the Aryan tribes moved south into the land known as Iran. This dating evidence comes solely from the short poetic works composed by him,[15] and preserved in a liturgy of the daily Zoroastrian act of worship, within the Yasna.

Al that can be reliably known of Zarathustra as a person is to be derived from these hymns. They show him to have been the founder of the old Iranian religion, the initiator of its beliefs and rituals, but also a prophet. He was the one who saw God in his internal vision and believed that, by preaching what he had thus apprehended, he could lead man to salvation and help to redeem the world from evil. Most remarkably, and to his great credit, Zarathustra never claimed to be a prophet. He never pretended to be a man sent by God or one chosen to heal the world. He never claimed divine origin or even any direct communication or special connection with God. Of fundamental importance here is the fact that he actually never pretended or declared that there was any connection between him as a human and the supernatural.

According to historical belief, he was a priest in his community, a priest of the deities who were worshipped before his time (pre-Zoroastrian deities). He claims that, one day when he was drawing water for a religious ceremony, he had in his mind an internal vision. According to him "good thoughts [humanah] appeared to him." This is not presented as an apparition or communication *sent* by the supernatural, merely visions from within the boundaries of his own mind. After these good thoughts appeared to him, he abruptly ended all matters with which he was occupied and left his community, opting for the solitude of the nature—the mountains and the woods—for reflection. After having lived for ten solitary years in remote areas of nature thinking and reflecting, he returned and faced humankind to declare and proclaim his teachings, teachings which he refused to attribute to supernatural agency of any kind. What he taught, instead, came to him through solitary reflection, his mind recognizing the true nature of things. This recognition is what he was presenting to humankind for their further consideration.

Zarathustra appears as a man of powerful intellect who founded a remarkably logical and coherent theology. He failed, nevertheless, to win a hearing from his own people.[16] Rejected by them and impoverished, he eventually had to leave them.[17] Eventually in his wanderings he reached another Iranian community, which according to the newest historical estimations, was living probably in the immediate north of the city of Marv of today. The king of this community was Kavi Vishtaspa [*Vishtaspa* in Persian: *Goshtasp* or man who has many horses]. He was impressed by Zarathustra's teachings, and accepted his religion.[18] In reality it is his wife, Queen Anahita, who first believed in Zarathustra, and who later persuaded the king to follow. In the beginning Zarathustra was imprisoned by order of the king and was subjected to harsh treatment, but did not lament his fate. Later the king accepted him, and after having settled at his court, Zarathustra saw his religion established, and some Yashts were composed during this period. Mary Boyce in this regard:

> Zoroaster's is the first individual voice to be heard out of the great family of Indo-European people, and his community deserves both gratitude, and respect for the faithful preservation of his words, which without aids of writing, from so long ago. Yet because his voice is a solitary one, speaking from the remote past, and because his utterances are in an otherwise unknown stage of a long dead language, much obscurity invests them.

> Where he does turn to address his hearers, urgently,
> it is not to teach them the elements of his beliefs,
> but to exhort them to act according to those beliefs,
> which the implication must be that they have already
> heard from him, expounded doubtless in good,
> plain, orations.[19]

The legend of the Prophet's life, although almost entirely hagiographical, probably contains some factual matter, such as his father's name, and his relatively long life—he is said to have died at the age of seventy-seven. According to the legend, Zarathustra had three wives, three son, and three daughters—a suspect symmetry, since three is the holy number in Zoroastrianism. According to the Zoroastrian rule and tradition, priests [in Greek: magi, singular magus] are required to be married; therefore, in Yasna 53 he speaks of his youngest daughter, Pouruchista.

It has been said by ancient sources that Zarathustra was laughing at his birth and that later in his childhood and youth he was a wanderer and seeker of truth. Zarathustra's spirit receives profound veneration, and his name is constantly invoked by his believers, who regard him, to this day, as the greatest of the holy men. Historians now place Zarathustra as a likely contemporary to Odysseus and King Agamemnon in the mid to late bronze age. Aristotle in the first book of his work *On Philosophy* says that the Magi are more ancient than even the ancient Egyptians and that, according to them, there are two first principles, the good spirit and the evil spirit, one called Zeus or Oromasdes the other Hades or Areimanus.[20]

Furthermore, Aristotle says of Zoroaster (Zarathustra) that he lived 6,000 years before Aristotle's own time, and that he was even greater than his teacher Plato. Aristotle, who himself was the teacher of Alexander the Macedonian, died in 322 BC. From this statement, we can see that the Greek philosophers and intellectuals knew about the Zoroastrian religion and its founder Zarathustra, but for whatever reason, they estimated the lifetime of the prophet to be set in the remote archaic period. We have to consider that, in a time when record-keeping was strongly limited—we are speaking mainly of the area of north Kwarazmia and the central Asian steppes—and consisted effectively only in writing on clay or stone or ox skin, the dimensions of time can be distorted or exaggerated.

Plutarch (46–120 AD), the Roman historian of Greek descent, was also a witness to Zarathustra. He lived during the time of the beginnings of Christianity, and he mentions these records, which presumably stood in relation to orthodox Zoroastrian observances—as did for, example a, black mass to accepted Christian rites. Plutarch writes:

> …this is the view of the majority and of the wisest, for some believe that there are two gods, and that they are rivals, as it were in art, the one being the creator of good, and the other of evil, others call the better of these a god and his rival a Daemon, as for example, Zoroaster the Magian, who lived, so they record, five thousand years before the siege of Troy. He used to call the one god Oromasdes and the other Areimanus, and showed also that the former was especially akin, among objects of perception, to the light, and the later on the contrary to darkness and ignorance, while in between the two was, Mithras, and this is why the Persians call Mithras the Mediator.[21]

Furthermore, the Greek historian and chronicler Theopompus, who lived 380 BC, in citing the writings of Plato, says,

> … And even Plato brings back Areimanus in bodily form from the Hades into the land of the living, as Zoroaster prophesies that some day there will be a resurrection of all the death.[22]

Theopompus knew of Zarathustra, and was himself the source of information concerning it for the other writers. Mary Boyce, one of the leading authorities on Zoroastrianism, in her book *Zoroastrianism: Its Antiquity and Constant Vigour* writes concerning the return of Zarathustra to this world as a saviour [Saoshyant, a messiah in modern-day] but also concerning the presumed geographic location of the Prophet's life:

> In the Young Avesta a truly Zoroastrian association with an identifiable place is that of the Myth of the future Word Saviour, the Saoshyant, with Sistan. This is attested in Yasht 19, which is largely devoted to the celebration of the khvarenah the fortune or grace send down on the chosen or the just mortals from on high. In one of its verses it is declared that khvarenah will accompany the victorious Saoshyant "... when he comes forth from the Kansaoya waters..." Yasht 19:91.2. This is clearly an allusion to the belief that the seed of the Prophet is miraculously preserved in the depths of a lake, and that one day a virgin, bathing there, will conceive his son, the Saviour (Saoshyant). Another verse in the same Yasht says that the "fortune of the kavis (kavam khvarenah) accompanies him who rules there where is the lake Kansaoya which receives the Haetumant." The Haetumant is the modern Helmand river, therefore this identifies Kansaoya as the modern Hamoun lake, into which that river flows.... In the verse which follows, eight other rivers from the same region are named, showing that this area (ancient Arachosia–Drangiana) played an important part in the transmission of Yasht 19... There is no suggestion in Yasht 19, or anywhere else

in the Avesta that Zoroaster himself lived in Sistan, or that this was the homeland of the kavis.... but that the prophet's homeland lay further away to the north..."[23]

Another place that has always been associated with the Zoroastrian faith is the ancient city of Ragha (modern-day Rey south of Teheran) This city, which existed from pre Achaemenid times, was also mention in Yasht 19 as follows:

Thus with all lands but Zoroastrian Ragha, in Zoroastrian Ragha there are only four masters. Who are this four masters? He of House, clan, tribe and fourth Zarathustra.

Historians believe that other cities may have existed with the same name in north-eastern Iran, and the Yasht 19 may have mentioned that other city or settlement, which does not exists any more today.[24] The meaning of this can only be that Ragha was, at some time, an autonomous holy city, ruled by Zoroastrian chief priest equivalent to a prince or bishop's rule of cities in medieval Europe. Robert Charles Zaehner was even of the opinion that Ragha was indeed the birthplace of the prophet himself:

Ultimately he found refuge with King Vishtaspa who was, according to Henning, the last paramount chief of a Chorasmian confederation finally overthrown by Cyrus. The only place in the Avesta, which is brought into connection with Zoroaster is Ragha, (the classical Rhages and modern Shahre Rey close to Teheran) which is described as Zoroastrian. It is then rather more than possible that Zoroaster was a native of Rhages in Media, and that he fled from

there to Chorasmia, where he finally found a patron
in king Vishtaspa.[25]

This theory has since been rejected. The interpretation of Ragha
being a centre of Zoroastrianism, and eventually being ruled by the
Chief Magus [or Mobedan Mobed in modern terms] receives some
credibility as this city remained an important centre of Zoroastrianism
until the beginning of the Islamic conquest and still has several famous
shrines of Zoroastrian origin, which date back before the Achaemenid
Dynasty, meaning before 750 BC. Later, after the time of Alexander the
Great, when one of his generals, Seleucus, had established himself as
the new ruler of Iran (circa 305 BC), the city of Rhages was renamed
Europos by the Greeks, and it was at this period of history that Rhages
was the administrative centre and the de facto capital of Persia.

Later again, the name Rhages was reinstated, and the city became
an important trading and strategic military centre for later rulers.
With its central position as the most important Median town, Rhages
attracted travellers from the eastern part of ancient Iran. It is known
that, before the conquest of Alexander, Rhages was governed by
a Median Satrap by the name of Atropates who, after Alexander's
conquest of the city, left with his troops for the north-west part
of the country, which was later called Lesser Media and again later
Atropatakan [the land of Atropates, modern-day Azerbaijan]. Because
Alexander never managed to take Atropatakan, Atropates was able
to keep his independence from the Macedonian unbelievers, and he
and his family clan ruled Atropatakan for centuries in a dynastic way
under Zoroastrian rule.

Ferdowsi's *Shahnameh* and the majority of the Muslim historians
accepted the city of Balkh to be Zarathustra's true birthplace, but not
so, Mary Boyce:

> ...none of this can reasonably to be held to go back
> to the time before the Macedonian conquest... It is

thus possible to turn back to the Avesta and to conclude from it that the one genuine Zoroastrian tradition about the homeland of the Prophet, Airyana Vaejah, was that, this lay outside the settled Iranian lands, some where more to the north.[26]

As for the date of Zarathustra's life time, according to Boyce:

...on the basis of linguistic comparison with the Rigveda, (the holy scriptures of Hinduism) the first Western scholar to identify the Gathas as Zoroaster's own words, held that the prophet could not have lived later than, 1000 BC, but various recent estimates followed setting him to have lived between 1000–1700 BC.[27]

Furthermore, the Gathas, with their two brief Mantras and the short Worship of the seven chapters Yasna Haptanghaiti, yield some significant indication about the society in which the prophet really lived.

This (community) appears to have considered itself to be ethnically homogenous. There is no reference to *alien people* [anairya]. The new proper names are all Iranian in character, and despite some religious divergences, worship and cult appear to have had a common basis. There is a firm social order, repeatedly referred to, whose units are the *family* [khvaetu], settlement and the *clan* [Airiyaman], and the land being claimed by the clan as its own being called Dahyu…. there are recurrent references to *power* [khshathra] exerted presumably in varying degrees by the head of each of these groups, and a

special term for those who wielded power on a larger
scale. One is *sastar* [commander]. This occurs in the
plural in the phrase "commanders of the land" and so
it is likely to be used for petty chieftains. In contrast
a reference to those who are bad rulers of the lands
(dushk sathrah) suggests that each clan or Dahyu
had his own ruler, one man in supreme authority...[28]

The controversy over what appear to have been Zarathustra's
extraordinary contribution to monotheism, and to religious
thought, in general, is largely due to the deficiencies in its written
sources. The first western chronicler to refer to Zarathustra as "the
only prophet arising from the Aryan race" (all the other mythological prophets were of the Semitic race) was the influential Austrian
Philosopher and writer Rudolf Steiner. A controversial personality
from the beginning, Rudolf Steiner (1861–1925) was a friend of the
Nietzsche family.

In 1896 Friedrich Nietzsche's sister, Elisabeth Forster-Nietzsche,
asked Steiner to organize the Nietzsche Archives in Naumburg. Her
brother by that time was in a "state of mental darkness" which is to
say *non compos mentis* [in German: unzurechnungsfaehig]. Elisabeth
Forster-Nietzsche introduced Steiner into the presence of her brother,
the catatonic Philosopher. Steiner was deeply moved and subsequently wrote the book *Friedrich Nietzsche: Fighter for Freedom*, and
it was later, through this relationship, that Rudolf Steiner was introduced probably into the knowledge of Zarathustra and his teachings.[29]

In a famous lecture entitled "Zarathustra" given in Berlin on
January 19, 1911, Rudolf Steiner probably mistakenly, tried to introduce Zarathustra to the western public, in mentioning him in his
lecture to be "the only Prophet arising from the Aryan race... who
started world civilization... a personality, who is still an enigma for
the historical science [in German: geschichtsforschung]."[30] He puts
Zarathustra's lifetime to be 8,500 years before his time. This was

due to his acceptance of Aristotle's and Plato's beliefs that Zoroaster had lived 6,000 years before their time—or 5,500 years before the Trojan war.

At a later date, as an enemy of the right wing political currents in Germany, Steiner warned against Adolf Hitler, and predicted that he would lead Germany into the catastrophe. The Nazis immediately branded him as a Jewish traitor—which was not true, as Steiner was not Jewish—and he died subsequently under mysterious circumstances in 1925.

Concerning the place of the prophet's birth and life, there are some geographical names mentioned in the Avesta. According to Professor Prods Oktor Skjaervo, from Harvard University:

> Seeking for the origin of the Iranians, that is, the peoples who spoke Iranian languages, there are two two mutually supporting approaches. One is the archeological approach, which consists in trying to identify Iranian-speaking peoples with archeological sites and remains, a second is the linguistic approach, by which the point of origin of the oldest Iranian literature and language is sought, and the third is the literary approach. Since the Iranians did not have writing, it has not been possible to identify them securely in the archeological record of Central Asia and Iran, although there have been speculations. As for the Avesta, it never refers to historical events, but it does contain series of geographical names.

> The Avesta contains two lists of geographical names in two texts: the hymn to Mithra and the first chapter of the Videvdad, in which lands made by Ahura Mazdâ are listed. The principal names in these two lists are the following:

1. Haraivian Margu (Margiane), Sogdian Gava, and Khwârazm (Chorasmia).

2. Gava inhabited by Sogdians, strong Margu, Bâkhdhri (Bactria) the beautiful with uplifted banners, Nisâya, which is between Margu and Bâkhdhri, Haraiva, Xnanta, inhabited by Verkânas (Hyrcanians), Harakhvati (Arachosia) the beautiful, and Haetumant (Helmand), rich and glorious....[31]

We see that the most western name mentioned in the Avesta is Hyrcania, which in historical times was an area and also an Achaemenian Province, being to the south and south-east of the Caspian Sea. We see that the horizon of the Avestan texts is central Asia, the region between the Caspian and the Aral seas, and the Helmand basin in southern Afghanistan. From the historical and linguistic evidence, as well as the geographical horizon of the Young Avesta, we can therefore tentatively conclude that the oldest Avestan texts originated among the ancient Iranians who inhabited the area between the Aral sea and modern Afghanistan in the second millennium BC. According to Professor Skjaervo:

> According to the tradition, under Khosrow (531–79 C.E.), the Avesta was divided into 21 books, or nasks, the contents of which are given in the Dênkard, a Pahlavi text compiled in the ninth century. From this it appears that only one of the books have been preserved virtually complete: the Videvdad; of most of the others only smaller or larger parts are now extant. The loss of so much of the Sasanian Avesta since the ninth century must be ascribed to the effect of the difficulties that beset the Zoroastrian communities after the Muslim conquest of Iran.[32]

There is no exact data available to us, regarding the death of the Prophet, but several sources have mentioned his end. These sources has to be regarded as non-historical, but mythological. It is said that the Prophet died at the age of 77. The general view is that he was murdered by a priest, who stabbed him with a dagger. The Persian national poet Abolghassem Mansour (940–1020 AD) better known as Ferdowsi [Arabic for the man from paradise] in his famous book *Shahnameh* mentions the death of Zarathustra, saying that he was murdered by the Turans or the Turs—horse riding people from the steps of central Asia, who attacked and invaded the kingdom of King Vishtaspa, where Zarathustra was living. Mary Boyce dedicates many interesting investigations concerning the way in which Zarathustra ended his life:

> In the surviving Avesta nothing is said of the Prophet's end, but in a Pahlawy passage from the Zand, his death is referred to in conventionally devout terms, as "the departure of Zarthusht of venerated spirit to the Best Existence, when 77 years had past from his birth ..." As we have seen, the wording of the *Shahnameh* verses, which tell of the sack of *Adar Nosh* (the sacred and ancient fire Temple) suggest a close rendering by Ferdowsi's sources of a Pahlawy original, and that original was apparently interpreted by some Zoroastrian scholastics themselves, in late Sassanian or early Islamic times, as telling of the death of their master, Zoroaster. An interpretation prompted by the reference in the same passage to the *Fire of Zarthusht*. Then in the way of scholastics, they would naturally have sought to establish the identity of the man, who struck the actual blow. In the Avesta *Arejat-Aspa* is chief of the Hyaona tribe, and in the Ayadgar Arjasp is addressed

accordingly as the Khyonan Shah, and his followers are Khyonians. But in the *Shahnameh* he appears as the *Turan Shah* or the *Turan Khoday*, that means Lord of the Tur people, the Avestan Tuirya.

There was a tendency in the Zoroastrian tradition, to regard the Tuiryas as the natural foe of the Aryans, because Franrasyan [in modern Persian: Afrasiyab], the Kavis great enemy, was of that tribe, and early Islamic writers attested that Arjasp, as Kay Vishtasps opponent, was regarded by some as a kinsmen of Afrasiyab, and so as himself a Tur. Further when in late Sassanian times, turks began to threaten Iran's north-eastern frontier, they and the turs confounded, and the Land of Turan became the general name for non-Iranian central Asia. From all this it follows that Zoroaster's putative killer, being one of Arjasps Army, could be classified as a Tur.[33]

1.4 ZARATHUSTRA—MYTH OR HISTORY

There is an ongoing discussion amongst linguists and historians, whether the historical personality of the Prophet Zarathustra really existed, or if he was just a mythical figure invented later by priests in subsequent generations. Some have suggested that later priests of that religion invented this myth of a Prophet named Zarathustra in order to justify or legitimize their religious inventions. This religion became an ideology that was later canonized and institutionalized by subsequent rulers. For example, a king, for strategic reasons converted into this religion, and he declared it later to be a national religion. At this point in its development the priests probably had to create and invent a prophet, in order to give more credibility and legitimation to their own proclaimed teachings. As it happens, academics today investigating the life and times of the Prophet Zarathustra are mostly linguists, and seldom historians. From their perspectives, sometime the linguistic evidence is more important than the historical fact. According to Skjaervo:

> Zarathustra is not a "historical" person in the sense that he belongs in a known historical context or that there are recognizable historical details associated with him. He is also not represented as a "real" person in the texts, much less so than, for instance, Jesus in the Gospels. There is therefore no advantage in assuming that he was a historical person who lived in such and such a place at such and such a time. The futility of such assumptions is indicated by the disagreements among Western scholars on these points.

> The Greeks called Zarathustra Zoroaster, hence the name of the religion. The followers of this religion are also called Mazdeans (or Mazdayasnians) after the Old Iranian term mazda-yasna, which literally means "he who sacrifices (performs a ritual of offerings) to Ahura Mazdâ." Correspondingly, the religion is also called Mazdaism or Mazdayasnianism.[34]

We have here the saying of Jean Cocteau (1889–1963):

> In deciding to distinguish between History and Mythology, I personally prefer Mythology. History is what they always taught us to be the truth, but in the end it turned out to be all lies, written later by the

winners. But Mythology, which was supposed to be
all lies, in the end turned out to be the truth.

As a principle, it can be said that myths are probably the echoes of
real happenings in times past, when recording of events were technically impossible and the recounting of historical events could only
be passed forward by word of the mouth from one generation to the
next. These doubts concerning the existence of the real person of the
Prophet Zarathustra surfaced only after the discovery and the deci-
pherment of the various rock inscriptions in different locations of the
ancient Persian Empire as we have seen above. These rock inscriptions were dated from the beginning of the Achaemenid dynasty
until the end of the Sassanian rule, from approximately 650 BC to 644
AD—a period of more than a thousand years. In all these records on
mountain rocks, Ahura Mazdâ was venerated as the creator God, but
the prophet Zarathustra, who emphasized him as the one true creator
God to mankind, was not mentioned at all. This fact being a matter of
heated discussion among scholars up to this date, the reason for this is
still unknown. Mary Boyce writes in this context that:

> "... Zoroaster's name does not appear in the
> Achaemenid inscriptions, perhaps because of the
> lack of precedent for referring to a Prophet in the
> ancient Near Eastern texts, which served their
> scribes as models. The same omission is found in the
> royal inscriptions of the later Sassanians, and even in
> those of their great high priest Kirder.[35]

Furthermore, in support of the Mazdayasnian beliefs amongst
Achaemenids, the Greek writers record that King Cyrus called one
of his daughters Atussa, which is a defective Greek form of an ancient
Iranian name Hutaosa, the name of the Queen of King Vishtaspa. This
queen was the first to become a follower of the Prophet Zarathustra,

and only after that did the King himself decide to follow and become the patron to this new creed. In so doing, it was the Queen Atussa who, in reality, was decisive in the spread of the Mazdayasnian religion. Here we have to wonder at the omission of the name of Zarathustra from all ancient historical records by past rulers, who at the same time, were believers in Zarathustra's creator God Ahura Mazdâ.

Consider that historians now estimate the time of Zarathustra's lifetime at around 2000–1400 BC, and the first rock inscriptions date from 521 BC, an interval of more than a thousand years. In this time, the memory of the prophet may only have been kept alive orally, for technical reasons from generation to generation. Probably, after a thousand years, the details of his person and his personal life would be partly forgotten or unrealistically distorted, and thereby ignored by rulers of the empire.

It is also possible that rulers of the Achaemenid dynasty, for example, seemed to be very self-confident, self-assured and egocentric, therefore we do not see the name of any other human being, other than the one of the supreme king himself to be mentioned. In the case of King Darius the great, in his very long inscriptions on the rock of the mountain in Bisotun for example, he mentions numerous battles, many victories, many conquests, but always only his own name.

Therefore, in the framework of royal egocentricity, which can be found often in history, it is probably not unusual not to find the name of any other person except that of the king himself on these carvings, not even that of Zarathustra. It is well-known that King Luis XlV of France has been quoted to have said after an accident: "Why is God doing this to me, has he forgotten how much I did for him?" Furthermore, we have also several rock carvings from the time of the Sassanian dynasty, wherein the same situation exists: only the king is mentioned, the only exception to this was the name of the very powerful high priest, Kerdir.

Finally one cannot ignore the fact that Zarathustra was not forgotten but venerated and remembered by the Persian people. We know that, for example, according Zoroastrian mythology in the time of the Sassanian dynasty, the small and holy lake Kansaoya (modern-day Lake Hāmūn) was suppose to contain the seeds of the Prophet himself. It was believed that a virgin girl, bathing in that lake, will give birth to the Messiah or Saoshyant.

According to the Zoroastrian belief, the virgin will give birth to the Messiah, who will come to save the world. That virgin will give birth to the prophet's son, and thus a descendant from the lineage of Zarathustra will return to the world in order to save it from the powers of the evil forces.[36] It is important to mention here that the Saoshyant is clearly mentioned in the Gathas. This scriptures are attributed to Zarathustra himself. But the birth of the Saoshyant by a virgin is a proclamation from later centuries, long after Zarathustra, probably from the time of the beginnings of the Achaemenid Period, which is to say 600–500 BC and long before the birth of Christ.

Importantly, Lake Hāmūn was, for centuries, during the Sassanian period, a sacred pilgrimage site for the common people, and girls and woman would bring flowers with them and throw them into the small lake. Candles were burned and prayers were said on the shore of that lake. In doing so, the population venerated the creator God Ahura Mazdâ in an indirect manner, but remembered and revered the person of Zarathustra, their Prophet, in a *direct* manner. As this lake is connected directly to person of the Prophet Zarathustra, but is only in a distant sense concerned with the creator God Ahura Mazdâ. This clearly indicates the vivid presence of the prophet Zarathustra's person in the mind of the population up to the time of the Islamic invasion in 644 AD.

If Zarathustra never existed, then the question arises: who wrote the Gathas in the Avesta?

Concerning the holy scriptures of Zoroastrianism, which are believed to have been written by Zarathustra himself, and its religious message, there are three differing opinions.

The first is that Zarathustra has never really existed and that the Avesta was written later by another person or persons, and the Myth of the Prophet Zarathustra was created later by priests and projected to the past, in order to legitimize their own ideas.

A second possibility is that the Avesta was written by poets, who did also sacrifice to the old gods. This is what Professor P.O. Skjaervo believes; he calls the writer of the Gathas "the poet-sacrificer". It is the view of Skjaervo that the Zoroastrian religion and its ideology as we know it today was evolved over time from the ancient Indo–European beliefs and shifted from the polytheistic religion of the archaic Aryan tribes in the steppes of central Asia into a monotheistic religion *by itself* with time passing. The ethical content of the religion was imagined and added at a later stage, and together with an non-existent but imagined prophet named Zarathustra projected in to the past by Priests and Magi.

The third and final possibility, of course, is that an individual named Zarathustra, about whom various historians, chroniclers, and philosophers of antiquity—Aristotle among them—have written, really existed. This individual composed the Gathas and instituted a wide range of moral principles. He introduced to mankind a one single Creator God by the name of Ahura Mazdâ (a being not himself created but was born out of himself). In so doing, this individual had to eradicate old polytheistic deities of the ancient Indo-European pantheon, who were worshiped before his time, in order to properly elevate Ahura Mazdâ. By introducing Ahura Mazdâ and his moral teachings to mankind, this individual set a precedent in the human consciousness, namely that of a central and unique creator God for all humankind. Probably this new development in human consciousness resulted in a beginning of a new period in human history, which some historians have called civilization.

Noted Zoroastrian scholar Professor Almut Hinze from the School of Oriental and African Studies at London University, posed the question of Zarathustra's existence in her inaugural speech on February 22, 2012. At the end of her speech she offered the following:

"... if Zarathustra did not really exist and he is just a phantom and a myth, created later, then the Iranian pre-Islamic religious situation would have developed the same way as did the religious situation in India, meaning we would have had a conglomeration of gods in Iran like Hinduism in India..."

Furthermore, Almut Hintze mentions here that, from prehistoric times, the Aryan tribes who were in the central Asian steppes and preparing to wander south, did have a: "sister belief system from both the Hindu–Iranian ancestors".

Almut Hintze is absolutely correct in this point, as the situation in India and Iran developed parallel to each other. We know that the Aryan tribes coming from the north divided, one group entering the Indian peninsula from the north, and the other group entering the Iranian plateau from the north of what is, today, Khorasan, somewhere between Herat and the east coast of the Caspian sea. Almut Hintze distinguishes two types of religions, or religious beginnings: the Revolutionary or the Prophetic religions versus the Evolutionary religions and suggests that

"it is not continuity, but *change* which requires an answer."

Those religions that broke from the past and experienced a drastic change in the religious belief are the prophetic or the revolutionary religions. These religions needed a strong and charismatic Prophet, for this individual had to weather this violent change and break with the past. In so doing, they created something new and revolutionary. These are religions like Judaism with the Prophet Moses, or Christianity with Jesus Christ and also the Islamic faith with the Prophet Mohammad. Without the strong personal appearances of those three personalities, these three religions would not have existed, and would have been just the continuation of the old and nascent beliefs of the people, whatever they might have been. Hinduism is an example of what Hintze calls an evolutionary religion. We know that Hinduism was the ancient, probably prehistoric belief of the Aryan tribes featuring various divinities and gods who existed in their belief and folklore from ancient times, from before they entered the Indian subcontinent. These ancient beliefs changed organically and incrementally from archaic times to the present in a constant evolution, and people still believe in them today. Almut Hintze mentions only Hinduism, but we can add to this also the ancient religion of the Pharaonic Egypt, which could not reform itself, and continued in the same way until its total demise with the advent of Christianity.

Looking back in time, we have indications from recently discovered evidence that sometime around 3000 BC the Iranian people had separated from their cousins the Indo-Aryans, with whom they shared a common religion and oral literary traditions, reaching back into proto-Indo-European times. It is believed that between 2000 and 1800 BC the two tribes started to migrate into the south, the one migrating south-east whilst the other south-west into the Iranian plateau.

Here we have to ask the important question: if a strong and determined individual hadn't existed amongst those Aryans entering the Iranian plateau from the north (an individual with strong convictions and a powerful and decisive will to change their religious beliefs, and to change the course of the ancient Aryan religious dogmas) then what would be the religious situation in Iran up to 644 AD. The Iranian religion would likely have been a parallel to the Hinduistic religion in India. Nothing other than an organic evolution of the old pre-Zoroastrian pantheon would have continued in Iran. It is clear that the Hindu religion evolved organically from its beginning to this date, but the Zoroastrian religion was formed by the intervention and revolution of an determined individual, who changed the course of the ancient beliefs and constituted a new ideology.

Here we can give another example, namely Catholicism. In the late medieval time, the Catholic Church was in crisis due to doctrinarians in its hierarchy who would not allow any change or reforms. At that time the Catholic Church was in a deep ideological crisis, and in 1414 AD, a very important reunion of all the major personalities of the Catholic Church took place in the southern German city of Constance. The famous Council of Constance, which lasted four years until 1418, had the opportunity to reform the Western Christian Church and to renew it. The problems of the Church were evident and had been long discussed. However, and on the contrary, the Council of Constance did everything to strengthen the old hierarchies and dogmas. This was due to the fact that those in positions of power were the main beneficiaries of the old hierarchies. In any case, the first person to seek a reform of the Church was a professor at Charles University in Prague by the name of Jan Huss (1369–1418) who, in his speeches, tried to convince the delegates to introduce some reforms to existing religious dogmas. Jan Huss, being an philosopher and a priest, was in reality an academic, and as such, he did not have the backing of a powerful king or local ruler to enforce his reforms.

Subsequently, the Council ordered him burnt at the stake, and he was the first to be executed for heresy against the doctrines of the Catholic Church, in what was later called The Reformation. At this point we see a clear confirmation of our theory that, without the revolutionary action of a determined individual, the status quo would continue indefinitely. For the Christian Church, the determined individual in this case was the strongly persuasive personality of Martin Luther (1483–1546), whose actions opened the doors to other reformists like John Calvin and Ulrich Zwingli both active in Switzerland. Following the events of The Reformation, a devastating war began between the Catholics and the Reformists, which was unprecedented in Europe, namely the famous Thirty Years War (1618–1648). This was probably the longest and most devastating war in European history.

We have seen that a revolutionary act had to be performed by whomever wanted to reform the Christian religion. The determined Martin Luther was such an individual. After having sparked The

Reformation of the Christian Church (its doctrines and traditions), he set off a series of events that culminated in an unprecedented conflict. This confirms the rule that religions, no matter in how deep a crises they are, cannot change simply with time or reform themselves from within, unless a violent or revolutionary act occurs, started always by an determined individual.

In the case of Zarathustra, after having introduced the supreme god creator Ahura Mazdâ to all mankind, he had to eliminate all previously venerated deities and archaic god whom he deemed unreal and without merit. The historical fact is that, even apart from efforts of the prophet Zarathustra, whose intervention revolutionized Iranian religious world, for over a thousand years the rulers of the empire had to fight with gods which were expelled from the pantheon but still worshiped by some. These archaic gods were now called *Daivas* [in Avestan: Daevas meaning demons or bad spirits or negative deities] or the *followers of druj* [liars—druj being Persian for lie]. It is important to note that, according to the Zoroastrian ideology, the biggest sin a human can commit is to lie—and we will see later in the chapter of the Arda Wiraz Namag, the deepest and most frightful corner of hell is reserved for the liars, and the followers of falsehood.

Even with the powerful efforts of Zarathustra, the divinities of the pre-Zoroastrian period could not be completely eradicated from the mind of the general public. It would take—as we will see in later chapters—millennia and the efforts of many ruling dynasties to press the population to stop the worship of those divinities and forget them. The task of eradicating the worship of pre-Zoroastrian gods [Daivas] required various drastic and calculated actions by rulers over those whom they ruled. Some of these actions were recorded by King Darius's son, King Xerxes [in Persian: Chashajar shah] who ruled 486–465 BC. He relates in one of his rock inscriptions:

> When I became king... there was (a place) where previously the Daivas were worshipped. Afterwards,

by the grace of Ahura Mazdâ, I destroyed that sanctuary of the Daivas, and I proclaimed: "The Daivas
shall not be worshipped!" And where previously the
Daivas were worshipped, there I worshipped Ahura
Mazdâ with the proper rites, in accordance with
the Asha.

(Xerxes, Persepolis H 35–41)

At this point we have to look carefully into the meaning of the
word *Daiva* (Daeva, Diva, Deus, etc.), which means practically the
same thing in all the ancient languages of the Western world, namely
God/Goddess. For generations linguists have been investigating the
roots of this single word, which originates from prehistoric Avestan
(the ancient Iranian pre-Zoroastrian language) and ancient Sanskrit
(which is one of the earliest Indo-European languages). We see for
example that the Imperial Rome used the word *deus* for god and *diva*
for goddess; in Italian it is *divo* and *diva*. In Lithuanian it is dievas
(god) and deivė (goddess). In Hindi: Dev (god) and dēvī (goddess).
In English, these same roots yield words *divine*, *divinity*, *deity* and the
verb *deify*.

The Daivas were the Indo-European gods in the archaic times
both in the east—India and Iran—as well as in Europe in the west. In
ancient Greece the word *Deus* became first *Zeus* and then *Theos*. P.O.
Skjaervo in *Introduction into Zoroastrianism* writes:

Scholars in the twentieth century compared the Old
Iranian religion with that of the Indo-Aryans in an
attempt to recover common Indo-Iranian beliefs.
Attempts were also made to isolate comparable
data throughout the Indo-European literatures to
identify elements that might be ascribed to the
remote ancestors of all the Indo-European peoples,

the proto-Indo-Europeans. By this research, it was established that the proto-Indo-Europeans sacrificed to heavenly gods, denoted by the word *deiwo*, known in a variety of Indo-European languages: Old Indic *deva*, Avestan *daêwa* and Old Persian *daiva*, Latin *deus*, Old Norse *Tyr*, contained in the day name (Norwegian) *tys-dag* "Tues-day," plural *tivar*. This word was in turn related to another word, *dyew*, denoting the bright sky, which was probably worshipped as a high god by several Indo-European peoples: Old Indic *dyau* "heaven" and *dyâus pitâ* "father heaven," Avestan *dyao* "heaven," Latin *Juppiter* from the vocative *dyeu-pater* "O father heaven," Greek Zeus from *dyêus*.[37]

Similarly these roots once informed the old Persian word *Daiva*, but Zarathustra, in order to eliminate all other deities next to his God, Ahura Mazdâ, turned the meaning of this word into its contrary. Accordingly, though this word—or its variations—has the same in most of the ancient languages, in all the Iranian and Persian languages in means something very different, and that shift can be traced directly to Zarathustra and his religion. From Zarathustra forward, *Daiva* was used to denote *monster* or *bad demon* or *devil*. Furthermore, Iranian rulers since the birth of Zoroastrianism have declared themselves to be persecutors, destroyers, and suppressors of the followers of the Daivas.

Amongst the pre-Zoroastrian gods now turned into demons was Indra. We see now two clearly defined groups emerging. On one side the positive, those gods worthy of worship are the mazda-yasna who are all a reflection of the true Asha; and on the other side the negative, unworthy of worship are the daiva yasna. There are two pre-Zoroastrian deities, Mithra and Anahita, are exempt and still worthy of worship. We know, for example, that the King Vishtaspa sacrifices to the Goddess of Anahita, asking for the success of the teachings of Zarathustra. Mithra and Anahita are subordinate divinities to Ahura Mazdâ—same as the angels in Christianity.

The inversion of such a fundamental aspect of the language was radical and likely could not have happened incrementally on its own. It would take the will of a strong influential individual to captain such a shift. In this case, change in the meaning of daiva was nothing less than a strategically calculated act by a powerful and authoritarian individual. It changed the course of history and created, for the first time ever, a monotheistic religion presented to all humankind. By the demonization of the existing Daivas, Zarathustra performed an act of unprecedented importance in the development of religious thinking.

Furthermore, it is evident from the style in which the Gathas are compiled that the writer (or poet-sacrificer as P.O. Skjaervo puts it) was a person powerful and authoritarian, and that only one person was involved in compiling this document. In particular and importantly, experts and linguists are united in the opinion that the Gathas were written by one person only, with authority, and at one time, and that this work was not a product of lengthy or slowly development in history.

This act of elevating one god as a central creator and father figure, can be seen as a fundamental turning point in human spiritual history. It marked the beginning of morality as the main guiding principle of human society. In a time when the rough and primitive struggle for survival was the only viable way of life, emphasizing the importance of morality and righteousness as the only way of life was a courageous revolutionary act.

Elisabeth Forster-Nietzsche in her Introduction to *Thus Spoke Zarathustra* quotes her brother as suggesting:

> Zarathustra was the first to see in the struggle between good and evil the essential wheel in the working of things. The translation of morality into

the metaphysical, as force, cause, end in itself, was *his* work. [...] Zarathustra *created* the most porten-tous error, *morality*....[38]

Zarathustra saw in the workings of the world a clear sign that evil was an independent force in itself that must be combatted and overcome at all times. Clearly the pantheons and religious beliefs of the great civilizations of antiquity—such as ancient Egypt, ancient Greece and the Roman Republic and later Empire—did not have a prolific and strong revolutionary reformer as Zarathustra. These religions and their gods, therefore, remained the same until the end, frozen in time, same with their archaic and outdated ideology. It is for this reason that those once almighty gods of the antiquity such as Jupiter, Zeus, and Amon-Ra (who ruled the Egyptian Pantheon for thousands of years with the other related gods) had to lose their power, surrender the stage of world history, abdicate and be forgotten. As Karl Marx puts it:

"Die mussen auf den Scheiterhaufen der Geschichte." [the English idiom equivalent: they must go into the dustbin of history].

The repudiation of existing deities and the elevation of Ahura Mazdâ as the one and only supreme creator God was a task taken on by various rulers in the Iranian Empire for a millennia. Despite the sustained efforts of various ruling dynasties, it took millennia to eradicate the ancient belief in those gods Zarathustra deemed to be false gods and demons. All this could not have happened by itself. As Hintze puts it:

> The evolutionary model can not explain why the previous Gods, the Daivas, changed into Demons.

In the Avesta, Zarathustra is presented as a mythical priest to whom Ahura Mazdâ confides into his mind the sacred texts and rituals and the other dogmas, for him to confront and declare the truth to the mortals. He was the one who, according to the Gathas, received in his mind Ahura Mazdâ's word and proclaimed it to mankind. We have seen that Zarathustra did not prohibit and dismantle *all* previous deities, but kept two of them as sub-deities to Ahura Mazdâ (comparable to Judeo-Christian archangels) namely Mithra and Anahita.

Mithra, who from pre-Zoroastrian times was regarded as the deity of friendship and contracts, and who also battled the forces of darkness so that the sun could rise and travel across the sky, was, in late Zoroastrianism, identified with the sun. We will see in later the chapters that this deity would endure and resurface in several other historical locations, as for example in the later Roman Empire, and also probably in the mind of the young Pharaoh Akhenaten.

The Goddess Anahita, a heavenly deity, representing fertility and childbirth, was the most important female goddess in the pre-Zoroastrian period.

Then, apart from these two important sub-deities, there were six other life-giving immortals, the Amesha Spentas.

According to modern historians, those Aryan tribes of the late Bronze Age who lived south of the Aral sea, divided and wandered south. One group to northern India, the other group to the north eastern Iranian plateau. These Aryan tribes were living a pastoral lifestyle, keeping animals or were herdsman, but probably were not agriculturalists in today's sense—as agriculturalists are not mobile but are, instead, tied to the land on which they are working. We see for example several times the mention of a cow in the Gathas. According to historical materialism the development of the human society has moved through a series of stages each with its own ideology and worldview.[39] Mankind started in the stone age as *hunter gatherers* which lasted for millions of years until to *pastoralism* or shepherd-based society and from there to *agricultural cultivation* and finally to a *commercial society*.

Each of these separate stages in human history has its own ideology or worldview and with it a different lifestyle and a different attitude of the individual towards the general society. For example, hunter gatherers were extremely mobile and constantly on the move for new hunting grounds.

Pastoralists, on the other hand, kept animals, but were not working on the land as such. The attitude of pastoral societies is that they are not protective of the lands they are living on, and therefore, they are not thinking in terms of protecting their lands and their own tribe or their own group of people. They are not thinking in terms of "you are not one of us, you are not a member of our tribe" —but rather— "every person has to cooperate together" for pastoralism needs the peaceful cooperation of the neighbouring communities.

Clearly, the society in which Zarathustra lived was a pastoral society. Therefore we see here an attitude of internationalism, instead of a protective attitude towards a limited community or a tribe. This attitude of internationalism is clearly visible in the Zoroastrian worldview. In this respect it is interesting to note that Friedrich Engels (1820–1895), in *The Origin of the Family, Private Property and the State*, wrote:

> The start of the existence of private property and subsequently the state, which was created in order to protect it, and the general beginnings of repression of humans by humans started with the founding of the Family. The initial start was the subsequent subjugation of the woman by the man. The beginning of the social class system, where the domesticated animals belonged to one person, and others had to graze and watch over them, was the consequence of the pastoral phase in human society…. […] The beginning of human repression all having started as the consequence of the pastoral way of life in the early stages of human development….[40]

In contrast the societies of *agricultural cultivators* are attached to the land on which they are working, for their efforts are long-term based, and they are more defensive of the fertile land they occupy. They have invested their time and efforts in to that land, and therefore, they are attached to it and they have to protect it. The religions deriving from this type of agricultural societies is tribally oriented (*God gave this land only to our tribe, you are not one of us*) meaning restricted to their own tribe or group, and therefore strongly defensive of their own tribe and their own fertile land. By contrast, the pastoral societies are more ready to extend their beliefs to non-members of their tribe or group, as they constantly encounter new groups of people and are dependent on their goodwill or their peaceful attitude. Zarathustra was clearly living a simple pastoral lifestyle, highly dependent on the healthiness of the environment, cleanliness of the scarce water reserve etc., and this is also evident from the Gathas. The elements of Water, Fire and Earth were regarded as sacred and thus ought to be protected, for the wellbeing and fundamental existence of the community depended on them.

We see that Zarathustra's teachings has no restrictions of tribe or race membership, but is a universal and international religion for all humankind anywhere and anytime. The Enemy is not the 'other' from outside the tribe but rather the one who lies and is dishonest, in other words the *Ahriman* [or as in the Avestan: *Angra Mainyu*, all meaning the evil spirits].

The ideal of the Zoroastrian worldview is *Ashawan* [World of the truth, *Asha* meaning *the truth*], and therefore, the creation of the material world is only a reflection of the spiritual qualities of the world of truth, or Ashawan. This means that the material world has been conceived only as a transcendence and a continuation of the ideal and spiritual world, which had been created and which existed before, all created by Ahura Mazdâ. Furthermore, the role of humans in the cosmic scheme is to support Ahura Mazdâ and his world, by keeping his moral laws, and through a principle of general conduct that comprises "thinking good thoughts, speaking good speech, and doing good deeds". Therefore, Zarathustra's worldview reflects the ideal cosmic order—as Nietzsche says in *Human, All Too Human*, "Every person is the best imitator of his ideal."

From this we can assume that an ideal and balanced worldview, which included such elements as the one central Creator God, the afterlife (Paradise and Hell), the Messiah or the Saoshyant, and the immortality of the soul, had been formed in the mind of a man, who saw this as an ideal and balanced world order. Altogether to be combined in a comprehensive ideology and introduced to mankind as a religion, it had been formed initially in the consciousness of an individual, who had been envisioning this in his mind as the ideal way of life for the human race in their future existence. It was Zarathustra who first recognized Evil as an independent force, in and of itself, that must be combatted at all times.

Who was this man we call Zarathustra? When exactly he lived is a matter of investigation for future generations of historians and linguists to determine. What concerns our investigation is that we can see that no compelling proof of the existence of the ideological and religious elements thought to be introduced by Zarathustra was existing anywhere before his time. On the other hand, the monotheistic religions of today have not introduced any significant new elements into their ideology, it is evident, therefore, that core elements of all of today's monotheistic religions go back directly to the Traditions of Zoroastrianism and its ideology.

As the consequences of logical and reasonable thinking—and after having considered all historical data available to us—we can argue that historical and linguistic research point to the fact that somewhere in the late bronze age, probably somewhere in south central Asia, Northern Kwarazmia, east of the Caspian sea, there lived an individual who declared, introduced and instituted some elements of his worldview as dogmas and subsequently presented them as a new religion. This was accepted and revered later by his followers as a new faith. Furthermore, the main elements of his dogma, without any new and important elements and additions, are still today being accepted

and worshiped in all the world's monotheistic religions under different names. According to P.O. Skjaervo:

> By the turn of the century, the view had taken firmly
> root that the Old Avestan Zarathustra was historical:
> a prophet, reformer, thinker, etc., while the Young
> Avestan and later Zarathustra was a myth or legend,
> but with several surviving historical details.

> It was also about this time that the argument from
> the vivid and personal description of Zarathustra in
> the Gâthâs became common. Thus, Karl Friedrich
> Geldner, author of the chapter on the Avestan litera-
> ture in the Grundriss, put it as follows:

>> In the Gāthās, [the personality of
>> Zarathustra] appears far less legendary
>> and comes closer to us as human ... The
>> relationship to his patrons, especially King
>> Vishtāspa and his advisors, stands out in
>> more lifelike fashion and more clearly.
>> The subjective and personal empha-
>> sis prevails....[41]

> [...] Recently, an argument has also been put forward
> based on the form and structure of the poems to the
> effect that the high degree of sophistication of the
> poetic techniques involved point to Zarathustra as
> their author.

> The Gâthâs contain the topos of an (apparent) "self-
> dramatization" of the poet as poor, persecuted, etc.,
> which belonged to the center piece of the proof of

Zarathustra's historicity to Bartholomae, Lommel, Boyce, etc.

A Poet's Complaint is found in Gâthâs 1-4. It is missing in the fifth Gâthâ, the structure of which differs from that of the others, and in the Yasna Haptanghâiti, which is a "collective" hymn. [...] The poet-sacrificer complains about his weakness and poverty, caused by his lack of earth, men, and animals, as well as lack of approval, apparently, by his own people. In the first line of 2.46.1 traditional scholarship has seen an indication of Zarathustra's intent to leave his home land and go to preach his message in another "land"... [...] All these passages have serious problems of interpretation and can obviously not be used to reconstruct Zarathustra's life.[42]

Returning again to Hinduism and Zoroastrianism, we have seen that the two branches of Indo-Aryans—which wandered to the south *separately*—had initially the same gods and deities, which had entered their pantheon from time of prehistory. The Aryans, who entered the Indian subcontinent brought their divinities with them, and these divinities and gods continued and developed organically through the millennia, and the belief in them is called today Hinduism. The word Hinduism has nothing to do with that religion itself or their deities, but it simply means in Old Persian the religion of the people of Hindustan—which is in turn a Persian word, meaning the *people who live on the river Indus*. We can therefore say that Hinduism is an ancient religion with no known founder and no known date of origin. By Hinduism, we simply refer to a wide variety of religious traditions and philosophies that have developed in India over thousands of years. Most Hindus today worship one or more—sometimes many—deities.

Here we have to carefully examine the development of Hinduism, as this is connected to the better understanding of Zoroastrianism and to the existence of the historical personality of Zarathustra himself. The earliest evidence for prehistoric religion in India dates back to the Neolithic period (5500–2600 BC). The beliefs and practices of the pre-classical era (1500–500 BC) are called the historical Vedic religion. This historic Vedic religion has been influenced by the proto-Indo-European religion. Today Hinduism does not have a unified system of belief encoded in a declaration of faith or a creed but is rather a umbrella term, comprising the plurality of religious phenomena originating and based on the Vedic tradition. Part of the reason why, in Hinduism today, all or nearly all the gods and the divinities have survived time and are still revered as they were revered in antiquity, is that each god has its temple and its group of priests. The survival of these priests depends on the faith and the donations of the believers in that particular deity. The priesthood is generally composed of members of the Brahman caste and manages the various temples on a hereditary basis. It is probable that this priestly class—which existed from the ancient times—kept the cult of each separate deity alive for personal reasons.

Explaining the continuation of the daivas as worshipful gods in India, versus their alteration in fortunes in the Iranian world, P.O. Skjaervo writes:

> This feature in particular distinguishes Zoroastrianism from Indic (and Indo-European) beliefs, and the fact that the Avestan daêwas and Old Persian daivas are no longer beneficent heavenly beings, but rather the agents of chaos, deception, and evil, has been explained by scholars variously. Most commonly, it has simply been assumed that the reversal of the fortunes of the daêwas was the work of a single man and due to a conscious and planned

departure from earlier beliefs. That man, they decided, must have been Zarathustra, and the "new" beliefs must have been part of his "reform" of the traditional religion.[43]

Here significantly P.O. Skjaervo does not gives an answer to his own above question. The truth here is that Hinduism did, in fact, also have a revolutionary individual, who intended to change the course of this religion, and he was initially also successful and accepted in India. But, over time, he was rejected by his own people, and Hinduism, in its current form, returned again into the mind of the general public as their main religious belief.

This man was the Buddha, whose religion is an offshoot of Hinduism. His religious teachings are still today being followed in many countries of South East Asia, Indochina and Sri Lanka, though not in India. Buddha, which means "the awakened one" or the "enlightened one", was just his title. He was, in reality, a prince and the son of a local king, who lived in the northern part of India, on the border modern-day Nepal. His real name was Siddhartha Gautama.

The dates of both his birth and death are uncertain, but his lifetime has been estimated to be around 470–400 BC. Buddha tried, just as Zarathustra did in northern Iran, to alter the course of the Hindu religion in India, but after some initial successes, he failed and was rejected completely at the end—at least in his own homeland. The majority of followers of Buddhism in Asia today are divided into two schools of thought. This being approximately two thirds into the Mahayana (great Vehicle) school, and on third into the Theravada school. It is widely believed that the Mahayana school of Buddhism is strongly influenced and based on Zoroastrianism, which is at least one thousand years older than Buddhism.

While sometimes referred to as a religion, Hinduism is more often defined as a religious tradition, and it is therefore viewed as the most complex of all the living and historical world religions, with roots reaching back into prehistory. The Hindu scriptures refer to the heavenly personalities as Devas, or Devi in feminine, or Daevatas taken together. We see here again that word from prehistorical times used also in Europe and in ancient Iran. Major Hindu scripture include the Vedas, Upanishads, Puranas, Ramayana, Bhagavad Gita, Agamas, and finally the great Mahabharata—which is in its own right, one of the greatest literary works of human history.

Suffice it to say that, had a strong personality not appeared to the Aryans wandering to the south into the Iranian plateau, and had he not have dismantled and destroyed the polytheistic pantheon which existed before his own time, we would have, in Iran, up to the Islamic conquest a parallel situation as in India. This situation being a religion subject to the evolution of the old existing deities, similar to Hinduism in India. Looking at our explanations above, we can reasonably conclude that the existence of the man Zarathustra was a logical necessity for the historical developments that occurred.

Without an individual such as Zarathustra, the historical events in Iran would have developed very differently. In this connection we should mention another argument, which could initially speak against the physical existence of the Prophethood in general, at least from a philosophical point of view. In the ancient world there were several thinkers and philosophers who were categorically against the principle of prophethood or any kind of mediating position between God and Man. One of these man was Zakhariah Razi (865–925 AD) who lived in the ancient city of Ragha. As a philosopher, mathematician, physician and one of the great thinkers of medieval Persia, Zakhariah Razi was of the opinion that the theological argument for the general necessity of prophethood (the position of a human mediator between God and the Humans) is illogical, unconvincing, against the general laws of nature, unreasonable and finally unnecessary.

Against the argument of the theologians, who claim that God, in his great Wisdom, can appoint or has appointed a person to warn his people against sin and wrongdoing, Zakhariah Razi argues that, if

God had been concerned about the virtue of the people he created, he would have, from the beginning, created them good and incapable of any sin and wrongdoing, in which case there would have been no need to send a prophet. Another philosopher of the medieval Islam, namely the blind Syrian anti-religious thinker and philosopher Abdallah al-Ma'arri (973–1058) rejects any kind of prophethood, and calls their claims to be illogical and against the laws of nature.

Before answering to these arguments, we have to recognize the fact that these kind of sacrilegious statements—made in the time of the omnipotence of Islamic doctrinal and ideological monopoly—were acts of exceptional courage and admirable devotion to the personal beliefs by these individuals. In medieval Europe and the Middle East, to be killed for a sacrilege was a daily occurrence, if we look at the history of the Islamic and also the Christian world of that period.

Returning to the argument of the illogicality of prophethood in general, we can say, in response, that no matter how we look at the supernatural component of prophetism in human history, the civilizational and social impact of personalities claiming to be prophets and mediators between the divine and the humankind was of extraordinary importance to the human societies and their civilizations. Human history has shown that the question of the physical and the historical existence of a certain prophet was absolutely irrelevant and without any importance to the cause of human civilization and human history as such. A mythos alone, once established in the consciousness of the masses as real, can and does alter the course of civilizations and creates realities which no real historical event would be able to.

Needless to say personalities such as Zarathustra, the Prophet Abraham, Prophet Moses, Jesus Christ and Mohammad had an impact on the historical events, which no factual emperor or dictator or revolution or even wars could match. Considering that these persons are, for some academics, merely mythological and not historical personalities, it is justified to say that the power of a myth can be stronger and more monumental and long-lasting than any historical event. To make or enact laws or moral rules by humans for themselves is not enough and does not carries the weight and power which a rule coming from higher authority carries. Humans tend to think of laws and social conventions that are made by humans for other humans as changeable, voidable, temporary and relative—made according the context of a certain time, geographical location and certain social condition. Whereas divine commands, coming as they do from a higher authority, carry an eternal and absolute power that is unchangeable and also unreachable to humans.

From early antiquity various historical rulers (the Pharaohs of ancient Egypt, Cyrus the Great and Darius, Roman Emperors and rulers of medieval Europe et cetera) had to abide by the moral rules and standards of their gods in order to unite and stabilize the societies in their nations. Even now, nations and societies are basing their moral and ethical laws to one extent or another on divine law passed down through religious tradition or another, which for them came from a higher authority. All these divine laws and commands were born from the mind of non-historical prophets who were mythological personalities.

Finally we have to mention here that Zarathustra had only an *internal vision* which occurred in his mind. It was not a conversation with God or any communication with a supernatural being, as in the case of other prophets. This makes his personality even more realistic, credible and logical. Therefore, even if the Prophet Zarathustra should have been only a myth and not an historic personality, because he stands at the beginning of all the other myths, he is probably the biggest myth of them all—the biggest myth that history has ever known.

1.5 RELIGIOUS BACKGROUND IN PRE-ZOROASTRIAN TIMES AND A SHORT LOOK AT MITHRAISM AND ITS HISTORICAL CONSEQUENCES

Concerning the deities worshipped by the Aryan tribes in south-central Asia in pre-Zoroastrian times, not much is known. Mary Boyce investigates this topic in her books briefly. Richard Foltz of Concordia University in Montreal in his interesting book *The Religions of Iran*[44] enters extensively into this subject. What is known, can give us an impression of the circumstances in the period immediately prior to the life of the Prophet. Professor Mary Boyce writes:

> The Iranians throughout their history never believed in personal gods, but they always believed in abstract and impersonal ideological divinities …[45]

The beliefs and religious rituals of the ancient Iranians can be reconstructed partly from the comparison with the closely related religion of Vedic India. Also partly from fragmentary evidence about other Iranian religions, as for example Old Persian and Scythian, and partly from archaic elements surviving in the Avesta and in Zoroastrian observance. We can generally say that in pre-Zoroastrian times the Aryan tribes were polytheists, who conceived of their gods as cosmic beings, essentially benign, and apprehended a universal principle, "arta or asha" which means essentially "that which ought to be" this should govern everything in the natural and human spheres. They acknowledged three Lords (Ahuras), who guarded Asha. Animatism dominated their way of perceiving the world. The gods they believed in had created the world in seven stages: sky, water, earth, plants, animal, man, and fire. Fire was perceived as the vital force which gave warmth and life, through the sun, to regulate nature.

Then, by the sacrifice, they set it in motion, with the new life always following death, and the cycle of the seasons in nature always beginning again. This state of the new life and the beginnings was thought to be unending so long as man did their part through sacrifice and worship. This notably by the daily performance of a priestly rite—the Yasna—by which the creations were purified and blessed. The essential rituals were offerings to fire and water. It is important to note that worship was performed mostly in the open, without temples, altars, or any images.

Regarding the worship of the Gods in pre-Zoroastrian times, Mary Boyce continues:

> As wandering pastoralists the Indo-Iranians had no temples, and worshipped mainly in the open, without altars or images. They uttered hymns or praise and thanksgiving, and prayers, while making sacrifice and food offerings. An important rite, enacted during the Yasna, consists of expressing the juice of an intoxicant (Avesta: haoma and in Sanskrit: soma) which, when consecrated, was offered to the gods, and drunk ritually by the worshippers. Daily offerings were made to the hearth fire and sources of pure water, and priestly offerings to the fire and water also formed a part of the Yasna rituals.[46]

At death, most souls were thought to pass as shadows to an underworld, needing food offerings from their descendants to sustain them, but some fortunate and exceptional souls, it was hoped, would ascend to join the gods in heaven. With this there was also a hope, at least for some, in a complete resurrection of the body within a year after death so that the soul, totally reincarnated, could thereafter fully enjoy again the pleasure it had known on this earth. Therefore, looking at the Indo-Iranian comparative studies, we see that these give us the possibility to distinguish a fount of religious concepts, beliefs, and practices that are common to ancient Iran and ancient India. It is therefore methodologically possible to reconstruct some elements of an Indo-Iranian religion by using some of the surviving evidence of ideas and practices that seem to be unrelated to the Zoroastrian tradition in Iran and to the later developments of religious thought in archaic India and yet, at the same time, have something in common.

These various religious elements are connected with rituals, the pantheon, myth and epochs, and concepts of death and the afterlife. Even the cosmography—that is to say, several different aspects of an ancient religion—though not the ones that enable us to reconstruct an organic system which derives from the standpoint either of doctrine or of ritual or with regards to individual or collective behaviour. The highly ritualistic nature of the Indian Vedic religion on the one side, and that of the religious world in which, by way of reaction and deliberate opposition, Zoroaster's message established itself on the other side, features a number of common points. These common points include, among others, the important ritual and symbolism of fire [in Persian: Ātar; in Sanskrit: Agni]. Furthermore, the main dogmatic elements in Zoroastrianism, where there are three distinct ritual fires, of priests, of warriors, and of farmers, and five natural fires, namely the one in men, animals, plants, clouds, and the earth. The Italian scholar Gherardo Gnoli says in this connection the following:

> "According to a conception that is of Indo-Iranian origin (Duchesne-Guillemin, 1961, pp. 36–37); the cult of sauma, Av. haoma-/Skt.soma; the purificatory rites involving the use of animal urine; some aspects of the more archaic funeral ceremony (Gonda, 1962, pp. 49–50); and some cosmographic, cosmogonic, and cosmological concepts (Boyce, 1975, p. 130 ff.). As for the cult of haoma in Iran and soma in India, several studies have long since

pointed out the features that help trace it back to a common origin (Hillebrandt;Henry), notwithstanding the specificity of its different developments in the two branches of the Indo-Iranians and in the relative ritual and sacrificial performances (yasna in Iran, yajña in India). Haoma or Soma is not only the name of a plant, or a mushroom (Wasson; Brough; Gershevitch, 1975; Flattery and Schwartz), but it is also the name of a deity or "one worthy of worship" (yazata in the Zoroastrian tradition) in the Avesta and in the Vedas, a divine priest (Boyce, 1975, p. 160). There are also some precise Indo-Iranian parallels between the "Son of the Waters" (Apąm Napāt in the Avesta; Apąm Napāt in the Vedas; Boyce, 1975, pp. 44–52) and the Avestan Nairyō.saŋha ("of manly utterance"; cf. Vedic narāśaṃsa; Gray, pp. 152–54; Gershevitch, 1959, pp. 205 f.). The same can also be said for the Waters (Āpas) and the other figures connected with ritual practice, sacrifice, and libations (Av. zaoθra; Skt. hotrá)…."

As we have seen in previous chapters, the Indo-Iranian name for god or divinities is in Vedic deva, and in Avestan daēva, that derives, like the Latin deus, from an Indo-European root meaning "shine, be bright." We have also seen that Zarathustra, perhaps as a religious reformer, condemned the polytheism of the past. This term came to signify in Iran "false gods and demons."[47] At the same time, in India, the term was also used to refer to some deities that were opposed to others, these were designated by the term asura [in Avesta: ahura] "lord"[48]. The original meaning of daēva can be deduced from, amongst other things, the Avestan expression *daēva/mašya*, which is markedly similar to the Vedic *deva/martya*, the Greek *theoi/andres* (anthrōpoi), and the Latin *dii/homines*, all of which mean "gods and men."[49]

In terms of Ahura or Asura [Lord], it was used in Iran and India alike for gods or men. In the Zoroastrian tradition it referred especially to the supreme god, Ahura Mazdâ, to Mithra, and to Apąm (Napāt), who are regarded by some as being the "Three Lords" of the Indo-Iranian pantheon.[50] Significantly in the Veda, as well as meaning divine beings in general, it often referred in particular to Dyaus Pitar "Father Sky" [in Greek Deus becomes Zeus --Old Greek: *Zeus Pater*; Latin: *Deus Pater* from which we get *Jupiter*].[51]

Recent studies of ancient Iran and Vedic India reveal various criteria of an ancient theology that goes back to a period we can define as archaic Indo-Iranian. At this point, the information provided by the historian Herodotus[52] refers to the deities of the Persians as contained in a pantheon that is to some extent Indo-Iranian. The sun, the moon, the earth, fire, water, the atmosphere, and the winds, as well as the whole heavenly vault, have a number of nature gods corresponding to them both in India[53] and in Iran. This can be clearly seen in the Avesta. Divine entities, heavenly or astral bodies, can be found there as deities of the heavens and more generally of nature, especially in the part containing the Yashts.

In Iran there were some particularly important beings 'worthy of worship' (as Almut Hintze puts it) that have, in various ways, an Indo-Iranian prehistory. These were for example such as Mithra (Yasht 10), Varuna (Yasht 14), Vayu (Yasht 15), Haoma (Yasna 9–11). In India the adjective (vṛtrahan) was especially used as an epithet of the god Indra, who was demonized in Zoroastrian Iran. These together with Saurva, the Indian Śarva, the equivalent of the violent, warlike Rudra, and Nåŋhaiθya, the equivalent of Nāsatya in the Rigveda. These deities appear next to Varuṇa as Aryan gods of the Mitanni kingdom in the important tablets found at Boğazköi in Asia Minor.[54]

Concerning the Indo-Iranian deity Mithra, the Indian equivalent of the Iranian Mithra is evident, although the Indian Mitra is undoubtedly a much more vague a figure in the Vedic pantheon than is the divine entity in the Iranian (yazata) in Yasht 10. This is also valid for the god (baga) in the Achaemenian inscriptions, the Mihr in Pahlavi text theology, or the deity in Iranian-Capadochian and Mesopotamian regions, where the cult of the Mithraic was very popular.[55]

Other useful fields for the reconstruction of an Indo-Iranian religion are myth and epochs. As well as the aforementioned Vṛtrahan, another highly significant example is that of the Iranian Yima, the son of Vīvaṇhvant, and the Indian Yama, the son of Vivasvant, king of the golden age in Iran[56] and ruler of an underground realm of the dead in India.[57] Equally important are the examples of the first man, Gayō. marətan in Iran and Mārtāṇḍa in India[58] and of other heroic figures, especially those belonging to the mythical dynasty of the Paraδātas or Pišdādians.[59] These were the Kavyān or Kayānian dynasty[60] whose heroes were connected with the haoma/soma sacrifice (the drinking of the hallucinogen, which appears also in our chapter concerning Arda Wiraz, the Zoroastrian priest, who travelled to the other world) and the victorious fight against, respectively, the dragon Aži Dahāka in Iran and the dragon Viśvarūpa in India.[61]

With regard to funeral ceremonies and beliefs concerning the afterlife, an Indo-Iranian comparative approach is still possible and useful. This for the purpose of reconstructing common elements in both cultures. It is therefore possible that the funerary customs, with the cremation of corpses in India and their exposure to vultures in Iran—and with the respective burials of the bones—became differentiated as independent, secondary developments, compared to an original practice of inhumation. Traces of this can also be found in Iran, where the Avestan term daxma, which was later used in the Zoroastrian tradition to denote the towers of silence, is thought to be derived from a root meaning *to bury*.[62] Both cremation and exposure, on the other hand, almost certainly had the purpose of favouring a rapid detachment of the spirit from the body so that it could then ascend to heaven.

Some hints of a paradisiacal existence and afterlife were not altogether unfamiliar to the archaic Iranians—although it cannot have been marked by strictly ethical values. A happy life after death must have been reserved for an elite of priests and warriors only, while the background of individual eschatology must have been dominated by the belief in a grey, shadowy survival of the spirits of the dead in a nether region. This was approached along the paths taken by the deceased ancestors.[63] There is an echo of a similar afterlife, which is neither good nor bad, in the Zoroastrian concept of an intermediate zone, halfway between heaven and hell, for those who have deserved neither too much nor too little in their life on earth.

For those who succeed in possessing Truth or *Asha* and who are therefore ashavan or ṛatāvan (the righteous) are assured of a state of blessedness. The very concept of asha and ṛata is an important theme of Indo-Iranian historical investigations. The term, which can be translated *truth*,[64] has also the meaning of *order* in the broad sense of the word. This meaning the cosmic, ritual, social, and moral order. The possession of asha/ṛata is the sign of a spiritual fulfillment that enables the ashavan/ṛatāvan (the one who has achieved the level of righteousness) to enter into a new dimension of life. This, in spite of its being characterized by a post-mortem state of blessedness, does not yet belong entirely to the afterlife. It can be said that such a person is an initiate or a seer, one whose intimate bond with the other life— which eludes the physical senses—gives him access to the mysteries of earthly life.[65] Furthermore, Zarathustra himself did not negate these concepts but gave them new ethical meanings. He used the language that was typical of the religious tradition in which he had been trained as an expert in the art of priesthood. The belief in an initiation for the purpose of acquiring the supreme *wellbeing of asha/ṛata* was therefore of Indo-Iranian origins. Importantly Zarathustra, before declaring his personal worldview as an religious ideology to his fellow humans, was himself a priest of the deities, worshipped before his time.

These deities formed the basis of an early Aryan mysticism[66] whose characteristic signs were an experience of the inner light and an inner vision that was seen by the "eye of the soul," meaning basically the one who sees the righteous way of human existence. This, in itself, shows that the Aryan tribes in Iran had a relatively sophisticated poly-theistic pantheon, which could have induced a man of Zarathustra's capabilities to become their priest. Therefore, historians now believe that Zarathustra himself not only was a priest of the deities worshiped before his time, but he was an innovator and a reformer of that same old religion.

Furthermore, we have seen above that the deities of Mithra and Anahita were established gods, worshiped well before Zarathustra's time. One more essential argument exists here, which proves that the existence of various other deities worshiped by the Aryan tribes before the time of Zarathustra were well established, and that is the fact that the Prophet had great difficulties convincing the popula-tion, *not* to worship those deities any more. He had to declare them to be demons, fundamentally shifting the population's perception of their former deities. This task took centuries to accomplish. This shows clearly that those deities worshiped by the Aryan tribes before Zarathustra had deep roots in the public memory, which reached to very ancient prehistoric times of the Indo-Aryan tribes, and were firmly established in their consciousness.

It is time now to delve, in greater detail into an important and ancient deity who existed well before the time of Zarathustra and was subsequently repurposed by the Prophet to continue his existence as a lesser deity still, as Almut Hintze put it "worthy of worship". This God was Mithra, the symbol for the honest contract or agreement, but more importantly the God representing the Sun. When the Prophet introduced Ahura Mazdâ as the ultimate creator to mankind, the other ancient deities had to the leave the historical scene. As such Zarathustra had declared them to be Demons and not worthy of worship (Worship of Demons Daiva Yazhna –Worship of the one rightfull God Ahura Mazda –Mazda Yazhna)). The excep-tion were two major deities, made subordinate to Ahura Mazdâ, namely Mithras and Anahita. Professor P.O. Skjaervo writes in this regard:

> In the Avestan Pantheon, there were several great
> gods, who also deserved sacrifices…. Among them
> were Mithras and Anahita…. Mithras battles the
> powers of Darkness so that the sun can rise and
> travel across the sky; in late Zoroastrianism, he is
> identified with the sun. Anahita is the heavenly river,
> presumably the Milky Way, the greatest female deity,
> who is in charge of fertility.[67]

These two ancient deities, being worshiped in pre-Zoroastrian times, and very popular from antiquity in their own rights, remained as the subordinated gods and helpers to the creator God Ahura Mazdâ. Comparable to the archangels in the later Christian terminology. We know, for example, that in the Bible at least four types and ranks of Angels are mentioned. These are, at the highest rank, the Archangels as the more important than the Angels after that the Cherubim and the Seraphim. In the Bible God may give a revelation or instructions through the medium of these heavenly messengers to humankind.[68]

Due to the continuous wars between the Roman Empire and the Parthians, and the long lasting contact of the Roman military with the civilizations of the East, this cult of Mithras was carried to the West, and to Rome by the Roman Army. Very soon it gained strong popularity among military personnel in the Roman Empire, and the upper class of the Roman establishment, including some Emperors, later became members of that cult. Having been one of the subordinate deities of Zoroastrianism in the Achaemenid period, Mithras later became the central God of a religion in his own right, after this transition to the western hemisphere, and to the Roman Empire. On the way west, various smaller kingdoms and countries in Cappadocia and Mesopotamia had adopted—and were sacrificing to—Mithras as a deity representing the sun. The God Mithras, being of Indo-European origin, was already worshipped by the Aryan tribes, who entered the Iranian Plateau, as early as 2300–2000 BC. Probably the earliest historical documentation regarding this deity existed from circa 1450 BC, which is in the Hittite texts. Mithra was worshipped, as we have seen above, in both northern India and the Iranian Plateau well before the time of Zarathustra. During the Achaemenid Dynasty, which ended with the invasion of Alexander of Macedonia to Persia in circa 334 BC, Mithras was worshipped alongside Ahura Mazdâ.[69, 70]

Later in the Roman Empire, Mithras took on the mantle of the primary God of soldiers, and was an important bonding element in the life of professional soldiers and military personnel. These soldiers were permanently separated from family and friends, and had to live—and possibly die—in far away and in inhospitable places. Temples for Mithras have been found in such remote regions of the Roman Empire as settlements close to Hadrian's Wall (between Scotland and England) in Brocolitia (modern-day Carrawburgh). In principle, Mithraism in the Roman Empire was associated with the sun—*sol invictus* [the invincible sun]—and its organization had the character of a union of selected people, or a fraternity in the style of the later Freemasons.

Mithraism, at this point, had lost its solely ethical character and content of the pre-Mazdean (Zoroastrian) religious and philosophical ideology. It had transformed itself into a cult with secret society features, such as secret initiation ceremonies, secret initiation rites (called mysteries) and a hierarchy of grades for the members to climb up and to achieve. Being very popular amongst the higher ranked military in the Roman Empire, various Emperors were members of that cult. Among these was Emperor Commodus (161–192 AD), the son of Marcus Aurelius, who was initiated into the cult in 190 AD. Later on, Emperor Diocletian (244–311 AD), being one of the most capable Emperors of Rome—and the only man ever sitting on the Roman Imperial throne to abdicate and to go into voluntary retirement, leaving the Imperial power to others by his own free will—was also a member of the Mithraic cult. Diocletian, furthermore, declared Mithras as being one of the state Gods of Rome, and a "guardian of the Roman Empire". Ultimately some historians believe that Emperor Constantine the Great, in his earlier career as a Roman Army officer, was a member of the cult of Mithras. This new cult in Rome became popular in the first century AD and ended with Christianity dominating the society in the Roman Empire by circa 380 AD.

The Mithraism in the Roman Empire, being in the style of a fraternal organization, had elements in it that were not known in the ancient Persian Mithraism. In the Roman Empire, Mithraism was an archetypal mystery cult. Like the antique ancient rites of Demeter, Orpheus, and Dionysus, the Mithraic rituals admitted candidates by secret ceremonies, the meaning and the detail of which were only known to those who were previously initiated. Like all other institutionalized secret initiation rites of the past and present, this mystery cult forced the initiates to be controlled, and put under the command of their superiors and ultimate leaders. The initiate was then informed about the secret Mithraic Password, which was the Password of his Degree only, and which he was instructed to use to identify himself to other members, and which he was to repeat to himself continuously as his personal principle and future guidelines.

There is currently a heated discussion among scholars as to whether the Mithraism practised in the Roman Empire derives from the same deity who was worshipped before the time of Zarathustra in ancient Iran, or a completely different religion that shared only the same name. Firstly, we have to consider here that in a time where written records were technically difficult to make and preserve, and all details and doctrines of a religion were passed on by word of mouth from one generation to the next, the metamorphosis of religions and their ideologies depended on the geographical location, living circumstances and environments of the people who believed in them. Thus in early antiquity a religion changing its geographic location with time could also transform some of its ideological aspects. Furthermore, in a time frame of at least two thousand years and the travel of that cult from north eastern Iran, and the central Asian steps to the capital of Imperial Rome, many unexpected changes or metamorphoses can and did occur. Nevertheless, we can see that the core of that cult did not change and that the main ideological centrepiece of that religion was still the veneration of the sun whose heat and light dominates our existence.

Discussions of the origins of Mithraism have, at times, been nationalistic and decidedly un-academic; we have to mention here Franz Cumont. A Professor at the very ancient University of Ghent in Belgium, Franz Cumont (1868–1947) undertook extensive travels in the Middle East— namely Syria, Mesopotamia, and Armenia—under stressful political conditions, with a combined French–American expedition and conducted digs on the shore of the Euphrates at the previously unknown sites of Dura-Europos, where he discovered a previously unknown Mithraeum (Mithraic temple). The conclusion of his life's work suggested that Mithraism in the Roman Empire was originated from the pre-Zoroastrian deity. Following Emile Benveniste, Cumont believed that "…the basis of Mithraism to be a primitive form of Mazdean Dualism, not transformed and purified by the Zoroastrian …reform. Furthermore, in his book *Lux Perpetua* (Eternal light) he was convinced that the belief in the celestial immortality, proclaimed by the Platonic, Pythagorean and Stoic philosophical schools, was in reality taken over by the Greek Philosophers from the Maguseans , by which he meant the later followers and priests of Zarathustra.

In 1910, the Catholic establishment in Belgium revolted against these kind of ideas, and as a result Baron Edouard Descamps, the Catholic Minister of Sciences and Arts, refused to approve the faculty's unanimous recommendation of Franz Cumont for the Chair in Roman History. Though Cumont had been a professor in that University for years, he was forced to resign his position at the University—and at the Royal Museum in Brussels—and leave the country. Furthermore, after his death, critics of his interpretation of Mithras as the descendant of the Persian deity Mithra began to be heard, and surfaced at the First international Congress of Mithraic studies in Manchester, England, in 1971. Recent academics in North America are speaking now about the origins of the Mithraic religion, variously as having originated somewhere in the eastern part of the Roman Empire –or– as a Greek Mythical cult of astronomical origin, which reached Rome.

The most probable explanation is that the Mithraic cult originated from the Aryan tribes who came from the central Asian steppes and invaded the Iranian Plateau, circa 2000 BC or earlier. This cult predated Zarathustra himself and was very successful in its own rights. Its deity was venerated from the central Asian steppes to Mesopotamia, Babylon, the Kingdom of Mitanni, and Assyria simultaneously and next to any other local deity of these societies. It is true that, as far as is known, the worship of the ancient Mithraic deity of the Aryan tribes was not associated with Mithras slaying a Bull with a dagger—from whose blood all other living creature emerges—this being an important doctrinal part in the Roman Mithraism.

Significantly an interesting detail is that, approximately six hundred years earlier, the Achaemenid King Cambyses II, son of Cyrus the Great, in the year 525 BC, after having conquered Egypt and declared himself as the new Pharaoh, stabs the sacred bull presented to him by the Egyptian High Priests with a dagger in the genuine Mithraic manner.[71] This to the amazement of the Egyptian High priests present, as the sacred bull was, in fact, the Mnevis bull, which according to the ancient Egyptian religious tradition, appears when the sun god Ra enters the world of the mortals, and transforms himself into a black Bull. The Mnevis Bull is in this case the embodiment of the sun god Ra. According to German professor, Reinhold Merkelbach:

...apart from King Cambyses II, also another Persian Achaemenid king did the same thing, namely shortly before the invasion of Persia by Alexander of Macedonia, the king Artaxerxes III, again stabs the sacred Bull, to the horror and amazement of the Egyptian population. This act had been politically very negative for the Persian invaders and occupiers in Egypt, therefore it must have had a mystical or religious ceremonial reasons.[72]

When the Bull appeared, "… Mithraic doctrine had to be repeated, and sacrifice of that animal had to take place, for the greater salvation of the World.…" Herodotus reports that the "…Persians, when sacrificing animals, were singing, and that a sacrifice of an animal without the presence of the singing priests is not ceremonious. …"
Reinhold Merkelbach continues in this regard:

> "…This ceremonious act is probably to be looked upon clearly as an sacrifice in the Mithraic tradition. This was a sacred ritual and sacrifice, which the king Cambyses thought to be obliged to do, as an official devotee of Mithra."

Reinhold Merkelbach bases his second bull sacrifice of the king Artaxerxes III on the writings of Plutarch.[73] Therefore a bull who is associated with the sun god as in Roman Mithraism was also known in the Egyptian tradition—although probably not in connection with Mithraism.

In 1869 the German scholar Karl Bernhard Stark came forward with a different explanation for the symbolism of the tauroctony [killing of an ox or a bull], which was earlier not accepted by Franz Cumont, and which was therefore completely ignored and forgotten by scholars for the coming decades.[74] Karl Bernhard Stark's theory was based on the simple fact that the figures which are visibly painted or marked in the Roman Mithraism next to the one of Mithras in the ceremony of the Tauroctony—bull, scorpion, dog, snake, raven, lion, and cup—all possesses a parallel among the celestial constellations. In particular a group of celestial constellation that are visible together at certain moments during the year. The bull is paralleled by the constellation of Taurus, the scorpion by Scorpio, the dog by Canis Minor (smaller Dog) the snake by Hydra, the raven by Corvus, the lion by Leo, and the cup by Crater. Additionally, the star Spica, the wheat ear, which is visibly the brightest star in the constellation of Virgo, parallels the ears of wheat often shown in the Tauroctony, visibly showing as if growing out of the tail of the bull.

These parallels, all visible and clear, cannot be coincidental, and the Mithraic Tauroctony must have been conceived and created with a group of celestial constellations in mind and as a representation of heavenly or cosmic bodies. In recent times, various academics such as Roger Beck, Alessandro Bausani, Michael Speidel and Stanley Insler, all agree with the explanations of Karl Bernhard Stark, namely that the Mithraic Tauroctony is a clear map of the existing celestial constellations. This, the astronomical component in the Roman Mithraism, is the new direction that investigations concerning this important cult of the later Roman Empire has taken academic and private scholars. Also the astronomical components of Karl Bernhard Stark in the Roman Mithraism, which Professor Roger Beck from the university of Toronto has investigated further, is not present in the ancient Iranian Mithraism.

The Mithraism practised in the Roman Empire believed that Mithras had slain a Bull as a sacrifice, and it was from the blood of that bull that all other living things had emerged. Richard Foltz is of the opinion that several details point to the fact that the Roman Mithraism was a continuation of the ancient Iranian Deity Mithra.[75] Foltz points to the fact that Professor John Hinnels is here also of the opinion that several important parallels exist between the Iranian and the Roman Mithraism, namely that at both rituals food—bread, wine, fruit—was offered according to ancient Iranian tradition, and also that participants were wearing animal masks. The wearing of animal masks was also an ancient Iranian tradition and was a part of the Mehregan festivals, which is associated with the "Now Ruz" celebrations of the Spring Equinox. Furthermore, Foltz suggests that the most important Iranian Festival of "Now Ruz" is in reality of Mithraic origin and derives from the festival of Mehregan and is not of Zoroastrian tradition, making it of pre-Zoroastrian Origin.

Furthermore, Richard Foltz believes that during the Arsacid period (247 BC–224 AD) of the Parthian Empire the local rulers of the eastern part of the Iranian Nation were in reality Mithraists (in Persian -- Mehrparast), whereas in the western part of the country the local rulers were Mazdaists, or Zoroastrians. Also, according to Parvaneh Pourshariati, that these differences in religious belief in the empire continued well into the Sassanian period and ultimately brought about the downfall of the Sassanian Dynasty. In reality, the Roman Republic and later the Roman Empire in the west and the Parthian Empire in the east fought continuous wars and were in constant contact during that period, namely from circa 250 BC until 250 AD. Therefore, if at that time, some part of the Parthians were still worshipping Mithra as their main deity, it would be reasonable to believe that the Roman Mithraism was derived from the Parthian influence. Mithraism was only one of the important intellectual influences that reached the Roman Empire from Zoroastrian Persia. We know that important influences have been detected coming from Mithraism to the new religion of Christianity. Various components of Mithraism have been incorporated into Christianity, probably in order to facilitate the conversion of the followers of Mithras into the new emerging Christian religion. Professor of theology, Michael Patella investigates extensively the parallels and influences of Mithraism on early Christianity.[76] For example, according to the Mithraic cult, which is at least two thousand years older than Christianity, Mithras was born on the 25th of December, to a virgin, with shepherds as his first worshippers. His rites include a baptism, and a sacramental meal. Mithras was, in the ancient Iranian tradition, an ally and subordinate to Ahura Mazdâ, the creator, in his fight against the forces of lie and falsehood, evil and darkness.

Here we come to another interesting aspect of that pre-Zoroastrian deity Mithras whose influence reached beyond the borders of the ancient Iranian Plateau and that of Imperial Rome. One of the remarkable personalities of human history was the Egyptian Pharaoh Akhenaten—instead of enjoying the life of a ruler of ancient Egypt, as he was venerated as a living god, he followed his ideas and personal beliefs, sacrificing and fighting for his personal conviction. What he exactly believed and intended to do was nothing less than to destroy the ancient Egyptian state religion of polytheism, wherein the Pharaoh himself and his family were believed to be of divine descent, and he the Pharaoh was venerated as a living god.

Instead he tried to change the state religion of ancient Egypt, by declaring that there is only one God who created everything and that this God was the sun—from which all life derives. He ultimately failed, and his religion was forgotten for over three thousand years. His personal faith and his name were erased from the official records by the priestly castes of Egypt, and he was forgotten in history until the 1930s when his name, ideology, his religion and his forgotten capital city of Amarna were rediscovered beneath the sands of the Egyptian desert by archaeologists.

Akhenaten's personality is still very much an enigma for archaeologists and historians, and only now historians are slowly trying to reconstruct the events around Akhenaten and his time. Here we are investigating the probability that Akhenaten and his religious ideology had a strong influence or was, in fact, strongly inspired by Mithraism and the Mithraic cults. The same Mithraic cult that was subordinated to the ultimate creator God Ahura Mazdâ by Zarathustra—the same sun deity that gave birth later to a new cult in the Roman Empire, this with the so-called ideology of the *sol invictus* [invincible sun].

In order to prove our point, here some details of the time and life of the Pharaoh Akhenaten. What is known about Akhenaten, and has been accepted by the academic community as being historical, are the following facts: Akhenaten was the son of the Pharaoh Amenhotep

III whose reign ended 1350 BC. Amenhotep III, apart from his main wife Tiye, who was an Egyptian woman of common descent, had six other known wives, who were the daughters of kings or rulers in the northern part of his Empires. They were as follows:

- Gilukhepa, the daughter of Shuttarna II the King of Mitanni. He married her in the tenth year of his reign. The Mitanni Kingdom was located in a region of North Western Mesopotamia, in what is today eastern Anatolia.

- Tadukhepa, the daughter of his ally King Tushratta of Mitanni. He married her around the year thirty-six of his reign.

- A daughter of Kurigalzu, king of Babylon.

- A daughter of Kadashman-Enlil, king of Babylon.

- A daughter of Tarhundaradu, ruler of Arzawa. a small kingdom in western Anatolia.

- A daughter of the ruler of Ammia, a small kingdom in the region of modern-day Syria.

It should be noted that, according to the ancient traditions of Egypt and their theological paradigms, it was usual for a Pharaoh to accept royal women much younger than himself as wives. This was both to strengthen the chances of his offspring succeeding him and to strengthen the bonds with other hostile neighbouring kingdoms. Akhenaten's father, Amenhotep III, was born 1391 BC and died 1350 BC. He became Pharaoh at the age of twelve and ruled approximately twenty-seven years. An authentic ancient Egyptian Sphinx portrait of Pharaoh Amenhotep III is now adorning Universitetskaya Embankment in Saint Petersburg, Russia.

At the time of the death of the Pharaoh Amenhotep III, in the year 1350 BC, his son Akhenaten (Amenhotep IV) was sixteen years old, meaning Akhenaten was born 1366 BC. The old Pharaoh had another son, who was Akhenaten's older brother, but he died at a young age. It is known by historians that when Amenhotep III died, his only remaining son, the later Akhenaten, was not in Egypt. After his death, his main wife (Akhenaten's mother) Queen Tiye became the reigning sovereign, in charge of ruling the Egyptian kingdom. The historian Flinders Petrie writes:

> "....it appears as if she, Queen Tiye were the sole regent after the death of her husband Amenhotep III, and before the arrival and the active reign of Amenhotep IIII (Akhenaten).[77]

Arriving at the Egyptian Capital Thebes, Akhenaten was a stranger there at the time he assumed royal power from his mother. He had spent his childhood and youth abroad, partly in Babylon and partly wandering from country to country in the courts of various kings in the Middle East. His name is never mentioned in inscriptions of his father Amenhotep III—although a prince-heir to the throne would be *expected* to have his name mentioned next to the ruling Pharaoh. He and his father are never pictured together on any bas-reliefs and monuments.[78] His father Amenhotep III had himself depicted together with his wife and daughter in enormously oversized figures, but no son was ever represented in this or any other family portrait. Then after the death of Amenhotep III and the rule of his wife Queen Tiye for several months, her son Akhenaten appeared suddenly on the scene and took over the rule of the Egyptian Kingdom from her. It has even been suggested, by W.M. Flinders Petrie,[79] that Akhenaten *usurped* the throne. Among the letters written on clay tablets found in the state archives of Tell el-Amarna in the Nile Valley there are letters from Dushratta, the King of Mitanni (modern-day Anatolia) who wrote to Akhenaten:

....and when my brother (Amenhotep III) died, they proclaimed it, and when they proclaimed I also learned. He was gone... and I wept on that day... But when Naphuria (Akhenaten) the son of Amenhotep.... wrote to me – I will enter upon my reign, I said: Nimmuria (Amenhotep III) is not dead. Now Naphuria (Akhenaton) his great son.... has placed himself in his stead.[80]

This clay letter written by the ruler of the Mittani kingdom to the new Pharaoh Akhenaten, reveals that, first of all, the death of the old Pharaoh was not made public to his son Akhenaten by a group of people which this letter calls as "they." And secondly, it clarifies a very important point, which is that Akhenaten was not in the Egyptian kingdom before and during the death of his father. If he *had* been present, he would have succeeded his father as the new Pharaoh. As he was not present in the kingdom, his mother took over the power for several months. Furthermore, Akhenaten must have travelled not in Anatolia—where the Mitannic Kingdom was located—but probably in the eastern part of the Middle East. Clearly, the king of the Mitannis would not have written such a letter to him, if Akhenaten was with him at the time of the old King's death.

Sometimes after gaining the throne of the Egyptian kingdom, the Pharaoh Amenhotep IV changed his name officially to Akhenaten. This action was a consequence of his religious reform—the replacement of the ancient Egyptian supreme god Amon-Ra with that of the sun god Aten. Additionally, Akhenaten took for his personal agnomen, or personal motto, "Living in truth," and whenever these inscriptions of "living in truth" is found in any statue or records, even when the name of the king on that inscriptions has been destroyed, it is to be concluded that the person meant was Akhenaten.

Immediately after gaining the throne, Akhenaten started a full-scale replacement of all the gods in the ancient Egyptian pantheon with that of the Sun God Aten, proclaiming Aten being the one and only God, who created everything, and upon who alone everything depended. Having devoted his entire being to the new God Aten, he declared himself the only chosen son of that God, and the entire world was created by his God. In the days of the previous Pharaohs Amenhotep II, Tuthmoses IV and his father Amenhotep III, live humans sacrifices were made. Akhenaten stopped immediately all live human sacrifices, and forbid even the hunt and killing of animals for pleasure.

In the fourth year of Akhenaton's reign, he definitely broke with the Priests of the God Amon-Ra. It was a violent and dangerous rift between an ancient powerful and well-organized religious establishment, and a young pharaoh, who at the age of sixteen had just taken over the throne of Egypt. The priestly class, extremely powerful, had ruled the kingdom for millennia in the name of the ruling pharaohs and had always stood between the Pharaoh himself and the royal family on one side, and the general population of the Egyptian Kingdom on the other side as an intermediary.

Monarchy and theocracy clashed head to head, Akhenaton decided to complete the break and return the capital city of Thebes to what it had been before the New Kingdom, and the rise of Amon-Ra as the Father of the Gods—namely to one of the ordinary and second rated cities of the kingdom. The eight great temples of Amon-Ra, which were the important centre point of the city of Thebes were closed, its priests removed from their positions, and all the nobles of the former pharaoh's establishment dismissed.

Furthermore, Akhenaton refrained from acknowledging that he was the son of Amenhotep III, but next to his name he placed in all public statues or records, the heraldic motto of his life, namely "living in truth" Ankh-em-Maat. However, after having been on the throne for nine years, Akhenaten suddenly declared that Aten was not only the highest God, but the *only* God, and that he, Akhenaton, was personally the only intermediary between Aten and the Egyptian People. At this instance, he ordered the inscriptions of plural gods, and the name of all the other deities in the entire kingdom to be erased or destroyed from all statues and public records.

Akhenaten negated his true origin, by proclaiming that his true father was the Sun God Aten. He was now the son of the Sun God. Historians are in agreement that Akhenaten's new religion was not a clear monotheism as we currently think of it, but that it certainly had monotheistic tendencies and characteristics. It is known that Akhenaten, during the Amarna period, erected in Heliopolis a grand temple to the sun god Aten, under the name Wetjes Aton, elevating the sun god Aten. This temple stood for millennia until it was disassembled and its stone blocks used for the city walls of medieval Cairo. It is said that, to this day, in some places of the city Gates of Cairo the ancient stone blocks and their inscriptions from that temple can be seen.

One of the interesting theories concerning Akhenaten comes from Sigmund Freud in his book *Moses and Monotheism* which was first published in London in 1939. Here Freud believed that Akhenaten saw himself as a new prophet and had decided to propagate the message of the Aten as being the one god who created the world. Subsequently—according to Freud—Akhenaten educated monks and sent them as emissaries and missionaries to the various nations and peoples known to him, in order for these nations and people to be converted to his new religion. In this book, Sigmund Freud suggested that one of Akhenaten's main priests and officials, a man by the name of Tuthmoses, which is a commond ancient Egyptian name, one of the main ideologues of the new religion, left Amarna after the death of Akhenaten. After changing his name from Tuthmoses to Moses, he chose the Hebrews—his chosen people—to convert them to the new religion, adding some Hebrew components to his new teachings. In effect, Freud believed further that Moses was an Egyptian missionary sent by Akhenaten to convert the Hebraic people to his new Monotheistic religion and that, in the end, Moses was killed by the Jews themselves, for forcing them into such a harsh religious belief.

Needless to say, this theory was not well-received by the religious Jewish community and various high profile member of the Jewish community approached Freud on the subject. Among others were Professor Abraham S. Yehuda, the American Jewish theologian; he visited Freud in his home in Hampstead in London, and requested that he refrain from publishing this book. Sigmund Freud, nearing the end of his life, refused, and the *Moses and Monotheism* was published in London in 1939. Six month after this book was published, on September 23, 1939, Sigmund Freud died in London at the age of 83.

The god Aten, though not among the dominating gods of the Egyptian Pantheon, did exist long before Akhenaten. He was representing the sun disc as a peripheral minor god—in the city of Heliopolis, an ancient and constant worship to the sun god was held from ancient times and well before Akhenaten. It was Akhenaten who first elevated Aten to position of supreme creator. The British New Testament scholar, and professor of divinity Jimmy Dunn, has written an interesting article, dealing with the existence of Aten as the Sun God, in pre-Akhenaten times.[81] In all the monuments dating from the time of the Pharaoh Akhenaten, the sun disc is depicted in the form of an eye, the high relief and the low relief illustrations of the Aten show it with a curved surface, therefore the late scholar Hugh Nibley insisted that a more correct translation would be globe, orb, or sphere rather than disc. There is a possibility that Aten's three-dimensional spherical shape depicts an eye. This phenomenon appears only in one other religion, namely Zoroastrianism, wherein the sun was called Ahura Mazdâ's eye.

In the fifth year of his reign, probably 1345 BC, when he was twenty-one years old, Akhenaten abandoned Thebes—the seat of the High Priests of Amon-Ra at the temple complex of Karnak—and moved the capital city of the Kingdom to the newly erected city of

Akhet-Aton. The name of the new capital meant "The place where Aton rises" and was pronounced very similarly to his own newly adopted name. At a later excavation on that location, one of the most spectacular archaeological finds at the new capital city of Akhet-Aton (later called Amarna by archaeologists) was made—the beautiful painted bust of Nefertiti, Akhenaten's wife and Queen. It was found by the German archaeological expedition, and this magnificent statue is now in the Berlin Antiquities Museum. Tutankhamen was the son of Akhenaten with his wife Queen Nefertiti. After having ruled for seventeen years, Akhenaton died—probably sometime between 1335 and 1333 BC. Akhenaton and his name were all but lost from history, only to be rediscovered in the 1890s, after the excavation of his capital city Amarna by Flinders Petrie and the English archaeological expedition.

Scarcely, ten or fifteen years after the death of Akhenaton, Akhet-Aton, the city he so lovingly created in middle of the desert, was taken over again by the desert sand. Napoleon Bonaparte visited the excavation site of the City of Amarna in November 1798 with a group of French explorers, historians and scientists. His entourage measured and prepared the first site map of the city of Amarna, which was later published in a series of publications under the name of "La Description de l'Egypt" between the years 1821–1830.[82]

It was not until 1891–1892 that the Petrie expedition uncovered the remains of the ancient city. Previously, in the year 1887, not far from that location, a local peasant woman, who was digging a waterhole in the ground, found several packings of clay tablets with unknown signs to her. These clay tablets turned out to be a part of the diplomatic correspondence of the Pharaoh Akhenaton's court—this peasant woman had dug into the lost archives of Pharaoh Akhenaten Administration. The more than three hundred and eighty clay tablets found, written in several languages such as cuneiform (used mainly in the Persian and Babylonian Empires), Akkadian and Babylonian, concerned the diplomatic correspondence of the Pharaoh with foreign kings and rulers. There were also letters from military outposts requesting reinforcements, and other important documents. This find was of greatest historical importance. These letters were published in a classical edition with a German Translation by the Scandinavian scholar J.A. Knudtzon in 1915.[83]

It is in general accepted that Akhenaten himself died after having been Pharaoh for seventeen years; he gained the throne at the age of sixteen and ruled for seventeen years meaning he died at the age thirty-three, circa 1335 BC. The cause and the circumstances of Akhenaten's end are still shrouded in mystery. After the death of Akhenaten, the cult of the God Aten and his religious revolution fell out of favour very rapidly and was very soon forgotten. One of the major reasons for this was the close co-operation of the priest clan of the God Amon-Ra and a military-man under the name of Horemheb. Horemheb was a man of common birth, who had probably advanced to become, under Akhenaten, the commander in chief of the Royal Guard. Some time after Akhenaten's death and the accession to the throne of Akhenaten's son, Tutankhamen, Horemheb advanced to become the commander-in-chief of all the armed forces of the kingdom.

After Akhenaten's end, and a short interval during which his son— the child Pharaoh Tutankhamen—probably ruled with his mother, queen Nefertiti, the new strongman Horemheb took over the power and ruled for fourteen years as the new Pharaoh of the Egyptian kingdom until his death in 1292 BC. After having gained the throne, the new Pharaoh Horemheb systematically destroyed and disassembled all temples built by Akhenaten, which were dedicated to his sun god the Aten. Akhenaten's sarcophagus was taken out of his tomb and was destroyed, and his body was reburied in an unknown location.

Horemheb after becoming the new Pharaoh, in co-operation with the high priests of Amon-Ra, did everything to cancel and destroy any kind of record, which contained the names of those who were in any way connected to Akhenaten, his god the Aten, and his city Amarna. All official records in monuments temples and governmental records, read that after the reign of Amenhotep III (Akhenaten's father), his immediate successor was the Pharaoh Horemheb. It was not until the late nineteenth century that this man, whose personality so much fascinated Egyptologists and historians, was rediscovered and some vague surviving traces of his reign—and his god—were unearthed by archaeologists.

As a conclusion we can say that the time and the life of the Pharaoh Akhenaten contain several facts that are obvious. First of all, Akhenaten's status as a religious revolutionary and self-proclaimed prophet has led to much speculations and theories. It is clear that Akhenaten cannot be named as a pure monotheist, as it is known that he did not actively deny the existence of other gods beside the god Aten—he simply refrained from worshiping them. The technical term for this kind of belief is Henotheism (the acceptance of multiple gods but the worship of one). He was, furthermore, expecting his people and his followers to worship *him* as an intermediary, in order to connect with Aten.

The idea of Akhenaten being a pioneer of the monotheistic religions has connected him somehow to the monotheistic religion of Judaism. The theories connecting Akhenaten to the Judaic prophets speculate that Akhenaten was, in fact, influenced by the Hebrews who lived in Egypt at that time. This theory can not be correct in any sense, as the Hebraic people until the Babylonian captivity—which was around 700 years *after* Akhenaten—were themselves believing in multiple gods, and a clear Judaic monotheism only started from the time after the Babylonian captivity, circa 587 BC. For the time before the Babylonian captivity, the religion of the ancient Hebraic people has been characterized by scholars not as monotheism but as a folk religion.[84] We will enter into this subject in greater detail in following chapters. Furthermore, the biblical names of the Prophet Abraham and the Prophet Moses are not historical, but they are mythological personalities, which means their existence is dependent on fate rather than historical reality.

Akhenaten's rule with his elevated Creator God Aten appear in history two and a half centuries prior to any archaeological or written evidence concerning the Hebraic presence found in that area. The Egyptian scholar Ahmed Osman claims that Akhenaten's maternal grandfather Yuya was the same person as the Biblical Joseph—forgetting that Joseph himself was a mythological personality added to the Hebraic scriptures more than a thousand years after Akhenaten's death. Ahmed Osman, being a knowledgeable Egyptian historian, writes in his preface to *Moses and Akhenaten:*

> I came to London from Cairo a quarter of a century ago, intending to devote most of my time to trying to establish links between the Bible and what we know, from a variety of sources, of the Egyptian history.[85]

What Ahmed Osman forgets here is that the Judeo-Christian scriptures, which introduce us to personalities such as Abraham, Moses, Josef and others—and who are without exception related to monotheism—are dated at the earliest to the time of the prophets Ezra and Nehemiah's return from Babylon to Jerusalem, circa 445–444 BC. Whereas, the events around the Pharaoh Akhenaten (died c. 1335 BC) and his religious revolution in favour of Aten the Sun God are approximately 900 years earlier in history.

Concerning the end of Akhenaten's religion and his new ideology among the Egyptian population, we have seen in history that religions or cults cannot be simply stopped or eradicated from the public memory and public belief from one moment to the other. Even after losing their ideological base, religious beliefs still remain in public memory or public worship for generations, until they are slowly forgotten. We have seen in earlier chapters that Zarathustra, after having declared most of the pre-Zoroastrian gods as the demons and thus unworthy of worship, it took nearly two millennia to eradicate those deities from public memory. Strangely, in the case of Akhenaten's new religion, it was different, as this new religion was immediately rejected and forgotten after the monarch's death. Therefore, we can conclude that there was something in this new religion and its ideology that was fundamentally alien to the Egyptian populations belief and was considered hostile to them and the Egyptian civilization.

In conclusion, we have seen that Akhenaten, the son of the Pharaoh Amenhotep III, was not present in Egypt at the time of the death of his father, as his mother had to take over the throne for several months, before her sixteen-year-old son (still Amenhotep IV) could come and take over the throne himself and become the new Pharaoh. Akhenaten was not in Egypt, and also not in the Kingdom of Mitanni, as it is evident from the letter of the King of Mitanni, Tushratta, which we have mentioned earlier. Historians do not know where Akhenaten was at the time of his father's death; it is only known that he was not in Egypt. Therefore, the question is where else can a boy and a hereditary royal prince of probably twelve to sixteen years stay where he is safe, protected and in good company.

The reasonable answer to this is that the young and only son of the ruling Pharaoh was very probably visiting and staying with his stepmother's families in the kingdom of the Hittites and or in Babylon, or both. We have earlier seen that Amenhotep III had married in total six women, who were the daughters of the Kings of various kingdoms in the Middle East, included the daughters of two subsequent kings of Babylon. Where would a Pharaoh trust to send his young and only son and successor after his older son had just died in his own lifetime. The answer is probably to the court of another king, trustworthy and closely allied to him by blood relations. Therefore it is reasonable to assume that young Amenhotep IV was in Babylon, for this city was, at that time, one the great centres of civilization, and the great Metropolis of the world of antiquity. Probably larger, more interesting and more crowded than any city outside Egypt, it was in any case more important than the capitals of the Mitanni or Hittite kingdoms. Therefore, it is very likely and logical that young prince was in Babylon. As travelling in those times was difficult, dangerous, and very time-consuming, it would be logical to assume that once a child travels a long distance—for example from Egypt to Babylon in Mesopotamia—he would stay there for some years, in the court of the local king whose daughter is at the same time his stepmother.

Wherever Akhenaten was in his youth, before returning to Egypt to take over the throne, he must have been exposed to and influenced by the Mithraic cult, surrounded as he no doubt was by people who worshiped the sun God Mithras. At the same time, he was not being similarly exposed to the Egyptian traditional gods. That probably was the reason why, upon his return to Egypt to take up the mantle of pharaoh at the age of sixteen, he had no consideration for the traditional Egyptian deities. If Akhenaten had lived in Egypt instead of living outside the country as a child, he would have known that the Egyptian pantheon included gods dedicated to the sun, worshiped in the City of Heliopolis, and that the sun god Aten, although a minor god, was well known and accepted by the high priest of Amon-Ra.

Therefore, all signs of Akhenaten sun god worship point to a connection of influence between Akhenaten and the Indo-European pre-Zoroastrian sun god Mithra. The proof that his sun worship of the God Aten had his roots not in the Egyptian pantheon but in gods of foreign origin is that, after his death and subsequent disposal by the Pharaoh Horemheb, his religion was regarded by the religious establishment and by the people of Egypt with a hostile attitude, therefore immediatly rejected and forgotten. Were his new revolutionary religious doctrine of the sun god Aten to have been based on gods existing and worshipped previously in the pantheon of the Egyptian people, the religious establishments and the general population would logically have tolerated it. As in the time of previous Pharaohs, for instance, various Gods were worshipped simultaneously and some of these gods were worshiped as the main god. Akhenaten's new Aten, however, though familiar in name,was completely rejected and eliminated in a hostile manner.

We have seen in later Egyptian history that, at various times, the population had a hostile attitude towards any religious influence or traditions coming to Egypt from the eastern part of the Middle East. Centuries later, when the Achaemenid kings conquered Egypt, as king Cambyses II did in 525 BC, and two of the Achaemenid kings[86] stabbed and killed a sacred bull in front of the high priests, in the manner of the Mithraic doctrine, the Egyptian public and the religious establishments was deeply perturbed. These acts were regarded as a direct affront to the ancient Egyptian religious tradition and deemed as a direct insult to the Egyptian gods and subsequently, Egyptian people. The question as to whether the stabbing of the sacred bull by the two Persian kings was indeed an act of Mithraic religious ceremony, or was done under some other motivation, is not clear. What is important for us here is that any influence by the newly emerging civilization of the Indo-European people in the Iranian plateau—including Mithraism and also the religion of the Prophet Zarathustra—was regarded by the Egyptian religious and cultural establishment as being alien to them, and was therefore at all times rejected.

The nearly two-century Persian–Achamenian occupation of Egypt, which lasted from 525 BC until approximately the invasion of Alexander of Macedonia, did not result in introduction of any of the Zoroastrian teachings—be it Mazdaism or Mithraism—to the Egyptian population. At that time the Egyptian population could neither be influenced by Zoroastrianism nor by Mithraism. The German archaeological publication Minerva reported that Zoroastrian fire temples had been unearthed in Egypt, if so, then they were erected for use of the Iranian–Zoroastrian community living in Egypt at that time. The Achaemenid kings on the contrary, had to try always to rule in Egypt in a manner which was acceptable and conformed to the ancient Egyptian religious traditions. This could be one of the explanations as to why the religious teachings of Akhenaten had ended abruptly with him—his religious ideology was influenced by a foreign eastern deity namely Mithras.

On the other hand, parallels between the religious doctrine of Akhenaten and that of early Mithraism are evident. Professor Roger Beck of the University of Toronto writes:

> For the Mithraic mysteries I shall propose, likewise, just two axioms (ultimate sacred postulates) Deus sol invictus Mithras this is the God's cults title and the normal formula for dedications, it establishes that the religions effective Power is God is the sun is unconquered is Mithras…[87]

Some names and other terminology of the Mittani Kingdom show close similarities to the Indo-Aryan belief, suggesting that an Indo-Aryan Elite imposed itself over the Mittani–Hurrian population over the course of the Indo-Aryan expansion during the period circa 2000–1500 BC. Documentation exists that point to the fact that, in a treaty between the Hittites and the Mitanni Kingdom, the deities invoked are firstly the God Mithra, and then secondary Varuna, Indra, and Nasatya.[88] Manfred Mayrhofer, professor at the University of Vienna, proved that extensive influence in the language and military expressions have come to the Mittani kingdom and the Hittites population from the Mithraic cults of the Indo-Aryan languages and civilization.

And finally it would be illogical and unreasonable to believe that a boy under the age of sixteen would create, alone in his mind, a complete philosophy of a new monotheistic religion in an environment firmly based on polytheistic beliefs. It would be reasonable and logical to assume that the boy Akhenaten, being between the ages of twelve and sixteen, living somewhere in Babylon or another location in the Middle East, was firmly subjected to the cult and the worship of the sun god Mithra, and had been grown up in an environment of Mithra worship. Later when he arrived in Egypt from the long journey of the Middle East, he started to implement and put into reality, as the new Pharaoh in his kingdom, the religious beliefs under which he had been

raised, namely Mithraism. Probably in order not to stir up any unnecessary reaction of the general public of his kingdom, he didn't use the
name Mithra, but in order to appease the population, he used that of
an already existing ancient Egyptian sun god, namely the god Aten.

As for the hypothetical connection between Akhenaten and the
ideology of the Prophet Zarathustra, Akhenaten died circa 1335 BC,
whereas according to Professor Mary Boyce, Zarathustra's lifetime
is been estimated to be 1400 BC or earlier.[89] This shows clearly that
Zarathustra likely lived earlier than Akhenaten, and their ideology
shows no common ground. There are no records or documentation
as of this date, which would connect the ideas of the two man to
each other.

2. DOGMAS AND TEACHINGS OF ZOROASTRIANISM

Before entering into the details of the Zoroastrian teachings, an important question has to be investigated: is Zoroastrianism a monotheistic religion, or is it a dualistic based belief? Are Ahura Mazdâ and Ahriman poised, balanced against each other, as equal but opposite forces —or— is Ahura Mazdâ set as a unique supreme being with Ahriman playing the subordinate role of a demon working against the will of its own creator?

According to Martin Haug (1827–1876), noted Orientalist and early scholar of Iranian studies:

> Zarathustra taught a pure, ethical monotheism—and a philosophical dualism. There was no evidence for rituals in the Gathas, that the teachings of Zarathustra was anytime corrupted by later Generations.[90]

The same is held to be true by Professors Mary Boyce[91] and John R. Hinnells[92]

Zarathustra believed profoundly in a just God and therefore in the justice of the just God—Asha [Truth] which has been called the decisive confessional concept of his religion—but the injustice in the society of his own time drove him to project its strict and final administration and consequences to the life hereafter. Fusing the two existing beliefs about life and death, he taught that all mankind, man and woman alike, could attain heaven by accepting his revelation and acting justly in accord with it (Y 46.10). But humankind must be judged when, on the third day after death, as in ancient traditional Iranian beliefs, the soul ascends at sunrise to the peak of Mount Hara, the Mythical Mountain at the centre of the earth. There, its good thoughts, words and deeds are weighed in a balance against the bad, and if the good are heavier, the soul crosses the broad Chinvat Bridge and passes up to the heavens. If the bad outweigh the good, the bridge contracts, and the soul plunges down through a chasm into the underworld, seen by Zarathustra as "a place of worst existence," a hell, where the Evil Spirit presides over retributive punishments. The blessed and the damned will remain in heaven or hell as spirits until Frashkokereti which is the day of the final and last Judgment. At that time there will be a general resurrection of the bodies, and the departed spirits will be reincarnated to undergo the last Judgment.

One fundamental aspect of the religious belief of Zarathustra is the principle of the innocence of all humankind. There is no concept of guilt in Zoroastrianism, like in Christianity, where all humans are guilty from the beginning, and are born with the concept of the original sin. Therefore the son of god has to come and by sacrificing himself on the cross, he has to redeem the sins or guilt of all humanity. According to Christian dogma, the person of Jesus Christ has taken the guilt of humanity on his person, sacrificing himself for the sake of humankind. This dogmatically important point is, since the time of Saint Augustine, a declared and accepted cornerstone of the Christian faith. Saint Augustine, one of the chief ideologues of the Christian faith, before converting to Christianity himself was a Manichaean priest, and the concept of humanity being born guilty was among the creeds of the religion founded by the Prophet Mani. We will talk about him in following chapters. When it comes to the Zoroastrian outlook on life Mary Boyce has this to say:

> The true realization that every thing good in this world is the affirmation of God is perhaps the kernel of Zoroastrian spirituality... A Zoroastrian is encouraged to live life to its fullest, in order that he may learn to preserve and enjoy the goodness of the seven creations... It is through an existential perception of the bounteous immortals that a Zoroastrian learns to formulate an ethical policy of the Good living. This awareness brings about a gnosis of what is indeed the right thought, the right word, and the right deed this being the key unquestionably to becoming an Ashavan the possessor of the truth.[93]

Significantly, fasting, asceticism and any kind of self-chastisement is a sin in Zoroastrianism, and all kind of celebrations and enjoyment in life are deemed to be part of the good creation by Ahura Mazdâ and in the spirit of the Ashavan the truth in this world. Furthermore, again on this matter Mary Boyce says:

> Zoroastrianism is opposed to any kind of asceticism in any form, partly because this involves a rejection of good things created by Mazdâ, which it is rational and grateful to take pleasure in, and partly because it tends to weaken the body and make it less able to receive Hauvatat and Ameretat and to pursue the active way of life proper to Ashavan. Fasting was accordingly a sin, as was any kind of self-inflicted form of suffering, and to be joyful was a virtue. Since

Mazdâ created joy, therefore sorrow has no place in his perfect world, which every Ashavan should be striving to help to create, in pushing back evil bit by bit. The breadth and vigour of Zoroastrian ethic, embracing spiritual, moral and physical health, is part of the religions strength and a vital element in it, as is that the aim of all just endeavour is not only to please God and to save one's own soul, but also to strive together with God to save the whole world. The faith is not man centred, but perceives all the creations as seeking, consciously or unconsciously, to reach the one glorious goal of Frasho-kerety.[94]

Zarathustra, as we know, had created a community which was united by clearly defined doctrines, shared moral endeavour, and common observances. Accordingly therefore, this unity and the conviction of his followers that all who would not accept his revelations were likely to be damned in eternity, must have been a provocation to the unconverted. Indeed it is believed that Zarathustra himself met with a violent end in his old age, stabbed by the dagger of a pagan priest while praying. In this regard, the Persian national Poet Ferdowsi writes in *Shahnameh*, which dates from the 980 AD, that the death of Zarathustra and the downfall of the Vishtaspa kingdom was caused by "…horse riding nomadic people from the east."

The Zoroastrian creed or daily prayer "the Fravarane" appears to have taken form during those early, difficult times and represents, it has been suggested, the declaration of faith required of each new convert. The ancient text begins:

I profess myself a worshipper of Mazdâ, a follower of Zarathustra, rejecting the Daevas, accepting the Ahuric doctrine, the one who praises the Amesha Spentas, who worships the Amesha Spentas. To

Ahura Mazdâ, the good, the rich in treasures, I
ascribe all things good. (Y 12.1)

The word chosen before all others to define a believer is
Mazdayasna, which means a worshipper of Mazdâ. This occurs eight
times in the longer version of the creed, (presented as Y 12) and only
four times it is mentioned as a *Zaerathushtri* which means a follower of
Zarathustra. The text then continues:

> I forswear....the company of Daevas and of the
> followers of Daevas, of demons, and the followers
> of demons, of those who do harm to any being by
> thoughts, words, deeds or outward signs.... Truly I
> forswear the company of all this as belonging to the
> Dorugh [the lie], as defiant (of the good)... even as
> Zarathustra forswore the company of Daevas... At
> all encounterings at which Zarathustra spoke about
> Mazdâ, together, ...so I forswear, as Mazdâ wor-
> shipper and Zoroastrian, the company of Daevas...
> As was the choice of the Waters, the choice of the
> Plants, the choice of the beneficent Cow, the choice
> of Ahura Mazdâ, who created the cow, who (created)
> the just Man, as (was) the choice of Zarathustra, the
> choice of Kavi Vishtaspa, the choice of Frashaostra
> and Jamaspa....by that choice and by that doctrine
> am I a Mazdâ Worshipper

These last lines emphasize the characteristic Zoroastrian doctrine
that by choosing the good, each individual is allying himself as a
humble fellow worker with God and the whole spenta-cosmos. Ahura
Mazdâ is honoured here as the Creator, here the Fravarane ends with
the believer engaging himself to uphold the threefold Zoroastrian
ethic, and the faith in general:

I pledge myself to the well-thought thought,

I pledge myself to the well-spoken word,

I pledge myself to the well-performed act.

I pledge myself to the Mazdâ-Worshipping religion, which is righteous, which of all faiths which are, and shall be the greatest, the best, the most beautiful, which is Ahuric, which is Zoroastrian…

Mary Boyce says, furthermore, that a Zoroastrian has to cover his head at all times in the presence of the sacred fires or at times of prayers, according to the religious dogmas, this as a sign of respect and devotion to the creator.

2.1 ASHA—THE TRUTH— OR THE TRUE COSMIC ORDER

One of the key words in the Zoroastrian ideology is the word of Asha which has been translated as truth, or cosmic truth, order, or maybe true cosmic order. Being one of the important concepts of the Avestan writings, it is one of the three short ritual formulas for prayer, which is called "Ashem Vohu". This prayer has twelve words, and could be approximately translated as: *Asha is best of all that is good*. The lines that follow these are a matter of discussion among linguists. Mary Boyce has translated it as:

…According to wish it is, according to wish it shall be for us, Asha belongs to Asha Vahishta…[95]

We see here that Mary Boyce does not translate the word Asha itself—whereas Humbach and Ichaporia translate it as *truth*. Other meanings also could be truth, cosmic order, or true order, or also sun-like beautiful order. According to Mary Boyce, the Indo-Iranians conceived their gods to be as cosmic and universal elements and therefore unlimited in time and space, but not as personal divinities. They apprehended an universal principle of what ought to be [in Avestan: *asha*; in Sanskrit: *rta*, variously translated as *order, righteousness, truth*]. This principle should govern everything, from the workings and laws of nature to the human laws including all of the human conduct. It was guarded, they think, by a great triad of ethical divinities, the lords [in Avestan: *Ahura*; in Sanskrit: *Ashura*]. The greatest divinity of them, known to the Iranians of antiquity as Ahura Mazdâ [Lord of Wisdom] was conceived, it seems, as the divine counterpart of the wise supreme high priest, who wielded authority in the tribe through his learning and his sacred powers. In the Rigveda he is referenced simply as 'the Ashura', and below him there were the two lessor divinities, Varuna and Mithra, Guardians respectively of the oath and the covenant, who came therefore to hypostatise truth and loyalty, and were active and doing Ahura Mazdâ's will. Equivalent to archangels in Christianity.

These two divinities, seem to be the divine counterparts of those tribal chieftains who were called the 'ashavan', meaning those who are possessing Asha, meaning those "...who are truthful righteous and posses the sense right order". Varuna as lord of the truly spoken words was venerated particularly as a creator god in his own right. His name was not mentioned in the known Iranian tradition, but mostly in the Indian tradition. Another powerful god of the Indian subcontinent, Indra, was worshiped as the divine counterpart of the warrior, invoking strength, courage and success in battle, for the Hindu worshipers of the Indian sub-continent. The Iranians in the pre-Zoroastrian times, also venerated 'nature' and 'cult' gods. They thought of the divine beings as generally benevolent.

At the beginning of the third Ghata we can realize that Ahura Mazdâ is the creator or father of Asha, and this is of greatest dogmatic importance. Ahura Mazdâ, the Wise Lord and the sun like Asha are worshiped together. It can be said that Asha is a key concept in the Zoroastrian perception of the cosmic principle. The opponent of Asha, is the lie, falsehood and the deception. One of the other aspects of Asha is the infinite light, which is the place of Ahura Mazdâ.

"...And the infinite light is the place and space of Ahura Mazdâ as it is called the endless light..."[96] This is also the reason that Zoroastrian priests (Mobeds) have always to turn their face to the source of light, any light available, when performing a religious ceremony. To compare with this, we see that in the Torah-Genesis 1:2 and later in the Christian Old Testament it says therefore:[97] "And God said—let there be light—and there was light, and God saw that the light was good..."

2.2 THE CREATOR GOD AND THE NAME AHURA MAZDÂ

The name Ahura Mazdâ, meaning the "Wise Lord" which was used for the first time by the Prophet Zarathustra, is the name for the uncreated supreme God, who created this world and the galaxies. It was Zarathustra, who for the first time had introduced him to humankind. His name, Ahura Mazdâ, was subsequently in the course of the history of the Iranian people and in the course of time subjected to various transformations. According to Professor P.O. Skjaervo:

> Ahura Mazdâ, by his thought and words and actions
> first ordered the Cosmos, and still upholds the true
> cosmic order, the visible image of which is the day lit
> sky, with the sun at its centrepiece. Ahura Mazdâ is

also the one who engendered many of the elements in the cosmos, and he is the ruler. His two epithets, Ahura and Mazdâ, which also make up his name, refer to these functions.[98]

Furthermore, according Mary Boyce:

> There is but one God, and he is the Creator.... God is absolutely good. This goodness in itself desires the goodness of others. God wishes that man should comply, in knowing Him. (Denkard 3.147)[99]

In the Gathas these epithets are still independent of one another, although either of them is likely to be followed by the other in the same strophe. In the Young Avesta, Ahura Mazdâ is clearly the name of the divinity, and whether there still was a feeling for what the words originally meant, was uncertain. By the Achaemenid period, the uni-verbation process was complete, and the name appears as Ahura Mazdâ, which in turn in Parthian and middle Persian became Ohrmazd, then still later Hormazd. In eastern Iran the name continued to be associated with the sun, even after the Islamic invasion, and even come to mean the sun itself. The same after the dethronement of the Zoroastrian supreme deity by other religions, meaning Islam and Christianity. It is significant that in Buddhist Khotan "Urmaysd" means the sun, and the same in Chorezmian "Remazd" and equally in modern language of sanglechi. But this is not to say that Ahura Mazdâ was the sun god, or he represented the sun, or he was the representation of light. Ahura Mazdâ was the Supreme Creator God, and all other gods or deities were inferior and subordinated to him.

There is the evil spirit, who is the ruler of the destructive forces Angra Maynu [in Middle Persian: Ahriman]. This ruler of the destructive forces, or of the dishonesty and the lie, is not equivalent to Ahura Mazdâ the uncreated supreme god. The rank or the place of the rulers of the evil forces is probably equivalent to that of the Devil. In the Gathas, which are the oldest texts of Zoroastrianism and are attributed to the Prophet himself, Angra Maynu is not yet a proper name, only in one instance—Yasna 45.2—do we see the words separately angra as destructive malign, and further down the word Mainyu mind spirit. We see in later Zoroastrianism that the daevas have been transformed into demons, but this is not jet evident in the Ghatas. Zarathustra sees the daevas initially as wrong gods or false gods that have to be rejected. Only later on, they are going to be named as demons. In the beginning, in Yasna 32.3, these daevas are identified as the offspring of evil thinking (akem manah), there is no mention of any Angra Maynu yet. In Yasht 19.96, a hymn that shows the Gathic injunction, Angra Maynu will be vanquished and Ahura Mazdâ will ultimately prevail. Importantly, there is no evidence in the Zoroastrian tradition that the destructive force, Angra Mainyu (or Ahriman), was ever a cultic competitor of Ahura Mazdâ.[100] This is an fundamental point, and it shows that Ahura Mazdâ was indeed the supreme and only creator God, and the evil forces under Angra Mainyu (or Ahriman) were subordinated to him.[101]

Mid March 2014 an article went through the world news media, which said that Astronomers had detected a very small electronic evidence which had remained from the initial start of the Universe namely the "Big Bang", which happened according to the theory 13.8 billion years ago. In connection to the news articles, Professor of Zoroastrianism at the University of London, Almut Hintze, wrote a comment which was printed in the *Financial Times*, Thursday March 20, 2014, p. 32:

Sir,

"At the beginning of time Ohrmazd created the world out of his own substance, which is eternal light." This passage from a Zoroastrian Middle Persian text on cosmology, the Bundahishn, compiled in the

tenth century AD but based on much older traditions, reads like a pre-scientific summary of the most
recent discovery... This sensational breakthrough
was reported on your front page on Tuesday (March
18, 2014). The discovery of the gravitational ripples
is very excited indeed, but it should not be forgotten that the Zoroastrian pre-scientific explanation
of the origins of the world not only pre-empted this
discovery but also viewed it within the larger picture
of the origins of the cosmos and of its goal, ideas
which scientists are still a long way from verifying
in measurable terms... alongside science, it is well
worth being aware of the humanities, religious traditions in particular. [...] The question of what the primordial light is with which the Big Bang happened is
still to be explored .... but pre-scientific answers are
already there in religious traditions. One approach
does not preclude the other, of course, and both are
vital. But in the current climate that underrates and,
as a result, underfunds the humanities, it is necessary
to be open and listen to both. —Almut Hintze.

2.3 AHRIMAN OR ANGRA MAINYU—THE EVIL AND DESTRUCTIVE SPIRITS

The opponents of the creator god, Ahura Mazdâ, are the demons and
the destructive spirits of the cosmic deception, the lies and dishonesty
and decay and the death. Angra Maynu is the principal agent and the
Evil Spirit—*Angra* means "dark or black" and *Angra Maynu* literally means "the dark or black spirit". When Ahura Mazdâ created
and established the light, healthy,and ordered universe, the evil spirit

Angra Maynu (Ahriman) in turn polluted it with their own evil things, namely sickness, darkness, dishonesty, lies, and finally death.[102] It is interesting in this context that, in order to elevate his supreme creator God Ahura Mazdâ, the Prophet Zarathustra had to destroy and degrade nearly all of the pre-existing divinities.

Therefore we can see that the agents of the evil spirits are, to some extent, the old pre-Zoroastrian Indo-Iranian deities, worshipped in the time before Zarathustra. In the Zoroastrian terminology, their demotion was caused by themselves in making the wrong choices, meaning them siding with the forces of the evil spirit and dishonesty and lie. These demons and dark spirits are the equivalent of the Devil in the Christian religion, although their position in Zoroastrianism is stronger than that of the Devil in Christianity. In Zoroastrianism it is Ahura Mazdâ, who has created the cosmos, but the forces of darkness and dishonesty— the Angra Maynu or Ahriman—are fighting the good creation, in this respect they seem initially to be on the same level as the good creator god Ahura Mazdâ. Some people are speaking here initially about a dualism in the religion founded by Zarathustra, meaning the good creation of the cosmos, and the evil forces are initially nearly on the same level, but in reality Zoroastrian ideology is of the position that Ahura Mazdâ is supreme to that of Ahriman or the evil forces.

In Zoroastrianism all humankind are born free and innocent without an initial or original sin, and have the choice to chose between the path of righteousness and the path of dishonesty, for which they are going to be held responsible in the afterlife. The supremacy of Ahura Mazdâ over his adversaries is evident in the fact that, at the end and the last day of judgment, the evil forces will fail, and Ahura Mazdâ will save the world and all the souls will be cleansed and return to the eternal God and will be united with him. And that will be the end of time.

2.4 THE IMMORTALITY OF THE SOUL AND THE AFTERLIFE

From the time of the pre-Zoroastrian period, the Aryan tribes in central Asia had their own religious customs and rites. With reference to death, it was believed that, in some exceptional cases, humans after death would be resurrected within one year, and would continue to live on this earth as before, and in some other cases their soul would be joining the gods in heaven.

This uncertainty and ambiguity has been given a believable and logical interpretation by Mary Boyce. She believes that, in the pre-Zoroastrian period, at a time of social turmoil and bloodshed and general lawlessness, harm and looting and damage to life and property to the tribe or the clan by strangers or the competing tribes was a constant event. We know that the war chariot, first historically attested circa 1500 BC, gave new mobility to predators, who were mostly well armed warrior bands from the eastern Asiatic steppes. In order to induce the stronger man to defend their own tribe and fight in the hostile confrontations with strangers, the priests and those "elders or wisemen" of the tribe had declared, on behalf of the gods, that those who will lose their life in the struggle for the defense of the tribe will be rewarded later by the gods. At a later date the gods will "resurrect them within one year of their death," or in other cases for individuals who did a very important deed for the community, their soul after death would join the gods.[103]

Basically, resurrection of the physical body, according to Mary Boyce, and the immortality of the soul was in exceptional cases possible in the pre-Zoroastrian religion, and in their general worldview. Zarathustra changed this, declaring the souls of all humankind as being immortal. According to Zoroastrianism, when a child is being conceived, the pre-existing soul, which is of divine origin, enters the body of the newly born, and after death, the soul leaves the body and enters the next stage in its existence to be judged in the next world.

The question of what happens to the soul after death, is documented in several Avestan (Videvdad chap. 19, and Hadokht Nask) and Pahlavi texts (Bundahishn chap. 30, and Mhenoy Karad chap. 2). The Pahlavi texts indicate that the damned will suffer unspeakable punishment in Hell.

In the book of Arda Viraz [Arda Wiraz Namag], it contains full details of these sufferings and punishments for the evil spirited and the treatment of those who were Righteous, who will be sent into the beyond to enjoy their existence in goodness and harmony. All souls after having passed over Chinvat Bridge will be conducted to heaven and hell, as well as the intermediate area reserved for those whose good thoughts and good actions equal their bad thoughts and bad actions.

After death the soul leaves the body and enters the afterlife to be cleansed, either in Paradise or Hell accordingly. After the souls having been purified and redeemed in the other world they will join the divine and eternal God again, and will be united with him until the end of the world and the end of time. We will mention here some passages from the *Menog-i Khrad* [The spirit of Wisdom] which is a compilation of works from the later Sassanian period. According to Mary Boyce, these writings are based on ancient material from the pre-Achaemenid times. Here we read of the fate of the soul, (from Pahlawy sources):

> Do not trust in life, for in the end death will over-come you, and dog and bird will rend your corpse, and your bones will lie on the ground. And for three days and nights you soul will sit at your body head. And at the fourth day at dawn, accompanied by the just Srosh and the good Vay and mighty Vahram, and opposed by Astvihad and the worse Vay and the demon Vizarsh .... It will reach the high and ter-rible Chinvat Bridge, to which everyone must come, just or wicked...When then the soul of the just man

crosses the Bridge, the Bridge becomes if as a mile wide, and the just soul crosses accompanied with the just Srosh. And his own good will come to meet him...When a wicked person dies, then for three days and three nights.... Through the great glory of the Creator, and at the command of him who is the judge and protector of the Bridge, it becomes a broad crossing for the just, ...and for the wicked it becomes a narrow crossing, just like a razor's edge....[104]

2.5 THE SAOSHYANT OR THE MESSIAH

The Saoshyant is a personality in Zoroastrian eschatology who will bring the final healing and renovation of the world [in Avestan: Frashokereti]; his name means the one who will bring benefit. The dogmas of Zarathustra and the Zoroastrian tradition envisage a future saviour, who will return to the world three times at one thousand year intervals. Three times he will be born to a virgin girl, who will bath in the sacred waters of Lake Kansaoya (modern-day Lake Hamoun). These waters, have miraculously preserved the seed of the prophet Zarathustra himself. Yasht 19.92 mentions Lake Kansaoya by name. The first saviour to come to the world will be called Hushedar. The second saviour is the Hushedarmah. The third ultimate saviour—the Messiah if you will—will be Saoshyant who will lead the humankind in its final battle against the forces of falsehood and evil. The story of the Saoshyant's conception and early life are described in the Denkard 7.10.15 ff.

In the Gathas, which are believed to have been composed by the Prophet Zarathustra himself, and are the most sacred hymns in Zoroastrianism, the term is used to refer to the Prophet Zarathustra's own mission, who will bring "benefit to humanity" The word

Saoshyant may have been a title applied to Zarathustra himself. (Yasna 46.3) The word Saoshyant appears also in the Younger Avesta, clearly so in Yasht 13.129. Also a plural form appears in Yasht 17.1. Professor P.O. Skjaervo writes:

> At the time when the third son of Zarathustra the real and final Saoshyant, has been born from a Virgin he will bring about the return to the origins, bringing about the perfect world Frashkerd. ... The Saoshyant will however, experience several setbacks. During the Millennium of Ushedar—there will be a terrible rain followed by a harsh winter lasting three years, during which almost all mankind is killed... Towards the end of the human existence the Fortune will come to the Saoshyant...and he will lead the battle against Evil. He will raise the death, and Zarathustra's son "Isadwastar" will gather all mankind, whose good and bad deeds are revealed.[105]

The role of the future Saoshyant The Messiah as the future saviour of the world is also described in Yasht 19.88–96. Where it is clearly written that he will achieve the Frashokereti meaning he will "make the world perfect and immortal", and evil and the lie (Druj or Dorough) will disappear forever.

P.O. Skjaervo continues:

> For three days and nights the evil will be tortured in hell. Then the heavenly dragon Gôchihr falls down from heaven and sets the earth on fire. The metal in the mountains is smelted and pours into a giant river, through which humanity must pass. The good pass through without discomfort, while the evil have the rest of their evil burnt out of them.[106]

The events of the final healing and renovation of the world are described in the Bundahishn (30. 1. ff) These events are described as:

> In the final battle with evil, the Yazathas-Airyama [Airyaman meaning Member of the Community in younger Avesta, Yasna 61.5] will melt the metal in the hills and mountains, and it will be upon the earth like the flow of a river, but the truthful and the righteous Ashavan will not be harmed (Bundahishn 34.18)

At the end of each person's life, everything a person has thought, spoken or done will be accounted for. If the good and the positive is more than the negative, then that person will go to a place called paradise, and if the negative is more, then that person will be condemned to hell.[107] But at the last day of Judgement—after the Saoshyant has been born by a virgin, and he has returned to the world and liberated humanity from all evil—all the souls will be cleansed and will unite with the eternal God forever, and that will be the end of the world and the end of Time.

In the end, the creator Ahura Mazdâ will be triumphant, and the one he has sent, the Saoshyant, will resurrect all the deaths and all bodies will be restored to eternal perfection, and all souls will be cleansed and reunited with the eternal God. That will be the End of time. Truth and righteousness (Ashavan) and immortality will thereafter be everlasting.[108, 109]

---

1. G.W.F. Hegel, *Phenomenology des Geistes* (Berlin, 1807)
2. D. Jason Cooper, *Mithras Mysteries & Initiation Re-discovered* (Kindle Edition, 1996)

3. Almut Hintze, "Monotheism the Zoroastrian Way," *Journal of the Royal Asiatic Society* Vol. 24, no. 2, (2014), pp. 225–249

4. Jenny Rose, *Zoroastrianism: A Guide for the Perplexed* (London: Bloomsbury, 2011)

5. Geush Urvana (Yasna 29)

6. Avesta: Ahunavaiti Gatha (Yasna 28–34)

7. Ziggurats are vast pyramidal structures with a flat top, built from burned bricks and mud bricks. These structures were common in Mesopotamia and southern Iran and contained probably temple complexes and some living quarters in the same building.

8. Alexander, King of Macedonia (356–323 BC), crossed the Hellespont (that narrow sea channel that lies between Geographical Europe and Geographical Asia) in 334 BC with an army of 48,100 soldiers, 6,100 cavalry, 120 ships with 38,000 crew.

9. Translation by L.W. King and R.C. Thompson, "The sculptures and inscriptions of Darius the Great on the rock of Behistun in Persia" (London, 1907)

10. R.G. Kent, *Old Persian: Grammar, Texts, Lexicon* (New Haven: American Oriental Society, 1950), pp. 137–156.

11. Xanthus of Lydia, *Lydiaca* (Fragment 32)

12. Plato, *First Alcibiades* (122a1)

13. Wolfgang Amadeus Mozart, *The Magic Flute* (1791)

14. Diodorus Siculus was a Greek historian born in Sicily. He was active from 60–30 BC, his main work being the *Bibliotheca historica* [Historical Library] 1.94.2

15. Gathas 1–5 (Yasna 28–34, 43–51, & 53)

16. According to records, Zarathustra was born into the Spitama clan.

17. "Where and which part of land shall I go to succeed? They keep me away from the family and the tribe. The community that I wish to join does not gratify me, nor do the deceitful tyrants of the lands. How shall I gratify you, O Mazda Ahura?" (Yasna 46.1)

18. As reflected in (Yasna 51.16)

19. Mary Boyce, *Zoroastrianism: Its Antiquity and Constant Vigour* (Costa Mesa: Mazda, 1992), p. 62

20. W.D Ross ed., *The Works of Aristotle, Vol. 12 (Select fragments)*, (Oxford, 1952), 7–6

21. Trans. J. Gwyn Griffiths, *Plutarch's de Isis and Osiride* (Swansea, University of Wales Press, 1970), pp. 191–3

22. (Citation by Aeneas of Gaza, Theophrastus, 77; text in Jackson, Zoroaster, 248; trans. in Fox and Pemberton, 109.)

23. Mary Boyce, *Zoroastrianism: Its Antiquity and Constant Vigour* (Costa Mesa: Mazda, 1992), p. 4

24. Ibid., p. 7

25. Robert Charles Zaehner, *The Dawn and Twilight of Zoroastrianism* (London: Weidenfeld & Nicolson, 1961), p. 33

26. Mary Boyce, *Zoroastrianism: Its Antiquity and Constant Vigour* (Costa Mesa: Mazda, 1992), p. 19

27. Ibid., p. 30

28. Ibid.

29. Rudolf Steiner, *The Story of My Life* (New York: Anthroposophic Press, 1928), chapt. 18

30. The lecture was later publish in *Die Drei* 1925–1926 (Vol. 5, No. 10) and was later still translated into English by Walter F. Knox and published first time in England in 1927.

31. P.O. Skjaervo, *Introduction to Zoroastrianism*—Course notes (Cambridge: Harvard,2006)pp.2–3http://www.fas.harvard.edu/~iranian/Zoroastrianism/Zoroastrianism1_Intro.pdf

32. Ibid., p. 8

33. Mary Boyce, *Zoroastrianism: Its Antiquity and Constant Vigour* (Costa Mesa: Mazda, 1992), pp. 12–19

34. P.O. Skjaervo, *Introduction to Zoroastrianism*—Course notes (Cambridge: Harvard, 2006), p. 2 http://www.fas.harvard.edu/~iranian/Zoroastrianism/Zoroastrianism1_Intro.pdf

35. Mary Boyce, *Zoroastrians: Their Religious Beliefs and Practices* (London: Routledge, 1979), p. 56.

36. Yasht 19.92

37. P.O. Skjaervo, *Introduction to Zoroastrianism*—Course notes (Cambridge: Harvard,2006),p.11http://www.fas.harvard.edu/~iranian/Zoroastrianism/Zoroastrianism1_Intro.pdf

38. Elisabeth Forster-Nietzsche "How Zarathustra Came Into Being." Translation Thomas Common (1921)

39. Friedrich Engels (1820–1895) in his article "Der Ideologischer Uberbau."

40. Friedrich Engels, *The Origin of the Family, Private Property and the State* Ernest Untermann, trans. (Chicago: Charles H. Kerr & Co., 1909)

41. Karl Friedrich Geldner (1852–1929) "Avestan Literature" in Geiger, W.–E. Kuhn, eds., *Grundriss der Iranischen Philologie*, 2 vols., (Strassburg, 1895-1901; repr. 1974) v.2, p.29

42. P.O. Skjaervo, *Introduction to Zoroastrianism*—Course notes (Cambridge: Harvard, 2006), pp. 52–54 http://www.fas.harvard.edu/~iranian/Zoroastrianism/Zoroastrianism1_Intro.pdf

43. Ibid., p. 18

44. Richard Foltz, *Religions of Iran* (London: Oneworld Publications, 2013)

45. Mary Boyce, *Zoroastrians: Their Religious Beliefs and Practices* (London:Routledge, 1979), foreword.

46. Ibid., p. 9

47. J. Duchesne-Guillemin, *La Religion de L'Iran Ancien*, (Paris, 1962) pp. 189 ff.

48. Kuiper, 1985

49. Benveniste.

50. Mary Boyce, *A History of Zoroastrianism: Vol 1, The Early Period* (Leiden: Brill, 1975) p. 48

51. Ibid., p. 23.

52. Herodotus - 1.131

53. Gonda, 1962, pp. 65 ff.

54. Thieme, 1960; Dumézil, 1961; Mayrhofer, 1966.

55. Franz Cumont; Vermaseren; Turcan

56. Christensen, 1917 and 1934

57. Mary Boyce, *A History of Zoroastrianism: Vol 1, The Early Period* (Leiden: Brill, 1975) p. 92.

58. Hoffmann, 1957

59. Ehsan Yarshater, 1983, pp. 420–36,

60. Christensen, 1931; Ehsan Yarshater, 1983, pp. 436–73

61. Mary Boyce, *A History of Zoroastrianism: Vol 1, The Early Period* (Leiden: Brill, 1975) pp. 97–100.

62. Hoffmann, 1965

63. Oldenberg, pp. 546 f

64. according to Lüders; Gershevitch, 1959

65. Gherardo Gnoli, 1979.

66. Kuiper, 1964

67. P.O. Skjaervo, *Introduction to Zoroastrianism*—Course notes (Cambridge: Harvard, 2006) http://www.fas.harvard.edu/~iranian/Zoroastrianism/Zoroastrianism1_Intro.pdf

68. Genesis 3:24; 2 Kings 19:5; Psalms 80:1; Psalms 99:1; Isaiah 37:16; Ezekiel 10; Hebrew 9:1–6

69. Marteen J. Vermaseren, *Mithras, Geschichte eines Kultes* (Stuttgart, W. Kohlhammer: Verlag, 1965)

70. Hugo Gressmann, *Die orientalischen Religionen im hellenistisch-römischen Zeitalter* (Berlin: de Gruyter,1930)

71. this according to Herodotus *Histories*.

72. Reinhold Merkelbach, *Mithras* (Saarbrücken: Verlag, 1894) pp. 34–35

73. Plutarch, *De Iside et Osiride* 11 and 31 (Deinon and Kolophon 690 F 21 Jacoby) de natura animaleum x 28.

74. Karl Bernhard Stark, "Die Mithrassteine von Dormagen" in *Jahrbucher des Vereins von Althertumsfreunden im Rheinlande* Vol. 46, pp 1–25 (1869)

75. Richard Foltz, *Religions of Iran* (London: Oneworld Publications, 2013)

76. Michael Patella, *Lord of the Cosmos, Mithras, Paul, and the Gospel of Mark* (New York: T&T Clark, 2006)

77. W.M. Flinders Petrie, *Tell el Amarna* (London, 1894) p. 38

78. A. Weigall, *The Life and Times of Akhenaten.* (London: Thornton Butterworth, 1922) p. 20

79. W.M. Flinders Petrie, *Tell el Amarna* (London, 1894) p. 38

80. Mercer, *The Tell el-Amarna - Tablets*, Letter 29.

81. Jimmy Dunn, *The Egyptian God Aten, Before and After Akhenaten.* http://www.touregypt.net/featurestories/aten.htm

82. Donald Redford, *Akhenaten the Heretic King* (Princeton, 1984)

83. Later an English translation of the Amarna tablets made by S.A.B. Mercer *The Tel el Amarna Tablets* (1939). Later still they were discussed in detail in Immanuel Velikovsky's *Ages in Chaos Vol. I* (1952) pp. 223–335

84. William G. Dever, *Did God Have a Wife?: Archaeology and Folk Religion in Ancient Israel* (Grand Rapids: Eerdmans, 2005)

85. Ahmed Osman, *Moses and Akhenaten* (London: Grafton, 1990) — In which Osman tries to prove, that Moses and Akhenaten are the same person.

86. Cambyses II mentioned by Herodotus; Artaxerxes III mentioned by Plutarch

87. Roger Beck, *The Religion of the Mithras Cult in the Roman Empire, Mysteries of the Unconquered Sun* (Oxford University Press, 2006)

88. Manfred Mayrhofer, *Etymologisches Wörterbuch des Altindoarischen* (Heidelberg, 1986) vol. 2 p. 358

89. Mary Boyce, *Textual Sources for the Study of Zoroastrianism* (University of Chicago press, 1984) p. 22

90. The Encyclopedia Iranica: "Martin Haug"

91. Mary Boyce, *Zoroastrians: Their Religious Beliefs and Practices* (London: Routledge, 1979) p. 202 ff.

92. John R Hinnels (1983) p. 111

93. Mary Boyce, *Textual Sources for the Study of Zoroastrianism* (University of Chicago press, 1984) p. 158

94. Mary Boyce, *Zoroastrianism: Its Antiquity and Constant Vigour* (Costa Mesa: Mazda, 1992), 96

95. Mary Boyce, *Textual Sources for the Study of Zoroastrianism* (University of Chicago press, 1984) p. 57

96. R.C. Zaehner, *Bundahishn 1.1* (1956–1976) pp. 34–35

97. Ibid.

98. P.O. Skjaervo, *Introduction to Zoroastrianism*—Course notes (Cambridge: Harvard, 2006) http://www.fas.harvard.edu/~iranian/Zoroastrianism/Zoroastrianism1_Intro.pdf

99. Mary Boyce, *Zoroastrianism: Its Antiquity and Constant Vigour* (Costa Mesa: Mazda, 1992), 153

100. Professor Almut Hintze in her inaugural lecture, delivered on Feb. 22, 2012, in the School of Oriental and African Studies at the University of London

101. C. Herrenschmidt, "Once upon a time, Zoroaster." *History and Anthropology* 3 (1987) pp. 209–237.

102. J. Kellens, *Le Pantheon de l'Avesta Ancient, Quatre Lessons au College de France* (Paris, 2000) pp. 31–94

103. Almut Hintze—A forthcoming of Monotheism—the Zoroastrian Way.—Journal of the Royal Asiatic Society.Modi, Jivanji Jamshedji Modi (1903), *Jamasp Namak ("Book of Jamaspi")*, Bombay: K. R. Cama Oriental Institute

104. From *Menog-i Khrad*, Chap. 2

105. P.O. Skjaervo, *Introduction to Zoroastrianism*—Course notes (Cambridge: Harvard, 2006) p. 56 http://www.fas.harvard.edu/~iranian/Zoroastrianism/Zoroastrianism1_Intro.pdf

106. Ibid., p. 57

107. Almut Hintze, *A Zoroastrian Liturgy: The Worship in seven Chapters (Yasna 35–41)* (Wiesbaden: Harrassowitz Verlag, 2007)

108. Mary Boyce, *A History of Zoroastrianism: Vol 1, The Early Period* (Leiden: Brill, 1975) pp. 234, 282.

109. Maneckji Nusservanji Dhalla, *History of Zoroastrianism* (New York: OUP, 1938), pp. 108, 165

3. ZOROASTRIAN ESCHATOLOGY AND WORLDVIEW

The Zoroastrian eschatology is the oldest in recorded history, pre-dating all visions of the end of the world in any other monotheistic religion. In the Avestan language, *Frashokereti* is the term for the Zoroastrian doctrine of the final renovation of the Universe. That is to say when evil will be destroyed, and everything else will be then in perfect unity with Ahura Mazdâ. The name *Frashokereti* [in modern Persian: Farashgherd] means "making excellent" or "making wonderful".[110]

This important question of eschatology in the Zoroastrian religious doctrine has been discussed, in some detail by various historians such as Robert C. Zaehner,[111] J. Duchesne-Guillemin,[112] and the Shaul Shaked[113] to name but a few. Concerning the Zoroastrian eschatology, Mahnaz Moazami writes:

> The apocalyptic and eschatological ideas are of considerable importance in Zoroastrian religion. The Zoroastrian tradition contends that complete happiness can come only with a return to the initial

state of the material world, that is, the reunion of the body and soul in a physical world restored to its original perfection. The concepts of the Savior, the destruction of evil, the establishment of the kingdom of good, the renovation of the universe, and the immortality of the soul form an essential part of the religious tradition and are expressed very clearly in the Avesta. The importance of these ideas seems to have increased considerably in the Middle Persian (or Pahlavi) writings. Texts relative to these matters are found in the *Bundahisn*, the *Denkard*, the *Selections of Zadspram*, the *Pahlavi Rivayat*, the *Dadestan i Denig*, the *Menog i Xrad*, the *Cidag Andarz i Poryotkesan*, and the New Persian *Zartust Name*.[114]

The eschatological dogmas in Zoroastrianism refer to two questions, firstly so-called *individual eschatology*, which deals with the life of the humans after their death, their individual judgments and their subsequent consequences, namely paradise or hell. Secondly, we have the *universal eschatology*, which refers to the resurrection and to the universal judgment and the rehabilitation of the world at the end of time, on a universal basis but not on an individual basis. Furthermore, the events of the final Apocalypse, which in reality describes the cataclysms which would lead to the events of the end of the world, would therefore lead us further to the figure of the World Saviour—or Messiah if you will.

We can clearly see that humankind has to undergo the final Judgment twice, the first time as an individual after death, and the second time as a member of humanity in general. This for humankind all happening the second time, after we have actually received already our own individual reward and or punishment in paradise or in hell. Having departed from this world, the righteous human being has to come back from Paradise to start life all over again. Therefore, having fulfilled their task upon this earth—having successfully completed the fight against the powers of evil and darkness—humankind seems pointlessly called back to the new phase of material life. Therefore, it seems that it is justified to conclude, with Duchesne-Guillemin,[115] that there are originally two doctrines involved in this case. The one of which is the immortality of the soul, the other is that of the resurrection of the body. It is possible, however, that it can be shown that the eschatological events described in Sassanian Zoroastrian scriptures form a coherent whole and are in harmony with all the other dogmas of the Zoroastrian worldview. It is correct to say that a description of an eschatological doctrine in which one of the major events is missing, would be unorthodox and incomplete. Two points in the Zoroastrian worldview are of particular importance, for the understanding of what seems to be the essential structure of its Eschatology.

One of them is the parallelism which exists between the events of the end of the world, on one side, and the mythology of the creation of the world and the creation of mankind on the other side. The other very important point that has a special relevance in this connection is the conception of the Zoroastrian cosmos, which in reality is consisting of two aspects namely *menog* and *getig* [in modern Persian: *minou* and *gity*]. This can be explained as the intelligible, the invisible, the spiritual on one side, and on the other side the material, the visible, and the sensible aspects of the Universe.

The happenings of cosmogony are, therefore, enacted here with as a constant interplay which happens in stages, between the menog and getig. Furthermore, there are, in principle, three stages which leads to the process of creation. Firstly, the creation in menog, which is a purely spiritual creation of the universe, meaning the universe has been conceived first in the idealistic form by the creator. The next two stages are both different aspects of the material creation of the Universe. Namely, there is getig in menog, and then there is the getig creation in getig. Importantly, the first moment of cosmogony is indicating as state of general spiritual existence before any material creation is performed. This means that following the first stage of actual creation—which is in the spiritual or ideal world—the prototype of the material world is being created as a copy of the ideal or spiritual form. The material world is been created according to the principles of the ideal world already existing before, which becomes later the final stage of the material world, meaning the final stage of getig. It is my contention that the existence of the universe *first* in an ideal and perfect form and *afterwards* as having been crafted according to that ideal form into this material world was a concept later adopted by Plato from Zoroastrianism.

Returning to our previous explanation, the events of the final apocalypse that lead towards the end of the world are conducted entirely in terms of the material world, meaning in getig. On the other hand, the final eschatological stage shows a synthesis which is achieved between the spiritual and the material world together. In other words, between the menog and the getig. This means the universe does not cease to exist, nor does it stop being material, but in reality the material existence of the world itself undergoes a fundamental change. Therefore, we can say that it is no longer an amalgamation of the forces of good and evil, nor is it anymore a mixture of the material and sensible world, but it becomes a completely new entity. This process is described thus:

> Ohrmazd will stand up together with Srosh the Righteous. Srosh's righteousness will smite (the demon) Az... and or Ohrmazd will smite the Evil Spirit. He will perform sacrifice, and the earth will rise to the height of the three spears.... At the fifth sacrifice it will reach the station of the stars and Garodman (the highest stage of paradise) will descend from its place down to the station to the stars.[116]

Furthermore, Ohrmazd (Ahura Mazda) and all the gods, and humankind will be together in one place. A complete and absolute harmony is being thus achieved between the different elements, which at this moment, constitute the various spheres of existence. Not only will the difference between the spiritual and the material spheres be abolished, but the difference between God and humankind is to be narrowed—as will the distance between life on this earth and paradise. The world is to shed the existence of humankind and some of its distinctive marks of materiality. There will be no more hunger, thirst, old age and death.

The above remarks are regarding the system of the universal eschatology—which is different from the individual eschatology and dealing with the fate of human kind after his death. The soul of humans after that has to encounter with the menog counterpart of the person to whom it belongs. It later undergoes a spiritual judgement and gets a spiritual reward and or punishment. Whether in *Garodman* [*paradise*], *Dusach* [*hell*], or in *Hamestagan* [*the intermediary sphere*], all of these three states of beings are the concept of menog. Humankind, which contains a combination of menog and getig goes through the process of the final eschatology in two different stages.

Firstly after an individual person's death, only its menog aspect survives, and only this part represents the person in the final judgement. Secondly, when the world and the universe comes to and end—and menog and getig are entered into new synthesis—the individual human also is involved in this new development, which will lead to the events of the final resurrection. The individual human moves in the first stage from his material existence to a new state of menog existence, and finally in the second stage, the individual person joins the world when it turns from a material existence to a purified menog like material form of a final eschatological existence.

Similar to the other monotheistic religions, in Zarathustra's religious doctrine—which was later adopted perhaps directly or indirectly *by* other monotheistic religious traditions—there is a clear definition of the end of time for this world conceptualized as "the ultimate victory of good over evil, and the end of the present age, or the end of the world." Time will definitely have a clear end, at which point the world, as is perceived today, will cease to exist.

In this regard, very realistically, the end of the world is been perceived by Zoroastrianism as a catastrophe of cosmic proportions,
where a big object will hit the earth from the sky, and will set the earth
on fire, whereupon molten metal will flow down from the mountains.
P.O. Skjaervo, in his *Introduction to Zoroastrianism*, mentions this event
in its original wordings from the Zoroastrian scriptures:

> Then the heavenly dragon Gôchihr falls down from
> heaven and sets the earth on fire. The metal in the
> mountains is smelted and pours down like a giant
> river, through which humanity must pass. The good
> pass through without discomfort, while the evil have
> the rest of their evil burnt out of them.[117]

Furthermore, the description of the end of the world in
Zoroastrianism is additionally described (though somewhat sketchily)
in the Bundahishn as follows:

> The fire God and the God Erman will melt the metal
> in the hills and mountains, and it will be upon the
> earth like a river. At that time the Dragon Gouchehr
> also will fall down on the earth from the sky, which
> it will be terrifying like a wolf does a sheep. All of
> humanity will pass through this river of molten
> metal.... (molten metal is also alluded to in a passage
> of Yasna 30. 7) The earth will rise to the station of
> the stars, and Garodman (Garo-demana 'House
> of Songs', or 'heaven'), will come down from the
> place where it is now to the station of the stars, and
> everywhere will be Garodman. (ud garodman az
> an gyag ku ast abaz o star paydag ayed ud hamag
> gyag garodman be bawed—Pahlavi Text. 107.5.6)
> Ohrmazd (Ahura Mazdâ) dwells with man and the

other Amahraspands dwell with the animals, fires, metals, earth, water and plants, over which they respectively preside.[118]

We see here that these words clearly allude to the end of this world for humans and animals and plants alike, as a natural catastrophe of cosmic proportions. This end, which will not only affect humans and animals and plants, but also the elements as waters and the earth, is not being mentioned here as solely to be the will of a personal but anonymous God or creator, but rather an end, which is subject to the laws of nature and logic, reasonably within the parameters of modern scientific probabilities.

In contrast to the Judeo-Christian and Islamic scriptures, the description of eschatology in Zoroastrian texts prefigures what has been highlighted by the modern scientific community and their descriptions as being the primary belief, of how indeed the world will possibly end. Meaning this is what modern scientist believe how the end of this world and all life form on this planet might look like—the end of life as we know it on this planet caused by a cataclysmic meteor strike on our planet.

Compared with the Christian narrative involving the Four Horsemen of the Apocalypse (Book of Revelation) each bringing a plague and/or pestilence, the Zoroastrian eschatological narratives, which are much older—dating as they do from the dawn of recorded human history—are perhaps scientifically more plausible and realistic. Furthermore, the plague and the pestilence of the Bible are not perceived to be the End of the World as such, merely the end of humanity, for plants and most animals would not be affected by pestilence and plagues and would probably survive. Whereas the Zoroastrian "End of the World" would realistically affect all life on the planet. Furthermore, in the last book of the New Testament—compiled in the fourth century AD in the Council of Nicaea—the revelation which John the Apostle receives is described literally as "The ultimate victory of good over evil, and the end of the present age... and the end of the world." These words are clearly a copy of—or at least strongly inspired by—the Bundahishn, which is based on the Zoroastrian scriptures of the Avesta.

Concerning the human body and the human soul, according to the old Avesta, the body of humankind consists of two matters. First is the *bones* which signifies the physical constitution of the humans, secondly the *Ushthana* which is the vitality or the life breath. In contrast to the physical body, the humans have three kind of Urwan [soul]. First there is the pre-soul or *farawashih*; this soul exists from before in an eternal general world of thought, once a person is conceived it is sent down to that body and into the world of the living. Then there is the breath-soul or uruuan; this is the soul that leaves the body at death, and wanders into the beyond to be subject of the judgment. Finally there is the vision-soul or Daenah; this soul is the mind of a human being, which allows him to enter into the world of thought and imagination. This kind of soul allows a human being to decide his way and to fulfill his deeds and his destiny in his life, for which he will be judged in the beyond. The Avestan word *Daenah* [in Pahlawy: den or deen] can also stand for religion, but here it has a different meaning.

One of the important aspects of Zoroastrian eschatology is the notion of time. Although time is infinite, meaning from infinite past to infinite future, the existence of humankind in its creation and in its ending is decidedly finite—having both a beginning and an end. We have seen in the chapter above, how the Zoroastrian ideology perceives the end of the world. The end of our existence is not the end of time, but simply the end of the world for us, the one which we humankind live in and call it Being. According to Zoroastrianism, time and the universe will continue to exist. After the end of time for us humans, the universe will continue to exist for infinite time. According to Mardan Farrukh:

> Prior to creation, Ohrmazd (Ahura Mazdâ) exists
> fully complete in his own self, such that his perfec-
> tion consists in his having no need for any advantage

or increase from the outside. Ohrmazd existed as
light infinite in infinite time.[119]

Sassanian Zoroastrianism historically distinguishes two separate
orders: the order of *nature* versus the the order of *intellect, consciousness*
and *will*. These correspond exactly to the Avestan *mainyu* and *gaethya*
[in Persian: *Minoo* and *Guity*] meaning *time* and *space*. Whether the infinite or finite basically belong to the order of nature, and for this reason
are independent from any human existence, or whether the notion of
time and space are present to its fullest extent, in human consciousness or not, doesn't change the reality of their existence. Ahura Mazdâ,
however, is not only eternal and infinite in time and space, but also possesses the perfect ideal and the perfect wisdom of his creation. It is clear
that the spirit of light and the spirit of darkness have proceeded from the
eternal One—and that the first is life and the second is death. We know
that life and death are part of the eternal cycle of nature and have no
dependency to the mind or the consciousness of human kind.

We have to investigate now the question of how the human intellect
and will evolved from the One who is eternal. First we must consider
the relationship between the infinite of time and space and the finite
nature of human existence, as this was perceived by Zarathustra. We
cannot go into any detailed explanation but must simply say that the
one developed out of the other or that Ahura Mazdâ, in his wisdom,
created finite time out from a segment of the infinite time.

At this point, some explanation concerning one of the interesting
chroniclers of Zoroastrianism, a man by the name of Mardan-Farrukh,
would be reasonable. This historian lived during the ninth century
AD, in a time when the persecution of Zoroastrianism by the Islamic
conquerers of Persia was at its peak, and the Zoroastrian community,
still at large in the country, was struggling for their physical and intellectual survival. The book of this man was entitled *Shikand-gumanic
Vichar*. His real name was Mardan-Farrukh e Ohrmazd datan being
the son of Ahuramazd-dad. The title of his book *Shikand-gumanic*

Vichar can be translated as *The Analytical Treatise for the dispelling of Doubts.* The date of his lifetime can be placed approximately to 875–935 AD, as he lived shortly after the death of the Caliph Al-Ma'mun, who reigned from 813–833 AD. Being a firm believer in dualism, his book has been cited by many chronicler, historians, and scientists occupying themselves with the teachings of Zarathustra. R.C. Zaehner relied largely on Mardan-Farrukh and translated part of his book into English and quoted him continuously in his magnum opus, *The Dawn and Twilight of Zoroastrianism.*[120] Furthermore, Mary Boyce says about him:

> A practicing layman who drew on priestly Zoroastrian
> Books in the Pahlavy, his work is distinguished by its
> clarity of thought and orderly arrangement. It creates
> a rationalist and philosophic climate.[121]

Contemporary Persian intellectuals, such as Seyyed Hossein Nasr and Mehdi Amirazavi also cite frequently from *Shikand-gumanic Vichar.* In his work, which was first translated into Sanskrit in 1100 AD, Mardan-Farrukh compares the three religions known to him at his time, which were Christianity, Judaism, and Zoroastrianism. He analyzed and commented on the pros and cons of all these three religions, providing a wealth of information for future historians concerning some Eschatological matters of the Zoroastrian religion and world view.

3.1 ZOROASTRIAN RITUALS

The principle of good and evil exerts a profound influence in the daily rituals, observances, and purity laws of Zoroastrian life. Diseases and physical corruption are regarded as parallel aspects and are equated with agents of the evil forces Ahriman and Angra

Mainiiu, and in general the Evil Spirit. Once a human is dead, his body becomes impure and polluted (with the agents of the evil spirit) and must be kept away from the pure, *living* beings. Death, which is brought about by the "Demon of death" (Astwihaad) is understood to be the ultimate infliction of the Wicked Spirit, and consequently Evil is thought to be present in all decaying matter. The human body is believed to be possessed after death by the *demon of the corpse* [in middle Persian: Druji i Nasha], and as such it is to be kept away from all that is pure, specially al living creatures. The dead corpse is handled only by professionals—*nasasalars* which in middle Persian means *corpse experts*—after death the body is moved to a funeral ground in a metallic carrier; being porous wood is prone to contamination by the dead body. Mary Boyce citing here the Zoroastrian original holy scriptures says:

> If walking or running riding or driving, these Mazdâ worshippers come upon a corpse in flowing water, what would you have them do? 27—Then said Ahura Mazdâ, "Let them halt, Zarathustra, with taking off shoes, with taking off cloths, ...Let them go forward, let them lift the body out of the water, ...let them lift out of the water and let them lay it on dry land. They shall not sin against the waters by casting into them bones nor hair nor spittle nor excrement nor blood.... 44—Where shall we carry the body of a dead man, where lay it down? Then said Ahura Mazdâ, "On the highest places, so that corpse eating birds and beasts will most readily perceive it.... 49—Where shall we carry the bones of a dead man thereafter, where shall we lay it down? Then said Ahura Mazdâ, "A receptacle should be made, out of the reach of dogs and foxes and wolves, not to be rained on from above with rain water."[122]

The ancient structures, knows as the dakhma gahs in Iran and dungerwadis in India, were situated on the outskirts of cities away from the general population. These were open-roofed cylindrical structures in the centre of which the bodies were placed, then the corpses are abandoned to carrion eaters (vultures and other carrion eaters). In Iran, this tradition was abandoned in the 1930s in favour of modern cemeteries. Zoroastrians hold earth, along with other elements such as water and fire as sacred creations of Ahura Mazdâ and therefore they can not be polluted. Vultures and other carrion eating animals are all good creations of Ahura Mazdâ, and they exist to perform their important and natural task in the struggle against the evil spirit—namely to oppose the spread of contamination and disease. In this context, concerning the death and the burial of the Achaemenid Dynasty King Cyrus the great, Mary Boyce writes:

> The tomb of Cyrus shows, however, with what care Zoroastrian kings prepared their sepulchres, so that there should be no contact between the embalmed body (according to Zoroastrianism unclean in death, even though there was no decay, as embalmed) and all the living creations. The tomb chamber is set on a high six-stepped stone plinth, which raises it far above the good and clean earth, and it is itself all made of stone. It consists of a single small chamber, thick walled windowless, ...and with a narrow low and small doorway. Over this doorway was set a carving of the sun, the symbol of immortality in the luminous Paradise, and Cyrus' successor and son Cambyses, endowed, as well as daily sacrifice of sheep, a monthly sacrifice of a horse, the special creature of the sun, to be made at the tomb of his father's soul (the Roman historian, Arrian VI. 29.7.).

These rites were maintained there for two hundred years, until Alexander of Macedonia conquered Persia, and the tomb was broken into and despoiled. One of those who entered it at that moment, reported that it contained a golden couch, a table with cups, a golden coffin, and numerous garments and ornaments set with precious stones... (Strabo—XV. 3. 7).

Nevertheless, it is known that the rulers of all dynasties in Persian history, especially the Achaemenids and the Sassanians, did not abide by this rule of the Zoroastrian traditional burial practices. Most emperors and rulers and also members of noble families in Persian history are known to have erected mausoleums or burial sites and to have buried their dead in the earth.

3.2 PRIESTHOOD IN ZOROASTRIANISM

Clearly rules and rituals in any religion are closely connected to the persons who would enforce and guard them. Thus it can be stated that, in any religious society, the priestly class necessarily must exist and occupied an important position in that society. They later gain power and form a unique priestly caste. The ancient Iranian tradition no exception to this, and the priestly classes during the Zoroastrian era played an important role in that ancient society.

In the prehistoric and ancient times in Iran, sacred fires were guarded by persons delegated for this specific duty. The sacred places wherein fires were kept were called *Atash Gah* [*fire houses*]. It is believed that a fire which was constantly burning, was guarded in this buildings by persons who would later become the *guardians of fire* also called, in Iranian, *Athravan* and later *Athurvan* as well as *Adur Pad*. These guardians of fire became later the priests, and this occupation became hereditary. This group emerged as the future priestly class.

Members of households in that community would visit the Atash Gah, to obtain their hearth or home fires. The Athravans were the notables in their communities and would be involved in the daily lives of the members of their community. Accordingly, the role of the Athravans later evolved into that of mediators, healers and advisers. These Athravans became, with time, a well respected members of their community. In the western parts of ancient Iran the Athravan were also called the *Magi* [from the Old Persian *Magush*], in Greek they were called the *Magos* (plural the *Magoi*) and in Latin *Magus* (plural *Magi*). In fact, the Roman historian and chronicler Strabo (63 BC–24 AD) called the Magi also Pyraethi, which means the *the keepers of the fire*. The Greek historian Herodotus notes that the Magi were one of the six Median group of people, and that they formed a separate tribe into themselves, specialized in hereditary priestly duties. According to Herodotus their main function initially were a keepers of sacred fires.

In some ancient religious texts, Zarathustra himself was referred to as being an Athravan. Later Zarathustra highlighted the fire as the central symbol of his teachings, and the class of Athravans became Zoroastrian Priests. They were not only the keepers of the eternal fire, but also the bearers and keepers of the Zoroastrian flame of wisdom and illumination and, accordingly, his worldview not only in Iran, but well beyond the borders of the Persian Empire. The Zoroastrian priest class were called the Magi in the Hellenistic world.

With time, as the general population looked upon the Athravan, or the keepers of fires as an neutral and trustworthy persons, what were initially Fire Houses became the designated places to resolve disputes and solve unlawful acts and actions. Thus the roles of Athravans and Magi were extended to cast them as overseers of common laws, and solvers of legal disputes for the general public. As the keepers of common law—a role which is still reflected in the title of the most high ranking Zoroastrian priests today—they were known as Dastur [in middle Persian: Dast-var]. While the King and the royal administration enacted and decided royal laws, the disputes of the common people and their daily problems were delegated to the authority of the Dasturs in the ancient times. With this, the keepers and maintainers of the community fires—as they were also well versed in the Zoroastrian faiths moral and ethical code—including the elders and more senior priests would have gained positions of respect and authority in the Zoroastrian community.

This evolution into roles of authority and position of judges in civil and personal disputes was a natural progression for the priestly class. The Dasturs were thus the highest rank of the Zoroastrian Priesthood. In Persian, the word *Dastur* means *to give an order*, or simply *the order*. Accordingly some of the Atash Gahs became the *Dadgahs*, in other words, the location of the *keepers of fire* became the location of a regular *legal court*, and were called *Atash Dadgah* meaning *Fire and Legal Courts*, or simply the *Courts of Fire*.

In the today's societies the name of Atash Dadgahs have lost its significance. Today the Atash dadgah has become the Dar-e Mehr or Darb-e Mehr. The word Mehr is derived from the name of Mithra, who was the personification of the light of the sun, the guardian of justice in contracts and other moral values, and the word Dar or Darb means the *door* or *gate*. Darb-e Mehr, therefore, could be translated as the Gate of Mehr (Gate of Goodness), or Gate of Mithra. In contrast to the royal laws, which were declared and instituted by the King or the worldly power, the common law was, in general, administered by the highest rank of Zoroastrian priesthood, the Dasturs. These royal courts—which were called in Iranian Darbar—would act also as courts of appeal or courts of last resort, when in session.

Very likely the name of Darb-e Mehr evolved from Darbar-e Mehr, essentially The Court of Mehr (Mithra) or the Court of Justice. Therefore from the Atash Dadgah—the courts of fire—a Dastur would have resolved common law, based on moral codes derived from the principles and values of the Asha and Zoroastrian ethics and also of the Mithraic values. Ultimately the Darbe Mehr would have served the dual purpose of place of worship, but also as a court and a place of justice. We can see that, parallel to this, in all the other ancient cultures of antiquity, it was the high Priest, who always acted as an mediator between civil disputes of the common people, therefore his authority was respected, and he was regarded as the ultimate Judge. There are various examples in history, where high priests make judgments even over Kings and Pharaohs.

As for the the Zoroastrian priesthood, there are fundamentally three ranks of priests. *Herbed* [*Herbad* in Iran; *Ervad* in India], Mobed [and the higher rank Mobedan e Mobed], and finally, the highest rank of the priesthood , namely the Dasturs.

Herbed is the title given to those priests who have completed the first level of training as Navar. Herbeds acts as assistant to Mobeds and Dasturs, and have also the authority to perform the ceremonies of the *Outer Circle* or the Dron, or Afarinegan which is part of the Jashan, or Jashne ceremony; the wedding and navjote and other outer ceremonies (performed outside the sanctum of the fire temple) are called the Pavi.

Mobed is the title given to priests who have completed their training as a Martab. The Mobeds, (and later the Mobedan e Mobed) are called the true upholders of the religion, and are trained to perform the liturgies of the *Inner Circle*. These are the Yasna, Venidad and the Visperad ceremonies, which are performed only within the Pavi areas, which is the Inner Sanctum of a Temple. All Navars, Herbads and Mobeds are subordinate to Dasturs.

Dastur as a title means the upholder and promulgator of the law, this word comes from the Pahlawy language, and is rooted in the word Dastabar. Dasturs are High Priests, and in addition to being learned in the entire Avesta and proficient in conducting all the ceremonies, Dasturs are the spiritual guides and leaders of the Zoroastrian community, and are their administrators.

4. THE ENVIRONMENT— THE WORLD OF ANIMALS & ZOROASTRIANISM

An important aspect of the Zoroastrian religion is its perception and view towards the natural world, environment, and animals in general. Historically, Zoroastrians were credited as having a benevolent attitude towards the nature and safeguarding of natural elements, specifically water, earth and fire. These three elements were regarded as sacred and hence humankind were expected to safeguard their purity. Animals too were afforded, in the Zoroastrian theology, of having a soul just as humans do, and had their important part to play and contribute in the cosmic and dichotomous order. Some scholars, including Richard Foltz of Concordia University in Montreal, have often related to the Zoroastrian religion as an ecological religion. Mary Boyce cites from the Vendidad the following:

> Yasna 26—If walking or running, riding or driving, these Mazdâ worshippers came upon a corpse in flowing water, what would you have them do? Then

said Ahura Mazdâ, " Let them halt, Zarathustra, with taking off shoes, with taking off cloths, ... let them go forward, let them lift the body out of the water... let them lay it on dry land. They shall not sin against the waters by casting into them bones nor hair nor spittle nor excrement nor blood.[123]

Yasna 38 is devoted to the worship of the waters. In Zoroastrianism, the reverence for water is almost as strong as that for fire, but because Zarathustra's ardent devotion to Ahura Mazdâ caused most of his utterances to be directed to him, it seems that the intensity of his feeling for fire—as the icon of Asha and the instrument of justice—meant that it is fire imagery and the worship of fire which permit the Gathas. Therefore when we see that, in Yasna Haptanghaiti, worship is offered to water, then this is declared in more traditional terms than that of the worship of fire. Furthermore, in Yasna 38, also there is the beginning of the worship of the earth "which bares us with the ladies" (the ladies here has the meaning of waters).

Mary Boyce:

Yasna 39—We worship Thy Ladies, oh Ahura Mazdâ, who are excellent through Asha. So we worship the soul and the maker of the cow Geush Urvana and Geush Tashan...[124]

Divine beings, of whom the later figures are also in the Gathas. These words have been identified as important appeasement formulae, uttered to assuage the spirits of the sacrificial animals (symbolized by the cow) which were thought after their consecrated death to be absorbed into that of Geush Urvana.

There follows the dramatic declaration that "we worship our own souls and those of the domestic animals." The worshippers also venerate the souls of wild animals which are not harmful, presumably because such animals too might be offered sacrificially. "We worship the soul of the just (Ashavan) wherever they may have been born of man and of woman, whose good inner selves (daenas) conquer or will conquer, or have been conquered."

This is a remarkable utterance, which takes the worshipers beyond the boundaries of their own small community, with reverence for virtue wherever it is to be found. Zarathustra's individual voice sounds here, among and through the traditional elements, with the characteristic stress on the spiritual equality of woman and man and the reference to the inner self, which, if it should be good, will triumph at the end at the Chinvat bridge.

For Zarathustrians, one of the most important ways of caring and ensuring the well being for the good creation was by maintaining, at all times, their purity and cleanliness. They highlighted that impurity in all its forms is the work of Ahriman or Angra Mainyu, the evil spirits. Much stress is given to the point of the Ahuric virtues, further declared by Mithra and Varuna, signifying justice and honesty and telling of the truth. Also, a great importance is attached to the virtues and responsibility of one's own thoughts, words, and deeds, self reliance at all times, caring for ones fellow man, and the caring for the good animals, who are, likewise, Mazdâ's creatures.

We have seen in previous chapters that Zoroastrian teachings are opposed to any kind of asceticism, partly because this involves a rejection of all the good things created by Ahura Mazdâ. As noted by Mary Boyce in *Zoroastrianism, its Antiquity and Constant Vigour*, fasting was regarded as infliction, since it weakens the body, and lessens its ability to overcome wickedness and disease. It was accordingly a sin, on par with any self-inflicted suffering. Zarathustra called on people to be joyful and happy, as happiness was a great virtue created by Ahura Mazdâ, and sorrow has no place in his perfect world.

Furthermore, it is a well-known fact that the Zoroastrian religion devotes considerable attention to the relationship between humans and the world of animals. Importantly all animal species are seen as being in one of the two categories, namely they are either beneficent to human kind or malevolent creatures. All animals are aligned and connected either with the forces of good or with the forces of darkness and evil, in the continuing cosmic battle. Human kind ought to treat each group of animals and each species accordingly, protecting the species and races of the beneficent animals whilst on the contrary, exterminating the malevolent animals.

It is therefore not surprising to see that the most prominent and highly revered animal in the Zoroastrian sacred scriptures, the Gathas, is the cow, who is therefore seen as the principal food supplier and nourisher of all humankind. The reason is that the ancient society and the environment where Zoroastrianism had lived was the pastoral society, wherein cattle raising and keeping of animals was the main source of nourishment for humans. It is for this reason that the cow is seen as being worthy of worship and, together with a group of other animal species, these animals are said to possess a soul, same as the humans.

Professor Richard Foltz has written an interesting article[125] in this connection and also Columbia University's Mahnaz Moazami.

Cattle are described repeatedly in Yasna 44.6 and 47.3 and 50.2 as being a continuous source of human joy. Not surprisingly, the treatment of cattle is also a measure of human morality. This means that people who do not look after their cattle properly, as it says clearly in Yasna 49.1, or those who do not breed cattle at all, as it stated in Yasna 49.4, are bad people. Keeping cattle and caring for their well-being is being presented in the Yasna as an aspect of the true cosmic order the Asha. In contrast, those humans who steal or abuse the cow, are connected to the evil doers or agents of Ahriman. Here

are some quotations from the Yasnas, all in the translation from
Helmut Humbach:

> Yasna 38.5—We address you as the waters, and as
> the fertile cows, and as the mother cows, who are not
> to be killed because they nurse the poor and provide
> drink for all beings they are best and most beautiful.

> Yasna 39.1–2—...herewith we now worship the
> soul (uruuan) of the cow and her fashioner, and we
> worship our own souls and also those of the domes-
> tic animals (pasu-kanam) which seek refuge with us,
> both with us to whom they may belong, and with us
> who may belong to them. And we worship the souls
> of those wild animals that are harmless (daiti kanam).

> Yasna 48.5–6—Let the best insight, which purifies
> birth also for mankind, be applied also to the cow.
> Thou breedest her for food for us. For the cow pro-
> vides us with good dwelling, she provides us with
> stability and mightiness .

Although the texts of the Gathas are, in many ways, difficult to
decipher and understand, we can see nevertheless the extraordinary
importance they accord to cattle. This is understandable, considering
that the birthplace of Zoroastrianism was the pastoral, nomadic social
economy of the pre-historic Iranians, for we know that their own survival depended almost entirely on the well being of their livestock.

Most important is the fact that benevolent animals, in general, are
believed in Zoroastrianism to have a soul, but it is not clear, whether
their soul, in the hierarchy of the living species, are in reality a level
below of that of humans or on the same level. As a principle, in contrast to other religions, the Zoroastrian religion clearly believes that

some animals posses a soul, but not the faculty of a moral or reasonable choice. This is in a clear contrast to the other Monotheistic religions, where animals are regarded as inanimate subservient and passive soulless creatures. Similarly the Islamic religion, contrary to the Zoroastrian faith, has accorded to the dog a status of impurity and rejection, although, according to Richard Foltz, the Islamic faith has also a notion or a hint of some animals having souls, which probably is influenced by Zoroastrianism.

Another animal that is revered in Zoroastrian texts is the dog. He appears in the hierarchy of beings even higher of that of the cow, ranking next to humans in the degree of the good creations. Significantly, Mary Boyce mentions that, according to later Zoroastrian tradition, if only one human is present for a religious ritual where traditionally two persons are required, a dog may sit in place as a substitute for the second person.[126]

Some other religious rituals actually *require* the real presence of a dog, as an example when a Zoroastrian dies, a dog must be brought into the presence of the corpse before the human's body can be considered and verified as dead. This ritual in Zoroastrianism is called sagdid which means literally the dog has seen it. The reason for that is, in Zoroastrian mythology, dogs are believed to be able to see into the next world. Another interpretation for this is, in the absence of a qualified medical professional, probably a dog would be better able than a human to sense whether a human is really physically deceased or not. Furthermore, a dog also must accompany the priest in the funeral procession for a dead human, and significantly, dead dogs themselves are given funeral ceremonies like those of humans. Zoroastrian tradition dictated that every household should give nourishment and food to the dog in their household, once a day, before humans themselves are fed. Dogs played an important role in the pastoral society of the ancient Iranians. In this struggle for the daily survival, the dog was an important tool and a companion of the humans in the pastoral age. The Videvdad and other similar Zoroastrian texts prescribe various harsh and severe punishments for humans who mistreat the so-called benevolent animals. This is particularly the case when it comes to the mistreatment of dogs, to which an entire chapter (13) in the Videvdad is dedicated.

We will speak in later chapters about the voyage of a Zoroastrian priest by the name of Arda Viraz to the other world. He visits Paradise and Hell in his dreamlike, unconscious mind. When visiting the other world in his dream, he sees the souls of the sinners in Hell, who had mistreated benevolent animals, and there they are the subjected to great punishments and severe sufferings. For instance he sees a man, who has abused a dog, and he is continuously being torn apart by the evil Demons.[127]

Interestingly, the Zoroastrian Myth of Creation, contained in the Bundahishn, depicts the eating of animals, meaning general meat-eating by humankind as a degeneration of the ideal form of the human nutrition. Therefore at the end of time, when humanity will live in a state of perfection and the good will prevail, meaning when the classical good period of humanity is restored, humankind will no longer eat meat. (Bundahishn 30.1–3) It is a tradition, among the Iranian Zoroastrian community, that members refrain from eating meat on four days every month, called Nabor. These days are Bahman, Mah, Gosh, and Ram.

On the other hand, traditionally a negative attitude has been developed towards animals, which are considered in Zoroastrianism as being wicked creations or evil animals, and who are considered to be the agents of the evil spirits. Mahnaz Moazami writes the following about these animals.[128]

In the young Avesta and middle Persian texts the term Xrafstra [in middle Persian: xrafstar] is used usually for reptiles and amphibians such as snakes, lizards, frogs and obnoxious insects such as beetles, flies, scorpions, and locusts. In general, any animal that crept, crawled, pricked, bit or stung and seemed hideous and repulsive to human beings, was called xrafstra. Predators such as felines and wolves are referred to as dadan, meaning "wild animals or wild beasts".

The killing of undesirable animal species, such as snakes and scorpions by Persians, is first recorded by Herodotus in the fifth century BC.[129]

There is an interesting prayer in Zoroastrianism, which is unique among ancient religions, namely the "Gaush-Urvana". This prayer is, in essence, the call of the animal soul directly to its maker, Ahura Mazdâ. In this prayer the animal soul asks the creator God (Ahura Mazdâ) of the purpose of he having created them, and also lamenting that:

> O Ahura, when you created this world and you created us the animals, you told us that the humans are your friends , and that they are going to protect you and help you, but they are actually not protecting us, they are harming us and killing us for their sole pleasure ....

> Therefore, O Ahura, tell us, what was the reason of your creation

Here some further short excerpts from the prayer of the Gaush Urvana, these words are believed to be written by the Prophet himself, which is reflected in the prayer Yasna 29

> 1—To you immortals the soul of the cow lamented (the cow, as a symbolic representative of animals)

> For whom did you create me?

> Who made me?

> The cruelty of fury and violence, of wantonness and brutality (of humans), holds me in bondage.

I have no other pastor but you, provide me then with good pasture.

10—To these people (the humans), O Ahura, grant strength and the rule of the Truth and Justice and also of Good Thought, through which comfort and peace may come about.

I have indeed recognized, O Mazdâ, that you are the first provider of these.

11—Where are Truth and Good Thought and their Rule?

Let them come to me now.

Acknowledge me, O Mazdâ, as fit for the great task.

O Ahura, aknowledge us and come down to us here because of our gift to you, which is the piety of the faithful....

5. INCESTUOUS MARRIAGES (XWEDODAH) AND THE ZOROASTRIAN RELIGION

No narration of the Zoroastrian religion and its doctrines would be complete without the mentioning the very sensitive matter of *Xwedodah* or incestuous marriages or incestuous sexual relations. Unfortunately the appearance and the myth of the moral and ethical teachings of the prophet Zarathustra has been tainted with an ugly spot, and brought into relation with this unfortunate and despicable custom. Incestuous relations existed in most of the ancient cultures and empires of the antique world, and it was also practised in a certain period of the Iranian history, namely during the Parthian and indeed the Sassanian periods.

Incest [from Latin: *incestus* meaning unclean, impure, and or unchaste] is generally understood as any sexual intercourse between family members and or close blood related relatives. This term could also apply to sexual intercourse between individuals who are in a close blood relationship without being from the same family, or those individuals who are related to each other by adoption or marriage. The incest taboo has been, in history, probably the most widespread and the strictest of all taboos. In both present days societies and in many past civilizations incest was regarded as a despicable and most immoral relationship. Most of the modern societies and civilized nations have laws forbidding incest or social restrictions on closely consanguineous sexual relationships or marriages.

So impressed was Sigmund Freud by the writings of Edward Burnett Tylor, who claimed that in all primitive cultures incest was, and still is, a universal taboo, that he wrote in his own book, *Totem and Taboo* (1913), some psychoanalytical views about incest from his own perspective. Sigmund Freud believed that incest is in reality a subconscious struggle between the father and his sons for the possessions of the mother, and or the mother and the daughters struggle for the same possession of the father.[130] Carl Gustav Jung who later became, in his own right, one of the noteworthy psychoanalysts of his time, has expressed in his own book opinions which could be regarded as a rebuttal to Sigmund Freud and his views. C.G. Jung's book *Psychology of the Unconscious* (1912), therefore hastened the widening split between the two great psychoanalysts, which became final in the year 1914.

By around the turn of the nineteenth century, many western anthropologists had begun investigating the remaining unexplored tribes and clans of indigenous people in south america and other remote areas. As a result of this, scientists came to the conclusion that the majority of primitive and so far untouched human tribes in isolated areas, have the same negative attitude towards incestuous sexual relations, and concluded that incest must be, in general, against the laws of nature itself. Whether incest is against the laws of nature or not—and whether incest is practised in the animal kingdom—is a matter of a separate discussion. What is clear, in this context, is the fact that humankind and their societies have generally at all times condemned this kind of relationships. If incest existed in some or all societies of the ancient world (as well as later history) then this was probably on the basis of isolated incidents, meaning as an exception but not as the rule.

Importantly, Professor Maria Macuch from Berlin University, an expert in this field, admits that the documentation which enables us to judge the incestuous situations in the Iranian history during the Sassanian period, is highly controversial. According to Macuch:

> "The third and most important reason for controversy relates to the nature of the evidence in the Pahlavi texts and the manner in which they should be interpreted. First of all, the bulk of the material is late, having been written down all in the Islamic period, which makes it difficult to decide, whether incest was really an age-old custom from the pre-Islamic era, which had to be preserved as an important Zoroastrian tradition, or whether its significance was mainly exaggerated in the post Sassanian era as a strategy to encourage endogamic alliances, and keep the Zoroastrian communities intact in a hostile environment. If it was an age old custom, as we have reason to believe, the main question is were incestuous marriages really concluded on a large scale in the Sassanian society, or should the praise they receive in later texts (in texts of post-Zoroastrian times) be interpreted as a result of the opposite, as a lack of enthusiasm on the part of Zoroastrians to enter these kind of marriages."[131]

The purpose of us mentioning this topic, is to clarify, in short, a few points with reference to the custom of incestuous relations in general, and the relationship of incestuous marriages to the teaching of the prophet Zarathustra in particular. It is not the scope of this investigation to present an analysis of incestuous relationship through history.

Firstly, the Prophet Zarathustra himself and his writings in the Gathas and the scriptures of the Avesta do not mention any thing about the acceptance of incestuous relations between humans in the society. It is therefore wrong to believe that, if in the Sassanian period of the Iranian history, circa 224–644 AD, incestuous relations in the society were not forbidden by law, this had anything to do with the teachings of the prophet Zarathustra himself or his religious doctrines. Zarathustra lived, according to recent historical estimates, approximately 1,600 years before the beginning of the Sassanian period in Iranian history. During this time, the Zoroastrian religious traditions were mainly preserved orally from one generation to the next. There is no proof of incestuous relations being legal in the society in the Achaemenid period, which ended circa 340 BC. The earliest appearance of this phenomenon in the society being recorded in foreign (non-Iranian) sources is during the mid-Arsacid period, which is to say circa 150 AD and onwards. Meaning a time interval of approximately 1,500 years between the presumed lifetime of Zarathustra, and the occurrence of incestuous marriages in Iran. In this period of time, any religion will go through unorthodox transformations or unwanted additions, especially when traditions are only preserved orally from one generation to the next.

We have to mention here two important sources, which can attest to the fact that incestuous marriages and relations were not a Zoroastrian religious phenomenon, but appeared probably in relatively isolated situations, much later in Iranian history for a limited time, and this independently of any Zoroastrian religious dogmas. The historian Herodotus of Halicarnassus, who lived during the time of the Achaemenid Dynasty in Iran, being famous for his Greek nationalism, writes in his *Histories*—when mentioning the marriage customs of the ancient Persians—that the nobility and upper classes had multiple wives and were keeping a number of mistresses. There is no mention anywhere about marriages or unions of incestuous nature in his accounts of the Iranians. As he was critical of the Iranians, he would not have missed this opportunity to mention this point about their customs, if he had any knowledge about it.

Furthermore, we have the documentation in the hebraic Mishnah which mentions that, in Iran, starting from the time of the end of the Arsacid period, circa 224 AD, when the rule of the Sassanian Dynasty started, incestuous marriages started to be practise and were not illegal.[132] This writing of the oral traditions of the Jews had to be done, according to the Talmud, as the persecution of the Jews and the passage of time, raised strongly the possibilities that the details of the ancient oral traditions, dating from the Pharisaic times (536 BC–70 AD) would be forgotten. The oral tradition of the Mishnah goes back at least until the time of the Babylonian captivity or earlier, therefore it can be considered as a highly historical document.[133] In 1168 AD, Moses Maimonides published a comprehensive commentary on the Mishnah, which was one of the first commentaries of its kind. Therefore, it is evident here that incestuous marriages were not practised or were probably not legal during the time of the Achaemenid dynasty.[134] That is the case also after that period, until circa 150–200 AD in Iran. For this reason, if incest was, in fact, practised in the Iranian society sometimes after 150 AD and onwards until at latest 644 AD, there is no proof that this had anything to do with the teachings of the Prophet Zarathustra or his religion.

Secondly, a detail which is of greatest importance in this context, and which has not been addressed by scholars, is the fact that, according to the laws of the Sassanian period—the same law codex which did not forbid incestuous marriages—sister and brother were defined not only as persons who shared one or both parents, but also as persons who, in childhood, had been given the breast or mother's milk by the same woman. More clearly, if a woman feeds her breast milk to two or more children, then all this children were, according to the Sassanian law, considered brothers and sisters regardless of parentage.

This legal notion highlights certain situations, pertaining to inheritance law and family law during the Sassanian period: "If two or more children are being breastfed by the same woman, they are considered in front of the law as being brothers and or sisters. Without consideration whether this children are blood related or not, and also without consideration who gave birth to this children." The law considers them to be blood related, and they inherit also in the same way as if they would be really blood related. In fact, to be breastfed by the same woman was considered, according to the law, as a blood relationship.[135]

We are basing all this on the *Madigane heẓar Dadsetan* [The Book of a Thousand Judgments] which was the central civil law codex of the Sassanian Period in Iranian history. In fact, importantly, in the later Islamic jurisprudence, marriage between a boy and a girl, who were nursed by the same woman is legally prohibited. Accordingly, in the Islamic religion too, two children from different mothers and fathers, who are nursed by the same woman are thus considered to be blood relatives. Still today in Iran, the word for brother and sister is Ham-shireh, which means exactly *from the same milk*.

This legal detail of the Sassanian law codex has a fundamental significance in the historical definition of the notion of incestuous relations in the Sassanian period in Iranian history. In fact, this new definition of the word brother or sister changes the whole aspect of the previous belief in incestuous relationships in Iranian history. In effect many cases of incestuous relations could possibly be referred to as a marriage between persons, who are, in fact, legally brothers and sisters, but not related biologically or by blood to each other. For example when a neighbours of a family dies, and the family takes over and keeps their small children with them in their own household, and later the families children and the children of the death neighbour marry each other. This would be considered legally as incest but not biologically. Another possibility is, after years the mother of the same family dies, and the father of the family marries the daughter of the neighbour, who has grown up in his house. The daughter of the neighbour is also legally his own daughter, but she is not biologically related to him. Interestingly Maria Macuch, in her book, which we have mentioned earlier, writes on page 138 "The only form of marriage not attested anywhere is that of mother and son..." What she means is, that this type of marriage has not been mentioned in the family and inheritance law codex and also has never been mentioned or has appeared historically. Theoretically therefore, if in some Sassanian period records, there have been a mention of the benefits or the praise of incestuous marriages, for example the praise for persons marring their sister, then it is possible that the meaning of that maybe "... that female considered legally your sister, is in reality the daughter of the dead neighbour, she was an orphan, who has been grown up in your family, in marring her you do a good and praiseworthy deed..." The extant encouragement and praise of the practice of xwedudagih in Pahlavi and Sassanid text perhaps alludes to a time honoured trend that is practiced within Iranian society today.

When an orphaned child is kept and raised by an extended family, who is not related to the parents of the child, his or her eventual betrothal to son or the daughter of the extended family is regarded as a highly praiseworthy and laudable act, both in cultural and religious terms. Albeit, from the legal point of view, the position of the adopted child within the family is, in fact, that of a blood relative, although this child is not related biologically or by blood to the other members of the family. This notion is practiced today amongst the traditional families in Iran and elsewhere in the Middle East and is regarded as praiseworthy. It is highly probable that wide spread practice of xwedudagih (marriage of legally brothers and sisters) in Pahlavi texts, attributed to the Sassanid period, may, in fact, had included this very popular trend practiced then and today in the Middle East.

In terms of incestuous marriages between to people who are legally but not biologically related to each other, we have to mention an interesting book by the name of *Vis u Rāmin*. This book, is said to be of Parthian origin, namely from the time of the Arsacid Dynasty. The Parthian Empire, which was the rival of the Roman Empire, existed from 248 BC to circa 224 AD, and was a society that lived according to the traditions of the Zoroastrian religion. In fact, all the details of the events and traditions mentioned in this book, refer to Zoroastrian customs. The events described in this book are believed by experts to be the life story of one of the minor Kings of the Parthian Arsacid Period, who lived in the first century AD in northeastern Iran. This story, which existed from that period of time, was later in the eleventh century (1040–1054 according to Vladimir Minorsky) rewritten by a Persian poet, by he name of Fakhruddin As'ad Gurgani, who transformed the story of this book into prose.

In brief, *Vis u Rāmin* is a classical love story about a girl named of Vis (or Viseh), who is the daughter of a nobleman from a local important family in the west of the Parthian Empire, and Rāmin, a young prince, who is the younger brother of the king of a region in the east of the empire. The king of that region, Mobed Monikan, is the ruler of Marv, and at the same time Rāmin's elder brother. The king himself is also in love with Vis and marries her, but this marriage is never consummated, for she finds constantly ways to avoid it. After a very long narrative, she has only had sexual relation with Rāmin, the only man she loved.

Interestingly, this book was regarded for centuries as a work which celebrates incestuous relations. Rāmin, the only man she really loved and had intimate relations with, had been nursed together with her, both as children, by the same nanny. The same maid woman had breast fed both of them, although both of them were from completely different families and from different parts of the Empire. The ancient pre-Islamic laws, as we have seen above, considered them legally to be brothers and sister, although they were not blood related.[136]

This book was first brought to the western literary attention by A. Sprenger, who had found a copy of it in India.[137] There are several old records relative to the book of Vis and Rāmin in Iranian Literature. The anonymous author of the *Majmal al Tavarikh* [the collected histories] locates the story of Vis and Rāmin in the time of the second Sassanian King Shapur, the son of Ardeshir and assumes that the king,

Mobed Monikan, was in reality a local king of the city of Marv during the time of Shapur of the Sassanians circa 248 AD. Again another Persian author, Hamdullah Mostofi, identifies Mobed Monikan as being King Behzan-Goudarz from the Arsacid Dynasty in circa first century AD.[138]

Vladimir Minorsky writes, that in the early thirteenth century, this book with the poems written by Fakhruddin As'ad Gurgani, was translated into the Georgian Language. Where it was a popular book under the name of *Visramiani* and in past centuries, had a long lasting influence on Georgian literature. Unfortunately due to the Zoroastrian characteristics of the events in this book, this work of Fakhruddin As'ad Gurgani was later not appreciated in Islamic Persia and was forgotten, only surviving in India, written in Persian language, where it was discovered in the 1850s by western historians.

In reading this book, one thing is immediately clear: the events surrounding the story of Vis and Rāmin are reflect the customs and traditions derived from the Zoroastrian period. For example, the very peculiar nature of the marriage customs that seems to be practised right at the beginning of the poem. These marriage ceremonies belong not only to the Zoroastrianism of 2,000 years ago, but they were still in use in the immediate pre-Islamic Persian royal dynasties.

Marriages that are now universally regarded as incestuous, were relatively tolerated among the pre-Islamic dynasties of Iran. A confirmation of the relative commonness, in pre-Islamic Iran, of marriages that would now be regarded as incestuous, is provided by the *Madigane heẓar Dadsetan* [The Book of Thousand Judgements]. The translation of the Pahlavi text, notes and glossary according to Anahit Perikhanian.[139]

We have seen above that Vis and Rāmin has shared criteria that made them, in the eyes of the law, brother and sister even though they were not blood related. That was the reason why this book was later classified as being immoral—it was considered to depict an incestuous relationship. Another clear indication, is the emphasis on pleasure and joy of life, which can be seen partly as surviving trait of the ancient Zoroastrian religious tradition. Until the Zoroastrian tradition was disrupted by the Islamic religion, physical pleasure and the joy of life had always been seen in the Zoroastrian society as a gift of the good principles of life and nature. As already mentioned, Zoroastrian tradition forbids any kind of fasting, self-mortification or chastity for religious reasons—living the life to its fullest is a duty to celebrate the good creation of Ahura Mazdâ. The joy of life, which was a gift from the creator Ahura Mazdâ, and the gratitude for its presence and its continuous cultivation, were seen as a serious religious duty.

There is another very interesting aspect to this ancient book, which was probably originally written in Iran around the time Jesus Christ was born or shortly thereafter. The story of this book and that of the ancient western nordic mythological tale of Tristan and Isolde are exactly the same—as if the one had been copied from the other. The Russian historian, Vladimir Minorsky, one of the recognized experts on iranian literature and *Vis u Rāmin*, writes:

> ...A comparison between the story of Vis and Rāmin and Tristan and Isolde is a tempting literary problem. Absolute similarities in characters, episodes, dramatic attitudes, and even the basic idea of love sweeping away all obstacles are obvious both in the Iranian story and its western counterpart.[140]

The question of whether the story of Vis and Rāmin—which according to experts as Vladimir Minorsky and Hamdollah Mostofi, was based on real historical events from around the time Tiberius was Emperor of Rome—has any connection to the European mythological story of Tristan and Isolde is a matter for further historical investigation and discussion. Historians came to the conclusion, that the story of Tristan and Isolde became known in Europe at the beginning of the twelfth century, after the Crusaders returned to Europe from the

Middle East.[141] Furthermore, some more important details have been investigated by Joan T. Grimbert.[142]

For over a century now, the academic and historian community has been suggesting a serious connection between Vis and Rāmin and Tristan and Isolde. The story of Tristan and Isolde became known in Europe approximately 150 years after Gurgani wrote *Vis u Rāmin*. This obviously based on the date of the first appearance of the poem of Tristan and Isolde, which has appeared in Europe circa 1225 AD, written by the Norman poet Béroul. The first scholar and historian to suggest a connection between the two books was Italo Pizzi (1849–1920). In 1890, another scholar Rudolph Zenker discussed the notion that these books maybe the same in his article "Die Tristansage und das persische Epos von Wis und Rāmin," which appeared in 1911—Zenker concluded that Vis and Rāmin is the major source of the Tristan and Isolde legend. Later, the french scholar Pierre Gallais in his article "Essais sur Tristan et Iseult et son Modele Persan" in 1974, also made a strong case for the basis of the Tristan legend to be that of Vis and Rāmin.

These scholarly arguments concerning the roots of the story of Tristan and Isolde were generally ignored by historians. *Vis and Rāmin* has been recently published in a new edition by Penguin Books with an excellent translation by Dick Davis, who was decisively assisted by his Iranian wife Afkham Darbandi. Dick Davis adds, by himself, an additional line of poem to this book, in which he says, "Ah Vis, across the centuries I heard your human cry, and vowed that I would do my part to see that it did not die."

Vladimir Minorsky, one of the respected experts on Iranian culture and history in the Imperial Russian Czarist era, lived for many years in Iran. In 1903, he entered into the service of the Ministry of Foreign Affairs in St. Petersburg and was sent to Iran on several assignments. In 1917 at the start of the Russian Revolution, he was the chargé d'affaires (meaning the person in charge) of the Russian Embassy in Teheran. After 1917, he went to Paris, and later, in 1937, he became a Professor of Iranian Literature and History at the University of London. Vladimir Minorsky was convinced that *Vis and Rāmin* sprang from real historical events, which happened probably during the reign of the Arsacid Emperors of Parthia. In his book Minorsky comes to the conclusion, that the real identify of Mobed Monikan—older brother to Rāmin—was likely a minor King by the name of Behzan Goudarz, who lived circa 50 AD in eastern Persia. According to Minorsky:

> In fact, at no period of the long history of Iran did the Material, and especially the geographical conditions, correspond to those described in Vis and Rāmin except at the time of the Parthian Dominion, which was under the rule of the Arsacid Dynasty...[143]

Later, when the events around the king and his name were forgotten by subsequent generations, this book took a life of its own as an independent love story and novel. Later, in the Islamic period of Iran, this book was completely forgotten and only survived in India, where only a few copies had remained.

Returning again to the topic of incestuous relationships in past eras, if we look at the history of the ancient world, incest can be found in every culture and in all ancient civilizations. After analyzing the generality of incestuous relations known to us in history, one clear picture emerges from the total data available to us. Namely that the incestuous relations in history were, to a large extent, isolated and monopolized in the upper ruling class of various societies, namely persons like kings, pharaohs, rulers, emperors and higher nobility. Of course part of the reason for this is likely that recorded history only tends to concern itself with the behaviour of the ruling class. In general, the lifestyle of the average person in antiquity was ignored by historians.

An interesting historical case of incest is the story of the Greek king Mausolus (377–353 BC), a Persian Satrap (Governor) of the city of

Halicarnassus, before fighting against the troops of Persian Emperor Artaxerxes in 362 BC. He later, at the end of his life, became the king of Halicarnassus [modern-day Bodrum, Turkey], the same city where the historian Herodotus came from. After the death of King Mausolus in 353 BC, his wife Artemisia, who was also his sister, burned his body and then swallowed his ashes with a warm drink, saying she wanted to be united for eternity with her brother and lover. The Roman chronicler Pliny reports that it was she who ordered a huge tomb to be built in his honour—which was in reality her own tomb, as he was already dead and inside her body. This monument was later known as one the wonders of the ancient world, and the word *mausoleum* derives from this episode in history.[144]

Nevertheless a clear picture emerges which confirms that there is no proof of any past (or modern) society wherein the populace of average citizens takes part in widespread incestuous relationships. All cases reported in later chronicles are probably occurrences of exceptional, individual bases. Maria Macuch and others who have investigated the phenomenon of incestuous relations in the Sassanian period (224–644 AD) are basing the grand majority of their investigations on the *Madigan e Heẓar Dadsetan* [Book of a Thousand Judgements]. Furthermore, in her own book, Maria Macuch writes:

> All the passages deal with legal problems from the field of inheritance and transfer of property, arising from the double or even triple status of the person involved within the family.[145]

What she means is, for instance, a person who inherits is the wife and also at the same time the sister of a man, whose father had died and he and she are going to inherit certain assets. Furthermore:

> Marriages between father and daughter as well as between brother and sister are mentioned here *en*

passant leaving the impression that they were per-
fectly normal forms of matrimony with no need to
comment on them further in any form. [...] The
only form of marriage not attested anywhere is that
of mother and son.[146]

When she says this was mentioned *en passant* [in passing by] she
means that this was mentioned without any emphasis and importance
to the fact of incest itself. As an example, if there should be a case
where a man marries his sister, then and in case of the death of their
father she would have two rights, once as the daughter and once as
the daughter-in-law. In any case this could mean a law, which would
cover rare legal cases or legal eventualities This lack of emphasis suggests that this is a meritorious thing to do, and it should be done by the
general population. If the clerical establishment of the Sassanian era,
at the time when the Zoroastrian faith was the state religion, had sanc-
tioned the practice of incestuous relations, or the tolerance thereof,
then this was clearly a deviation from the true and initial dogmas of
that religion. It was also clearly an alien phenomenon to the spirit and
the teachings of the Prophet Zarathustra.

6. ZOROASTRIANISM
IN HISTORY

6.1 THE HISTORIAN HERODOTUS,
ALEXANDER THE GREAT,
AND ZOROASTRIAN IRAN

At this point we have to mention the famous Greek historian Herodotus. For indeed, narratives and primary sources on information of events relating to Ancient Persian history and the Greek–Persian relations of antiquity are known for the most part only through his efforts. His fundamental work, entitled *Histories* is a cornerstone of our knowledge for a certain segment in world history.

Herodotus was a Greek nationalist born in Halicarnassus [modern-day Bodrum in Turkey], a city under the occupation of the Persians, in fact, Herodotus was born a Persian citizen, for Halicarnassus was, at the time, part of the Persian Empire. Herodotus considered the Persians as enemies. Nevertheless, he is undeniably one of the most significant contributors of knowledge of the ancient world civilization.

His importance as a historian and chronicler cannot be questioned, for his contribution to history is irreplaceable. Herodotus was born circa 484 BC and subsequently left his native city and lived in various other areas in the Greek world, but mainly on the island of Samos where he died in 425 BC. His masterwork—in fact the *only* work he produced—the *Histories,* was written in the Ionian dialect, although Herodotus was of Dorian origin, as originally Halicarnassus was an ancient Dorian settlement. Herodotus claimed to have "… for the first time in history, investigated all his sources categorically and systemically…" but in reality (he claimed later) that he was "…reporting only what had been told to him." *The Histories* deals with the origins of the Greco-Persian wars and includes a wealth of geographical and ethnographical information; it is structured as a dynastic history of four Persian kings of the Achaemenid Dynasty, namely:

- Cyrus, 557–530 BC: Book 1

- Cambyses, 530–522 BC: Book 2 and part of Book 3

- Darius, 521–486 BC: the rest of Book 3 and then Books 4, 5 & 6

- Xerxes, 486–479 BC: Books 7, 8 and 9.

Some commentators believe that Herodotus' initial intention was to write a history of Persia and the personal biography of the Emperor Xerxes—whom apparently he admired—but later transformed his book into the narratives of the Greco-Persian wars. Herodotus says of himself in this regard, "Digressions are part of my plan."[147] The first person who referred to Herodotus as "the father of History" was the famous Roman Senator and orator Cicero. On the other hand, various ancient scholars and chroniclers have called him "the father of lies," the latest being David Pipes.[148]

Discoveries made since the end of the nineteenth century by historians have both added to and detracted from his credibility as an impartial historian. In this point we have to say, in general, that looking back at the circumstances in which he lived, and considering that mass-communications, news publications, written documentation of any kind and public libraries and printed books were not available to him at all, he did a tremendous work to collect data and information to master his task as a historian. Living on a relatively isolated island on the Ionian Sea, he was dependant mostly on hearsay and the narratives of other individuals, telling him of events they had heard from others—which had happened generations ago in far away regions of the world. Interestingly, the antique Persian word for the country of Greece, which is still in use today in Persia, is Iounan, which is derived from the word Ionian, for the first Greeks the Persians encountered were the people of the Ionian Islands. Considering the fact that Herodotus was a Greek nationalist who had to flee his occupied home city, it is reasonable to expect that this would somewhat colour his narratives of Persian history.

Herodotus, for unknown reasons, never directly mentions the Zoroastrian religion in his *Histories*, although by mentioning various Persian customs, it is a clear indication that these customs are derived from the Zoroastrian religious tradition. He mentions, for example, that in contrary to the Egyptian Priests who respect all type of life forms and animals, the Persian Magi kill animals such as snakes, scorpions and various insects. This act of the Magi is a clear indication that they are following the Zoroastrian religious tradition, according to which, some animals are considered agents of the evil forces (the Xrafstra in Avestan), who had to be combatted at all times.[149, 150, 151, 152, 153]

An example of the difficulties in writing balanced histories via second-hand sources and with an unavoidable nationalistic bias.

In the year 525 BC, the Persian Achaemenid Empire under the king Cambyses II, who was the son of Cyrus the Great, conquered

Egypt. According to Herodotus, Cambyses was confronted by the Egyptian high priest because of his treatment of a sacred Bull. King Cambyses II, according to Herodotus, to the amazement of the Priests assembled, is said to have taken his dagger and stabbed the sacred Bull in a genuine mythraic manner. Herodotus, who was at that time living on the island of Samos, reports this event, which happened in Egypt eighty-one years before his time.[154] Upon the Persian King stabbing the Bull with a dagger, the Egyptian population, including the high priest are, according to Herodotus, shocked by this sacrilegious act. Herodotus, who is here very critical of the Persian rule in Egypt under King Cambyses, mentions that the Egyptian high priest and the priesthood were at all times highly critical and rejected Cambyses who, after having conquered Egypt, had changed his name into an Egyptian name, calling himself Pharaoh Mesuti-Ra, meaning *the son of the God Ra*. The Persian–Achamanian Empire ruled Egypt as the Egyptian twenty-seventh dynasty for 193 years until the conquest of Egypt by Alexander the Great. In this regard, the Egyptologist James Dunn writes:

> " Modern Egyptologists believe that many of these accounts, which Herodotus has written are strongly biased, and that Cambyses II's rule was not nearly so traumatic as Herodotus, who wrote his histories seventy-five years after Cambyses's death, would have us believe... the Egyptians were particularly isolated, as their Greek allies against the Persians had abandoned them and defected to the Persian side, including Phanes, and then also the famous king Polycrates of Samos with a large fleet, supposing to help the Egyptians had joined the Persian army.[155]

We have to consider here that Herodotus lived on the island of Samos, the same island whose King Polycrates—being the ally of the Egyptian pharaoh—betrayed them and sided with the Persians when they invaded. A recently discovered inscription on a statue, which was kept previously for centuries in the Vatican museum collection in Rome, was recently deciphered. This statue, which had not been previously afforded any attention, shows the bust portrait of none other than Udjadhorresnet the Egyptian high priest and leading government official during the time of the Persian king Cambyses II in Egypt. The German academic Ursula Rossler − -Khoeler , who translated this inscription, talks about the following translation of the statue's inscription. The original words of the high priest himself are as follows:

> Regardless of the death of the Apis-Bull, it should be noted that the animal's burial was held with proper pomp, ceremony and due respect... His Majesty gave orders to give divine offerings to the god Neith the Great, the mother of all the gods, and so to the great gods of "Sais"... His majesty knew of the greatness of Sais that it is a city of all the gods who dwell there on the their seats and forever... I have introduced His majesty to the Egyptian culture and traditions. So that he might take on the appearance of a traditional Pharaoh...[156]

The high priest Udjadhorresnet goes on to say in his autobiography—which was written on a green basalt naophorus stone statue—that Cambyses II was well received by the Egyptian religious establishment, and he had, in fact, brought all the respect necessary to their ancient traditions and gods. It is in this point obvious that Herodotus writings were not accurate and, in fact, biased agains the Persian king Cambyses II. Furthermore, concerning the death of Cambyses II, Herodotus mentions that the Achaemenid ruler had, on the same location where he had stabbed the sacred bull, at some later date while dismounting from his horse, stabbed his own left thigh with the same dagger. Later, also according Herodotus' narratives, Cambyses dies due to infections or complications to the self-inflicted wound on his thigh.

In reality, most ancient historians are now united in the opinion that Cambyses II had to fight the influence and forces of his younger brother Bardiya, or most likely a Zoroastrian priest under the name of Gaumata posing as Bardiya who wanted to usurp the throne from him. Cambyses had died years later in this armed confrontation, and is buried in Damascus or some close location.[157] Herodotus here had to know that the Egyptian Pharaonic kingdom had fallen to the Persians, in part because of the betrayal of their Greek allies, who had abandoned the Egyptians in order to side with the Persians. Maybe this was the reason that his judgement of Cambyses was unfavourable. In any case, in narrating the historical events, one of Herodotus' favourite saying was: "It is always the circumstances that rules the man, it is not the man, who rules the circumstances."

As for the legendary Alexander of Macedonia, called Alexander the Great, he has fascinated historians of the western world for 2,300 years. Starting with various Roman military men of antiquity and Emperors and since then, it was the dream of many men of power and rank to follow in the foot steps of Alexander the Great. His marble statues show him to be beautiful and noble, equal to the gods of the Greek pantheon.[158] He conquered the Barbarians of the east and had advanced to the gates of the Central Asian steppes, and on the return had subdued part of western India. He had never lost a battle, and cities, such as Alexandria in Egypt, were founded by him, and named after him. The greatest minds of the time—philosophers and artists alike—were his admirers and worked for him. Aristotle was his teacher, and Lysippus, one of the greatest sculptors of antiquity, had worked for him, and sculpted his image. The philosopher Aristotle supposedly told him that "the Persians are one of the two pillars of civilization, if you destroy the Persians, then the world belongs to us alone."

Alexander's greatest Biographer, Arrian of Nicomedia, describes
Alexander as "The strong and handsome commander, with one eye
dark as the night, and one blue as the sky." In the Roman republic and
Roman Empire, it is said that Julius Caesar, one of the greatest Roman
Emperors, wept at his Mausoleum. Famed military commanders
such as Lucullus, Pompeius, Lucius Vinicius Crassus—the same man
who put down the Spartacus revolt—and emperors such as Trajan,
Hadrian, Caracalla, Gordian III and many others tried to imitate him,
but all without success.

The historical Alexander—as opposed to the legendary one
so fawned over by the western academic community—merits an
intense investigation. The British Encyclopaedia writes the following
about him:

> "Already in his lifetime the subject of many fabulous
> stories—he later became a hero of full-scale legends
> and stories, bearing only the sketchiest and slightest
> resemblance to his historical carrier."

It is useless to say that from the time of Alexander (he died in
323 BC in Babylon) or even shortly afterwards, there are no documentation or historical records at all. The records of the closest
chronicler, who was —a man who greatly admired Alexander—the
Greek Diodorus Siculus, wrote his chronicles in circa 30 BC, or
approximately 300 years after Alexander's death, and his documents
had been already lost in early antiquity. And yet, other chroniclers,
centuries later, without having seen his records, still quoted from
him uncritically. The writings of the other chroniclers, for example
Quintus Curtius Rufus—who lived circa 125 AD and who copied
from Diodorus Siculus without having even seen his records—were
also lost already in antiquity.

Among academic historians, it is agreed that the most reliable
recount of the events around Alexander the Great are from Arrian

of Nicomedia, a Greek historian, living in Rome between 86–160 AD; nearly 500 years after the death of Alexander. This historian, being a self-confessed Greek nationalist was, like Herodotus, from the city of Halicarnassus which was continuously occupied by Persians. Therefore he similarly harboured deep animosity for the Persians. In 131 AD, he was appointed by the Romans as the governor of the Black Sea province of Cappadochia, and ultimately the commander of the Roman legions on the frontier with Armenia and Parthia, essentially acting as the commander of the Roman troops on the frontier with the Parthian Empire. It was here that he wrote the *Anabasis Alexandri* [Campaigns of Alexander]. Arrian's intention was mainly to idealize Alexander and to make a myth out of him. He does not make the claim of objectivity, when he says, "Alexander's greatness is worthy of praise and glory, and should be known by future generations."

In general the Greeks of antiquity have looked upon the Persians as their biggest enemy; the wars between the Persians and the Greeks were a matter of historical and existential importance for the Greeks, whereas for the Persians rulers and military, this was just a peripheral military adventure on the borderline of their domain of influence in the west. The western historiography and academic establishment have always taken the accounts of Greek chroniclers and historians with reference to all matters concerning wars and other events with the Persians, uncritically as the absolute truth. This would be the same, as giving the history of the Jewish people over to be written by the Palestinians. In his memoirs, Winston Churchill correctly says, "History will be very kind to me, because I intend to write it myself." Mustafa Kemal Pasha, more commonly known as Kemal Atatürk, says also in one of his speeches, "to write history is as important, as to make history."

In this connection, A.B. Bosworth, one of the recognized experts on the history of Alexander of Macedonia, interestingly criticizing Arrian of Nicomedia:

"Arrian makes it quite plain, that his work is designed as a literary showpiece...Arrian has written a panegyric (literary work), rather than a serious work of history."[159]

The American Historical Review, writes about Professor A.B. Bosworth:

"Bosworth has emerged as one of the greatest living scholar of Alexander, perhaps among the best ever."

In any case, all the statues depicting Alexander, in famous museums now, are copies made from a statue, which was initially made as a Garden decoration, probably for the gardens of Tivoli close to Rome. This statue was an idealized and imaginary recreation of Alexander's features, and was made centuries after his death having nothing to do with the real Alexander. If Lysippus, the famous sculptor made a portrait of Alexander, then that portrait is now lost. So is the famous mosaic picture, depicting the battle between the Persians and Alexander's Army in the Pompeian villa known as The House of Faun, which is from approximately 210 years after the real events shown, and is just an artistic imagination of the real events. These are all the signs of the glorification of a man, about whom the real historical facts are on one side, and the idealized nationalistic thinking is on the other.

Nevertheless, one of the main proofs of the conquests of Alexander in the eastern and north eastern Persian Empire—which is the present day Afghanistan and north of that—is the discovery of coins with Greek inscriptions dating from the time shortly after Alexander. It is known that Greek settlements has been proven to have existed in the region of the northern Bactria. Smaller Kingdoms existed in what is today northeastern Afghanistan, and they minted coins with Greek inscriptions until the beginning of the Sassanian period circa 224 AD. A city mentioned in the Alexandrian records by the name of

Alexandria on the Oxus apparently and founded by the Alexandrian troops, was later excavated under the ruins of the a city by the name of *Ai-Khanoum* [literally: Lady moon] This city was founded circa 300 BC and was a focal point of Hellenism in northeastern Afghanistan. Its king was Eucratides I, whose coins, bearing Greek inscriptions, have been recovered on that site. The architectural remains of the city showed Greek, but also Persian Zoroastrian influences. Later it was totally destroyed circa 145 BC by nomadic horse raiding invaders from the northeastern Asiatic steppes.

According to history, Alexander III, King of Macedonia and later known as Alexander the Great, crossed from Europe to Asia (via the Hellespont) on 334 BC with an army of 48,100 soldiers, 6,100 Cavalry, 120 ships with a crew of 38,000 men, and marched from there to the east. Moving further east, he had caught the Persian king in a weak moment, defeated the troops of the Achaemenid King Darius in 331 BC near the modern-day city of Mosul, and continued on to Babylon, Susa and finally to the centre of the Achaemenid power base, the City of Persepolis—which he burned in 330 BC. When in the 1930s the ruins of Persepolis were excavated, before reaching the remains of the palaces, thick layers of coal and ashes were found. According to the Greek-Roman chronicler Diodorus Siculus, after the fall of Persepolis to Alexander's troops, all male persons were killed and woman and children were sold into slavery. The historian Michael Flower writes in this regard the following:

> Aristotle had allegedly advised Alexander to be a leader to Greeks and a despot to the barbarians, to look after the former as after friends and relatives, and to deal with the latter as with animals or plants... According to Aristotle, Barbarians, as the Persians, were natural slaves in that they were by nature more servile than Greeks. This was because they were deficient in reason logos..."[160, 161]

This saying by the great Aristotle is according to Plutarch, *On the Fortune of Alexander*. Plutarch was another philhellenic Greek chroniclers, who was speaking about the Persians as the enemy of his nation. Thus, in the framework of nationalistic emotions and pride, these kinds of statements by chroniclers can have a negative effect, and can deviate from the historical truth. This is especially true if all the ancient historians depicting the events are from the same political side and are referring to their common enemy. It is known that the famous Greek courtesan, Thais, who had accompanied the Greek troops and was with Alexander in Persepolis, persuaded him to burn down the Palaces of the Achaemenians, and when Alexander hesitated, she herself threw in the first torch as a revenge for the Persian war against the Greeks.

It is interesting in this regards, that Parmenion, an old and trusted General of Alexander, and probably his closest adviser, recommended he not burn the city and the palaces of Persepolis. His argument being that he should not be regarded as a conqueror and destroyer, but simply this new territory should be regarded as a new part of his future empire—that there should be a continuation of Macedonian rule over this part of the world, with him as the new ruler. Among the advice which Parmenion had previously given Alexander was that he marry and have an heir before starting the military campaign against Asia. Had Alexander listened and secured an heir and successor before starting his conquests, it would have had far reaching consequences for the Empire and the territories conquered by Alexander after his sudden and premature death.[162]

Alexander had already declared himself to be the Ruler or King of Asia in Arbil, a city in the west of the Achaemenid Empire, in modern-day Iraq. This title–King or Emperor of Asia—never existed in the Persian-Achaemenid vocabulary. Parmenion, being one of the closest army commanders to Alexander, was an experienced general and well respected both by the Macedonian and the Greek soldiers. Descended from a Macedonian noble family, he was the most trusted army commander and a close friend of Philip, King of Macedonia and Alexander's father. During Alexander's campaigns in Asia, he was commanding the left flank of the army, which included the famous Thessalian cavalries, while Alexander himself was in charge of the right flank. We see here that Parmenion was second-in-command of the Macedonian–Greek armies, and from the advice he gave Alexander, it is evident that his aim was to give to the newly conquered territory an aura of Imperial-Monarchic continuity. His aim was—in the vast newly established Greco-Macedonian Empire—to institutionalize the Monarchy in perpetuity, in this case including and gaining the cooperation of the population of the new territories. Some historians and authors have suggested that Parmenion, in this regard, spoke on behalf a group of senior army commanders.

Had Alexander listened to his advice, it would have had far reaching consequences in history, but events developed differently. Parmenion's son Philotas was suspected to be involved in a conspiracy against Alexander's life, and so he was arrested and executed. At the same time, fearing collusion between father and son, Alexander gave orders to assassinate Parmenion himself, who at that time was in Ecbatana, in the far west of the former Persian Empire. In the year 330 BC Parmenion was therefore killed.

Most historians today agree that it was likely Callisthenes, an old rival and enemy of Parmenion, who was the source of the conspiracy theory that claimed both Parmenion and his son—a conspiracy that has otherwise never been proven. Callisthenes was a historian, who had fallen from grace with Alexander.[163]

Plutarch himself a historian who live in later centuries after Alexander, also had a negative attitude towards Parmenion, as he probably suspected that the latter had a conservative influence on Alexander[164] In the David Gemmell novels, *The Lion of Macedon* and *The Dark Prince*, the author deals with the life of Parmenion and suggests that he may have been, in fact, Alexander's true father—as opposed to Philip. This of course is only a speculation, and not historical. Furthermore, the historian Ernst Fredericksmeyer writes:

> Alexander ...who among other misdeeds ordered the destruction of one of the two existing copies of the Avesta, which had fallen into his hands, while ordering the other copy to be taken to Alexandria for translation into the Greek script for everything in it dealing with Philosophy, astronomy, medicine and agriculture. If indeed Alexander found these two copies, and ordered one of them to be destroyed, while preserving the other one for the benefit of the Greek science, then it would be a clear evidence that he meant to suppress the Acheamenid (Zoroastrian) religious tradition...as it accords with Alexander's known scientific curiosity and his wilful destruction of Persepolis.[165]

As we have seen in the previous chapter, according to the witness of the Zoroastrian Priest Arda Wiraz, one the copies of the Avesta, and the scriptures of the Gatha were kept in a tower, called the so-called *Fortress of Writing* [in Middle Persian: Dezh-e Nebi] probably meant to be another name for a library. This ancient library was in the city of Estakhr e Papakan which was destroyed by the order of Alexander. The historical evidence show that Alexander, being not favourable to religion in general, was particularly hostile to Zoroastrianism and had ordered temples and sacred places and ancient religious documents destroyed. There are indications that he regarded *himself* to be a divine being. As we have seen in earlier chapters, he ordered the murder of all priests and also that the ancient fires in temples be extinguished. Furthermore, the grave of Achaemenid King were vandalized. In later Zoroastrian records, Alexander was the only person, to share with Ahriman the same title, namely gujastag which means, the Accursed.

Interestingly the Italian political commentator Niccolo Machiavelli (1469–1527) dedicated the fourth chapter of *Il Principe* [*The Prince*] to the question of why the Persian Satraps (or sub-rulers) did not immediately revolt against the Greek invaders after the Persian King Darius III's death. His theory is that there are two types of kingdoms. The one being like France (by way of example) where the landowning nobility is well established and strong, and semi-independent from the king's power. The king's authority is based on them; therefore, it is relatively easy to become king in France, but very difficult to keep this position and rule the country, for the nobility would not accept it and would revolt against any new king not endorsed by them. The second type of kingdom he suggests is like the Turkish Ottoman Empire. The Turkish Sultan is the absolute ruler of the Empire, and all other political personalities are, no matter how high in position, subject to his orders. The power of these kingdoms is absolutely dependant on the power of the absolute ruler—should the absolute ruler fall, then these political personalities will disperse. Machiavelli was of the opinion that the last Persian Achaemenid king before Alexander— namely Darius III Codomanus, who ruled from 336–331 BC—was an absolute Monarch, and all other political personalities of the Empire were dependant on him. Therefore, after the Darius's fall, the political system of the Empire collapsed. Machiavelli says, therefore, that to conquer this type of kingdoms is very difficult, but once conquered, it is relatively easy to rule.

Alexander died in Babylon in 323 BC, and shortly after that, a lengthy series of wars divided his conquests between his generals. Alexander's main secretary, a man of influence and respect, the known scholar Eumenes of Cardia[166] was on the opinion that Alexander's son from Roxana—a Persian princess from Bactria—should be declared as the new ruler of his Empire as Alexander IV. In the beginning, Eumenes seemed to have been successful in reuniting the various army factions, and a new ruler for a new Empire was taking shape. After some initial success, however, in 316 BC, Eumenes was betrayed and killed, and a few years later, princess Roxana and her son were also murdered.

This had to be expected, for the majority of the army commanders did not see the child of an Iranian woman to be the true and rightful successor to Alexander's Empire, notwithstanding the fact that Alexander was the child's father. It was clear from the beginning that this son of Roxana did not have the authority to resume the succession of a recognized Greek ruler, whereas had Alexander's son been from a legitimate Macedonian royal Princess, the generals and the army would have been conscious, from the beginning, of a continuation of the existing monarchy. If Alexander had had an heir from the beginning, his death would have been regarded by the commanders of the army only as a link between two monarchs, the past and the future. We see here that Parmenion's initial advice to Alexander to marry and have a successor, before starting the campaign against Asia, was of historical importance—important too for Zoroastrian Persia.

The most serious damage the invading moslem Arab Bedouins did to the Iranian people was to deliberately destroy and burn the ancient records and historical books and documents of the Persian nation. The Arabs in so doing, delivered the Iranian people to be dependant on the historians of their ancient enemies, the Greeks, for the knowledge of their own glorious past.

6.2 ZURVANISM

Zurvan [from the middle Persian meaning *time* or *old age*] was perceived to be the God of infinite Time and Space. Zurvanites believed that Zurvan existed alone before all things. Thereafter he was the father of the twin brothers Ahura Mazdâ, as the good spirit, and Angra Maynu (or Ahriman) as the destructive and dark spirit. Zurvan was regarded as being a neutral God, without gender and neither good nor evil; therefore, he had created the twins as negative and positive antipodes, meaning Ahura Mazdâ and Angra Maynu were equal but separate divinities under the supremacy of Zurvan. The core of the Zurvanite ideology puts Zurvan as the supreme god, with Ahura Mazdâ as the middle god, and Angra Maynu the fallen twin brother. In contrast to this, the Zoroastrians believe Ahura Mazdâ to be the uncreated transcendental creator. Zurvanism as a religious belief—now long since extinct—was a sect of mainstream Zoroastrianism. The historical origins and details of Zurvanism are still unknown, but it is clear that in response to some perceived inconsistencies in the sacred texts of Zoroastrianism itself, this new ideology was introduced probably some time in the second half of the Achaemenid Dynasty. Our knowledge of the Zurvanite heresy comes only from non-Zoroastrian sources. Mary Boyce is the opinion that Zurvanism was a deeply entrenched and harmful heresy to Zoroastrianism, one which was to later weaken Zoroastrianism in its struggles against Christianity and Islam.[167] The cult of Zurvan appears to have had few rituals, as Zurvan was believed to have been a remote being, later entrusting his powers in the world to his son Ahura Mazdâ or Ohrmazd. The Zurvanite belief system produced no change in the existing Zoroastrian worship. Three of the most reputable authorities in the field of Zoroastrianism have occupied themselves with this theory of twin brothers and its connection to Zurvanism, namely Mary Boyce, R.C. Zaehner, and W.B. Henning.

Zurvanism's principal characteristics is the belief that both Ahura Mazdâ and Angra Maynu (Ahriman) were twin brothers, with the first being the representative of the eternal good and the second being the representative of the eternal evil. Furthermore, this choosing the sides was by free choice, that is, Angra Maynu chose to be evil: "It is not that I can not create any thing good, but I decided that I (would not)." Zurvanism was partly promoted by the rulers during the time of the Sassanian Dynasty (226–651 AD), but its success was very short lived, and by the tenth century AD it was completely extinct and forgotten.

The question as to whether, in Sassanian times under the influence of greater Hellenistic philosophical influence, the Zoroastrian Zurvan was an adaptation of the ancient Greek deity of Time, Kronos, is not know. The earliest documentation of the cult of Zurvan is found in the *History of Theology* Attributed to Eudemus of Rhodes (c. 370–300 BC). Herein Eudemus describes a sect of the Persians that considered Space / Time to be the primordial father of the two rivals Oromazes of Light and Arimanius of Darkness.[168] In terms of Zurvanism in the Sassanian period, we have only Christian Armenian sources; the Kardir inscriptions at Ka'ba-ye Zartosht and the edict of Mehr Narse are the only Sassanian period sources that reveal anything about Zurvanism in that period. A book entitled *Ullemaye Eslam* [scientists of Islam] title notwithstanding is a book by a Zoroastrian and the only Persian language book that mentions the father of the twins theory. This book is from the twelfth or thirteenth century AD. Furthermore, the tenth century AD Denkard does not mention Zurvanism at all. Of the remaining Pahlawy texts only two—*Menog-i Khrad* and the Selection of *Zatspram*—both of them from the ninth century AD reveal a slight Zurvanite tendency.

The second document mentioned, is the last and latest Zoroastrian scripture that provides any information on Zurvanism. There is no hint of any *worship* in any of the texts of the Avesta, even the fact that the texts, as we have them today, are the result of Sassanian times redaction. Charles Zaehner is of the opinion that, in general, the Sassanian Monarchs were not Zurvanites, and the Mazdaean Zoroastrianism had always the upper hand during the time that the canon was written down.[169, 170] Two references to Zurvan are present in the Vendidad, and although these are late editions to the canon, they again do not establish any evidence of the cult.

The cult of Zurvanism does not appear in any listing of the Yazatas according to one of the great priests and scholars of Zoroastrianism, Maneckji Nusserwanji Dhalla (1875–1956). Among others, two of his important works are *History of Zoroastrianism* (New York, 1938) and

Zoroastrian Civilization (New York, 1921). Both books were published by Columbia University press and have been reprinted several times since first published. He was a liberal-minded Head Priest, who was critical of the orthodox refusal to accept converts.

Several theories exist regarding the development of the Zurvanist cult. Robert Charles Zaehner and Jacques Duchesne-Guillemin are of the opinion, that due to the religious liberalization of the late Achaemenid period, this cult developed out of the Zoroastrian mainstream ideology. Henrik Samuel Nyberg thinks that Zurvan existed as a pre-Zoroastrian divinity and was later incorporated into Zoroastrianism. The third opinion, which has followers such as Franz Cumont and Hans Heinrich Schaeder (also Walter Bruno Henning and Mary Boyce) suggests that Zurvanism is the result of the contact between Zoroastrianism and several of the Babylonian/Byzantium religions. Following the fall of the Sassanian Empire, and the emergence of Islam in 644 AD, the Zurvanist cult and its theory of the Twin Brothers faded away and ceased to exist by the tenth century. In contrast to the mainstream Zoroastrianism—essentially Mazdaism—which continued to exist. Why the cult of Zurvanism vanished remains again a matter of academic discussion. Arthur Christensen, thinks that the rejection of Zurvanism after the Islamic conquest, was a response and a reaction to the strong authority of Islamic Monotheism, that brought about the deliberate reform of Zoroastrianism, which aimed to establish a stronger orthodoxy, this theory shared by Mary Boyce.

6.3 THE PROPHET MANI AND HIS RELIGION MANICHAEISM

One of the interesting personalities who appeared on the political–religious scene at the beginning of the Sassanian era is the Prophet Mani (216–276 AD). Mani was the prophet and founder of a religious cult, called Manichaeism, which was in reality an offshoot of Zoroastrianism. It was a gnostic religion of late antiquity, which initially enjoyed great success and spread rapidly in eastern Asia, Europe, and in North Africa. This religion has been extinct since the fourteenth century in the west, and probably sometime later in north East Asia.

Until the mid-twentieth century, little reliable information Mani was known, and all knowledge about him was legendary or hagiographical, meaning we had to rely on the accounts of early Islamic historians or chroniclers, who had relied again on other chroniclers. These were for example the Persian Islamic librarian and philosopher Ibn al-Nadim, who wrote *Fihrist* on which al-Biruni based his subsequent book. Therefore the reports of Ibn al-Nadim about the life and work of Mani seemed to be the most reliable existing. In the year 1969, in upper Egypt, a Greek parchment codex dated circa 400 AD was discovered. This document is now known as *Codex Manichaicus Coloniensis* because it is conserved at the University of Cologne in Germany. This document combines a complex account of Mani's personality and career and spiritual development, his religious teachings, and contains some fragments of his writings. This documents and other evidence discovered in the twentieth century establishes Mani as a noteworthy and influential historical personality.

Mani was descendant of an ancient Iranian family that moved from the city of Ecbatana (modern-day Hamadan) to the western Iranian city of Ctesiphon. His father was born in Ecbatana, and his mother, Mariam, was a Parthian-Christian woman. Mani was born in Ctesiphon circa 216 AD. At the age of twelve and again at the age of twenty-four he had the visionary experience of a heavenly twin of his, calling him to leave his father's religion—which was Zoroastrianism—and teach the true message of Christ.

In the year 240–241 AD he traveled from Ctesiphon in the west to India—or rather to a place he thought to be India, but was in reality Afghanistan, the region of Bhamian, which at that time was strongly under Buddhist influence. He returned shortly afterwards, then wandered again for about eighteen years, reputedly in central Asia, Tibet and probably again in India. From the very beginning, he sought to unite and to synthesize the great major religions of his time into one new religion founded by him. He called himself the Apostle of Jesus Christ, but gave—at the same time—credit to other religious leaders and prophets. Therefore, as a consequence of this synthesis, he thought of himself as representing a Christian in Christian lands, and a Zoroastrian in Persia, and a Buddhist in Buddhist regions. Mani believed that salvation was possible through education, self-denial, fasting and chastity, and a strict vegetarian life.

He firmly believed that he was the reincarnation of Zarathustra, Buddha, Jesus and Krishna at the same time. Therefore, his mission on this earth was to complete the work of these individuals. In principle, Mani was a believer in the creeds of the early Christian sect of the Gnostics. Historians also note that Mani declared himself to be an Apostle of Jesus Christ. This means, as a Gnostic, he believed in a gnosis [secret knowledge] that derived from a direct, personal experience between the human and the divine. The Gnostics believe that there is a direct bond between the consciousness of every human directly and the divine, and therefore no other intermediary, as extensive religious organizations, is needed.

Returning to Persia from the east, he joined the court of the Sassanian King Shapur I, to whom he dedicated his only work written in Persian, the *Shabuhragan*. King Shapur I, although not impressed by his new religious teachings—and himself firmly a Zoroastrian believer—patronized Mani and welcomed him at his court. Mani was allowed to preach his new religion all over the Sassanian Empire; the king was not investigative of this this new religion, and rather ignored it, for his general policy was distinguished by a tolerant attitude toward all religions, including Judaism and Christianity. Furthermore, Mani was allowed to accompany king Shapur I in some of his wars and campaigns against the Roman

Empire—where he had probably met the high priest Kartir (about whom we shall speak later).

Interestingly at the same time, one of the major philosophers of antiquity, the famous Neoplatonist Plotinus (205–270 AD), was apparently included in the entourage of the Roman Emperor Gordian III on the other side of the war front. At the Battle of Misiche (modern-day Fallujah) in 244 AD, the armies of the Emperor Gordian III lost the battle to Shapur of the Sassanians, and subsequently the emperor himself was killed by his own Praetorian Guard, and the commander of the Guard, the Praetorian Prefect Marcus Julius Phillipus—known as Philip the Arab—was declared the new Emperor by the Guard. Philip the Arab (he was born in what is modern-day Syria), the new Roman Emperor, made subsequently a new peace treaty with the Sassanian Emperor Shapur I. After Shapur's death, his successor, Hormizd I, also continued this policy of religious tolerance. Hormizd's successor, however, the new Sassanian king, Bahram I, was fully under the influence of the Zoroastrian Chief Priest Kartir, a strict and doctrinaire Zoroastrian, who influenced the King to persecute any non-Zoroastrian creed—any deviation from the existing ancient Zoroastrian dogma was especially suspect to him, and worthy of persecution. Kartir pushed for the elimination of Mani and his followers, the so-called Manichaeists. As such Mani was arrested and imprisoned on the orders of Kartir and died shortly afterwards in prison in the year 277 AD. Mani's followers immediately depicted Mani's death as a crucifixion in conscious analogy to the death of Jesus Christ.

Although Mani declared himself to be an Apostle of Jesus, his religion was, in reality, an offshoot of Zoroastrianism, for he also declared it to be the *Religion of Light* and the ultimate fight between good and evil. Thus he believed in God and the Devil, Heaven and Hell, the three time epochs (three time epochs each of one thousand years), the individual judgment at death, the final defeat of evil, the last Judgment, and the life everlasting for the blessed in the presence of the creator. All these components (save the three time epochs) being components of Zoroastrianism.

The canon of Mani included six works originally written in Syriac, and one in Persian, the *Shabuhragan*. While none of his books have survived in complete form, numerous fragments and quotations survive. According to Mani teachings, the Manichaean community was divided into two group of people, The Elected and the Hearers. The Elected, was further divided between male and female Monks, who were in the position of authority and expected to lead society, there were priests of different hierarchical degrees, and they were to lead a life of austere devotion, and remain celibate, vegetarian and poor. The Hearers, the population at large, had to revere and care in any aspect for the Elected, and if they could prove themselves worthy, become one of the Elected themselves.

In 763 AD the ruler of the Uyghur Empire (modern-day Chinese province of Sinkiang), Khagan Boku Tekin (759–780 AD), adopted Manichaeism as the state religion of his Empire. This religion was known there centuries before, until it was elevated as the state religion, and remained at that position, until the collapse of the Uyghur Empire circa 840 AD. Further east, this religion spread to Chang An, the capital city of the Tang Dynasty in China. In the Sung and Yuan Dynasty in China, remnants of Manichaeism continued to exist, and transformed later itself to the famous sect of the Red Turbans. Special influence of Manichaeism has been detected in Manchuria and the Mongolian–Turkic tribes, and it has been said that most Mongolians were, until the twelfth century, under strong influence of Manichaeist ideas. Noting Mani's travel to the Kushan Empire, several religious paintings in Bamiyan are attributed to him, at the beginning of his investigative travels. Professor Richard Foltz, from Montréal's Concordia University, attributes Buddhist influence in Manichaeism:

The Buddhist influence were significant in the formation of Mani's religious thought. The transmigrations of the souls became a Manichaean belief, and the quadripartite structure of the Manichaean community, divided between male and female monks (the Elects) and the lay followers (the Hearers) who supported them, appears to be based on the Buddhist Sangha.

Manichaeism, in contrast to its success in east Asia and the west, was not successful in Persia from the beginning and was rejected by the Zoroastrian religious establishment, who looked at it as a distortion of the ancient Zoroastrian doctrine. Contrary to this, Manichaeism continued to spread with extraordinary speed through both the east and the west. It reached Rome through the Apostle Psattiq in 280 AD, who was also in Egypt in 244 and 251 AD. Manichaean Monasteries existed already in Rome in 312 AD during the time of Pope Miltiades. In 296 AD, seeing Manichaeism as a threat to Rome, the Roman Emperor Diocletian issued a decree against the Manichaeans:

> We order that their organizers and leader be subject to the final penalties and condemned to the fire with their abdominal scriptures…

The fourth century historian Hilary of Poitiers wrote, that a majority of Manichaeans fled to southern Gaul (France) where they were a significant force. In 381 AD Christan monks requested of the new Roman Emperor Theodosius I (347–395 AD), that he strip Manichaeans of their civil rights, and in 382 AD Theodosius I issued a decree, according to which all Manichaean monks had to be killed. In 391 AD, Theodosius declared that the Christian church is the only legitimate religion of the Roman Empire. He was the same Emperor who ordered the destruction of various non-Christian, Ancient Pagan temples and structures in Rome, and in Ancient Greece, in 393 AD he forbad and banned the continuation of the Olympic Games, which would only start again in 1896.

Saint Augustine 354–430 AD, the important Christian theologian—and later a very influential father of the Christian church, was born in the Roman Province of North Africa (modern-day Algeria) and became a Manichaean at the age of seventeen. Later he was a Manichaean priest and later still—after the death sentence for all Manichaean monks by the Roman state—converted and was baptized to Christianity in the year 387 AD at the age of thirty-three. He was a Manichaean for thirteen years and, according to his own *Confessions,* spent nine of those years a member of the Hearers.

Modern scholars believe that Manichaean ways of thinking influenced the development of some of Saint Augustine's ideas, such as the nature of good and evil, which has its roots in Zoroastrianism; the idea of hell; the separation of groups into elect, hearers and sinners; and finally the strong hostility to the flesh and sexual activity in general. There is some indication,that the Prophet Mani was born lame and disfigured, and some historians have suggested that his pessimism and disgust at the human body was a psychological reaction to his condition. As a principle Augustine believed that humans were born with a original sin, and had to redeem themselves in the course of their lives. Many of the ideas in Saint Augustine's teachings successfully entered in to Catholic Christian doctrine. Ideas such as original sin that was strongly associated—by him—with sexuality; predestination; the idea of an elect of the saved; and the damnation of unbaptized children can all be traced, at least partially, to the gnostic ideas of the prophet Mani.

Many of these key concepts, especially the central one—the original sin of man—show a striking similarity to Manichaean doctrine. As pursued later by the western Christian churches—especially in the medieval Europe—the strong distaste for the human body, the disgust for and guilt about sexuality in general, the association of sex and sin, the obsessive idealization of the spirit, and the distain for all the material, were in reality all markedly distant from the original teachings of Jesus. Saint Augustine, remarkably, before he converted to Christianity, was himself a devout Manichaean, had converted others to the sect, and at the end, before his conversion to Christianity, was a Manichaean priest.

Also interesting is the fact that the Manichaean worldview believed in a cycle of three times 1,000 years—at the end of each one thousand year epoch the world would descend into in general chaos, death and destruction, and would have to be renewed again, the close of the final epoch (three thousand years after the birth of Mani) would signal the end of the world. Subsequently Saint Augustine originally believed that Christ would establish a literal 1,000 year kingdom prior to the general resurrection—the so-called doctrine of premillennialism and the second coming of Christ.

In Iran, on the other hand, according to Alessandro Bausani, a noted scholar of Persian religions, the Zoroastrian religious establishment, under the heavy-handed leadership of the mobadane-mo bad (the priest of priests) Kartir was, from the beginning, opposed to Mani and his sect. It is a fact that the Manicheistic ideology—which in itself was an offspring of Zoroastrianism—has had significant influence on the Catholic and with that the Christian religions ideology in general. All this through the personality of Saint Augustine, who later became the Cardinal of Milan, and the chief ideologue of the Christian faith. Original sin, the second coming of Christ (after one thousand years), the sinful aspects of sexuality (and with it the human body) and the healing power of abstinence from the sins of the flesh can all be traced directly back to Manichaean roots.

A noteworthy detail in connection with the Manichaean religion is the sudden conquests of the Mongolians in Asia, who were strongly under Manichaean influence, especially due to their contact to the Uijgur Empire—geographically next to their territory. Suddenly, in the years following 1210–1220 AD, the Mongolians started to leave their motherland, where they had lived for millennia, and started to wander with their families and all their possessions to the four points of the compass, but mainly to the west, south-west, south, and southeast. The notion that their supreme leader, Genghis Khan, led and ordered his troops merely to conquer foreign nations and topple Empires is not convincing.

As we know, the Mongols did not send troops just to conquer other nations and then return back to their home country, but groups of entire Mongolian tribes, with their families—wives and children, the elderly, entire households including domesticated animals were following the troops at a safe distance in the back on horses. All this was led by a supreme ruler Khan, in most cases one of the sons or grandsons of Genghis Khan. Kublai Khan to the south, Hulagu Khan to the west etc. These groups of people not only were moving away from their original homeland, but it had the appearance that they, in fact, were fleeing with firm intentions never to return to their original homeland again.

In looking back at past history, we can clearly see that these people were fleeing their old habitat, and were looking at new places to live and to settle. Kublai Khan, whom the Italian traveler Marco Polo met personally during his journey to the east, the grandson of Genghis Khan, and the new ruler of the greater Chinese Empire, never returned to his old homeland Mongolia. Similarly the other Mongolian tribes, who went west, invaded and conquered the Middle East, starting from 1212 AD, also never returned to Mongolia. It is significant that, from the extensive Mongol tribes and their rulers, only Genghis Khan himself, at the end of his life, returned to his homeland to die and that from all the Khans and military commanders under him, he called only one of them back, and only this one returned—his formidable general and old friend, Subuthai.

Concerning the mongol invasion of the Persian Empire at the time and the destruction of the eastern part of Persia, horrific details have been reported. The Iranian historian Manuchihr Parsa Dust writes[171] that during the massacre in the city of Marv, a woman with a child approached a soldier and asked to speak with a commander, after having been brought into the presence of the commander, she said, "I have five beautiful pearls, if you spare me and my child, I will give

a small mountain Valley. In the centre of this small valley is a small but very deep mountain lake with artesian fountains. It is believed that this site was a sacred Zoroastrian temple location starting from the Achaemenid period. Initial archaeological excavation has revealed traces of a fifth century BC occupation during the Achaemenid period. A stone temple was built at the shore of the lake in the Sassanian period, which was dedicated to the Goddess Anahita. Several sanctuary and temple stone structures or buildings of Sassanian era origin have been found at this location. Furthermore, the Sassanians kings, at the beginning of their rule (c. 240 AD) build massive stone walls, and thirty-eight towers around the lake by the third century AD, which still stands today apart from the several other ancient buildings and temples. According to ancient tradition, the temple on this mountain valley was keeping the sacred eternal flame of the Zoroastrian creed. The Sassanian kings, after their coronation at their capital Ctesiphon (near modern-day Baghdad) had to travel on foot to this remote and inaccessible mountain location, to receive the divine investiture at the sanctuary of the eternal flame, which according to Myth, left no ashes, and from which all other sacred fires were ignited.

The valley of Takht-e Soleyman is an exceptional testimony to the continuation of the cults, related to fire and water, for a period of several millennia, probably starting even before the time of the Achaemenids. This site, which was not known to the western archaeological community, until first "discovered" by the English traveler Sir Robert Kerr Porter in 1819. Later a Swedish archaeological expedition visited the site in 1958, and later again a German group, R. Nauman and D. Huff in 1970, did some initial work on the site. Takht-e Soleyman, which is located in southern Azerbaijan province represents an outstanding example of Zoroastrian sanctuary. Herodotus writes in his *Histories*, which was compiled before 425 BC:

> As to the usages of the Persians, I know them to be
> these. It is not their custom to make and set up Statues

> or Temples or Altars… but they call the whole circle
> of heaven God (Ahura Mazdâ) and to him they offer
> sacrifice on the highest peaks of the mountains

How does the valley of Takht-e Soleyman intersect the Manichaean religion? The answer is intriguing, if somewhat circuitous; apart from the various ancient buildings and stone structures, next to the lake there has been discovered a building which was build as a combination of a palace and a fortification. The stone blocks were taken from the other ancient buildings, partly damaging them. The newly build palace–fort complex had two octagonal towers, and inside the building, the walls were decorated with glazed tiles and ceramics.This newly erected complex has been dated to between 1225–1250 AD and was erected during the time of the beginning of the Mongol invasion of Persia—built by order of the Mongolian ruling Ilkhans (the Mongolian Khans who occupied Persia). This separate palace complex—only discovered during the 1958 visit by the Swedish archaeological expedition—had one interesting peculiarity that initially puzzled the archaeologists: they could not find any entrance.

This palace–fort had no entrances or doors leading from outside the structure to inside. After having opened an entrance in the stone wall, and gained access to the building, they found out that all entrances or doors to the building from outside had been closed from the inside by big stone blocks—all doors, windows and entrances had been completely sealed up, as if the occupants were afraid of people coming to invade or storm the building from outside. Inside the enclosed building complex they found several human remains, and the skeletons of various horses. All these remains were dated to approximately the mid thirteenth century AD. The human remains were those of a limited number of middle-aged man of Asiatic or Mongolian race, in addition the remains of a bigger number of younger females of western or Byzantine origin. Among the objects found, were coins of Byzantine Emperor Theodosius II (408–450 AD), western or Byzantine style woman's clothing, various ornamental horse saddles, and a vast collection of clay and ceramic objects for the keeping and the storing of food and drinks on a long term basis. These findings were not deemed to have any historical significance, and were regarded as irrelevant, ignored and soon forgotten, as everybody was looking for fire temples.

It is worth considering that, according to Manichaean doctrine, the world was poised to come to an end at the close of the third epoch. Saint Augustine, after he converted, had believed that the time of Christianity would end after the first thousand years, ushering in the second coming of Christ. The Mongols were both racially and culturally closely related to their neighbours, the Uighurs, who had accepted the Manichaean religion as the state religion of their Empire. It is, therefore, reasonable to conclude that the Mongols either believed in the same religion or were at least strongly influenced by it—and perhaps believed that the end of the world was due thousand years after the appearance or the birth of the Prophet Mani.

Bearing that in mind, I would argue it no coincidence that, in 1227, a thousand years after the start of Manichaeism, all the Mongolians united under their supreme leader Genghis Khan and started to leave—or perhaps flee from—their original homeland never to return.

In terms of the fortification on the mountain valley of Takht-e Soleyman, it is again reasonable to conclude that a number of the Mongol Khans and top commanders wanted to escape the End Times and, therefore, had this complex erected in that extremely remote and inaccessible place, where nobody could reach or attack them. There they barricaded themselves in that building complex with things they loved—western white girls and beautiful horses—and waited for the world to end.

6.4 THE EMERGENCE OF THE SASSANIAN DYNASTY AND SOME IMPORTANT ZOROASTRIAN PRIESTS

It seems that the rise of the Sassanian Dynasty to power is somehow hidden in historical obscurity. One thing is clear, however; the Sassanian family were, from ancient times ,the hereditary guardians and priests of the temple of Anahid. This possibly was one of the ancient Achaemenid period temples of Anahita, which existed at that time in the city of Istakhre in the province of Pars. This shows that the Sassanian Family was, from earlier times, a hereditary landowner–priest family in that city. Papak, the head of the Sassanian family, revolted probably in 210 AD, and seized power from the local governor, who was a vassal of the Parthian kings, and also his son Ardeshir [in Greek: Artaxerxes] later succeeded to his usurped position. The Arsacid king Artaban V [in Persian: Ardavan V] refused to recognize the authority of Ardeshir, therefore, in 224 AD, a battle ensued and Ardeshir was victor, and the old king Ardavan V was killed thus firmly establishing Sassanian power. There is no doubt that the ancient existing priest class, whose ancestors had led the Zoroastrian community under the Achaemenids, felt themselves fitted to retake their old position again in the new society, especially as they regarded the new ruling clan as one of their own. This was the reason that the new rulers had the full support of the Zoroastrian priests class, and their influence over the general population. The new ruler of the empire, Ardeshir (born 180, ruled 224–241 AD) of the house of the Sassanians, was very fortunate to have, as his chief priest—and possibly also adviser—a man whose energies and abilities seems to have matched his own. This man was the *herbad* Tansar, (herbad is the title of a high ranking Zoroastrian cleric). The High Priest Tansar had one fundamental problem; whereas the previous rulers, the Arsacids, at their rise to power, had played the role of a champion against the

Pagan Seleucids (Seleucus was a General of Alexander the Great, who ruled Persia after Alexander's death), the Sassanians had to justify the overthrow of co-religionists. Therefore, Tansar had to convince the people of the nation, that the Sassanians were indeed better Zoroastrians than the rulers before them.

A document of historic importance for understanding the events of that time is the *Tansar Nameh* [*Letter of Tansar*]. This letter—which has survived through various redactions and translations—was written from Tansar to Gushnasp the local king of Tabaristan, an area south of the Caspian sea and separated from the rest of the country by the high Elburz Mountains. Gushnasp was previously a vassal king or Satrap of the Arsacid rulers, who ruled that mountainous region in the north of Iran, which to invade or subdue by force was very complicated and difficult. Therefore the new King of Kings Ardeshir, had decided to convince rather than subdue this local ruler to submit to him. Tansar wrote on King Ardeshir's behalf, in the year 224 or 225 AD, a letter to the local king in the north, trying to persuade him to yield to the new regime. This existing letter was an answer to a previous letter from Gushnasp, and in it Tansar counters one by one the concerns and the doubts of Gushnasp, which the northern king had expressed in regards to the new situation. In the religious field, it seems he had accused Ardeshir "of forsaking tradition; and right though this may be for the world, it is not good for the faith" (Tansar Nameh 36). To this Tansar counters with a double defence.

Firstly, he writes, not all the old ways were good, and the new ruler Ardeshir being "more richly endowed with virtues than the ancients... his custom is better than the custom of the old."

Secondly, he points out that the faith had decayed so greatly as a result of the destruction wrought by Alexander's intrusion that there had been no certain knowledge under the Arsacids "of its ancient laws and ordinances, and so it must needs be restored by a man of true and upright judgement... for till religion is interpreted by understanding it has no firm foundation."

Full licence was thus claimed for Ardeshir to make what changes he pleased, these being equally approved by Tansar. That this *carte blanche* was courageously opposed by some of his coreligionists, is shown by Gushnasp's further upright protests against "the excessive bloodshed, which he orders among those acting against his judgment and decree." To this Tansar replies that the people had become wicked, and that they were therefore to blame for the frequency of punishment and slaughter and not the new King of Kings:

> Bloodshed among people of this kind, even if of a prodigality that seems to have no bound, is recognized by us as a life and health, like the rain which quickens the earth... for in days to come the foundation of state and religion will be in every way strengthened through this... (Tansar Nameh 40)

The question is what were the religious measures, admitted to by Tansar, that Ardeshir tried to enact and enforce by means of bloodshed. There are a number of sources in early Sassanian history, and so it is possible to clarify various ways in which Ardeshir, in cooperation with the priests-class, must have distressed and angered the general Zoroastrian population.

Firstly, in place of the former loose fraternity of regional communities, a single and central Zoroastrian religious administration was created under the authoritarian control of the Persian government. Together with this went the establishment of a single canon of Avestan texts, approved and authorized by Tansar personally. This important step is mentioned in the Pahlavy *Denkard*:

> His Majesty the King of Kings, Ardeshir the son of Papak, following Tansar as his religious authority, commanded all those sacred and scattered teachings to be brought to the court...

These sacred documents preservation and collection, of course, had been ordered by the previous regime, namely the Arsacid king Valakhsh.

Mary Boyce writes:

> Tansar set about his business and selected one tradition and left the rest out of the canon, and he issued this decree:
>
>> "The interpretation of all the teachings of the Mazdâ worshipping religion is our responsibility, for now there is no lack of certain knowledge concerning them. (DKM–412–11–17–ZZZ 8) Again in another passage of the same work it is prophesied that, no peace will come to the land of Iran, until they give acceptance to him, Tansar the Herbad, the spiritual leader, eloquent, truthful, and just. And when they give acceptance to Tansar, ... those lands if they wish will find healing instead of divergence from Zarathustra's faith." (DKM–652–9–17)

Apart from the very difficult task of changing the ancient Achaemenid calendar—which was one of the innovations introduced by Tansar about which we will speak in following chapters—another hugely controversial measure, enacted by the Sassanians from the beginning of their rule, was to forbid the use of images in worship. During their epoch, statues were removed from consecrated buildings, and whenever possible, sacred fires were installed in their place. It seems that the Sassanians had been committed iconoclasts from well before the time of their rise to power. The Muslim historian

Al-Mas'udi states that, although their temple in the city of Istahkhr had once—before the Sassanian's came to power—contained idols, these had been removed in the past by orders of the Sassanian family, and fire installed in their place.[173]

It is generally believed that the rule of the High Priest Tansar was very positive for the reorganization and documentation of the Zoroastrian ideological dogmas and the daily rules followed by the empire's society. It is believed that it was during the time of the High Priest Tansar that the game of chess started its journey from the Sassanian court to the western world. Probably originating in India and sent from there to the Sassanian court as a gift by one of the minor kings, its historical and documented appearance in the world started only from the court of the Sassanian Kings. In German, the name of that game is *schach*, which comes from the Persian word Shah [King]. Furthermore, in German the term *schach matt* for the party who loses the game, comes from the ancient Persian *Shah martt* or *Shah mortt*, which means *The King is dead*. In English this has become Check Mate.

Another important high priest merits mentioning here: the *moobedane -moabed* [*priest of priests*] Kartir. Kartir was a highly influential and powerful Zoroastrian religious leader of the late third century AD, and he acted as an adviser to at least three Sassanian Emperors. It is said that the high Priest Kartir was among the advisers of King Shapur I, when that king with his troops encountered the troops of the Roman Emperor Gordian III in battle. If true, then the High Priest Kartir and the Prophet Mani were together with King Shapur I when the Persians and the Romans fought in the Battle of Misiche in 244 AD. That means the two adversaries, Kartir and Mani, knew each other personally and had travelled together. Later on, Kartir ordered the execution of Mani and his followers. According to his own inscriptions, Kartir rose to power during the reign of Shapur I (241–273 AD) and was present on all travels of the Sassanian Emperor. After the death of Shapur I, his son Hormizd I—who only ruled for one year—gave Kartir a position of absolute authority in religious matters and the title moabedane -moabed (the priest of priests) a position Kartir ruthlessly used to consolidate his power and destroy and punish any lower ranking Zoroastrian priest whose opinion he considered contrary to his own. Being a strict religious doctrinaire, Kartir was strongly opposed to Mani, and it was at Kartir's insistence that the new emperor, Bahram I, ordered Mani to be imprisoned and probably killed.

It was under the rule of King Narseh (ruled 293–302 AD) that the High priest Kartir died—after which a period of religious tolerance was started again by the Sassanian rulers. Scholars are in dispute over the question of whether Kartir was looking favourably at the newly developed cult of Zurvanism, which started at the time of the reign of Shapur I, around the years 250 AD.

6.5 THE TEACHINGS OF MAZDAK, THE ANTI ARAB UPRISINGS OF BABAK KHORRAMDIN IN 816 AD, AND THE KINGDOM OF MARDAVIJ

One of the interesting and noteworthy personalities who arose from the Zoroastrian religion was the prophet Mazdak. Mazdak was born circa 465 AD and died 524 or 528 AD. The descendent of a long line of Zoroastrian priests called Mobeds, Mazdak announced himself to be a prophet of Ahura Mazdâ and proclaimed that the creator God Himself had instructed him to reform the Zoroastrian religion. In the beginning, his teachings were very successful and extremely popular. Vast segments of the empire's population sympathized strongly with his new ideas and were ready to follow him. The ruling Sassanian king of the time, King Kavadh I [in Persian: Ghobad] who ruled from 488 until 531 AD, converted to the cult of Mazdakism. Furthermore, the king ordered his Arab vassals to adopt the same religion; the Arab kingdom of Al-Hira who succedet the deposition of the previous king al-Mundhir by the Kindite chief al Harith followed the oreders. Once the king—and with him the Sassanian government apparatus—had accepted Mazdakism, the Prophet Mazdak could start a wide-ranging program of socio-economic reforms that would very soon start to transform the whole society of the Sassanian Empire. In reality the King was not informed about the extent of Mazdak's reform, as we see shortly.

The origins of the socio-economic teachings of Mazdak were apparently the ideas of an ancient Mobed (Priest) who lived generations before Mazdak by the name of Zaradusht-e Khuragen (no relation to the prophet Zarathustra).[174] Later these ideas were taken up by Mazdak the Elder, an ancestor of the later prophet. Finally the Prophet Mazdak (Mazdak the Younger), who was the son of Bamdad, took over the ideas and completed them in the form of the Mazdakism known today. The ideology of Mazdakism and the teaching of the self-proclaimed Zoroastrian prophet Mazdak is nothing less than the first known ideology of radical socialism and communism in history. Mazdak tried to start a radical socialistic reform in the society not unlike the later communist takeover in Russia in the beginnings of the twentieth century. The only difference between Mazdakism and Marxism was that Mazdak was a Mobed and a descendent of a long line of Zoroastrian clerics who ruled on a hereditary base and tried to convince the general population that this radical socialistic reforms was, in fact, ordered by the creator God Ahura Mazdâ himself.

A great deal of information concerning the Prophet Mazdak and Mazdakism are derived from the Persian historian Abdul-Karim Shahrestani[175]. His famous work entitled *Ketabe al malal wa al nalal* [*The Book of Sects and Creeds*] was one of the earliest systematic studies of religion and their philosophies up to his time and is notable for its scientific approach.[176] It must be said, furthermore, that Shahrestani was not sympathetic to Mazdak and his teachings, but rather spoke of him in his book with a strong critical attitude. According to Shahrestani, Mazdak declared that:

> God who had originally created and placed all means and resources of his creation at the disposal of humankind, had intended that this resources be used specifically for the existence and the wellbeing of all humanity together. With the principal divine purpose and specific instruction, that all human kind should divide the world resources among themselves on equal basis. But later on, after this instruction by the creator god, those who were strong among the public had wronged the weak, their intention being the domination and economic oppression of the others. In so doing, causing temporary an inequality and injustice in the human society. This inequality which turned into injustice empowered the "five demons" (greed, vengeance, wrath, envy and falsehood) to deviate the rule of the creator God Ahura Mazdâ and his right path for humanity which is righteousness and justice, into the realm of the evil spirit Ahriman, whose intention in turn is the corruption and destruction of the human society. To prevail over powers of evil, justice had to be restored, and Mazdak allegedly planned to achieve this by making all wealth common and to redistribute all the assets and resources available in the human society on equal basis.

Mazdak's followers are considered to be the first real socialists in human history by their emphasis on community property and community work, with the benefits accruing to all people equally on the bases of their natural needs. This being markedly similar to both twentieth-century Marxism and Communism.

If we look at the social structure of societies in the time of the Sassanian dynasty, we see that all wealth—in essence the agricultural land—was concentrated in the hand of a small group of nobility and the priestly class. Under the pretext that this, in fact, was God's will, the priestly class and the nobility were oppressing the general population, who worked hard but were still living on the borderline of survival. The teachings of the prophet Mazdak, therefore, was primarily against the priests and clerical establishment, who were one of the great agricultural landowners. Mazdak's demands contained a number of actions to expropriate the whole priestly establishment from their agricultural land. Furthermore, Mazdak's teachings contained a number of rules to reduce and eliminate Zoroastrian religious formalities which were only used to enrich the clergy. In Mazdak's own words:

.... the true religious person is the one who understands and relates correctly to the principles of the universe and the 'Asha' (the Truth). Real religiosity is therefore based on a personal and direct relationship between the human being and the God, without any intermediary...

This description suggests, that Mazdakism had in reality a typical Gnostic religious ideology.[177]

Concerning the general philosophical teachings of the Prophet Mazdak, extensive investigations have been made, we can here mention, only in short, his doctrines related to economical matters, as these had a long-lasting effect on further development of the Zoroastrian Iranian society. In general, Mazdak's teachings entailed vast economic and social reforms that included the expropriation of agricultural land from the nobility and clergy and the distribution of the same to the peasantry who worked on them.

Under Mazdak's influence, Kavadh I consented to open the vast royal grain warehouses and to distribute the grain among the starving population. Furthermore, it was an important step taken by Mazdak to abolish and to forbid the widespread custom of polygamy by the rich and powerful, which had resulted in a lack of wives for the poor. Mazdak advocated a program of social pacifism, a strong anti-clericalism, and some sort of utopian communism. He emphasized good conduct, which involved a moral and simplistic life, with no killing and no meat eating of any kind, declaring that meat contained substances derived from the powers of darkness. In later centuries, the Zoroastrian clerical establishment remembered Mazdak, above all, as a dangerous heretic and an enemy of the true faith,[178] comparable only to Mani and to the Islamic Prophet Mohammad.[179]

It is now evident, that Mazdak's economic and social reforms declared and implemented nationwide would polarize and dangerously divide the general population of the empire. On the one side, there was the nobility, the ruling upper classes, and the priest and clerical clans who were among a small minority controlling the wealth in the society; and on the other side the general public of peasants and workers who formed the great majority of the population and had to struggle for their survival. From the beginning it was clear that King Kavadh I, who had initially been persuaded by Mazdak to help him in his reforms, was unaware of the consequences of these wide-reaching proposed socio-economical reforms. What is more probable, is that Mazdak did initially not reveal to him the full scale of his economic reforms he intended to put into reality.

These consequences became all too evident once his agricultural reforms started. In any case, two factors worked against him and turned the opinions of the general public against him, ultimately bringing about his downfall and the failure of his social programs. After Mazdak had already started his reform, rumours circulated that it was as part of his dogma, Mazdak's social reforms would eventually include the total elimination of all kind of private property in the society—that in effect all private property in the society would have to be made available for the community. This rumour—probably true—put the upper and ruling classes of the Empire in a state of instant panic; not to forget that at the head of the land-owning and the feudal ruling classes of the empire was the king himself and his family. Probably this was the main argument to convince the nobility to start to revolt against Kavadh I, who subsequently had to flee the country and went into exile to a small kingdom in the eastern borders of the empire.

The other very important factor, which ultimately destroyed the Mazdak's power base—though at one time he could count on the support and sympathy of the broad masses and the general population of the Empire—was the argument brought forward by the nobility and the priestly clan that the main point of Mazdak's social reforms included, what they called "free love and free sex for all men." These hostile sources made allegations that Mazdak's teachings, included the sharing of women thereby resulting in sexual promiscuity and confusion in the line of descent for future generations. These, of course, were standard allegations used against all heretical sects in history, and the calculated reaction by the general public is always the same: a negative panicked backlash. There is, of course, no proof that Mazdak *ever* said or planned anything of this kind. The ideological notion of a class without private property of any kind had taken its toll and had destroyed the Prophet Mazdak—whether this was his ultimate goal, however, is uncertain.

In 496 AD, Kavadh I had to flee the country in order not to fall victim to the revolt of the priestly establishment and the nobility. He was obliged to seek refuge in the kingdom of his former enemies, the Hephthalites (in modern-day southern Tajikistan), who in 496 AD gave him asylum and protected him. After four years in exile—once the revolt against the economic programs of Mazdak had partly calmed down—King Kavadh I returned to his country and to power. However, soon afterwards, he voluntarily abdicated in favour of his son Khosrow-Anushirawan. His son, the new King Khosrow I [in Persian: Anushiravan Adel], confronted with a vast population who were openly sympathetic to the social programs of Mazdakism, had to wait for several years—until he had stabilized his own personal power base in the empire—before initiating his plan to destroy Mazdak, his religion and the popular movement surrounding him. In 524 or 528 AD, the king made a declaration to Mazdak and his close followers to the effect that he intended to make a new arrangement with them. The Prophet Mazdak and a number of his followers were invited to take part in festivities—at which point the royal guard unleashed a massacre in which most followers and adherents of Mazdak were killed. Approximately 3,000 Madakis, included the prophet himself, were arrested. Ferdowsi in his book *The Shahname* describes the end of Mazdak as following:

> ...and buried all prisoners alive with their feet upwards sticking out of the ground, in order to present to the Prophet with the spectacle of a human garden. Mazdak himself was then executed... The oldest son of the old King Kavadh I, the brother of the present king, was also killed in this massacre.

After these events, King Khosrow I (501–579 AD), having recognized the urgent necessity of economical reforms in the society, started to implement a number of social economical reforms, which in reality were partly taken of Mazdak's own teachings. The Iranian history knows this king under the name of Anushiravan-e-Adel or Anushiravan Dadgar [Anushiravan the Just]. He was a contemporary and a rival of the Byzantine Emperor Justinian. Though Mazdak and his followers were eradicated, the ideas of his movement did not stop, but continued to occupy the minds of the society in the empire for generations after him.

The entire episode and events surrounding Mazdak and his socioeconomical teachings show us very clearly that, during that time of history, there existed a very serious and dangerously deep divide between the social classes in the empire. The rich and powerful—a small minority—oppressed the vast majority of general population. This was the standard characteristics of all ancient feudalistic societies. It was this class struggle which had weakened the society in a dangerous way and made it vulnerable to the invasion of the Arab Invaders who would conquer and destroy the Sassanian Empire approximately a hundred years later. Mazdak and his socio-economical ideology was, in fact, nothing other than (as Karl Marx would no doubt see it) a product of the circumstances in which the Sassanian society found itself at this time in history. Among the known historical personalities who were probably deeply influenced by the teachings of Mazdak was Salman Farsi. His original Iranian name was Rouzbeh Marzban, and he was born approximately thirty years after the death of Mazdak in Ispahan. We will speak about him in later chapters. Extensive historical investigations have been done concerning Mazdak and his socio-economical teachings.

After the invasion and the conquest of the Sassanian Empire by the Arabs in 644 AD the subsequent systematic destruction of the ancient Zoroastrian culture and civilization by the invaders was implemented. It was at this time that several continuous uprisings by the ancient Zoroastrian establishment and the Persian people against the Arab invaders has been reported in history. Eventually all these uprisings were put down at the end by the Arab–Islamic military, although some of them, at the beginning, were successful for some limited time. One of these uprisings, which merits mentioning here, and which should not be forgotten in the history of Zoroastrianism, was the revolt of the Zoroastrian and Mazdakite revolutionary Babak Khorramdin.

After the Islamic conquest of Persia, the peasant population was still hopeful to receive the land on which they were working, belonging to the big landowner families. The Mazdakite doctrines, still alive, became later mixed with currents of radical Shi'a Islam and continued to influence and give rise to powerful religious revolutionary movements in later periods. In the ninth century, nearly two hundred years after the Islamic conquest of Iran, a young man by the name of Babak Khorramdin (795–838 AD), an egalitarian with an ideology of a left-wing socio-religious doctrine originating from Mazdakism, led a revolt against the occupiers and rulers of Persia of that period. These were the Abbasid Caliphate with their centre of power in Bagdad. This social movement led by Babak Khorramdin had originated from the social-agricultural ideas of Mazdakism, pertaining to the expropriation of agricultural land from the big feudal landowning families. After being initially very successful, Khorramdin defended victoriously a large territory, controlled by him in the region of the today's Iranian Azerbaijan. For approximately twenty-seven years, Babak Khorramdin ruled and administrated a considerable amount of territory on an independent basis, implementing not only the agricultural-social ideas of Mazdak, but more importantly abolishing the Islamic religion from his territory and re-introducing Zoroastrianism into the general population.[180]

Babak Khorramdin was from an ancient Zoroastrian family in Azerbaijan. He was born in the village of Balal Abad, which is close to the ancient city of Artavilla—now called Ardabil. On becoming a teenager, Babak received traditional Zoroastrian initiation rites of passage into the faith, which are held in a fire temple—understand that this in the time of the Islamic–Arab domination of Iran.[181]

At around the year 816 AD, Babak started preparation for a wide scale military revolt against the Arab occupiers. He raised followers and erected camps for the military training of his forces. His followers and his soldiers comprised peasants and working men who were promised land belonging to the big landowners. Soon afterwards, the followers of Babak, militarized and armed, started a wide scale military campaign against the Arabic castles and military garrisons in that area. After his initial success, he immediately distributed all agricultural lands expropriated from the previous landowners. His declared general policy was to create a classless society where the gap between rich and poor would not exist, and where all economic oppression would be eliminated, this being the genuine teachings of the prophet Mazdak, revived 300 years after his death.[182] The historian Gardizi reports that Mazyar Sepahbod, who was the hereditary King of Tabaristan, Mazandaran, and Gorgan—meaning the northern part of Iran—and who had abandoned Zoroastrianism for Islam, decided now, to return to the ancient religion of Zarathustra.

In 819 AD, the Arab Caliphates, being alarmed at this new situation, sent from Bagdad an army under the general Yahya ibn Mu'adh against Babak's forces, but this army was defeated by the Babak revolutionaries. Two years later, in 821 AD, a second army was sent from Bagdad under the command of General Isa ibn Muhammed ibn Abi Khalid—these armies were *also* defeated by Babak. Again in 824–825 AD, a bigger army under the senior general Ahmad ibn al Junayd, was ordered to subdue Babak. The armies of Babak defeated this army as well and captured the commanding general.

In 828 AD, the Caliphs in Bagdad decided to dispatch a new army, but this time commanded by a Persian general under the name of Muhammed Tusi who was ordered to apprehend Babak. This time the Arab armies under the command of Muhammed Tusi defeated the forces of Babak Khorramdin but could not capture Babak personally; he had fled. One year later, Babak returned with a new and bigger army and on June 9, 829 AD, decisively defeated the armies of the Persian general Muhammed Tusi at the battle of Hasht-adsar. General Muhammed Humayd Tusi was killed with all his troops. After these events, the Caliphs in Bagdad, for ten years did not respond to the events in Persia. We can say that basically big parts of the ancient Persia was ruled by a man who was re-introducing Zoroastrianism combined with Mazdakite socialistic land reforms.

In 836 AD, Al-Mu'tasim, the new Caliph in Bagdad, decided to dispatch a new army against Babak, again commanded by a Persian general, who was very well familiar with the geographical and political situation in Persia, and who had prepared this new invasion for years well in advance. This new general was Haydar Kavus Afshin,[183] the head of one of those feudal families, whose lands had been taken away by the Babak movement. The new Persian General, after years of preparation, attacked the forces of Babak and defeated them decisively. Babak, however, again managed to escape and did not surrender despite an offer of amnesty by the Arabs—saying that Arabs seldom kept their word and lived by deceit. After these events, Babak fled to Armenia and asked for refuge from the Armenian prince of Khachen, Sahl Smbatean [in Arabic: Sahl ibn Sunbath]. After initially keeping their word, the Armanians later delivered Babak to the Arab troops of General Kavus Afshin for a large reward. Babak Khorramdin was then executed in a cruel fashion, his arms and legs being cut off one by one. It is said, that when one of his arms was cut off, he himself, with the other hand still attached to his body, took his own blood and smeared it on his face, saying "… I don't want my followers to see my face in agony."

After the execution of Khorramdin in 838 AD, the ruler of eastern Tabaristan and Mazandaran, Mazyar Sepahbod, was also captured and executed.

In 927 AD, approximately 89 years after the fall of Babak Khorramdin, as a result of the internal turmoil and infighting among provincial rulers in Iran, an experienced army commander by the name of Mardavij (born 890 AD) and a descendant of Argushe Farhadan—the ancient King of Gilan—gained the position of the new ruler of Iran. The new General Mardavij, shortly after gaining power, encountered the forces of the Caliph, who were sent from Bagdad to defeat him. After three subsequent battles, first in Hamadan, second in Kashan and the last near the city of Esphahan, Mardavij destroyed all the forces of the caliphate and marched with his troops victoriously on December 2, 931 AD, into the city of Esphahan.

After having settled into Esphahan, Mardavij declared it the capital of the new Kingdom on Iranshahr, this being the name of the nation given by the Sassanians to Iran. He started to reintroduce the ancient Zoroastrian religion, declared himself to be the new king, and took the Crown of King Khosrow when he was holding court. A practising Zoroastrian, he declared that his goal was to expel all Arabs and Islam from Persia, and to re-establish Zoroastrianism and the rule of the ancient Iran-Shahr (Sassanian) Empire. Some times later Mardavij started to assemble new troops, with the intention of attacking Bagdad, removing the Caliphate and restoring the ancient Persian Empire. He declared that, by crowning himself in the ancient capital of Ctesiphon as the new king of kings, he would bring back the ancient Sassanian Empire with a new dynasty.[184]

On March 17, 935 AD, only four years after entering Esphahan, and only days before the start of his new military campaign against the Caliphate, Mardavij was murdered by his Turkig-Sogdian troops. The tomb of Mardavij [in Persian: Gonbade Mardavijz] still exists in Amin Abade Rey, a suburb of Shahre Rey—the ancient city of Ragha.[185]

6.6 THE ZOROASTRIAN PRIEST ARDA WIRAZ—OR THE FORGOTTEN WITNESS

At this point, we have to mention in short the name and the work of a man who, for various reasons, maybe merits that his name should not be forgotten in history. He is a Zoroastrian priest by the name of Wiraz, who lived probably during the reign of the Sassanian king Ardashir Babagan 226–240 AD and who produced a remarkable work of literature, entitled *Arda Wiraz Namag* [in Persian: *Arda Wiraz Nameh*; in English: *the book (or the report) of Arda Wiraz*].[186] The date when Arda Wiraz lived is still in doubt and estimates vary between 220 to 320 AD, but it is certain that he lived during the beginnings to the midst of the times of the Sassanian Dynasty Kings. Recently historians tend to place his birth during the time of king Ardeshir I, circa 226 AD. A summary of the *Arda Wiraz Nameh* is as follows:

Wiraz, a Zoroastrian priest and a man of virtue and righteousness, was chosen by his fellow priests, out of his entire community assembled at the sacred fire in the temple at Adur Farnbag, and was required to drink Mang (a strong hallucinogenic laced wine that is still consumed today) which rendered him unconscious and in a hallucinating condition. The assignment, given to him by his fellow priests, was to undertake a journey to the next world, and then again to return to this world, in order to report and prove the truth and authenticity of the Zoroastrian religion. His seven sisters strongly objected to his being pushed into this ordeal, but eventually they assented. After having drank the Mang, Wiraz fell into a state of unconsciousness for seven days and seven nights, and during this time, his sisters and the other priests watched over him, gave him water, and reciting the prayers from the Avesta and Zand. When finally, after seven days, Wiraz's soul returned to his body, he gave this report.

His soul traveled to the next world, and was received and accompanied by the Zoroastrian Archangel Bahman. There he was greeted by a beautiful woman by the name of Den, this woman representing his faith and virtue. After crossing the Chinvat Bridge, he traveled through different levels of heaven and hell. At this stage he was guided by Srosh, the second archangel, to the three stages of the moon track and then to the sun track and finally to the star track. These places were outside the heavens, being places designated for the virtuous and faithful souls, who at the last instance have failed to live according to the ethical rules of the Zoroastrian faith.

In Heaven, Wiraz was brought into the presence of the supreme creator Ahura Mazdâ, who spoke to him, by indicating and showing to him the souls of the blessed. All human beings in this stage were living an idealized version of the life they once lived on the earth, some as an agriculturalist, others as a craftsman and then also some who were in their previous existence rulers and Kings and others.

Afterwards he descended in to hell, to be shown the punishments and sufferings inflicted on the sinners and the wicked. In the deepest most distant corner of hell, he saw souls that suffered the most tremendous punishment inflicted on them. Frightened and moved he asked, who those souls belonged and was told that they were the biggest of all the sinners, their sin was the lie and falsehood.

At the end, his visionary visit and journey completed, Wiraz was once again brought into the presence of the supreme creator Ahura Mazdâ, who told him finally, that the way to lead a life of truthfulness and righteousness is the only true way of existence. Furthermore, that the religion of Zarathustra is the only proper and true way of life, and that it should be preserved in both prosperity and adversity until the end of time.

Charles F. Horne writes:

...of its author we know nothing except what his book tells us. He has sometimes been connected with a religious scholar who wrote commentaries on the Avesta during the time of the Sassanian Empire... The entire vision is truly Dantesque, and while we do not know its age, we can say confidently and with certainty that it is many centuries older than the work of Dante Alighieri... so profound, even to this day is the Parsis (follower of Zarathustra) faith in the reality of Wiraz's vision, that when this work is read in their religious assemblies, the man weep and the woman cry in horror over its description of the sufferings and pictures of the damned in hell...[187]

We have to remember, here, that hell is not an eternal punishment according to the Zoroastrian faith, but only until the general renovation of the World—the Frashigird. The main purpose of our narration of this interesting work is that, at the beginning of his book, Wiraz gives us some indication of the sacred Zoroastrian scriptures, which were destroyed at the orders of Alexander the Macedonian (Alexander the Great) during his invasion of the Persian–Achaemenid Empire. We see that he calls Alexander of Macedonia "the Roman" as in the beginning of the Sassanian period, starting 224 AD, the main Enemy of the Persians were the Byzantines, who were called by the Persian population *Rumi* or the Romans. At that time, the Romans and the enemies of the Persian people were called Rumi.

Furthermore, in the early Sassanian period, the general belief was that Zarathustra had lived approximately 300 years before the coming of Alexander to Persia, (Alexanders invasion of Persia started c. 340 BC) therefore Wiraz says in his book that, for the first 300 years, the religion of Zardosht (Zarathustra) was in purity, but afterwards, meaning from the date of Alexander's invasion and shortly afterwards, the evil spirit (Alexander) made man doubtful of this religion. Here is the beginning of the original text of his book, the *Arda Wiraz Nameh*:

> IN THE NAME OF GOD – They say that, once upon a time, the holy Zartosht spread his religion, which he had received, current in the world, and till the completion of 300 years, the religion was in purity, and man were without doubts.... But afterwards, the accursed evil spirit, the wicked one, in order to made man doubtful of this religion, instigated the accursed Alexander, the Roman, who was dwelling in Egypt, so that he came to the country of Iran with severe cruelty and war and devastation, he also slew the ruler of Iran, and destroyed the Metropolis and the Empire, and made them desolate.
>
> And this religion, which s ancient records, namely all the Avesta and Zand, written upon embellished and prepared cow-skins, and written with gold ink, was deposited in the Archives, in Estakhr e Papaekan, and the hostility of the evil destined, wicked Ashemouk, hostile, ill fortunate, deceitful Alexander, the Roman, the resident of Egypt, he burned them up, and he killed several Dasturs and Judges and Herbads and Mobeds and upholders of the religion, and the notables and the wise of the country of Iran. He cast hatred and strife, and one with the other, amongst the nobles and the leaders of the country of Iran, and he himself was also destroyed, and he ran down to hell.
>
> And after that, there was confusion and contention among the people of the country of Iran, the one

with the other. And so they had no Lord, no ruler, no chieftain, nor Dastur who was acquainted with the religion. And so they were doubtful in regard to God. And religions of many kinds, and different fashions of belief, and scepticism, and various different codes of law were promulgated in the world...

And the soul of Wiraz went, from the body, to the Chinwad Bridge of Chaksat –i—Daitik, and came back the seventh day, and went again onto the body. Wiraz rose up, as if he had arose from a pleasant sleep... and those sisters, with the Dasturs of the religion and the Mazdayanians, when they saw Wiraz, became pleased and Joyful, and they thus said, "Be thou welcome, Wiraz, the messenger of us Mazdayanians, who art come from the realm of the dead, and return to this realm of the living..."

The Dasturs directed thus: "Bring a writer who is wise and learned, and an accomplished scribe" ....who was brought and sat before him, and whatever Wiraz said, he wrote clearly and explicitly. And he ordered him to write thus, "...in that first night, Shrosh the pious and Adar the archangel came to meet me, and they bowed to me, and spoke thus, "Be thou welcome, Arda Wiraz, although thou has come when it is not thy time." I said, "I am a messenger..."

Another quote from the original text of the book says:

...then I saw the souls of those whom serpents sting and ever devour their tongues, and I asked thus "What sin was committed by those, whose souls suffers so severe a punishment?" Shrosh, the pious, and Adar the angel, says thus "These are the souls of those liars and untruthful speakers, who in the world spoke much falsehood and lies and profanity…"

The narrative of Arda Wiraz is unique in that is written earlier than all other comparable documentations and parallels found in the Zoroastrian scriptures. The records in the Denkard 7, for example, are from a much later period, towards the midst of the Sassanian period, then we have the famous rock inscriptions of the chief high priest Kerdir (about whom we are going to speak in later chapters) around the beginning of the third century AD, which are also from two to three generations after Wiraz. This puts the work of Arda Wiraz in a date earlier than all of the mentioned Zoroastrian religious scriptures. The *Arda Wiraz Namag* like many of the Zoroastrian works, underwent some redaction, and it assumed its definitive form in the ninth century AD. It was copied in the handwritten form, translated into Latin and Greek and probably existed in many libraries and book collections of the Middle East and eastern Mediterranean cultures of the fifth or sixth century AD and onwards. It was translated into several western European languages,[188, 189, 190] most importantly into Latin.

It is here that we have to make a few comments regarding this interesting text, which is until today general unknown to the western academic and literary circles. Firstly, this small book, although clearly a work of some kind of fiction, is quite original, unique and a first of its kind, and was originally intended as a religious book written by a priest for the faithful of the Zoroastrian religious community. It is still revered as such in Zoroastrian religious circles.

Secondly, the fact that the original and old sacred scriptures of the Zoroastrian faith—having really existed, having been written with golden letters on ox skin and kept in a tower of the Fortification in the city of Estakhre Babakan—were transmitted to us by the writer of this Book, who himself was a priest, has some historical importance.

It is true that there is no other witness about this fact from the Iranian chroniclers and historians side, but it is reasonable and logical to assume that original or very old scriptures of the faith were kept in some secure location by the Achaemenid Empires government authorities. Therefore, this fact is generally accepted to be true and historical. The ancient city of Estakhre Babakan, existed and was known in antiquity, but does not exist anymore since the time of the invasion of Alexander. Furthermore, importantly, we will see in the next chapter—which deals with Alexander of Macedonia's invasion of ancient Iran—that there is a confirmation from the Greek historical records, that there existed two sets of ancient copies of the sacred Zoroastrian scriptures in the Achaemenid Empire before Alexander's Invasion. One of them being destroyed by Alexander's orders, the other being send to Greece for further translation and investigation by Greek scholars.

Thirdly, the fact that the Zoroastrian priest Wiraz drank mang is of interest, for scientists and historians still are investigating the exact meaning and composition of this drug. The word *mang*, in Persian, means *to hallucinate* or *to be unconscious* (but not dead or physically injured). The drug, whose composition is unknown to us today, was also used in ancient India, had a herbal composition, and was mentioned also in Zoroastrian scriptures. A similar drug *Haoma* (or in Rigveda called *Soma*) was a drug, known since antiquity, that had a herbal composition and was also a hallucinogen. Recently, in some pottery remains found in the ruins of the palace at Persepolis—destroyed by Alexander in 334–335 BC—traces of the remnants of Haoma has been found. This Drug was mentioned in Aramaic scriptures in relation to so-called Haoma ceremonies.

Fourthly, we know that the famous Italian writer and poet Dante, in what is considered to be his masterwork, *La Divina Commedia* [*The Divine Comedy*] has written exactly the same story. Dante, whose real name was Durante degli Alighieri, lived 1265–1321 AD meaning approximately more than one thousand years after Arda Wiraz wrote his book. This fact is being ignored completely by the western literary academic establishment, but a strong possibility exists that one or some of Wiraz's books, translated into Latin and Greek, had somehow made it to the libraries of the western world, there to be discovered by Dante, or someone knowledgeable of this book, had maybe informed him about its contents. Of course, this is just speculation, but of particular importance is the fact that Wiraz's name should have a Latin word attached to it. Considering that his original and ancient Persian name was Arda Wiraz, meaning, the truthful Wiraz. Curiously the Latin word Arduus means 'truthful'. This would hypothetically mean that his name had been given to him, or that he was simply called under this name, by people who spoke Latin or were westerners in a linguistic sense. In any case, the possibility exists, that his book was known in western circles of the time—or was to be found in some ancient Latin libraries—and that Arda Wiraz was the name they called him in latin. According to history, Dante was very knowledgeable in Latin literature and passed his youth studying the Latin classics. The main achievement of Dante was the sanctioning of the new Italian language, which was the vulgarization of the Latin into Italian.

In any case, same to Arda Wiraz, Dante meets God in heaven and visits hell where he sees the Prophet Mohammad. In Paradise he meets the Byzantine Emperor Justinian (482–565 AD), who according to history ordered the Jewish community to change their religious rituals in Synagogues in order to conform with Christianity. He also ordered the drowning and burning of non-Christians in his presence, namely the Manichaeans and Samaritans who did not want to convert to Christianity. This worldview of Dante Alighieri was, of course, all according to the spirit of the time in which he lived. It is remarkable that Dante puts some of the persons perceived by him to be bad human beings into hell, for example, the Prophet Mohammad. Others he deemed to be praiseworthy, such as the Byzantine Emperor Justinian—who ordered large summary executions of non-Christians—Dante places in heaven. For Dante, the criteria to be a good human or a bad human was simply to be a Christian or a Muslim. Whereas, for Arda Wiraz, as we have seen, righteousness and honesty was the criteria of a human being to be praiseworthy and be admitted into heaven, but not religion, as the followers of falsehood and the liars are those who are burning in hell. Arda Wiraz did not personalize his journey to the afterlife. There are no known personalities mentioned by name, whether in hell nor in Paradise. Not even Alexander the Great, whom he mentions to be the cursed one.

Fifthly, according to Zoroastrianism, falsehood and lying were the greatest sin, and therefore, not surprisingly, the most deepest corner of hell, where snakes bite the tongue of those sinners—as we saw in Wiraz's narratives—was reserved for liars and falsehood. Interestingly, also in the classical era of the Roman Empire, lying to the Emperor was regarded as grand treason punishable by death.

6.7 THE BABYLONIAN CAPTIVITY— CYRUS THE GREAT AND ITS HISTORICAL CONSEQUENCES

We have seen in the previous chapters that kings of the Achaemenid Dynasty, as they themselves declared in the rock carvings and other inscriptions on their tomb monuments, were believers in the supreme God Ahura Mazdâ and the Zoroastrian religion in general. Yet, similar to their later successors, the Sassanids, the Achaemenids never mentioned in their inscriptions the name of Zarathustra himself. In the case of the King Cyrus the Great too, it is generally believed that there is now direct evidence that King Cyrus personally indeed practised Zarathustra's creed. His liberal and tolerant view towards all religions practised in his Empire have led some scholars to consider Cyrus as being a Zoroastrian King, committed to Zoroastrian God, Ahura Mazdâ.

Others believe, however, that Cyrus, in fact, seems to have honoured also non-Zoroastrian gods. The reason for this suspicion on the part of these historians is that the so-called Cyrus Cylinder appeals to the help of the Babylonian gods of Marduk, Bel, and Nabu. The Cyrus Cylinder is a clay cylinder with written carvings on it, found in the ruins of Babylon in 1879 AD by a British expedition. This was a political declaration to the people of Babylon by the Persian Achaemenid King Cyrus the Great, considered by historians, to be the first human right declaration of its kind ,when he conquered Babylon in 539 BC. Part of the text carved on the cylinder now kept in the British Museum in London, reads as follows:

> Pray daily before Bel and Nabu for long life for me, and may they speak and say a gracious word to Mardouk, and say "May Cyrus, the king who worships you, and his son Cambyses."[191]

In Babylonian texts, as well as those contained in Jewish sources, we have clear evidence that King Cyrus initiated a general policy of religious tolerance in his empire. He brought peace and prosperity to the Babylonians, who were conquered by him in date in 539 BC. In Babylonia, he is credited with having restored the Babylonian Gods in their respective sanctuaries. Indeed, it is very likely that Cyrus's respect for the divinities of the Babylonians was, in fact, politically motivated to appease the population of that conquered city and gain their cooperation and sympathy. As a result of Cyrus's policies, Babylon not only continued to exist as an independent satrapy within the King's empire, but also prospered under Persian rule.

Here we come to the Chaldean or the so-called Neo-Babylonian Empire, which caused the downfall of the Judean Kingdom and the destruction of the temple in Jerusalem in 597 BC. The ruler of the neo-Babylonians, King Nebuchadnezzar II (634–562 BC), reigned from 605 until 562 BC as supreme King of the Neo Babylonian

Empire. He was the oldest son and successor of King Nabopolassar [in Persian: Nabou-pol-nazar], who died in 605 BC, and who had delivered Babylon from its dependency from the Assyrian Kingdom and destroyed the city of Nineveh. In 605 BC, when king Nabopolassar died, his son Nebuchadnezzar [in Persian: Nabou-khod-nazar] had already defeated the Egyptian army at the Battle of Carchemish that same year, and had brought Syria and Phoenicia under the control of the neo-Babylonian Empire. Nabopolassar died in August 605 BC, and his oldest son Nebuchadnezzar returned from the battlefield to take over the throne. Shortly afterwards, Nebuchadnezzar attacked and defeated the Cimmerians and the Scythians in northeast of Babylon. Immediately to the north and south-east was the powerful Median empire, with whom Nebuchadnezzar had ensured peace, having married Ameythis, the daughter of the King of the Medes. An attempted invasion of Egypt in 601 BC ended in failure, however, in 597 BC, Nebuchadnezzar II attacked the Kingdom of Judah, and after conquering Jerusalem, deposing King Jehoiakim, and putting down a rebellion of the Jews in 587 BC, he destroyed both the city of Jerusalem and the first Temple. Subsequently, Jerusalem fell on March 16, 597 BC. Many of the prominent Jewish citizens, along with a sizable portion of the population of Judea, were deported to Babylon. This period in Jewish history is called the Babylonian exile. King Nebuchadnezzar, according to Babylonian mythology, at the end of his life, called his son and his court, and on his deathbed foretold to them the fall of the Babylonian Empire. He died in April of 562 BC, and was succeeded by his son Amel-Marduk.[192] The Babylonian exile (597–538 BC) of the Jewish people is remembered in the following manner by the Jewish Virtual Library:[193]

> The Chaldeans [meaning the Babylonians], following general Mesopotamian practice, deported the Jews after they had conquered Jerusalem 597 BC. The deportations were large, but did not involve the

entire nation. Somewhere around 10,000 people were forced to relocate to the city of Babylon [once Bab-el meaning Gate of God], the capital of the Chaldean empire. In 586 BC Judah itself ceased to be an independent kingdom...This period, which actually begins in 597 BC, but is traditionally dated to 586, is called the period of the "Exile" in Jewish history, and ends in the 538 BC, when the Persians overthrow the Chaldeans and conquer its capital, Babylon...

On October 29, 540 BC, after a long campaign against Babylon, the Persian king, Cyrus the Great of the Achaemenid dynasty, personally entered the city of Babylon as its conqueror and arrested the Babylonian King, Nabonidus. King Cyrus's treatment of the Jewish people he thus liberated is well known and has been reported in the Torah. The Ketuvim ends in second chronicles with the decree of Cyrus and tells us the story of the return of the exiles to Jerusalem from Babylon, along with a commission from the king for the rebuilding of the Temple. The Jewish holy book of *Ketuvim* [*writing*] is the final and the third section of the Tanakh—after the Torah and the Nevi im.

This is what Cyrus king of Persia says: "The Lord, the God of heaven, has given me all the kingdoms of the earth and he has appointed me to build a temple for him at Jerusalem in Judah. Any of his people among you may go up, and may the Lord their God be with them" (2 Chronicles 36:23).

This edict is also fully reproduced in the Book of Ezra

In the first year of King Cyrus, the king issued a decree concerning the temple of God in Jerusalem:

Let the temple be rebuilt as a place to present sacrifices, and let its foundations be laid. It is to be sixty cubits high and sixty cubits wide, with three courses of large stones and one of timbers. The costs are to be paid by the royal treasury. Also, the gold and silver articles of the house of God, which Nebuchadnezzar took from the temple in Jerusalem and brought to Babylon, are to be returned to their places in the temple in Jerusalem; they are to be deposited in the house of God (Ezra 6:3–5).

As a result of this very favourable policy toward the Jews, Cyrus was honoured as a righteous and dignified King. (Isaiah 45:1–6) He is the only Gentile, to be designated as the Messiah, a divinely appointed leader, in the Tanakh.

I will raise up Cyrus in my righteousness: I will make all his ways straight. He will rebuild my city and set my exiles free, but not for a price or reward, says the LORD Almighty (Isaiah 45:13)

As these documents show, Cyrus did ultimately release the nation of Israel from its exile without compensation or tribute. The famous Jewish historian Josephus[194] writes about events that had happened approximately 680 years before his time, in his *Antiquities of the Jews* book 11, chapter 1 the following:

...In the first year of the reign of Cyrus, which was the seventieth from the day that our people were removed out of their own land into Babylon, God commiserated the captivity and calamity of these poor people, ...for he stirred up the mind of Cyrus and made him write this throughout all Asia.

Thus said Cyrus the King, since god Almighty has appointed me to be the King of the habitable earth, I believe that he is that God, which the Nation of the Israelite worship, for indeed he foretold my name by the prophets, and that I should build him a house in Jerusalem, in the country of Judea.- This was known to Cyrus by his reading the Book, which Isaiah left behind him of his prophecies. For this prophet said that God had spoken to him in a secret vision: "My will is that Cyrus, whom I have appointed to be King over many and great nations, send back my people to their own land, and build my temple."...Accordingly, when Cyrus understood this, and admired the Divine power, an earnest desire and ambition seized upon him to fulfill what was said, so he called for the most eminent Jews who were in Babylon, and said to them, that he gave them leave to go back to their own country, and to rebuild their city Jerusalem, and the Temple of God, for that he would be their assistant, and that he would write to the rulers and governors that were in the neighbourhood of their country of Judea, that they should contribute to them Gold and Silver for the building of the temple, and besides that, beasts for their sacrifices...

Here a short footnote concerning the Jewish presence in Persia, namely the fact that after the conquest of Babylon by King Cyrus the Great of the Achaemenids, a small group of Jews, in addition to those who returned to Jerusalem, went from Babylon to Persia and settled there in the ancient city of Ecbatana (modern-day Hamadan). These were the third group of Jewish immigrants to the Persian Empire. The first group being in antiquity before the time of the Achaemenids, the second group circa 720 BC when a large number of Jewish people came to Persia, due to the conquest of the northern Kingdom of Israel by the Assyrians. And a fourth group came after the Roman–Jewish wars at the time of Emperor Hadrian in 132–136 AD.

Returning to King Cyrus, he was, furthermore, praised in the Tanakh[195] as a Messiah [in Hebrew: Meshiach] for freeing all the slaves, humanitarian and religious equality, and costly reparations made to the Jews. Cyrus died ten years later, in 530 BC, in battle against local tribes of the Asian steppes in the north eastern part of his Empire. According to Mary Boyce:

> This was only one of the many liberal acts recorded by Cyrus, but it was of particular moment for the religious history of mankind, for the Jews entertained warm feelings thereafter for the Persians, and this made them the more receptive to Zoroastrian influences. Cyrus himself is hailed by Second Isaiah (a prophet of the Exilic period) as a Messiah, that is, one who acted in Yahweh's name and with his Authority. "Behold my servant whom I uphold (Yahweh himself is represented as saying) Cyrus will bring forth Justice to the Nations ....he will not fail... till he has established justice on the earth" (Isaiah 42:1–4). The same prophet celebrates Yahweh for the first time in Jewish history as the Creator, as Ahura Mazdâ has been celebrated by Zarathustra. "I, Yahweh, who created all things...I made the earth ...and created man on it ...Let the skies rain down justice... I, Yahweh, created it..." (Isaiah 44:24; 45: 8,12) The parallels with Zoroastrian doctrine and scriptures are so striking that these verses has been taken to represent the first imprint of the influence that Zoroastrianism was to exert so powerfully on post Exilic Judaism.[196]

As the history of the great Jewish people has been in several points in antiquity connected to the history of Zoroastrianism and the Iranian Empire, it is necessary to enter into this topic more in detail. Therefore, we have to give here a closer look at the ancient Hebrew holy book the Torah. In connection with archaeology and the Torah, Israel Finkelstein and Neil Asher Silberman, in their formidable book, *The Bible Unearthed* state the the following:

> When we speak of the bible we are referring primarily to the collection of ancient writings long known as the Old Testament, now commonly referred to by scholars as the Hebrew Bible. It is a collection of legends, poetry, prophecy, philosophy, history and law written almost entirely in Hebrew with a few passages in a variant Semitic dialect called Aramaic, which came to be the mainly used language in the Middle East after the period of 600 BC...these are the products of a continuous process of composition that stretched over hundreds of years. Although the earliest material in this collection, namely the Psalms and lamentations, may have been assembled in the late monarchic times, that is soon after the destruction of Jerusalem in 586 BC, most of the writings were composed much later, from the fifth to second century BC, meaning in the Persian and the Hellenistic period...by the late eighteenth century AD and even more so in the nineteenth century, many critical biblical scholars had begun to doubt that Moses had any hand in the writing of the bible whatsoever. They had come to believe that the bible was exclusively the work of later writers. These scholars pointed to what appeared to be several different versions of the same stories within the book

of the Pentateuch, suggesting that the biblical text was actually the product of several recognizable writers. A careful reading of the book of Genesis, for example, revealed two conflicting versions of the creator (Genesis 1:1–3 and 2:4–25) and two quite different genealogies of Adam's offspring (Genesis 4:17–26 and 5:12–28) and two spliced and rearranged flood stories (Genesis 6:5 and 9:17). In addition, there were dozens more doublets and sometimes even triplets of the same events in the narratives of the wonderings of the patriarchs, the Exodus from Egypt and the giving of the Law...[197]

Furthermore, in the same book:

In these times and places during and after the Babylonian captivity, the text of both the Pentateuch and the Deuteronomistic history underwent far reaching additions and revisions, arriving what was substantially their final form. The events and process that took place in the century and half after the conquest of the Kingdom of Judah—as we can reconstruct them from the historical sources and archaeological evidence—are therefore crucial for understanding how the Judeo-Christian tradition emerged...This is also the moment in our history when we must change our terminology; the Kingdom of Judah becomes Yehud, the Persian (Aramaic) name of this Province in the Persian Empire, and the people of Judah, the Judahites, will henceforth be known as the Yehudim... After that Yehud remained in the hands of the Persians for over two centuries, until the conquest of Alexander the Great in 332 BC...[198]

And also:

> Ezra was send to make "inquiries about Judah and
> Jerusalem" by Artaxerxes King of Persia, who autho-
> rized him, to take with him an additional group of
> Jewish exiles from Babylon, who wanted to go there.
> The Persian King provided Ezra with funds and
> judicial Authority... The other hero of that time was
> Nehemiah, the cupbearer or high court official of the
> Persian King.... The King granted Nehemiah per-
> mission and appointed him to the post of Governor,
> and soon arriving in Jerusalem (around 445 BC)
> Nehemiah set out on a night-time inspection tour of
> the city... Their efforts and the efforts of the other
> Judean priests and scribes which took place over the
> one hundred and fifty years of exile, suffering, soul
> searching and political rehabilitation—let to the birth
> of the Hebrew Bible in its substantial final form.[199]

Concerning the Aramaic language, so-called "Imperial Aramaic"
was the official language of the Persian Achaemenid Empire. The
Hebrew Alphabet of today, which started to be used by the Jews after
the Babylonian Captivity, is also adopted by the Jews from the ancient
Persian, Aramaic Alphabet (Imperial Aramaic alphabet). This alphabet was used by the Persians in all their official documents and correspondence through out the Empire, which at that time stretched from
the Indus River to the Mediterranean. Here we come to a sensitive
part of our investigation, namely the religious beliefs of the Hebraic
people in the pre-Babylonian period. In general terms, if we look circa
600 BC and before, it is clear that the religious picture in the various
eastern Mediterranean cultures show a lot of similarities and parallels
to each other. Namely the Egyptian, the Greek–Hellenistic, and the
Republican Roman (which was build culturally on the Etruscan and

the Greek world) show clear parallels. Namely "The Main Deities" of those cultures each one had a consort or a wife, and was related to other deities. As an example the Father of the Gods, Zeus in Greece, Amon-Ra in Egypt, and Jupiter in Rome, all had consorts. Obviously there existed, in the eastern Mediterranean world, various kingdoms and separated nations with their own deities and their own gods, for example the Babylonians or the Assyrian Empire or the city state of Carthage, which were all in the same situation. We see in those cultures, that their gods lived in harmony with other gods, who were equal, or inferior to them, and each deity had his own Domain. We see here clear parallels, as an example Poseidon the Greek God of the Sea was the brother of Zeus, who was the Father of the Gods in Greece. The same in Rome where Neptune was the God of the Sea. Then we have the God of the Underworld, Pluto in Rome, same position as Hades in Greece, and Osiris in Egypt.

Interestingly these deities were not international and universal gods who were made for all humankind, like Zoroastrianism, but only restricted to the members of that particular nation or society or that tribe. Clearly, the rituals of the sacrifices for these gods also show similarities in all the three nations—Rome, Greece and Egypt. Here we come to the conclusion that most probably the Hebraic cultural and national domain could not have been isolated from the other cultures in that region, as they were located geographically in between those civilizations, and therefore must have been strongly influenced by them. Probably, as the religions of the other neighbouring cultures were so to speak "the latest in cultural and religious development" of that time, it is logical and reasonable to assume that the Hebraic people had a similar pantheon of gods and were believing in a moderate polytheistic style religion. The Jewish professor of archaeology at the university of Arizona, William G. Dever says in this regard:

> Like the people of ancient Israel themselves, the folk
> religion of ancient Israel is extinct...sometimes filled

with nostalgia for what I suspect is a "biblical world
that never was"…for the religion of ancient Israel I
shall use the general term folk religion.[200]

Another work to be considered in this case, is the book of Ziony
Zevit.[201] All these above mentioned religious developments were
before the Hebraic people's contact with the Zoroastrian religious
worldview at the time of the Babylonian captivity.

Concerning the ancient history of the Jewish people, until before
the end of the Second World War in the year 1945, the history and
religion of the Jewish people, who had no homeland but lived scattered in various countries in the world, was a matter of mostly Jewish
academics and historians living and working in a country not of their
own, and their investigations were limited to the ancient scriptures
and documents. It was only after the tragic events leading to the
Holocaust, and the subsequent establishment of the state of Israel, that
the Jewish people started to investigate in their own country and, in
their own ancient domain, the history of the ancient Hebraic people
and their religion. These serious and comprehensive investigations,
were based mostly on archaeological excavations and research on the
original historical sites and locations, which in previous times was not
possible for them. Subsequent to these recent investigations, a number
of new publications and archaeological and historical documents were
published and made available to the general public. Therefore these
new and mostly archaeological reports and books opened a completely
new horizon and perspectives into the historic world of the Hebraic
people in the period prior to 600 BC. The history of the Hebraic
people was, in past centuries, believed to be the events recorded in the
Torah, the Talmud and the other scriptures. Those scientific investigations and historians, who where looking for other sources, had limited
possibilities, to investigate or to prove their point, but the contrary
happened now. After the founding of the state of Israel, from the 1960s
onward, a new generation of historians, mostly Israelis and Jewish

themselves, started to investigate the history of their own people from the archaeological and scientific historic perspective. Since then, a certain number of new publications have reached the public, which try to shed some new light on the religious history of the Hebraic people for the time before the beginning of the Babylonian captivity. Israel Finkelstein and Neil Asher Silberman's, *The Bible Unearthed* being a good example.

In 1967, Israeli scholar Raphael Patai put forward the results of investigations, which have since gained a very strong support among historians and scholars. Raphael Patai was the first historian to suggest that the ancient Israelites worshipped both Yahweh and Asherah together—this theory means in essence, that Yahweh, the God of the ancient Israelites, had indeed a consort by the name of Asherah.[202] This new theory is based on the recent discovery of various amulets and figurines unearthed primarily in the ancient Canaanite coastal city called Ugarit (modern-day Syria). All of these artefacts reveal that, in fact, Asherah was a powerful fertility Goddess in her own rights, and the consort of the main god of the time, Yahweh. According to the inscriptions from Kuntillet Ajrud that refer to the God Yahweh of Samaria, it is believed that Yahweh was the God of the northern kingdom of Israel.[203] Additionally the third edition of Raphael Patai's book contains new chapters concerning the Shekhina.

Furthermore, importantly, Asherah's connection to Yahweh is spelled out in the Bible, and also the eighth century BC inscription on pottery found in the Sinai desert at a site called Kuntillet Ajrud. This inscription pertaining to a petition for a blessing, crucially the inscription asks for a blessing from *Yahweh and his Asherah*. Here was the evidence that presented Yahweh and Asherah as a divine pair. Recently a handful of similar inscriptions have since been found, all of which helps to strengthen the case, that the God of the Bible once had a wife. Raphael Patai, born in Budapest (1910–1996) studied at the Rabbinical Seminary of the University of Budapest emigrated to Israel in 1933 and received a doctorate from Hebrew University of Jerusalem in 1936. Interesting details are also mentioned in Joan E. Taylor's *The Asherah, the Menorah, and the Sacred Tree.*[204] And another academic, Francesca Stavrakopoulou from the University of Exeter in England, presented on December 21, 2011, a BBC Television documentary under the name of *Polytheism in ancient Israel.* Francesca Stavrakopoulou, who is a Professor of Hebrew Bible and Ancient Religions, has presented on BBC several other theories, among others, she said the following:

> Asherah was a Goddess of fertility, and she was represented by the Etz Haim, the Tree of Life; the same tree was modified and later became the Menorah. [...] It is an accepted historical fact that the Jews became monotheistic during the Babylonian exile...

This new discovery was positioning the religious beliefs of ancient (pre-captivity) Hebrew people in parallel with the other civilizations of the eastern Mediterranean region. Just as the Greek, Roman, Assyrian, Phoenician and the Egyptian-Pharaohnic civilizations did, the Hebrew people believed, according to this theory, in multiple deities, and their chief god had a consort. We know, in fact, that in the domain of the ancient Hebrew people, before 600 BC, various divinities were worshipped. Apart from Asherah, whom the majority of biblical scholars now belive was worshipped as the consort of Yahweh, apart from Yahweh and El, who were each one the main gods of the two regional groups of the Hebraic people, there were other deities worshipped, from which we mention here only some important ones:

BAAL

Ba al is a Semitic word, meaning the *Lord*, the *Master*, or The *Owner*. This God was a patron and a protector of cities in the Levant and Asia minor and northern Hebraic inhabited regions. The priests of the God

Baal are mentioned in the Hebrew Bible numerous times, including in a confrontation with the prophet Elijah (1 Kings 18:21–40). This confrontation is also mentioned in the Quran (37:123–125). The encyclopaedia Britannica mentions here that:

> The knowledge of Baal's personality and functions derives chiefly from a number of tablets, uncovered from 1929 onwards at Ugarit and dating to the middle of the second millennium BC.... The Judge Gideon's name was Jeru-Baal (Judges 6:32) and King Saul had a son named Ishbaal (1 Chronicles 8:33)

In Zondervan's *Pictorial Bible Dictionary* it states that:

> At first the name Baal was used by the Jews for their God without discrimination, but as the struggle between the two religions developed, the name Baal was later given up in Judaism as a thing of shame.[205]

The sense of competition between the priestly forces of Yahweh and Baal in the ninth century BC is nowhere more directly attested than in 1 Kings 18, where the prophet Elijah is offering a sacrifice to Yahweh. Baal's followers did the same. Another interesting detail is that in (2 Kings 1:2–6) the name of Baal-zebub [In Hebrew: Baal-Zeviv] is mentioned as the name of the God Ekron. Later this name was turned into the negative as Belzebub (the demon, or Lord of the Flies). Same as in the time of Zarathustra with the Deavas, who were turned into Demons by Zarathustra himself.[206] The Jewishencyclopedia.com, and also the *Easton's Bible Dictionary* contain some details concerning this topic. The name of Baal appears also in the Quran:

> And Elias was most surely of the Messengers, he asked his people; do not fear, will you call upon Baal

and forsake the best of creators, Allah is your Lord,
and the Lord of your fathers (Surah 37:123–125)

Yehezkel Kaufmann, the well respected Israeli Biblical scholar and
philosopher concludes: "… Thus, for example Yahweh and Baal were
later merged into one."[207]

DAGAN

A west Semitic God of grain and crop fertility. *Dagan* was the
Hebrew and Ugaritic common word for *Grain*, and the God Dagan
was the legendary inventor of the plough. He was the most important God in the pantheon of the Canaanites, and his cult is attested as
early as 2,500 BC. According to the texts found at ancient Ugarit, he
was the father of the God Baal. At a later period, Dagan was apparently second in importance only to the main God El, who was the
supreme God.

ADON

From the early Bronze age, Adon was a Deity in his own right, and the
word *Adonai* [*my Lord*] derives from it. The later Greek mythological
personality Adonis is also derived from the Hebrew deity Adon.[208]

MOLOCH

The name of this deity in ancient Semitic mean *King*. Moloch was
worshipped by the Canaanites and the Phoenicians as a God and was
associated with a particular kind of child sacrifice by parents. In later
periods, Moloch figures in the book of Deuteronomy and in the book
of Leviticus as a form of idolatry to be rejected. Leviticus 18:21 says
clearly, "And thou shalt not let any of thy seed pass through the fire
to Moloch."

It is known that, in later periods, all references to ancient divinities in the holy scriptures were erased and censured, meaning not copied anymore. Additionally, oral tradition is usually only written down as text when the society is seriously threatened, or in historical turmoil—as for example in the time after the Babylonian exile and also after the period of the Roman Jewish wars in the time of Emperor Hadrian. Therefore, the memory of the ancient God's were omitted with time.

In this connection we have to mention the case of the Jewish military garrison on the island of Elephantine in the southern part of the Nile. The island of Elephantine was, from ancient times, used as a military outpost to protect Egypt against the Nubians in the south. The name of Elephantine derives from the fact that, once, this island was the trading centre of the ivory trade. At the time of the Persian occupation of Egypt, which started from 525 BC to approximately 193 years later circa until Alexander of Macedonia's invasion of Egypt in 332 BC, a Jewish military garrison and Jewish community existed on the island. This Jewish military presence was securing the southern part of Egypt on behalf of the Persian Achaemenid Kings, who had conquered Egypt in 525 BC and declared themselves to be the new Pharaohs of Egypt. This Jewish community and the military presence on the island had probably existed since around 650 BC—from the time of the King of Judah Manasseh, who reigned from 687–642 BC—when the Egyptian Pharaoh Psammetichus I planned a campaign to conquer Nubia. From the legal documents and other papyri found in caches, written in Aramaic, it is evident that the Jewish community there maintained their own temple (House of Yahweh). But there exists clear evidence in this community of polytheistic beliefs, which functioned alongside the Egyptian deity Khnum. The association of the God of Israel with the Egyptian Deity of Khnum, a ram headed pagan God, is reminiscent of the blowing of the Ram Horn at Rosh Hashanah.[209] According to Israeli scholar Yehezkel Kaufmann:

The religion of the Jewish Garrison of Elephantine
as reflected in the Elephantine papyri is an interesting
phenomenon in his own right, it must not, however,
be viewed as representative of the ancient popular
religion of Israel...[210]

This garrison was founded before the Persian conquest of Egypt
in 525 BC, the Jews of Elephantine had spent over a century isolated
in an alien environment by the time of the writing of the papyri.
No Israelite writing was found among them. They had become
assimilated linguistically and had intermarried with their neighbours. Whatever idolatry they brought with them from their native
land was thus highlighted in these circumstances. Their religion
can therefore be used only in a most qualified way to reconstruct
the popular religion of Israel before the Babylonian captivity.
Concerning the situation on the island of Elephantine, the Jewish
community there was isolated from the motherland, and the Jews
there did not stay current with developments in the religious affairs
of Jerusalem—which had evolved there after the return of the
Jewish people from Babylon. Therefore, we see here clear signs that
said community's religious practises had still a polytheistic character
and that this reflected the ancient pre-Babylonian religious situation of the Jewish people. The Israeli scholar Yehezkel Kaufmann
writes extensively about Elephantine.[211] Furthermore, Ziony Zevit
has done some interesting research concerning the pre-Babylonian
religion of Israel.[212]

Returning to the Babylonian captivity of the Jewish people, we
must examine the key Jewish personalities who had an important role
in the new relationship between the Persian rulers and the Jewish
people. We can mention here three main historic figures: Nehemiah,
Ezra, and Zerubbabel.

NEHEMIAH

He is the central figure in the Old Testament *Book of Nehemiah* which in effect describes his work rebuilding the city of Jerusalem and purifying the Jewish community. He was the son of Hachaliah (Nehemiah 1:1) and probably was of the tribe of Judah. In the years 445–444 BC, which was the twentieth year of the reign Achaemenid King Artaxerxes of Persia, Nehemiah was a member of the king's entourage, a close member of the king's court at the capital city of Susa. He is frequently mentioned in scriptures as being a cupbearer to the King; this is a ceremonial position, signifying his closeness to the King. The Book of Nehemiah is, in essence, the memoirs of Nehemiah. This document written largely in the first person was, according to scholars, written not earlier than circa 400 BC. Nehemiah says here that, after having learned that the walls of Jerusalem had broken down, he asked the Persian King for permission to return to Jerusalem and rebuild its walls and to improve the city. The King consented and appointed Nehemiah the Governor of Jerusalem. Nehemiah remained in Jerusalem for twelve years as the governor, during which time, according to his own words, he rebuilt the walls of the city within fifty-two days. He names each city wall he restored one by one. He ruled with justice and righteousness (again, according to himself), repopulated the city, and purified the Jewish community. At that time, the Persian Empire had some uprisings and revolts to deal with in Egypt, which King Cambyses II had previously conquered in 525 BC. Therefore the Persian King needed a strong and reliable ally in Jerusalem, a governor whom the king knew personally and who could be trusted. It is evident that Nehemiah was not a priest, for there were portions of the temple where he could not enter—portions reserved for priests. After twelve years as governor, he traveled to Susa, the capital of the Persians, which was approximately 150 kilometres east of the river Tigris, but then returned to Jerusalem again, at which time he was "greatly angered" at the people, for he saw that "they had fallen back in to their old evil ways."[213, 214, 215, 216, 217]

EZRA

The Prophet Ezra (c. 480–440 BC) was a high priest and the son of a high priest. According to the Hebrew Bible,[218] he returned from the Babylonian Exile and reintroduced the Torah in Jerusalem. (Ezra 7–10 and Nehemiah 8). Ezra also known as Ezra the Scribe and is a highly respected figure in Judaism.[219] The *Book of Ezra* describes how he led a group of Judean exiles living in Babylon to their home city of Jerusalem (Ezra 8:2–14), where he cleansed the community of mixed marriages.[220] The books of Ezra and Nehemiah were originally one scroll, but at later date they were divided into two discrete works. Some initial parts of the book of Ezra were written in Imperial Aramaic, which was the Persian Official language (for example, 4:8–8:16 and 7:12–12:26) but the remaining was written in Hebrew, for Ezra was skilled in both languages. Ezra himself, a descendant of Seraiah the high priest, was living in Babylon when, in the seventh year of the reign of Artaxerxes (c. 457 BC), the King of the Persians sent him to Jerusalem "to teach the laws of God to any who did not know them" (Ezra 7:25).

Ezra led a large group of exiles back to Jerusalem. Chronologically it is believed that Ezra was the first to be send to Jerusalem by the Persian Kings. It was years later, independently from Ezra, that king Artaxerxes sent Nehemiah to Jerusalem to rebuild the city walls and serve as Governor. It is generally believed among scholars that Ezra and Nehemiah seem to have no knowledge of each other, for their mission did not overlap. Nehemiah's appointment as the Governor of Jerusalem occurred years after the assignment given to Ezra by the same King.

In contrast to Nehemiah, whose assignment by the King Artaxerxes was political and administrative, the appointment of Ezra was highly religious and ideological. Being the descendant of a high priest, and being a high priest himself, qualified Ezra to start rebuilding the temple and compiling and cataloguing the books of the Hebrew scriptures. Jewish tradition has credited the Prophet Ezra with these two important religious tasks.[221] The Iranian-Islamic historian Ya'qubi, who lived in Eastern Iran, disagrees and writes, in 898 AD, that it was Zerubbabel who compiled the Torah, and not Ezra. Zerubbabel was an Exilarch[222] in Babylon, and it was he who had been appointed prior to Ezra to return to Judea by the Persians. Also Edward Kessler is the opinion that it was Zerubbabel—appointed earlier by King Darius as the Governor of Judea (Judah)—who started the works to rebuild the temple in Jerusalem. The fourth book of Ezra (Esdras 4), which deals with Hebraic Apocalyptic visions and contains the prophesies of the times of the destruction of Jerusalem and the Babylonian Captivity and the events of 557 BC, was according to scholars, written in the years 100 AD in Hebrew and Aramaic combined, i.e. hundreds of years after the above events.

ZERUBBABEL

The grandson of Jehoiachin, the second last king of Judah, Zerubbabel was a descendant of the Davidic royal line. The Kingdom of Jehuda—Memlekhet Jehuda—was also called the southern Kingdom and had become an established state circa 900 BC. This in contrast to the Northern Kingdom of Israel. Zerubbabel too, at the orders of the King Cyrus, returned to Judah from Babylon with 42,360 Jews. This, according to the Book of Ezra, happened between the years 538 to 520 BC. He was the first to return from Babylon—his assignment to return given to him by Cyrus the great only a few months after he had conquered Babylon; this places his return nearly a hundred years before the assignment of Nehemiah as the Governor of Jerusalem. Zerubbabel also laid the foundation of the second temple in Jerusalem soon after his return. In all the documents where Zerubbabel's return is mentioned, he is associated with the high priest Joshua son of Jehozadak. Together, these two man led the first wave of Jewish returnees from exile and began to build the temple. As already mentioned, the Islamic historian Ya'qubi attributed the new compilation of the Torah to him as well, rather than to Ezra. It is evident that the Persian King Cyrus regarded Zerubbabel as the successor of the ancient kings of the Davidic bloodline, and looked upon him as the main political authority of the Jewish people.[223] In the Prophecies of the Prophet Haggai it says:

> Zerubbabel is to be made either the representative of YHWH, or the new King who will restore the monarchy, or the new world leader....[224]

Furthermore, there is also mention by Ezra at the beginning of his book, that "...King Cyrus the Great entrusted the temple vessels to Sheshbazzar.[225] There are some conflicting opinions about the identity of Sheshbazzar, whether it was the same person as Zerubbabel or not. The majority of historians believe now Sheshbazzar to be Zerubbabel's uncle, who acted on his behalf. In any case, the Kingdom of Judah was, prior to the Babylonian conquests, an independently ruled Kingdom. Zerubbabel was thus appointed to be the independent governor of Judah by the subsequent King of Persia. It is therefore historical, that in the second year of the rule of King Darius I (520 BC), Zerubbabel and the high priest Joshua, son of Jehozadak, were given the task to rebuild the second temple. We can say here that historians, therefore, believe that Zerubbabel was, in reality, the most important personality in the revival of the Jewish society after the return from Babylon, and that the importance of Ezra and Nehemiah are partly due to their own writings, or memoirs, as in the case of Nehemiah.

In Freemasonry, Zerubbabel is also accorded an important position, for he is seen to be the successor to the Kings of the Jews and a prince of Judah. He is, in the Masonic tradition, the grandson of King

Jehoiachin, who had been deposed by Nebuchadnezzar and carried as captive to Babylon. In him, therefore, was vested the regal authority, and on him as such, the command of the returning captives was bestowed by King Cyrus. Accordingly, King Cyrus the Great presented Zerubbabel with the sword of his grandfather King Jehoiachin as the sign of his authority as the future King of Jehuda. This was the same sword which Nebuchadnezzar had received from King Jehoiachin at his surrender.[226]

As for the notion that the ancient Hebrew people themselves transformed their own religion from polytheism to monotheism, or that the polytheistic religious doctrines transformed themselves to monotheistic one, or that a slow development took place, which resulted ultimately in a change of the religious beliefs from polytheism to monotheism, this is, as we have seen in previous chapters, historically unrealistic. In looking at history, we can conclude that no religion has ever been able to change course by itself, or to reform its doctrine without the involvement of revolutionary means combined with tragic events and dramatic circumstances for the involved societies. The reform or change of any religion is technically not possible because the doctrines of each religion are being kept constantly within allowed parameters, and any ideological deviation in the doctrine of any religion at any time in history was, and is, immediately erased or persecuted by the responsible authorities or priesthood.

This is just as it was at the beginning of Zoroastrianism, when a determined individual had to fight the traditional forces—we see here, that Ezra, Nehemiah and Zerubbabel all had difficulties in their efforts to persuade the people not to fall back in to their old and evil ways. All three of these determined individuals were knowledgeable about the Zoroastrian religious doctrines and worldview, for they had witnessed it personally in their dealings with the Persian Authorities. Apart from this, the Jewish people themselves, now in Babylon, had been introduced to the Zoroastrian religion immediately after the fall of Babylon to the Persians. This fact is also clearly evident from that date forward in the Hebraic scriptures, for we find various analogies and similarities between the Zoroastrian doctrines and the Hebraic scriptures. For example, according to Zoroastrian doctrine:

> In ancient traditions of Zoroastrianism, the mobeds (Priests), when performing a religious ceremony, turn their face always to the source of light, any light. As infinite light is the source of the creator Ahura Mazdâ. In the Bundahishn it says clearly:
>
> > ....Thus it is revealed in the Good Religion. Ohrmazd (Ahura Mazdâ) was on high in omniscience and goodness; for infinite time he was in the light. The light is the place and space of Ohrmazd (Ahura Mazdâ), it is called the Endless Light...[227]

The counterpart of this can be found in the Book of Genesis 1:2 which says explicitly:

> And God said, "Let there be Light," and there was Light. And God saw that the Light was good...

Furthermore, we know that the Zoroastrian religious rule dictated that all humans at all times have to cover their head at all religious places and events, in order to emphasize their obedience and respect to the creator. This rule has not only been taken over by the Hebraic people, but also the Christian clergy abides by it to this day.

The ancient religions of Pharaonic Egypt, the formidable Pantheon of the Hellenistic civilization, and ultimately Imperial Rome's all-powerful gods all had to perish and be forgotten, without them having had the possibility to reform themselves from within. Those old gods simply lost their credibility, were forgotten with time, and were replaced by the new Christian religion, and by the new Christian God. The same happened to ancient Hebraic deities, such as Asherah, Baal, Dagan, Adon, Moloch and others. Their names were blackened, as Zarathustra had done with the ancient deities worshipped before his time. The Hebraic people had now only one God, it is historical, that some scribes of the Torah called him Yahweh, others called him El or Elohim.

From the study of some of the archaeological and historical publications of recent times, we can conclude that, after the return from Babylon, and over the next few centuries, the Jews were increasingly influenced by Zoroastrian religious concepts. For example, in the old Testament's Book of Job, although Satan appears as a doubter among the angels, there was no mention of resurrection of the dead, no eternal salvation or damnation, all rewards for humans were in this world. However, later in the Inter-Testamental era, new changes were made.

We know that it was Saint Paul's ability to split the council of the Jews, by declaring his belief in the resurrection of the dead and thereby obtain the support of the Pharisees against the Sadducees— the following quarrel panicked the Romans into rescuing Saint Paul from the Council Chambers (Acts 23:6–10). There is a discussion among historians, now, concerning whether the word Pharisee in reality stands for Parushim (meaning Persianizers) or those Jews who came from Persia. The word *Pharisee* is, in reality, a defective Greek pronunciation of the ancient Hebrew word *Parusheem*, scholars have suggested, that this term may, in fact, mean Persianized Judeans, for the term Persians in biblical Hebrew is *Paras*.

Saint Paul gained the support of the Pharisees, for they too believed in the resurrection after death, as did the Persian Jews in the Roman Empire, who knowing the Zarathustrian ideology, believed in the resurrection. It is reasonable to conclude here that, after the Babylonian captivity, and the Hebraic people's contact and knowledge with the

Zoroastrian religion, the ancient polytheistic gods of the Jewish people were abandoned, and their new religious beliefs became in reality an adaptation of the Zoroastrian religious ideology.

---

110. Mary Boyce, *Zoroastrians: Their Religious Beliefs and Practices* (London: Routledge, 1979), p. 27–29

111. R.C. Zaehner, *The Dawn and Twilight of Zoroastrianism* (London: Weidenfeld & Nicolson, 1961), p. 302

112. J. Duchesne-Guillemin, *The Western Response to Zoroaster (Oxford, 1958)*, p. 86

113. Shaul Shaked "Eschatology and the goal of the religious life in Sasanian Zoroastrianism", in: J. Bleeker and R.J.Z. Werblowsky (eds.), *Types of redemption* (Supplements to Numen) (Leiden: E.J. Brill, 1970), pp. 223-230.

114. Mahnaz Moazami "Millennianism, Eschatology, and Messianic figures in Iranian Tradition" *Journal of Millennial Studies* (Winter 2000) (Columbia University), p.1 http://www.mille.org/publications/winter2000/moazami.PDF

115. J. Duchesne-Guillemin, *La Religion de L'Iran Ancien* (Paris, 1962), p. 352

116. Bamanji nasar vanji Dhabhar ed., *The Pahlavi Rivayat accompanying the Dadistan-i-dinik* (Bombay, 1913), p. 156

117. P.O. Skjaervo, *Introduction to Zoroastrianism*—Course notes (Cambridge: Harvard,2006),p.57http://www.fas.harvard.edu/~iranian/Zoroastrianism/Zoroastrianism1_Intro.pdf

118. (Bund –TD 1–fol 96 r— translation Anklesaria page 289)

119. Mardan Farrukh, a Persian theologian writer of the ninth century AD. His book *Shikand-gumanik vichar* is an excellent partly Zoroastrian book and an important historical document.

120. R.C. Zaehner, *The Dawn and Twilight of Zoroastrianism* (London: Weidenfeld & Nicolson, 1961)

121. Mary Boyce, *Zoroastrianism: Its Antiquity and Constant Vigour* (Costa Mesa: Mazda, 1992), p. 153

122. Mary Boyce, *Textual Sources for the Study of Zoroastrianism* (University of Chicago press, 1984), p. 65

123. Ibid.

124. Mary Boyce, *Zoroastrianism: Its Antiquity and Constant Vigour* (Costa Mesa: Mazda, 1992)

125. Richard Foltz, *Zoroastrian Attitudes Towards Animals* (Leiden: Brill, 2000)

126. Mary Boyce (1977), p. 142

127. F. Vahman, *Ardā Wirāz Nāmag: the Iranian 'Divina Commedia'* (London: Curzon, 1986), p. 213

128. Mahnaz Moazami, "Evil animals in the Zoroastrian religion" History of Religions (2005), p. 302

129. Herodotus *Histories* 1:140.

130. It is interesting to note that this was the work that started the split between him and his favorite pupil, Carl Gustav Jung.

131. Maria Macuch, "Incestuous Marriages in the Context of Sassanian Family Law." in *Ancient and Middle Eastern Studies: Proceedings of the Sixth European Conference of Iranian Studies of the Societas Iranologica Europaea (Vienna, 19–22 Sept 2007)* eds. Maria Macush, Dieter Weber, and Desmond Durkin-Meisterernst (Wiesbaden: Harrassowitz. 2010b), p. 134

132. The "Mishnah" is the first written redaction of the ancient Jewish oral tradition, and it was called "The Oral Torah" The first work of Rabbinic Judaism, it was written down circa 220 AD by the famous Rabbi Yehuda Ha Nasi.

133. The two main commentaries on the Mishnah are the "Babylonian Talmud" and the "Jerushalmi Talmud", but neither work covers the whole Mishnah.

134. The Achaemenid Dynasty ended with the invasion of Iran by Alexander of Macedonia circa 332 BC.

135. The word Ham-shireh is still used today in the Iranian language, and it has two different meanings, the one is sister and the other is two persons who have been breast-fed by the same woman.

136. In the excellent translation by Dick Davis, *Vis and Ramin* (London: Penguin, 2008)

137. A. Sprenger led later to the publication of the english text of this book- (ZDMG—8—1854—page 608) by Nassau Lee's –Bibliotheka Indica in 1854—6.

138. Vladimir Minorsky, as we will see later comes to the same conclusion.

139. This text translated from Russian into English by Nina Garsoian in *Biblioteca Persica* (Costa Mesa:Mazda, 1997).

140. Vladimir Minorsky, "Vis u Ramin: A Parthian Romance," *Bulletin of the School of Oriental and African Studies*, vol. XI, 1943–46, pp. 741–63

141. Gregory Steward (Trans.) Thomas of Britain, *Roman de Tristan* (New York: Garland Publishers, 1991)

142. Joan T. Grimbert, *Tristan and Isolde, a Casebook* (New York: Garland Publishers, 1995)

143. Vladimir Minorsky, "Vis u Ramin: A Parthian Romance," *Bulletin of the School of Oriental and African Studies*, vol. XI, 1943–46, p. 22

144. Simon Hornblower, *Mausolus* (Oxford: Clarendon Press, 1982)

145. Maria Macuch, "Incestuous Marriages in the Context of Sassanian Family Law." in *Ancient and Middle Eastern Studies: Proceedings of the Sixth European Conference of Iranian Studies of the Societas Iranologica Europaea (Vienna, 19–22 Sept 2007)* eds. Maria Macush, Dieter Weber, and Desmond Durkin-Meisterernst (Wiesbaden: Harrassowitz. 2010b), p. 138

146. Ibid

147. Herodotus *Histories* (Book 4:30)

148. David Pipes, "Herodotus: Father of History, Father of Lies" http://www.loyno.edu/~history/journal/1998-9/Pipes.htm

149. *New Oxford American Dictionary*: Herodotus, Oxford University Press

150. Aubrey de Selincourt (trans.), *Herodotus: The Histories* (London, Penguin Classics, 1972) , p. 41

151. A.R. Burn, *Herodotus: The Histories*, (London, Penguin Classics, 1972), p. 23, citing Dionysius *On Thucydides*

152. Preparation of the Gospel, X, 3

153. Henry R. Immerwahr, "Herodotus" in: *The Cambridge History of Classical Greek Literature: Greek Literature*, P.Easterling and B.Knox (eds), (Cambridge University Press, 1985), pp. 430, 440

154. Herodotus's report is written down seventy-five years after the death of King Cambyses II.

155. James Dunn, "Cambyses II, the First Persian Ruler of Egypt And His Lost Army" http://www.touregypt.net/featurestories/cambyses2.htm

156. Ursula Rossler-Kohler, *Zur Textcomposition der neophoren Statue des Udjahhorresnet im Vatican* (Gottingen, 1985), pp. 43–54.

157. Josephus, *Antiquities* Xl 2.2

158. Alexander's marble statue stands in the Louvre and a larger-than-life statue in the Istanbul historical museum.

159. A.B. Bosworth, *Alexander the Great In Fact and Fiction* (Oxford, 2002)

160. Michael Flower, "Alexander and Panhellenism" in: A.B. Bosworth, *Alexander the Great In Fact and Fiction* (Oxford, reprinted 2010), p.21

161. Aristotle, *Politics* (1252, 5–9; 1255–1260, 12; 1285, 20–4)

162. Elizabeth Carney "Artifice and Alexander History" in: A.B. Bosworth, *Alexander the Great In Fact and Fiction* (Oxford, reprinted 2010) pp. 266–269

163. Cauer (1894), pp. 33–35; Berve (1926), p. 303; Hamilton (1969); Atkinson (1980), p. 398; Bosworth (1988), pp. 41–44; Heckel (1992), p.21

164. Plutarch, *Life of Alexander* (33.6)

165. Ernst Fredericksmeyer, "Alexander and the Kingship of Asia" in: A.B. Bosworth, *Alexander the Great In Fact and Fiction* (Oxford, reprinted 2010), p 150.

166. Eumenes of Cardia was a Greek general and a scholar 362–316 BC. Earlier in his life he was the private secretary of King Philip II of Macedonia, the father of Alexander.

167. Mary Boyce, *Zoroastrians: Their Religious Beliefs and Practices* (London: Routledge, 1979), p. 69

168. Maneckji Nusservanji Dhalla, ??? (1932), p. 331–332

169. R.C. Zaehner, *Zurvan, a Zoroastrian Dilemma* (Oxford: Clarendon,1955) p. 48

170. J. Duchesne-Guillemin, "Notes on Zurvanism" *Journal of Near Eastern Studies* 15/2 (Chicago: UCP, 1956), p. 108

171. Manuchihr Parsa Dust, Shah Esmail e Awwal (sherkate sahamieh entesharchapkhane haidari) ISBN 964-5735-11-4

172. *The Catholic Encyclopaedia*: "Nestorius and Nestorianismus."

173. Al-Mas'udi, *The Meadows of Gold*, p. 1403

174. "Mazdakism" in: John L. Esposito, *The Oxford Dictionary of Islam* (Oxford: OUP, 2003), p. 198

175. Shahrestani died on July 20, 1171 AD at the age of 81 years in his hometown Shahrestan in Khorasan, northeastern Iran. Shahrestani had studied in Nishapur and was a high ranking official and Deputy Chancellor for Sultan Sanjar, the Seljuk ruler of Persia.

176. Abdul Karime Shahrestani, *Ketabe al malal wa al nalal (The Book of Sects and Creeds)*, pp. 192–194; 663–666.

177. Mary Boyce, *Zoroastrians: Their Religious Beliefs and Practices* (London:Routledge, 1979), p.130.

178. *Zand-i Wahman Yasn*, 2:1

179. Denkard 3:345

180. Ehsan Yarshater, "Mazdakism" In: *Cambridge History of Iran: The Seleucid, Parthian and Sasanian periods 2*. (Cambridge, 1983), p. 994

181. The historian Gandizi also reports that Afshin Kheydar was a descendent of an ancient Zoroastrian noble family of Tabaristan.

182. The Arab historian Abu Mansur al-Baghdadi, being an enemy of Babak and his reforms, mentions that the followers of Babak, now called the Khurrami, were openly of the Mazdakait school.

183. It is important to note that *this* Afshin is not identical with the *other* Afshin, who was the friend of Babak; Afshin being a common name in Persia.

184. W. Madelung, "The minor Dynasties of northern Iran: In: *Cambridge History of Iran* (Cambridge, 1983), p. 213

185. Manouchehr Saadat Noury, in a research article on Mardaviz.

186. Interesting that the name Arda Wiraz finds roots in both Latin [arduus: truthful] and proto-indo-European [wer: man], meaning that the Arda Wizaz Nameh could be translated further as Truthful Man's Book.

187. Charles F. Horne (ed.) *The Sacred Books and Early Literature of the East: Volume VII Ancient Persia* (London: Parke, Austin, and Lipscomb, 1917)

188. M. Haug, E.W. West, *The Book of Arda Viraf* (Bombay & London, 1872 – reprinted Amsterdam, 1971)

189. M.A. Barthelemy, *Arda Viarf Namag, ou Le Livre de Arda Viraf* (Paris, 1874).

190. P.H. Gignoux, *Le livre de Arda Viraz* (Paris, 1984)

191. Cyrus Cylinder, English translation line 35

192. A clay tablet now in the British museum, confirms these events. (Praeparatio Evangelica 9.41—Berossus and Abydenus in Eusebius.)

193. "The Jewish virtual library" is a division of the American–Israeli Cooperative Enterprise. http://www.jewishvirtuallibrary.org/

194. The historian Josephus (Josef ben Matityahu: b. 37 AD d. 100 AD) was the son of a *rabbi* [in Persian: *chacham*], who is famous not only to be a conservative, but also a Jewish nationalistic oriented chronicler.

195. Isaiah 45:1–6

196. Mary Boyce, *Zoroastrians: Their Religious Beliefs and Practices* (London:Routledge, 1979), 51–52

197. Israel Finkelstein and Neil Asher Silberman, *The Bible Unearthed* (New York: Free Press, 2001), p. 5

198. Ibid., p. 298

199. Ibid., p. 30

200. William G. Dever, *Did God Have a Wife?: Archaeology and Folk Religion in Ancient Israel* (Grand Rapids: Eerdmans, 2005)

201. Ziony Zevit, *The Religions of Ancient Israel, A Synthesis of Parallactic Approaches* (London and New York: Continuum, 2001).

202. Raphael Patai *The Hebrew Goddess 3/e* (Detroit: Wayne State University Press, 1990)

203. Karel van der Toorn, *Dictionary of Deities and Demons in the Bible* (Leiden: Brill, 1995)

204. Joan E. Taylor "The Asherah the Menorah and the Sacred Tree" *Journal for the Study of the Old Testament Nr. 66* (University of Sheffield—Dept. of Biblical Studies, 1995)

205. Zondervan *Pictorial Bible Dictionary* 1976 ISBN 0-310-23560-X

206. Karel van der Toorn, *Dictionary of Deities and Demons in the Bible* (Leiden: Brill, 1995), p. 154

207. Yehezkel Kaufmann, *The religion of Israel* (University of Chicago Press, 1960), p. 123

208. "Gesenius" in: *The Hebrew Lexicon*

209. A. van Hoonacker, *Une Communaute Judeo-Arameenne a Elephantine, En Egypte, Aux Vi Et V Siecles Av. J. -C* (London, 1915)

210. Yehezkel Kaufmann, *The Religion of Israel* (University of Chicago Press, 1960), p. 149.

211. Ibid., p. 153

212. Ziony Zevit, *The Religions of Ancient Israel, A Synthesis of Parallactic Approaches* (London and New York: Continuum, 2001)

213. "Nehemiah" in: *The Jewish Encyclopaedia*: (New York: Funk and Wagnalls, 1906)

214. Israel Finkelstein, "Jerusalem in the Persian (and Early Hellenistic) Period and the Wall of Nehemiah." *Journal for the Study of the Old Testament 32: 501–20* (2008)

215. Lester Grabbe "Ezra" in: *Eerdman's Commentary on the Bible* (2003)

216. Ibrahim Omer, *The History of Elephantine.*

217. Ian Shaw, *Oxford history of ancient Egypt* (New York: OUP: 2000), p. 206

218. The Encyclopaedia Britannica: "Ezra"

219. Emil G. Hirsch, Isaac Broyde, "Ezra the scribe" in: *The Jewish Encyclopaedia* (New York: Funk and Wagnalls, 1906)

220. Edward Kessler, Neil Wenborn, *The Dictionary of Jewish–Christian Relations* (Cambridge 2005), p 398.

221. Mary Joan Leith, "Israel among the nations: the Persian period" in: *Oxford History of the Biblical World* (Oxford: OUP, 2001)

222. Exilarch was a political administrative person equivalent to a Governor for all the Jewish population living in the Persian Empire.

223. Janet E. Tollington, *Tradition and Innovation in Haggai and Zachariah 1–8* (Sheffield Academic press, 1993), p. 132.

224. Wolter H. Rose, *Zemah and Zerubbabel: Messianic Expectations in the Early Postexilic Period* (Sheffield Academic Press, 2000), p. 211.

225. Diane Edelman, *The Origins of the Second Temple and Persian Imperial Policy and the Rebuilding of Jerusalem* (London: Equinox, 2005), p. 104

226. The Masonic Dictionary: "Zerubbabel" http://www.masonicdictionary.com/

227. R.C. Zaehner -TM (1956–1976) at page 34–35 Bundahishn 1.1

7. THE FALL OF THE SASSANIAN EMPIRE AND THE TWILIGHT OF ZOROASTRIANISM

Die Weltgeschichte ist das Weltgericht.
[The world history is the world Tribunal.]

Friedrich Schiller (1759–1805)

Looking at the history of greater Persia, we see that the last great dynasty ruling the Empire as a Zoroastrian ruler before the fall of the country to the Muslim invaders, was the Sassanian dynasty. The Sassanians ruled that part of the world commonly known as the Persian Empire from 224 AD until 651 AD.

The Sassanian rule, which succeeded the Parthian rule of the Arsacid dynasty, endured for a period of more than 400 years. This dynasty was founded by King Ardeshir I in 224 AD.

The Sassanians called their own country *Eran Shahr* which (in Middle Persian) means *The Aryan Empire*. The Sassanid era, during the late Antiquity, is considered to have been Persia's most important and influential historical period; it constituted the last great Iranian Empire before the Muslim conquest. In many ways the Sassanid period witnessed the peak of ancient Persian and Zoroastrian Civilization. The Sassanian cultural influence extended far beyond the Empires territorial borders, reaching as far as Western Europe, Africa, China and India, and it played a prominent role in the formation of medieval art both in Europe and Asia.

The last king of the Zoroastrian Persia, King Yazdegerd III, died in 653 AD in the city of Marv, and that was the official beginning of the Islamic Persia; he was the twenty-ninth and the last ruler of the Sassanid Dynasty. He had not only lost an Empire to the Arabs invaders, but he witnessed the end of Zoroastrianism as a state religion that had dominated the Persian Society for approximately 2,000 years.

It is reasonable to say that the fall of the Persian Empire to Islam was consequently the reason that Central Asia, the Caucasus, the Indian Peninsula, and the Ottoman Empire became Islamic. This means that the fall of Iran was the key factor in the success of Islam as a world religion. We know that, since the first century before Christ and early antiquity, the river Euphrates was not only the borderline between the Persian Empire and the Roman Empire but also the line between the Sassanian Zoroastrian World and the Roman (and later Byzantine Christian) world. When the Muslim Arabs crossed this borderline and the destroyed of the Zoroastrian world, the historical dimensions changed, and we entered a new phase in world history. It is therefore very important, in the context of Zoroastrianism, to investigate the detailed events which really caused the downfall of the Sassanian Persian Empire and, with it, Zoroastrianism as a world religion. Often people think that it is one big event changes the course of history, but in most cases it is not one big event, but a collection and succession of smaller historical factors taken together as a whole. This is certainly the case with the fall of the Sassanian–Zoroastrian world to the Arab invaders. A combination of different factors, all unfolding together, put the Sassanian Persian Empire in a most vener-able position and caused the end of Zoroastrianism as a state religion. Therefore, let us go into more detail in looking at some historical events in that part of the world approximately 550 to 650 years after the birth of Christ.

7.1 THE PERSIAN INTERVENTION IN YEMEN

It is historically know that, prior to 300 AD in Northern Ethiopia and Eritrea, there was a kingdom by the name of Aksum. Since the late iron age, this kingdom controlled the commerce between the European countries and later the Roman Empire in the north and Ancient India in the south east. In 320 AD, the population of this region converted to Christianity, and as early as the fourth century, this kingdom called itself Ethiopia. At this time, Yemen was ruled by a Jewish King by the name of Dhu-Nuwas, but by the years 522 or 525 AD, a group of Christian Ethiopians lead an attack across the sea to Yemen. An Ethiopian General named Abraha conquered Yemen and took control of the Yemenite throne, crowning himself King, and creating there an independent Christian Kingdom. Again after Abraha's death, one of his sons Mad-Karib, took over the throne.

It was at this time that, in Byzanz, the famous Emperor Justinian I (reigned from 527 to 565 AD) was in power. During his reign, Justinian tried to revive the empire's greatness and reconquer the lost western half of the classical Roman Empire. This brings us to his reli-gious policy, which consisted basically of suppressing and destroying all religious minorities in the Byzantine and west Roman Empire, and forcing all minorities to accept Christianity or to be executed and or severely punished. Justinian's religious policy reflected the imperial conviction that the unity of and empire unconditionally needed the unity of faith, and it appeared obvious to him that this fate could only be the orthodox Christianity.

Justinian famously routed out Paganisms even on a small scale. For example, in the oasis of Awjila deep in the the deserts of Libya, there was a last remnant of the long lost Pharaonic Empire's religion. In that very isolated oasis, people were still worshipping Amon-Ra, the creator god of the Egyptian-Pharaonic Pantheon. Emperor Justinian insisted on the Christianization and elimination of this pocket. Then there was a small island in the Southern Egyptian part of the Nile (near the boarder to the Nubian kingdom) by the name of Philae that housed an ancient Pharaonic monastery. This very small island by the first Cataract was said to have been the burring place of the famous Pharaonic god Osiris. It was said that people in that monastery secretly still worshipped the ancient God Osiris or Isis. Troops were sent, for Justinian also insisted on the eradication of this Pagan pocket. In Constantinople itself, on one occasion, a group of Manicheans, after strict inquisition, were executed in the emperor's presence—some by burning and other by drowning. It was at this time that Persian King Khosrow I ruled (531–579 AD). He was the twentieth Sassanian Emperor and the most famous of the Sassanian rulers. Although he had ordered the execution of the social reformer Mazdak, he is still regarded as being one of the most outstanding and prolific of the Sassanian rulers of ancient Iran.

During this time, the Persians dominated the trade routes between the west and China and India. All routes, from the Indian Ocean and from Central Asia and South Russia had to pass from the Iranian main-land—although competition with the Byzantines was at times intense. Sassanian settlements in Oman and Yemen testify to the importance of the trade with India, but the silk trade with China, as we shall see, was mainly in the hands of the Sogdians, centred at Samarkand and Bokhara in northeastern corner of the Sassanian Empire and Kwarizm.

King Khosrow I [in Persian: *Anushiruwan-e-dadgar* meaning Anushiruwan the Just] was liberal towards Christians of the realm of eastern Christianity in his Empire. He also welcomed refugees from the Byzantine Empire such as the philosophers from the school of Athens, which had been closed by Justinian in 529 AD due to un-Christian teachings in that Academy. This school, (Plato's Home was called *Academos*) existed from the time of Plato (circa 450 BC), according to some historians. After the closure of the Athens Academy by Emperor Justinian, all the teachers were welcomed by King Khosrow I and travelled to the Iranian Empire. The introduction of the game of Backgammon to the west from Persia occurred during this time. In a recent archaeological excavation of a city in ancient Iran called Shahre Souchteh (the burned city) that dated back to 3000 BC, remnants of the game of backgammon has been found.

Returning to the situation in Yemen, we have seen that in this atmosphere of religious zealousness, the Byzantine Emperor Justinian had decided to convert all the population of the Arabic peninsula to Christianity. Considering the rule of an Christian kingdom in Yemen, whose Kings were the descendant of the Ethiopian-Christian general Abraha, Justinian dispatched a bishop from Egypt to Yemen, with the order to actively pursue the Christianization of all the inhabitant of the Arabic Peninsula included Mecca and Medina. This was the year 576 AD, at that time the prophet Mohammed, the founder of the Islamic faith, who lived in Mecca; was six years old.

The hostilities in the north between the Byzantine and the Iranian Empire were matched by their competition in the Arabian peninsula, especially in Yemen. There, in 572 AD, the Christian Ethiopian rulers of Yemen sent an army against the Himyarites clan—allies of the Persian Empire—who were at the time the dominant power in the Arabian Peninsula. This was about the time when the Prophet Mohammed was still a child. At this time, the Himyarites, who were cooperating with the Iranians, defeated the Christian Ethiopians and immediately sent for help from Iran. At the same time, the Ethiopians who had lost the war, asked for help from the Byzantines who immediately dispatched ships and supplies. Here we see the struggle for the Arabic peninsula between Christianization and the Zoroastrian influence.

In order to counter the Byzantine intervention in Yemen, the Persian King Khosrow I sent a small army of 750 men under General Vahriz with a fleet of ships to the city of Aden, and from there to Sanaa. The famous chronicler Procopius reports that Saif, who was the son of Mardkarib, a Persian adviser to General Vahriz on this expedition, was installed by General Vahriz as the new King of Yemen, circa 576 AD.

Thus the Sassanians were able to establish a base in the Southern Arabian peninsula and control Yemen—and with it, the sea trade with the East. In 579 AD another expeditionary army was sent from Persia to Yemen and completed the successful annexation of southern Arabia and Yemen as a Persian province—a move which lasted until the Islamic conquest of Persia. We see here that, without the intervention of the Persian King Khosrow I in Yemen, the Arabic peninsula would have been Christianized by the very serious efforts of the Byzantine Emperor Justinian. It is reasonable to say that, without the intervention of the Persians in Yemen and the Arabic Peninsula, the Prophet Mohammed (b. 570 AD) would had been raised as a Christian. It Is interesting to note that the famous Italian poet Dante Alighieri writes in his *Divine Comedy* that when he was in the other world, and visiting paradise, he encountered there the soul of the Byzantine Emperor Justinian.

7.2 THE LAKHMID KINGDOM

We have seen that, for approximately 550 years prior to the Islamic conquest of Persia, the river Euphrates was most of the times the borderline between the Roman (and later the Byzantine) Empire in the west and the Persian Empire in the east. This was, of course, in constant change as one or the other party was advancing eastwards or westwards in military conquests. Furthermore, from antiquity onwards—but especially during the time of the Sassanians—there were smaller independent kingdoms or small political entities who existed between the two big powers, acting as a buffer zone between the Byzantine and the Sassanian Empire, with their allegiance and loyalties changing from one side to the other according to the political situation. By the end of the fifth century after Christ, there were two of those semi-independent principalities which served the Byzantine and the Persians as a protection from Beduin attacks from inside the Arabic peninsula. The Byzantine clients were the Ghassanids; the Persian clients the Lakhmids. The Ghassanids and Lakhmids feuded constantly, which kept them occupied, but that did not greatly effect the Byzantines or the Persians. In the sixth century, various factors destroyed this very useful balance of power that had held for so many centuries.

Both of these small independent principalities were Christian Arabs. The Ghassanids, who had a Monophysite form of Christianity, were regarded as heretical by the established Byzantine Orthodox church. The Byzantines attempted to suppress their heresy, alienating the Ghassanids and sparking heavy rebellions on their desert frontiers. The Lakhmids, however, were acting as client state to the Sassanians and had been for generations. They had assisted Khosrow II [in Persian: *Khosrow Parviz*] during his flight, at the time of the attempted revolt and power grab by Bahram Chobin in 581 AD. The revolt of Bahram Chobin revealed strong weakness in the power base of Khosrow II and the Sassanian ruling family, and it became evident that the provincial feudal rulers and the nobility of the country were looking for their own independence and were unwilling to support the throne. Still, they all agreed on one point, they preferred to have a Sassanian prince as Ruler of the Empire, rather than a newcomer on the Throne. Nevertheless, according to Richard Nelson Frye, when Khosrow II, in 600 AD, requested troops of the Lakhmid King to assist him during his invasion of the Byzantines, the Lakhmid King Nu'man III in his capital al-Hirah (located approximately at modern-day Karbala) refused. At this, Khosrow II ordered the execution of the king, and the destruction of the Lakhmid Independent state, and the annexation of their territory as a part of the Sassanian Empire.[228]

The Lakhmids therefore revolted and turned against the Persian King Khosrow II. In 602 AD when the Lakhmid King was executed by the orders of Khosrow II, the dynamic of power in that area shifted against the Sassanians. The Lakhmid Kingdom turned away from the Sassanians, and became effectively semi-independent. Looking for new allies, they started to act as spies for the new emerging powers in the Arabic Peninsula, namely the Muslim Arabs. Richard Frye's opinion is that the annexation of the Lakhmid Kingdom by the Sassanians was one of the main factors behind the fall of the Sassanian Dynasty to the Muslim Arabs. He further thinks that the Lakhmids agreed to act as informants and spies for the Muslims against the Persians, their former allies, specifically after being defeated by the Arabs in the battle of Hira by Khalid ibn al-Walīd.

Earlier when the Sassanian army were allies with the Lakhmids Kingdom, al-Mundhir III ibn al-Nu'man, the Lakhmid King, and his army joined with the Sassanian army and defeated the famous Byzantine General Belisarius at the Battle of Callinicum in 531 AD.[229] Later one of the sons of the king of the Lakhmids, Prince Arslan bin Malek bin Barakat, was sent to the coast of Lebanon by the Muslim rulers in 634 AD, where they were responsible for guarding the coast and protecting it. There they established a small independent political entity, and ruled the area of modern-day Beirut for 476 years (634 AD to 1110 AD). A certain prince Arslan bin al-Mundhir founded the principality of Sin-el-fil in 759 AD in Beirut, and this was the base of the foundation of the modern greater Lebanon. The Arslan Dynasty is still one of the most powerful Lebanese families and is now considered to be a hereditary Druze leadership Dynasty. The last in succession to that line is Emir Talal Arslan, born in 1989.

7.3 THE GEOGRAPHIC LOCATION OF CTESIPHON, CAPITAL OF SASSANID PERSIA, AND ITS CONSEQUENCES

One of the obvious reasons, why the Sassanian Dynasty and their Iranshahr Empire was so vulnerable to attacks from both the west and southwest—which played a part in having been fatally defeated by the Islamic invaders—was the location of their capital Ctesiphon. If we look at the map of the Persian Empire at that time, we see that Ctesiphon is, in fact, in the extreme western part of the territory, which the Sassanians ruled. According to history, the borderline of the Iranian Empire in the west, with their main rival and competitor, the Byzantine Empire, was the River Euphrates, and Ctesiphon was only fifty kilometres east of that and thirty-five kilometres south of what is Bagdad today. To the east of Ctesiphon, the Persian empire stretched to the eastern borders of today's Afghanistan, approximately 2,350 kilometres away. This was a strategically disastrous situation and ultimately helped decide their downfall.

Of course, the Sassanians had other palaces in other cities in the eastern part of the empire, for example they stayed most of the summer in *Ecbatana* [in Persian: *Hamadan*] and in the winter months in Ctesiphon for the mild weather. Khosrow II irresponsibly insisted on being most of the time in Ctesiphon and using it as his capital city, perhaps because of his wife's emotional closeness to Constantinople. As she was after all a Christian woman and the eldest daughter of the byzantine Emperor Maurice.

The city of *Ctesiphon* [Ctesiphon is Greek, in Persian: *Tisfun*, in Arabic: *Taysafun*] had a very rich history, first mentioned in the Book of Ezra as Kasfia. Strabo (64 BC–24 AD), a famous Roman historian of Capadochian origin, has described the city extensively. Unfortunately, as of today, the only things remaining in that location is the ancient palace of King Khosrow II called *Taghe Kasrah* [Arch of Khosrow]. The Iraqi government today calls Ctesiphon Salman Pak city in honour of a man called Salman Farsi. In antiquity, this city had been several times conquered by the Roman Empire. Trajan, one of the formidable military leaders and Emperor of Rome, captured Ctesiphon in 116 AD, and then later his successor, Emperor Hadrian, returned it to the Persian Empire at a peace treaty in 123 AD. At that time, the conquest of that city was of little political consequences for the Parthians, as there central power base, lay further east in Khorasan. The Roman Emperor Septimus Severus, later destroyed the city completely, and carried away its inhabitants to Rome, where they were sold as slaves. These historical events *should* have alarmed the Sassanian rulers, especially Khosrow II, but unfortunately for the Zoroastrian-Persian nation, this historical lesson and Ctesiphon's vulnerability was ignored.

At this point we have to mention an episode from earlier history, which proves the theory that the location of the Parthian Empire's capital—too far in the west—was strategically a great mistake, which invited tragedy. The Roman emperor Caracalla (Marcus Aurelius Severus 188–217 AD), after having gained the power in Rome as the new Emperor, saw himself to be the heir of Alexander the Great and subsequently plotted the conquest of the Parthian Empire. First he proposed to marry the daughter of the Parthian king *Artabanus* V [in Iranian: *Ardavan*] and to make an agreement of "Eternal peace" with the Parthians. The Parthian King was surprised, but agreed to this, and in October of 216 AD Caracalla proposed a wedding in the Parthian capital, where all the Parthian nobles and princes would be assembled.

The Roman historian Herodian[230] reports that the Parthians accepted, and at the end of 216 AD, a wedding ceremony was held in Arbela (modern-day Iraq) one of the main western cities of the Parthian empire. Arbela was not the capital of the Parthians, although an important city in the west of the empire. At the end of the wedding night, the most of the Parthian group, including the nobility, a part of the Parthian Royal Guard and the bride—who was the Persian king's eldest daughter—was by order of Caracalla, slaughtered by the Roman Praetorian Guard. The Parthian King Artabanus and a small group of his guard managed to escape.[231] Caracalla, angered at this, ordered the destruction of the Royal Parthian Tombs in the west of the country, where all the previous Parthian kings were buried. King Artabanus, in the meantime, fled to Khorasan and consolidated his forces in the east of the Empire. Only one year later, Artabanus returned with an army from the eastern part of the empire, forcing Caracalla to retreat further west to Carrhae. On April 8, 217 AD, Caracalla was murdered by a member of his own guard.

Caracalla's successor as roman Emperor was Macrinus, the Preatorian Prefect (Commander-in-chief of the Imperial Guard). Macrinus and the Roman Army were subsequently defeated by the Parthians at the Battle of Nisibis, and a peace treaty was signed between Rome and the Parthians, in which Rome had to give up all the recent conquests, and had to pay a heavy penalty to the Parthians.

Had Arbela, so far in the west, been the capital of the Parthian Empire, Caracalla's treachery might have delivered the whole of the Parthian Empire in one bold stroke. This historical detail, however, was lost on the Sassanians.

Concerning the city of Ctesiphon, it is widely believed that the famous *Thousand And One Nights* was actually written and started in the city of Ctesiphon, meaning Ctesiphon was in reality the city of Isbanir mentioned in that book. *The Thousand And One Nights* was a famous Iranian book of the Sassanian period; its name in Iranian was *Haẓar Afsaneh [thousand stories]*, and later Arab translators who translated it into Arabic changed the name to various Arabic names as *The Arabian nights* or *Alf khurafa* or *Alf layla*. The earliest mention of this book is from the tenth century. An Persian librarian by the name of ibn al-Nadim, was compiling a catalogue of books that the Arabs, after conquering Ctesiphon, had found in the Sassanian royal library in the palace.[232] He notes the translation of a Persian book into Arabic by the name of *Hazar Afsaneh* [The Thousand Stories]. He mentions, in his catalogue, that the Sassanian Kings of Persia enjoyed always tales, fables and stories in the evening, read and told to them by young girls of the court before sleeping. Ibn al-Nadim explained the premise of the book *Hazar Afsaneh as following*:

Namely, a Persian king by the name of Shahriar, after having been told, that his brothers wife had betrayed him, in his anger kills off a number of wives after their first wedding night with him, being afraid of them betraying him. Finally the Vizier [Vizier is Persian for Minister] informs him, that no virgin girl is anymore ready to marry the King. At this point the Viziers own daughter Sheherazad [a common Persian girls name] proclaims, that she is ready to marry the King. After being very hesitant, the Vizier consents to this. Sheherazad starts to tell a story to the King at night, but does not finish it at the end of the night. The next day she finishes this story and starts to tell an other story, which again is not finished at the end of the evening and so forth. This goes on for one thousand nights, and at the end the King declares his admiration and love to Shehrzade.

Another chronicler, Al Masudi, also from the tenth century, mentions the *Hazar Afsaneh* and the name of the main protagonist of the book as Sheherazade and says that the name of the Arabic translation of that book had been changed to *Alf khurafa* or *Alf layla*. Probably the premise and most of the episodes existed from Sassanian times, and were later Islamicized after the Arabic conquest of Persia. The first English language edition of that book dates from 1706, at which time it was published under the title *The Arabian Nights Entertainment,* probably because they translated it from the Arabic to English and they did not know what the origin of this book was. At a later date, probably some new episodes, fitting to the Islamic environment were added to the original story. As the old proverb says, "A success has hundred fathers, whereas a failure is always an orphan."

Furthermore, in the same library, two other notable books were found: *Xvatay Namah* [Book of Kings] and *Kar-namag i Ardashir i Pabagan* [Book of Deeds of Ardeshir, Son of Papak]

Xvatay Namah, compiled in the period of the Sassanian dynasty, contained a compilation and collection of the history of the Kings and Heroes of Persia from the ancient, mythical times up to the time of the death of the Sassanian King Khosrow II in the year 628 AD. It was an important chronicle of the Sassanian Dynastic rule over their Empire, probably with documentation, such as agreements and other documents attached. Its chronicles for the time *after* the death of the last Sassanian king were not historically accurate, as it was added later by the Islamic conquerors or their representatives. In this book of the Sassanian period, the personality of the Iranian folk hero Rostam was already included. It was this important and historical document which was later taken by Abolghassem Mansour (known as ; Ferdowsi) and transformed into the famous *Shahnameh*. The original document was in prose form, but Ferdowsi transformed it into poetry. Ferdowsi himself added some materials containing the history of the overthrow of the Sassanian Dynasty by the Arabs up to 644 AD and later.

The other notable book catalogued by ibn al-Nadim was the *Kar-namag i Ardashir i Pabagan* which was originally written during the late Sassanian era and gave accurate description of the events of how Ardeshir I and the Sassanian Dynasty came to power. This book, also of great importance to the Iranian History, is regarded as historically accurate due to its timely proximity to the events. This work, written in Middle Persian, was also used by Ferdowsi for the *Shahnameh*.

Importantly the first Governor of the city of Ctesiphon, the ancient capital of the Sassanian Kings, was Salman Farsi, who was appointed to this position by the Caliph Ali Ibn Abu Taleb. Salman arrived in Ctesiphon and ultimately died there and is buried there according to Islamic historians. Contrary to the Arabic Islamic custom, to burn and destroy all libraries in the Persian Empire, as it was done in various other cities as for example in Herat and in Bukhara, in this city the

Imperial Library and Archives of the Palace of the Sassanian Kings was saved for further generations by the Intervention of Salman Farsi. Salman was the first Governor of Ctesiphon after it fell to the Arab invaders.

But returning to our investigation of the City of Ctesiphon, several archeological expeditions have been made from Europe to that site, including a German oriental society and University of Pennsylvania team led by Oskar Reuter who excavated in Ctesiphon in 1928–29 and later again 1931–3; and a University of Turin team under A. Invernizzi and G. Gullini who worked at the site in the 1960s mainly doing restoration at the palace of Khosrow II.

7.4 GENERAL SHAHRBARAZ

General Shahrbaraz and the events surrounding his time are of crucial importance for the understanding of the downfall of the Sassanian Empire and the end of the Zoroastrian religion as the main faith of the Persian Nation. To start some years earlier, the Byzantine Emperor Maurice, who was in power from 582 AD until November 27, 602 AD, played an important part in the events of those years. Being a famous and successful general in his youth, Maurice fought with success against the Persian Sassanian Empire. Once he became emperor, Maurice brought the war with Persia to a victorious end; the eastern borders of the Byzantine Empire were vastly expanded and, after 200 years, the Byzantines were no longer obliged to pay the Persian Empire thousands of pounds of gold annually in tribute (as per the agreement with Khosrow II) to keep the peace with them as they had done in the previous decades.

Earlier in 590 AD, Prince Khosrow of the Sassanian clan together with the commander in chief of the Persian armies at the time, General Bahram Chobin, revolted and overthrew King Hormiz IV.

This was done ostensibly to seat Prince Khosrow on the throne. General Bahram Chobin, after having overthrown the reigning King, decided to take the throne for himself and ordered the arrested and execution of Prince Khosrow, his ally in this revolt. Prince Khosrow subsequently fled to the Byzantine court, and sought refuge with Emperor Maurice in Constantinople. The Senate of the Byzantines, consulted in this matter by Emperor Maurice, advised him to imprison Prince Khosrow and deliver him to General Bahram Chobin, arguing that the general was holding all the powers and was already sitting on the Persian throne. Emperor Maurice decided against the advice of the senate, however, and sent with Prince Khosrow an army of 35,000 men for him to gain back the throne of Persia. In the year 591 AD, a combined Byzantine and Persian army which was commanded by two Generals John Mystacon and Narses, defeated Bahram Chobin's forces near Ganzak at the Battle of Blarathon.

This was a clear, decisive victory for the future King Khosrow II, who, after this victory, was declared the new Emperor of Persia. Following these events, the new Emperor Khosrow II, married Myriam, who was the eldest daughter of the Byzantine Emperor Maurice. Khosrow II further had to reward Emperor Maurice for his help, and gave to him some vast territories, which previously belonged to the Persian Empire. These territories were western Armenia and up to the lakes Van and Sevan including the large cities of Martyropolis, Tigranokert, Manzikert, Ani, and Yerevan. The new treaty between Emperor Maurice and his new son-in-law extended the Byzantine Empire to territories, never before part of Byzantium. Additionally this was much cheaper to defend in the future due to the new peace agreement between the two Emperors. As mentioned before, millions of soldi (a late Roman gold coin) were saved by not paying the tribute which they were paying previously to the Persian Empire.

The reign of Maurice is a relatively well-documented period of Late Antiquity. The historian Theophylact Simocatta says that Maurice stands out as one of the last Emperors, whose Empire still bore strong resemblance to the Roman Empire of the last and previous centuries and that with his death the classical Antiquity ended forever.

Unfortunately things from this point on did not go well for Emperor Maurice. One of his army generals commanding the western army, a man by the name of Phocas, under the pretext that funds were cut for the army, rebelled against him. Maurice and his family were arrested and imprisoned, and on the November 23, 602 AD, after having Maurice's sons all executed in front of him, Maurice too was beheaded. Maurice's wife and daughters were forced to enter a monastery and become nuns for the duration of their lives. General Phocas then declared himself Byzantine Emperor.

It was at this time that hostilities again started between Persia and the Byzantium, for Khosrow II used these events as an immediate excuse for renewed war against the Byzantine empire. Khosrow II had been deeply disturbed by the brutal murder of his friend and father-in-law Maurice and his family and was moved to avenge those deaths—and use it as a political gain for his Empire.

In any case, in the year 603 AD, he declared war against the new Emperor Phocas. Soon thereafter, the ruler of the Byzantine Empire changed yet again. A man by the name of Heraclius became the new Emperor, and ruled from 610 until 641 AD. Heraclius was of Armenian descent, and his father, Heraclius the Elder, had been appointed by Emperor Maurice as the Exilarch of North Africa with the seat in Carthage. Previously, Heraclius the Elder was a key general in the war against Bahram Chobin in 590 when Maurice helped Khosrow II to gain his throne. Heraclius, the son, came from Carthage by ship with his troops, and when approaching the capital, the Emperor Phocas's elite bodyguards—called the Excubitors and commanded by Priscus, the son in law of Phocas—deserted to Heraclius, and therefore Heraclius could enter the city without further resistance. Heraclius personally executed Phocas and was crowned Emperor on October 6, 610 AD.

It is here that we meet the greatly talented and capable Iranian army commander, General Shahrbaraz, whose real name was probably Farrokhan, the son of a certain Ardeshir, and who was a member of the house of Mihran, one of the seven ruling Parthian Clans of ancient Iran. It is said that he was married to Mirhan, the sister of King Khosrow II for whom he acted as the commander-in-chief of his armies. He had two sons by Mirhan, Niketas and Shahpur-i Shahrbaraz. General Shahrbaraz's date of birth is not exactly known, but he died June 9, 630 AD. The name Shahrbaraz, was not his real name and meant probably the *King's Boar* or the *Empire's Boar*. Alfred Joshua Butler, in his book *The Arab Conquest of Egypt and the Last Thirty Years of Roman Dominion*[233] suggests that the name of this general was just a title. In any case, in a new sets of wars between the Persians and the Byzantine Empire, General Shahrbaraz lead the Persian armies in a wide scale invasion into the territories of the east Roman Empire, defeating the armies of Emperor Phocas. This was, as we will see shortly, the beginning of a new period of approximately thirty years of warfare and great hostilities between the Byzantine and the Persian Empire, which not only greatly weakened the two ancient Empires, but opened the way for the newly emerging Islamic movement to be victorious.

In the subsequent wars, the Persian armies under General Shahrbaraz advanced into the heartland of the Byzantine Empire and conquered Damascus, Jerusalem, Egypt and the whole Capadocian peninsula (modern-day Anatolia) and besieged the city of Constantinople which withstood the Persian army only due to its formidable fortifications and walls. This wide scale invasion started in the summer of 613 AD. The entire part of the Asian Byzantine Empire was now under the control of the Persian Armies under General Shahrbaraz. According to some sources, with the Persian general standing at the gates of Constantinople, Heraclius thought of abandoning the city and moving the capital of the empire to carthage in north Africa. Furthermore, in Jerusalem, having conquered this city on July 17, 614 AD, General Shahrbaraz carried away a number of Christian relics—among them, what was considered at that time to be the true and Holy Cross of Jesus Christ—which were all sent to the Persian capital of Ctesiphon.

It was the powerful head of the Byzantine church, Patriarch Sergius, who convinced Emperor Heraclius to negotiate a peace treaty in exchange of "one thousand talents of gold, one thousand talents of silver, one thousand silk robes, one thousand horses, and one thousand virgins girls for the Persian king personally." After this peace treaty was signed, the Byzantine Emperor started to rebuild the army by slashing non-military expenditures, devaluing the currency, and with the backing of the church under Patriarch Sergius, melting down and selling church treasures.

All this conquests were made under the command of the formidable General Shahrbaraz,, but we will see later, that General Shahrbaraz at the end betrayed his king and nation, which had tragic consequences for the Persian Empire. It is the opinion of the historians, such as Parvaneh Pourshariati and others, that two factors could have had a great influence on the decision of General Shahrbaraz to betray the Sassanian rulers and the nation. Firstly the old local and provincial ruling houses of Iran, at that time of its history, were mostly descendant of the Arsacid rulers, meaning the dynastic rulers of the country, who were in power before the Sassanians took over. In fact, these local ruling houses did not feel they owed any loyalty to the Sassanian, and regarded them as usurpers to the Persian throne. The local ruling clan that Shahrbaraz belonged to was, in fact, already in power when the Sassanians took power in the country. Secondly, it is now believed by historians, that the ancient Satraps[234] of the eastern part of the Persian Empire, namely in Khorasan, were probably not Zoroastrians, but were still mainly Mehr Parast (worshippers of the Mithraic cult) and that the worship of Mithras had still endured in some pockets in the eastern part of the Empire.

7.5 THE CONQUEST OF JERUSALEM AND THE ESTABLISHMENT OF AN INDEPENDENT JEWISH STATE BY THE PERSIANS ON JULY 17, 614 AD

In April of 613 AD, the success of Persian troops under General Shahrbaraz meant that Egypt and the Asiatic parts of the Byzantine Empire now lay under Persian control. It was then that Emperor Khosrow II decided on an important strategic move, namely to establish an independent Jewish political entity in Jerusalem, to give back the land of Judea and Samaria (Israel) to the Jews, and probably to establish there an independent Jewish kingdom, which would assemble all the Jews in their old ancestral land. Until this date the province of Palestina, and the city of Jerusalem were a part of the greater Byzantine Empire. Importantly before the year 614 AD, Judea and Samaria and Jerusalem itself were under the control of the Roman Republic , the later Roman Empire and subsequently the East Roman Empire later called the Byzantine Empire for over 700years.

Here again we have to mention an interesting footnote to history: one of the ancestors of Khosrow II—namely King Yazdegerd I—was married to a Jewish woman named Sushan Docht, meaning that all subsequent Kings of the Sassanian Dynasty were technically speaking within the Jewish faith. Furthermore, throughout the Sassanian Dynasty the entourage and the advisers and the high government officials of the court of Sassanian Kings were mostly Jewish. The Jewish Queen Sushan is buried together in the mausoleum of Esther and Mordekhai, which still exists today in the city of Hamadan in western Iran. It is for this reason that traditionally the Persian Kings of the Sassanian Dynasty were not only favourable but also strongly influenced by the Jewish presence in Persia. In contrast, to the Christian Byzantine Empire—which constantly pressured the Jewish community to convert to Christianity *especially* under the reign of the

Emperor Justinian—the Zoroastrian Persia and the Sassanian Empire had always respected the independence of the Jewish community and their faith in Iran. In the Persian Empire until the time of King Khosrow II (590–628 AD), the Jewish population enjoyed a free and semi autonomous existence. This Jewish entity was run by an Exilarch who, being Jewish himself, was the chief administrator of the Jewish community. This Exilarch was appointed by the king and was responsible only to him, but he was running the affairs of the Jewish community independently and according to the Jewish customs and laws. He was raising taxes and had Jewish personnel under him who were helping him in his administration and keeping order, this in the style of an police force, which was under the order of the Exilarch.

In the summer of 613 AD, the Jewish community leaders, and a man by the name of Nehemiah ben Hushiel, the son of the reigning Exilarch, were involved in the King's plans, concerning the establishment of an independent Jewish state in Jerusalem by the Persian Government. The Jewish community leaders in Persia raised an army of 20,000 men who were recruited among the Persian Jewish population, which was put under the command of Nehemiah ben Hushiel. This group was armed and trained by the Persian Army and was subsequently a part of the Persian Troops, under the command of General Shahrbaraz, the commander-in-chief of the Persian armies in the west.

Towards the beginning of his reign, King Khosrow II was favourable to the Christians, however, when the Byzantine Emperor Maurice was murdered in 602 AD by his subsequent usurper General Phocas, King Khosrow II launched an offensive against Constantinople, ostensibly to avenge Maurice's Death—but clearly his aim included the annexation of as much Byzantine territory as was feasible. His armies invaded Syria and Asia Minor, and in 608 advanced into western Anatolia. In 613 and 614, Damascus and Jerusalem were besieged and captured by General Shahrbaraz. Soon afterwards, another Persian army commander, General Shahin marched through Anatolia, defeating the Byzantines numerous times, and then conquered Egypt in 618.

The Byzantines could offer but little resistance, as they were torn apart by internal dissensions, and pressed by the Avars and Slavs, who were invading the Empire from the north west, across the Danube River. King Khosrow's forces also invaded Taron at times during his reign, and In 613 AD, the Byzantine army suffered a crushing defeat in Antioch, allowing the Persians to move freely and swiftly in all directions. This surge caused the cities of Damascus and Tarsus to fall, along with Armenia.

More seriously, however, was the loss of Jerusalem, which was besieged and captured by the Persians in three weeks. According to some Christian sources, countless churches in the city, including the Holy Sepulchre were burnt and numerous relics, including what was believed at that time to be the True Cross, the Holy Lance and the Holy Sponge, present at the time of Jesus Christ's death, were carried away and were now in Ctesiphon, the Persian capital. The Persians remained poised outside of Chalcedon, not too far from the capital Constantinople, and the province of Syria was in total chaos. After General Shahrbaraz's victory in Palestine and Jerusalem in 614 AD, another important Persian army leader General Shahin made further military advances into Central and Western Anatolia towards the Black Sea. It is also General Shahin who is credited with the siege of Alexandria and the conquest of Egypt for the Persian Empire in the year 619 AD.

There are three history works which are important in this connection, "The Persians in Asia and the End of Antiquity" by Clive Foss,[235] *Causes of the Downfall of the Sassanian Empire* by Virasp Mehta,[236] and *Heraclius: Emperor of Byzantium* by Walter E. Kaegi.[237]

After the Persian victory in Anthiochia, the joined Sassanian–Jewish army arrived to the Province of Palestina after having conquered Caesaria Marithima. The Persian Army, which included the Jewish troops under Shahrbaraz, after having arriving in Jerusalem, were joined by new Jewish volunteers under the leadership of Benjamin of Tiberias, who was, according to Jewish sources, one of the local wealthy and influential Jewish leaders. Together the troops under the leadership of Shahrbaraz, joined again by the Jews of the southern part of the country and supported by local band of Arabs, marched on Jerusalem.

The city of Jerusalem—founded in the early antiquity as Uru-Shalem, named after the Canaanite God Shalem (the God of the Dusk)—was strongly fortified and had impregnable walls. After a siege of twenty days, on July 17, 614 AD, Jerusalem fell to Shahrbaraz and his combined troops. Here we have limited information as to what really happened in the following years. It is clear that the Jews were given full authority to run their own affairs of Jerusalem and the lands around it by the Persian commanders, after the combined army gained complete control of Jerusalem and the countryside. At this time, much of the territories of the ancient Judea and Galilee became an autonomous Jewish Province in the framework of the Sassanian Empire. It is estimated that approximately 150,000 Jews were living, at that time, in that autonomous entity scattered in forty-three different settlements through out the territory. According to the Jewish sources, after Jerusalem and the territory surrounding it had been conquered by General Shahrbaraz, he appointed Nehemiah ben Hushiel as the new ruler of Jerusalem and the territories around it. This new Jewish political entity, which was intended later to be declared as a new Jewish Kingdom by the Sassanians, lasted nearly fifteen years, from July 17, 614 AD, until November of 628 AD. Nehemiah started the work of making arrangements of rebuilding the Temple and sorting out the genealogies of candidates to establish a new High Priesthood. According to sources, a great number of Christians living in Jerusalem at that time were killed and many churches destroyed by the Jews, or the combined Persian–Jewish forces.

At this time King Khosrow II—whose plan was to probably elevate Nehemiah ben Hushiel to be the King of Jerusalem and thus establish a strong ally in the newly formed Jewish Kingdom—was murdered, in February 628 AD, after which everything changed.

In the year 629 AD, after the death of the Persian King Khosrow ll one year earlier, and the betreyal of the Persian General Shahrbaraz, when the Byzantine troops had successfully counter-attacked the Persian positions, Emperor Heraclius entered the city of Jerusalem. There the situation escalated for the worse and resulted in a wide scale massacre of the Jewish population throughout Jerusalem and Galilee by the Christians. Resulting with tens of thousands of Jews escaping from Palestine and Jerusalem to Egypt.

The historian Eutychius (887–940 AD) records that the Emperor Heraclius would have kept peace with the Jews, but that fanatical Christian monks put pressure on him to start a massacre. When Heraclius didn't listen, the monks started to fast until Heraclius obeyed. Heraclius is said to have dreamed that the destruction of the Byzantine empire would come through the circumcised people. He therefore proposed to massacre all Jews who would not become Christians, and he is reported to have written a letter to Dagobert, the King of France, to do the same with the Jews in his country. By that time the Jews in the Byzantine empire were under such pressure by the Christians that the Tiburtine Sibyl had predicted that, in a 120 years, there would be no Jews anymore in the Byzantine empire as they would all be converted to Christianity. As for the dream of Emperor Heraclius, it *would* be the circumcised people who would destroy the Byzantine Empire, this dream—if he really had such a dream—came true, for the Muslim Mongols, who were also circumcised, were the ones who destroyed the Byzantine empire.

It is mentioned in several chronicles that, after these events, the Jewish population of Jerusalem perceived themselves as being abandoned by the Persians, and that this being regarded as a betrayal. In reality, the tragic reversal in the fortunes of the Persian Empire—which started with the execution of the old King Khosrow II—affected the destiny of the newly established Jewish homeland planned by the Sassanian Kings. We have seen that, during the reign of the Sassanian rulers of Persia, the Jews living in Iran not only did so in peace and safety, but that they occupied vast territories of the countryside and had their own independent administration ruled by a Jewish administrator—an

Exilarch who basically ruled a state within a state. Only nine years after the conquest of Jerusalem by the Christians, in the year 638 AD, the Byzantine Empire again lost complete control of Jerusalem and Judea, but this time to the Muslim Arabs under their ruler the Caliph Omar.

At this point we have to mention a very important turn of events, which proved to be a decisive catastrophe not only for King Khosrow II but for the whole Persian Nation—the betrayal of the commander-in-chief of the Persian armies, General Shahrbaraz.

Shortly after these events, the newly emerging Islamic movement gained momentum, and as for Zarathustra the Prophet, who had previously started a chain of events which deeply influenced three world religions, he and his message would be banished from being an official religion of an Empire, and would have to continue its existence in the obscure and dark corners of mythology.

In any event, the great Persian General Shahrbaraz, practically now the commander-in-chief of all the Persian Armies rebelled and betrayed his king and nation. This happened in late 626 AD or early 627 AD. The General formed an alliance with the enemy of the Persians—the Byzantine Emperor Heraclius—against his own country Persia. The details of this episode in Persian history are vast but not entirely transparent.

7.6 THE KHAZAR INVASION OF NORTHERN PERSIA—THE THIRD PERSO-TURKIC WAR OF 627 AD. AND THE DOWNFALL OF KING KHOSROW II

At this point we have to investigate one of the important factors that contributed to the fall of the Persian Zoroastrian society at the time of the Sassanian rulers to the invading Muslim Arab invaders. With the Persian war effort against the east Roman Empire disintegrating, the Byzantine Emperor was able to convince the Gokturks of the western Turkic Khaganate to invade Persia from the north and occupy and plunder Armenia and Azerbaijan. The French historian René Grousset who is looked upon as an expert on the history of the people of central Asia, in his famous source book *The Empire of the Steppes a History of Central Asia* (probably the best book ever written about the history of the Central Asian people), writes:

> At the beginning of the seventh century, the south-western part of the Russian Steppe and Dagestan, had witnessed the rise of the Khazar empire. The Khazars were Turkic people who previously had worshiped Tangri and were governed by Khagans and Tarkhans. Barthold suggests that they represent a branch of the western Turks, and they were already a powerful nation in 626 AD, as their Khan Ziebel, at the request of the Byzantine emperor Herclius at a meeting in Tiflis, lent the Byzantine emperor 40,000 men to make war on Persia. A reinforcement with which Heraclius laid waste the Sassanian Province of Azerbaijan. The alliance thus formed between Byzantium and the Khazars was renewed many times by royal marriage. Emperor Justianian II at the time of his exile (695–705 AD) took refuge with the Khazar's and married one of the Khagans sisters, who became the Basillissa Theodora.[238]

Comparing this to 334 BC, when Alexander the Great crossed the Hellespont, setting foot in Asia with 43,000 man and 5,500 horses. Following the first siege of Constantinople by the Avars from across the Danube and the Persians from the east, the Byzantine Emperor Heraclius, who was politically completely isolated, tried to ask the Christian Armenians in the Caucasus to assist him against the Persians, but this was not possible because the Orthodox church in Constantinople had declared them as heretics.

Furthermore, the king of Iberia (no connection to modern Iberian peninsula but rather in the Caucasus, modern-day republic of Georgia) did not respond to his (Byzantine) advances and stayed loyal to the Persians. Seeing this situation, Heraclius sent, in the year 625 AD, an emissary by the name of Andrew to meet the Khagans of the Northern steppe Turks, called the Gokturks. At that time, the ruler of the Turks was Tong Yabghu, with their western Turkic kingdom, which was geographically north east of the Caspian Sea. Heraclius offered them great riches and gold to be had in the Caucasus (meaning the city of Tiflis), Armenia and Azerbaijan. Approximately sixty years before, the same western Gokturks, under their leader at the time, Istami, who were used to receiving, from the Persians, a cut from the silk trade passing from China to the west through Persia, found themselves at odds with the Sassanian emperors who refused to pay any cut to them anymore. The new Khagan had decided, therefore, to take matters into his own hands and to secure the Chinese–Byzantine trade route along the silk road to continue to work for him. We must mention here that, previously, there were two Perso-Turkic Wars and that these hostilities mentioned here now were the beginning of the Third Perso-Turkic War.

At this time the western Gokturks allied themselves with the kingdom of the Khazars. Concerning the Khazars, we have to say that these were a kingdom of people of Slavic-Turkic race, ruled by a king who was called Khagan. The Kingdom of the Khazars, at this time, believed probably in some pagan religion, but by the years 1100 AD they adopted the Jewish religion and became a Jewish kingdom. Later on, under the pressure of the Tartars from the East, they moved west towards the area of today's Hungary, and later on to Poland, and are commonly known as the Ashkenazi Jews of today. The Hungarian writer Arthur Koestler's book *The Thirteenth Tribe*, which is an important document in itself, describes this issue in detail.[239] The Khazars were formidable warriors and horsemen, and this is not the first time that they allied themselves with the Gokturks, who lived in the steppes immediately east of them in Central Asia.

Returning to the Third Perso-Turkic War, in early 627 AD, the Gokturks and their Khazar allies attacked the city of Derbent in the Northern part of the Caspian Sea, with a combined army of 40,000 men. The newly erected and impressive castle and the fortifications of the City of Derbent, built by the Sassanians, was the only entrance to the very fertile land of Aghvania which is modern day northern Azerbaijan. The combined army under Tong Yabghu, took Derbent and a terrible looting and destruction of the city went on for days. In this connection, the Armenian historian, Movses Kaghankatvatsi, who was an eye witness to these events writes the following:

> "Like waves in the sea, the Turks fell on the town of Chora (Derbent) and they destroyed it completely. Seeing the terrible threat posed by this vile, ugly horde of attackers with their slanting and lidless eyes, and their flowing hair like that of woman, the inhabitants were seized by terror...."

The fall of the fortress of Derbent, that had been considered by the inhabitants of the area as impregnable, sparked a general panic all over the country. The next objective of the Turkic-Khazar offensive was the kingdom of Georgia, whose ruler, Stephanos, was a tributary to the Sassanian emperors. Again, here the invaders encircled, besieged and conquered the Capital city of Tablisi. The city was looted and its citizens were massacred. The Persian governor of the city and the nobles of the Georgian ruling houses were tortured to death in the presence of Tong Yabghu. Shortly after these events, Heraclius and his army joined the army of Tong Yabghu. Here Heraclius personally met the Mongol leader, whose name in the Byzantine sources is mentioned as Ziebel.

In the meantime the situation for the Persian king became more dramatic, as Heraclius, who was well informed of what transpired within the Sassanian Camp, and had knowledge about the intrigues between the various powerful personalities in the court, masterfully exploited the situation.

Knowing of the tensions between the King Khosrow II and General Shahrbaraz, Heraclius managed to convince the general that his king has grown jealous of him, and that he had, in fact, intercepted a message from Khosrow II to the other generals, in which he had ordered the arrest and execution of General Shahrbaraz. As to what extent this intrigues had any factual foundation is a matter of further historical investigation. The result was that Heraclius, in so doing, succeeded in neutralizing this very capable army commander General Shahrbaraz.

In October of 627 AD, the Byzantines started an attack on the Persian troops in Mesopotamia where they defeated the Persian Army under General Rahzadh at the battle of Nineveh. Shortly after that, the Byzantine army turned south and destroyed Khosrow II's famous palace at Dastagird and was only prevented from attacking the capital city of Ctesiphon by the destruction of several bridges on the Nahrawan Canal. Khosrow II, having been betrayed by his important Paladins, Shahrbaraz and others, was overthrown by his eldest son Kavadh II, in 628 AD, who immediately started peace negotiations with the Byzantines.

On the night of February 25, 628 AD, with General Shahrbaraz already acting against the king, a group belonging to the Counsel of the Nobles ordered Khosrow II's eldest son, Khavadh II, who was previously imprisoned by his father, to be released, and proclaiming him as the new king. This Council of the Nobles were essentially the representatives of the seven ruling houses of the Empire.

The newly appointed King Khavadh II was in very bad health and close to death due to his long years in prison. The new king, in order to protect his infant son of seven years, Ardeshir, whom he wished to succeed him, immediately agreed to peace negotiation with the Byzantine's and, as a gesture of good will, sent (what was perceived at that time to be) the True Cross of Jesus Christ with a Priest negotiator to the camp of Heraclius, the Byzantine Emperor.

It is said, that the new king, Khavadh II [in Persian: Qobad Siroy], was a very cruel and ruthless person. Perhaps this was caused due to his long years of imprisonment by his father; or perhaps because his father had intended on appointing another son as his successor. Whatever the reason, upon gaining the throne, Khavadh II ordered the immediate arrest of his father, after which he orders all his brothers and half-brothers executed in his presence. He did this,in order that his own infant son would become King after him.

King Khosrow II had a favourite wife by the name of Myriam, a Christian with whom he a son by the name of Mardanshah, and the wish of Khosrow II was always to see *this* son succeed him.

Khavadh II had Mardanshah, his half brother brought into the prison and executed him in front of their father. King Khosrow II was subsequently also executed on February 28, 628 AD. These events were recorded by the Armenian bishop and historian Sebeos, and by the historian Tabari. Abu Ja'far Muhammad ibn Jarir al-Tabari was born in Amol, Tabaristan, a small city near the caspian sea. His main book as historian, was *Tarikh al-Rusul wa al-Muluk* [History of the Prophets and Kings].[240]

King Khavadh II died after ruling less than a year. His son, who was seven years old, succeeded him as the new king Ardashir III [Ardeshir lll -- in Greek: Artaxerxes III]. The seven-year-old heir was placed under the direction of a regent, Mir-Hasis once the chief purveyor of Khavadh II.

Eighteen months after the seven-year-old boy had become the new king as Ardeshir lll, he was murdered by orders of General Shahrbaraz on April 27, 629 AD. Shahrbaraz then declared himself to be the new king of kings of the Persian Empire. Shortly after taking over the Persian Throne, Shahrbaraz, in a gesture of good will to the

Byzantines, gave away vast territories previously belonging to the Persian Empire, to Heraclius. At this point, the Counsel of the Nobles of the Persian Empire was again convened and assembled, and on June 9, 629 AD, General Shahrbaraz was himself arrested and executed by the army commanders for grand treason to the Persian Empire. His body, in chains, was dragged through the dusty streets of Ctesiphon by horses. General Shahrbaraz, who had betrayed the Empire and murdered the seven-year-old king in order to became King himself, rules for only five weeks, from April 27 to June 9, 629 AD.

At this point, Purandokht the daughter of Khosrow II was chosen again by the Counsel of the Nobles from among many candidates as the most suitable person to wear the crown of the Empire. It was June 9, 629 AD, and the first time a woman became the ruling Queen of the Sassanian Persian Empire. The probable reason why she become the first woman to sit on the Persian Sassanian Empires throne, was the execution of all her brothers and half brothers by the former King Kavadh ll. She was the daughter of Khosrow II by Miriam and thus sister of Mardanshah, whom her father had seen executed in front of his own eyes. Her mother was the Christian woman Miriam, herself the eldest daughter of Maurice, the former Emperor of Byzantium. The new Queen Purandokht had a very difficult task, for the Empire was in a chaos. As the thirty-first Sassanian ruler, she could not save Zoroastrian Iran from the collapse that followed. In December 631 AD, Queen Purandokht signed a peace treaty with the Byzantines ending hostilities. Her reign lasted only sixteen months; she was, according to records, a good and a capable queen for the Persian Empire.

Queen Purandokht was deposed by a cousin who was then subsequently (and quickly) deposed by Purandokht's younger sister Azarmidokht, who in turn ruled less than a year.

Looking back at the events concerning the famed General Shahrbaraz, we can say that nothing can justify his betrayal of his king. It was an act that held dire consequences not only for the old

Persian Empire, but also for the Zoroastrian religion. It is very likely, had Shahrbaraz remained loyal and the country remained intact under Khosrow II, that the Sassanian Persian armies would have been in a much better position of repelling the Arab–Islamic invaders. Instead Khosrow II was demoralized by this betrayal, and as a consequence of this, and the chaos that followed, the leading powerful ruling Clans of the Empire withdraw their support from the king and plotted his downfall. This all is confirmed by Parvaneh Pourshariati in her successful book The Decline and Fall of the Sassanian Empire.[241] Contrary to this, Walter E. Kaegi in his book *Heraclius: Emperor of Byzantium* sympathizes with Shahrbaraz, calling the old king Khosrow II "suspicious, impatient and arrogant". Maybe all kings—and especially those under great pressure and responsibility—are and must be suspicious, impatient and arrogant. Perhaps, that is their prerogative.

7.7 THE START OF THE ARAB–PERSIAN HOSTILITIES

When western academics initially were investigating the Muslim conquest of Persia, they mostly relied on the accounts of the Armenian Christian Bishop Sebeos, and after that, the most significant work was that of Arthur Christiansen and his *L'Iran Sous les Sassanides*.[242] However recent investigations by Parvaneh Pourshariati[243] provide us with a detailed account of the problematic nature of the events of those days. According to Pourshariati, contrary to what was previously assumed, the Sassanian Empire was highly decentralized and was, in reality, a federation of local independent provinces ruled by powerful families in a dynastic way for centuries.

These powerful semi-independent members of the confederation, whose representative the Kings of the Sassanian dynasty were, unexpectedly withdrew from the confederation. Two Parthian provincial ruling families the kust-e-khwarasan and the kust-e-adurbadaghan withdrew to their respective strongholds and refused to fight under the banner of the Sassanian Kings. They were approaching the Muslim invader to make their own and separate peace agreements, and in so doing, weakening the Sassanians and the central government of the Empire.

The Arabs mounted three attacks against the Persian empire. The first came in 633 AD when General Khalid ibn al-Walid invaded the lands formerly known as the Lakhmid kingdom, in the southern Iraq of today. Following the transfer of general Khalid to the war of the Muslims against the Byzantine empire, the Muslims eventually lost their advances against the Iranians and the Iranian counterattack was successful. Parvaneh Pourshariati argues that the Arab conquest of Mesopotamia took place not as has been conveniently believed in during the years between 632 and 634 AD, after the accession of the last Sassanian King Yazdegerd III (632–651 AD), but much earlier in the year 628–632 AD.

The second Muslim invasion began in 636 AD, under Sa`d ibn Abi Waqqas when a key victory of the Arabs at the battle of Qadisiyyah made them the permanent masters of the western part of Iran. At this time, the Zagros mountains became the natural borderline between the Rashidun Caliphate and the Sassanian Empire, this was in 642 AD.

The third and final invasion into Persia was directed by the Caliph Omar personally from Medina in a series of well co-ordinated attacks against the Sassanian positions. These attacks were successful, and that was the final end of the Sassanian Zoroastrian Empire and the beginning of the total domination of Iran by the Islamic conquerors. This great triumph, which occurred in 644 AD, contributed to the reputation of Omar as a great military and political strategist.

The last Sassanian King was Yazdegerd III, who came to the throne on June 16, 632 AD. It is believed that Yazdegerd III's older daughter, Shahrbanu, was the wife of Hussein ibn Ali, the revered son of Imam Ali of the Shias. Yazdegerd III's second daughter, Yazdandad, was married to the Jewish Exillarch Bustanai ben Haninai. Furthermore, the Bahai religions founder, Baha ullah, (his real name was Mirza Hossein Ali Nouri 1818–1892 AD) who was living and died in today's Haifa, traces his own line back to Yazdegerd III's third daughter. The Sassanian Dynasty ended with the death of King Yazdegerd III at the age of twenty-seven in 651 AD.

By 651 AD, most of the cities and provinces of Iran were in the hands of the Arab conquerors with the only exception of the provinces south of the Caspian Sea and Transoxiana. Many cities in Iran, at a later date, staged various revolts and defence against the invaders, but in the end without any great success. Even after the Arabs had subdued the country, in many cities, the people rebelled, killing the Arab governors and attacking the Arab soldiers, but the Caliphs sent, from the Arabian peninsula, reinforcements and these rebellions were put down and the Islamic rule was ultimately imposed.

After the Arab conquest of the Persian countryside and the cities, the main target of the Arab invaders was to destroy all libraries and records of previous history. It is a historical fact that, according to orders, in cities like Herat and Bokhara and in Eastern Iran, for months, bath houses were lit and fired with books that contained historical records of ancient Iran. The most important aim of the Arab invaders was to prohibit the Persians from continuing to speak their own ancient language. Every Persian had to learn Arabic and the punishment for speaking Persian was death. It is said that, were it not for Ferdowsi and his famous book Shahnameh, which is written in the old Persian, the Persians of today would speak Arabic and would have lost their identity and culture—but that again is another story.

8. THE ZOROASTRIAN PRIEST SALMAN FARSI AND THE EMERGENCE OF ISLAM

In writing this chapter, it is not our intention to enter into the history or the ideology of the Islamic religion, nor is it the aim of this book to comment in the least about the life of the Holy Prophet Mohammed. The aim of this chapter is to investigate the life and personality of Salman al-Farsi, or Salman the Persian, in connection to his identity and his roots, having been born as a Zoroastrian and having become a priest of that religion in his early years. Following his life up to that point, as we will see, he became a close friend and advisor to the Prophet Mohammed and it is believed that he exerted a considerable, if not decisive, influenced upon the formation of the new world religion later called Islam. The knowledge of Salman's destiny is not only relevant to the end of the Zoroastrian era in the Persian and Middle Eastern world, but as we will see, his considerable influence in the forming of the new religion of Islam must be seen in context of a disillusioned Zoroastrian priest, who was seeking new way to reform the religion he knew, namely Zoroastrianism.

Salman al-Farsi is undoubtedly one of the most obscure historical personalities, and his importance in the history of the Middle East has been grossly under estimated, as has his influence upon the emergence of the Islamic religion. It could be said that traditional Muslim scholars and historians have purposely ignored the personality of Salman Farsi. There are only a handful of sources available about him, predominantly by three separate interest groups, these include Muslim commentators, Iranian Nationalists, and Zoroastrians. Each one has sought to highlight its unique portrayal of Salman al-Farsi, and accordingly there are a handful of publications by each one of these groups. These publications try to shed some light upon this personality, but their proclamations and assertions tend to obfuscate rather than illuminate. The more copious and the great majority of these publications belong to conservative and ideologically committed Islamic Shiite sources, whose viewpoints are religiously conservative and thus effectively ahistorical. Salman al-Farsi in Iranian Muslim Shiite publications is generally referred to as the Hazrat-e Salman-e Farsi, meaning the Saint Salman Farsi.

Those who are familiar with the history of the Middle East are often struck by the exceptional successes of the Arab armies, under the banner of Islam, in conquering a vast empire in a short period of time. This conquest was made possible after the weakening and the subsequent fall of the Byzantine and the Sassanian Empires, who had fought each other for decades. The fall of the Sassanian Persia was a key factor in the Arab victory and the establishment of Islam as the major world religion. Prior to their success as conquerers, the Arabs were never a major player in the history of the Middle East. From early antiquity, they were dominated and often controlled by major external powers such as the Egyptian Pharaonic Empire, the Roman Empire, the Persian Empire, and the Byzantine Empire—later the Ottoman Empire, the British Empire, and finally the American foreign policy interested priorities.

In the following, whilst examining the events leading up to the fall of the Sassanian Persia to the Muslims, it will become clear that a Persian young man, the only son of a well-to-do landowner family, and an ex-Zoroastrian priest by the name of Rouzbeh Marzban, later called by the Prophet Mohammad *Salman Farsi* [Salman the Persian], played an important part, not only in the conquest of Persia by the Arabs, but also in the emergence of the Islamic religion.

According to the traditional Islamic historiography, Salman belonged to the innermost circle of the companions and friends of the Prophet, and the Prophet considered him a member of his own household.

In looking at the life of Salman Farsi, we encounter many conflicting reports; the date of his death has been especially debated among Muslim Scholars. Therefore, if we take everything into consideration—and if we accept only those facts which are common and acceptable to all parties involved, namely the committed Islamists, the Iranian nationalists, the Zoroastrian traditionalists, and the secular historians—the following picture of his life emerges.

Salman al-Farsi was born in Persia in the year 568 AD in a village called Jiyye, which was a suburb of the ancient city of Ispahan. Islamic and Arab sources indicate that he was, in fact, his father's only child. His father was a rich Zoroastrian feudal landowner—he had peasants working for him—with good connections to the Zoroastrian religious and political establishment. Salman's Iranian name was Rouzbeh Marzban; and later on his name was changed, in Mecca, to Salman the Persian by the Prophet himself, hence in Arabic Salman al-Farsi. Some Islamic accounts state that Salman's father was a Zoroastrian priest, and as priesthood was a hereditary office in Zoroastrian societies, Salman himself was introduced into the teachings of Zoroastrianism and was later appointed as a priest. If his father had not been a priest before him, it would have been impossible for the young Salman Farsi to become a priest himself. Even today, in the Zoroastrian communities around the world, the noted hereditary tradition and condition for Zoroastrian priesthood continues.

At the age of sixteen, therefore, he had been introduced to the ideologies of the Zoroastrian religion, and was prepared for the priesthood. In the Zoroastrian faith, young men are appointed at a very early age for priesthood, and even that practice and tradition among Zoroastrians continues to this date. By the age of twenty, four years after beginning his training in the Zoroastrian religion, he was appointed as a Zoroastrian priest. At this point the conservative Islamic sources note that:

> Salman showed interest and curiosity concerning the Christian religion, this was probably because of the singing and the music that had been prevalent in Christian churches, which he visited out of curiosity..."[244]

It is documented that, in and around Ispahan at that time, there were numerous villages and settlements populated by Jewish communities. Ispahan itself, which at that time was called Sepahan, had begun as an army garrison with military fortifications. Concerning the Christian presence in that city at that time, nothing is known. If they did exist and Christians lived there, they most likely were Nestorians—a sect deemed heretical for their belief in the discrete dual nature of Jesus.

In an important article on the Jews in Persia of that period it is argue that Salman Farsi was the younger brother of the Jewish Exilarch Nehemiah ben Hushiel and that his real name was Shallum. The brother of the same Nehemiah ben Hushiel, who was the commander of the Jewish Army, and was involved in the conquest of Jerusalem in 614 AD. Although the village of Jiyye was also populated by Jews at that time, it is very unlikely that Salman Farsi was Jewish himself, for the following two reasons. Firstly, he became a Zoroastrian priest at the age of sixteen, and secondly, as will be discussed later, he is sold as a slave to Jewish landowners. It is unlikely that Jews buy as slaves other young Jewish men, for this is considered a transgression of the Laws of Torah. Nevertheless, this prouves that Salman Farsi was later a known personality in the Jewish community.[245]

The French Catholic and religious writer Louis Massignon (1883–1962) has called him *Salman-i Pak* [Pâk in Persian meaning *clean, pure* or *innocent*] which also tries to shed some light into the life of Salman Farsi, and it was also he who mentions that Salman's family name was, in fact, Marzban—therefore, Rouzbeh Marzban.[246]

Returning to Salman Farsi, in a book published in the city of Qum in Iran, the Shi'a Muslim scholar Syed A.A. Razwy states that Salman-Farsi "…went into a Christian church, renounced his Zoroastrian faith, and was immediately converted into Christianity." This statement, which reflects the belief of the traditionalist Islamic camp, seems to be an unrealistic and probably an exaggerated account. The Christians of that region and of that time were Nestorians, which was a dyophysite sect regarded as being heretical by the then mainstream Greek (Byzantine) Orthodox church. According to Razwy's book:

> Salman, as he converted into Christianity, had to leave immediately and at night, against the will and the knowledge of his father, his city and his country and never to return….[247]

To suggest that Salman was obliged to suddenly leave his country just because he became a Christian does not seem to be convincing, for the Christian community enjoyed the protection and the respect of the authorities of the Sassanian Empire. Nevertheless, a point which all the parties seem to accept is that, by the age of around twenty, Salman Farsi, against the will of his father, left suddenly his home and his city, and went alone with a caravan to the city of Damascus in Syria. The different accounts on Salman Farsi agree that he left the house of his family and his hometown, against the will of his father and after a quarrel, albeit the details and the reasons for his quarrel will probably never be known. It is clear, however, that this difference of opinion between Salman and his father, and the reason he had to leave his country so suddenly and never to return, was of utmost importance.

All accounts and historians agree, as we will see later, that Salman did, in fact, return at the end of his life to Iran as the adviser to the commander in chief of the Arab–Islamic Armies. Similarly, all accounts agree that, after leaving his hometown, he lived in a monastery as a Christian monk near Damascus for approximately ten years, meaning after his conversion into Christianity. Monasticism and living in monasteries at that time, were often the ways in which man, who wanted to disappear from public life hid. In ancient times there was no place better than a Christian monastery for one to live anonymously, under a new name, and without consideration of their past. Thus Salman spent approximately ten years, until the year 598 AD, living near the city of Damascus in a monastery as a Christian monk. This point is also agreeable to all parties.

At this point it is necessary to digress and focus upon the self-proclaimed Prophet Mazdak, whose ideology was an offshoot of the Zoroastrian religion, and whose teachings are considered to be a uniquely radical egalitarian economical and agricultural ideology. Mazdak's religion gained popularity during the early sixth century in Iran, but he, along with his followers, were arrested and executed by the Sassanian authorities in 528 AD.

As was discussed extensively in the previous chapters, Mazdak's teachings as a social reformer were later greeted with hostilities by the Sassanian establishment and the ruling regime of the time. This new economic and social ideology, which Mazdak labelled reformed Zoroastrianism, is often regarded as extreme left or an Iranian proto-Communist ideology with respect to economic, and private property.[248] The important point here is that, due to pressures from the great feudal and landowning families, this sect was later forbidden by the Sassanid Regime, and all its followers together with those who sympathized with this new ideology were severely persecuted. Even the suspicion of being a sympathizer was sufficient to be executed or banished and send away to far away places in deserts and inhospitable regions for life. At that period of the Iranian-Sassanian history, social tensions had driven many young idealists and intellectuals into the camp of the left-wing Mazdakite ideology.

If Salman Farsi, as a young man, was indeed a follower or at least a sympathizer of this new Mazdakite sect, which is very likely, then this may explain his sudden decision to leave his hometown, never to return while the existing regime was in power. And also the difference in opinion that he had with his father before leaving the country would look more logical.[249, 250] Mazdak and his teachings propagated, as the core of his economical teachings, a radical agricultural land reform, meaning that all agricultural lands belonging to the landowning priest-class had to be taken away from their owners and redistributed freely among the workers and peasants who work on this land. In general his ideology was considered to be a radical egalitarian economical movement, and after his death in 528 AD, his political and economical ideas, which as an ultimate consequence planned by him, would have included the elimination of all private property, remained very popular for centuries among the poor and working class population of the empire. After Mazdak's death, the masses of poor farmers and workers were also joined by idealistic young people from the upper classes, and formed a left wing oriented political movement.

Several years after the death of Mazdak himself, the Sassanian King of Kings Anushiravan Adel (Khosrow I) started wide-ranging agricultural reforms in order to defuse the dangerous class inequality in the nation's society. At the same time, all the followers of Mazdak's movement and their sympathizers were identified and severely punished by the Sassanian governmental authorities. People who were suspected to be sympathizers of this movement were arrested and severely prosecuted; therefore, a large number of young people had to leave the country and to go in exile. Salman himself was born 568 AD, and at the time of his youth; the Mazdakite movement was in full bloom. Mazdak himself had died 528 AD, approximately one generation before Salman's birth.

It is, therefore, reasonable to suspect that the young idealistic Rouzbeh Marzban (Salman Farsi) was probably involved in some kind of political or ideological movement related to Mazdakism. If so, then this forced him to leave his country at once, not to return while the present regime was in power. He was at odds with his father, who was a member of the Zoroastrian priest clan and a feudal landlord— exactly the group of people targeted by the Prophet Mazdak as being the oppressors of the farmers and working class population. Salman himself was also young enough, at the age of twenty, not to realize the consequences of his ideological actions for his own future and the reputation and the existence of his father and his own family.

There is also another detail, which would indicate that the involvement of young Rouzbeh/Salman obliged him to leave the country so abruptly. If Salman was, in fact, his father's only child, as Syed A.A. Razwy writes in his book, then there must have been a very urgent reason for him to leave his family and home. A father would not let his only child leave the country and never come back without a compelling reason—such an imminent danger to the life of his son and or himself. For a feudal landowner the loss of his son and heir this was of the greatest emotional importance. In other words the disagreement between them must have been severe.

As of this moment there are not enough historical documentation, to prove the connection of Salman Farsi with the Mazdakite movement of that period, but circumstantial evidence points in this direction.

Returning to Salman Farsi, after approximately ten years living as a monk in Damascus, the records become unclear. Now the Islamic scholar Syed A.A. Razwy mentions that he left Damascus and lived, as a Christian, in three different cities in Southern Iraq, Mosul, Nasibin and Ammuria. It is nevertheless clear, that he traveled in the middle East without returning home, but the length of his stay in these three cities, which at the time were under the influence of the

Byzantine empire is not clear. What is certain is that probably at the age of thirty- or thirty two or earlier, (circa 600 to 603 AD) he decided to return again to Damascus, with the intention of travelling south. It is known that all caravans going to the south or the north were all assembled and started from this city. Having returned to Damascus, he met some people from the Makhzoom clan, a part of the greater tribe of Quraysh from Makkah. We know that these clans all made their living by trading goods between Makkah and Yathrib in the south and Damascus in the north. After having reached Damascus, Salman asked the Arab caravan leaders whether he could join them heading south to Yathrib (modern-day Medina). With Salman joining them, the caravan set foot toward Yathrib. A few days later the caravan arrived at an oasis by the name of Wadi-ul-Qura in the Hijaz.

The caravan leaders announced that they would stop here for several days and ordered the travellers to unload their baggage in order for the animals to rest and to take food and water before the continuation of the journey to the city of Yathrib.

It is at this point that Salman was apprehended by the caravan leaders and put in chains. They saw him alone and unprotected, not belonging to any clan or group which could give him protection. Then they sold Salman as a slave to a Jewish merchant, and the caravan left for Yathrib without him. Also this point is acceptable to all parties.

At this point we must mention that Salman could not have been any more than thirty to thirty-two years of age, for it is said that the Jewish masters bought him with the intention of putting him to agricultural labor in date farms. At that time a man of more than thirty-five was no longer young or strong enough to work for hard labor. Furthermore, if Salman was indeed a Jew, his new Jewish master—having heard Salman's outcry and statements saying that he is not a slave but a free man and a Jew—would probably not have bought him, but would have even liberated or helped him.

Eventually Salman was, in fact, brought to Yathrib by his master. There he was again sold to another Jewish wealthy land owner by the name of Uthman ben Ashhel from the Banu Qurayzah clan. This man had, in Yathrib, a big agricultural farm and was cultivating dates. It is unknown exactly how many years Salman lived as a slave of his new master, but it is clear that he was soon elevated to the position of personal servant to the Jewish family thus joining the household where he learned not only to speak but also to read and write Hebrew. This point again is also acceptable by all parties.

After years having lived in the household of Uthman ben Ashhel, Salman was not only familiar with the customs and way of life of the Jews, but started to become knowledgeable about their religious customs and beliefs, and importantly having also gained knowledge into the holy Jewish scriptures and religious writings. Also, this point is acceptable by all parties.

At this point we have to mention that, in the Middle East, in ancient times—and even today—people of different religious beliefs were living in completely separated communities. According to ancient Middle Eastern tradition, which is still valid today, matters of religion and identity are kept absolutely separate and private in the communities. As there were no means of mass communication or even printed books, matters of religion and customs of the different communities were kept very confidential and practised behind closed doors. Christians or Jews, if they had in their household their own religious books, they were handwritten and kept in a secure place, away from strangers. People of different religious groups lived separated from each other behind big walls. They could see each other in public, but would never mention matters of religion or identity to an outsider or a person from another faith or community. That was as valid in ancient times as it is today in the Middle East. Mostly religious communities had their own separate quarters where they lived together, separated from other religious groups. This was the case in the Middle East until the beginning of the twentieth century.

Therefore, an individual's knowledge of the religious dogmas, beliefs and practices of another group were limited to the point of being almost non-existent. This often gave way to wild rumours and malicious creations, which were the roots of centuries-old animosities between the different religious communities.

Returning to Rouzbeh Marzban, we see here that he was in a stage in his life where, according to his own mind, he had made all experiences he needed and had learned all he wanted to learn—and he had arrived there by a unique path. Born and raised as a Zoroastrian he was, based on his family, inducted into the priesthood; converting to Christianity, he then spent many years as a Christian monk, only to end up, through misadventure, in a Jewish household as a servant.

If we look at the past destiny of this man, it would be logical to conclude that Rouzbeh Marzban came, at that stage of his life in his own mind, to a point where he drew a big line under his past and decided to look into the future. He was working hard pysically, but his mind was at ease. Here, if we reconstruct his state of mind, we could say that, as a man of multiple experiences and knowledge, he concluded that it was time to combine all the data gained in his life, to take all information, and with it to form a new ideology for a new world religion or world order—at least that was probably his dream. He had to take action and to put into reality all he had learned and experienced in his adventurous life so far.

We have to accept this as logical consequence in the life of this man and recognize here that, had Rouzbeh not been a determined and energetic idealist, but at least a courageous adventurer, before taking the caravan south to the Arabian Peninsula, he would have just returned home where a good life and a family and position would have waited for him, as after his friend Mohammad had purchased him as a slave from his master after fifteen years and set him free. Very likely all old accusations or pending political matters would have been mostly forgotten by this yime. This would have been especially true after so many years, for his father had probably passed away, and he would be the heir and the new master of his estate.

The argument of the Islamist camp—namely that Rouzbeh took the caravan from Damascus to Yathrib (Medina) because he had heard about the coming of the new Prophet Mohammad and his teachings and wanted to meet him—cannot be valid. The Prophet Mohammad became known only after he started to preach of the first supernatural visions revealing him as the Prophet. This events historically started in the year 610 AD—and Rouzbeh was already seven years a slave in Yathrib at that point. The pertinent question here is when did the Prophet and Rouzbeh actually meet. This date is unknown to us, but what is known and well documented is the fact that the Prophet Mohammad and Rouzbeh actually met and became very close friends. This fact is also acceptable by all parties.

It is furthermore accepted that eventually Mohammad, who had been friendly with Rouzbeh for some time, paid his master and owner in order to buy him as a slave and gave him his freedom, this was actualy well before Mohammad declared to be the Messenger of God.

From the moment Salman Farsi, as the Prophet Mohammad called him, became a free man, he was a well respected member of the Prophet's inner circle and a close adviser to him. Salman was just a few years older than the Prophet; he had learned and personally experienced a great deal about monotheism from the different religious perspectives. It is safe to assume that he had long reflected about what had to be changed and done differently, and how to correct the different religious systems he knew. All was prepared and ready in his mind to start a new ideology, suitable for the new age and the new environment in which he was living.

Three historical episodes clearly show that Salman Farsi and the Prophet Mohammad were, in fact, not only close friends prior to the start of the Islamic movement—or the first Ajiaat or supernatural messages he received—but also that the personal knowledge and advice of Salman was asked for, welcomed, and accepted by the Prophet.

The first historical episode occurred in 627 AD when Yathrib (soon to be Medina) was still the capital of Islam. A group of Arabs from Makkah, with a cavalry and infantry of ten thousand men, were threatening to attack the city. There plan was to hit the positions of the Prophet in an coordinated hit and run strategy, thus obliterating the new Islamic movement in one massive attack. Here Salman approached the Prophet and proposed that a trench should be dug around the fortifications of the city. This proposition was accepted at once by the Prophet, and he gave orders, so that the trench could be dug, which proved to be strategically important. The enemy cavalry was immobilized. It proved, that the trench was too deep for the horses to leap over, and the attack was repelled. After the death of the leader of the invaders, Amr ibn Abd Wudd, their front fell apart. This was finally a great victory for the Prophet.

The British Lt. General Sir John Glubb, (1897–1986), one of the architects of the British colonial policy in the Middle East, who at the same time was also an expert on Arab history, writes:

> The Arabs had no experience in siege warfare, as Bedouins they were only knowledgable to the strategy, called the hit and run in the general desert war and hostilities. The only mode of fighting with which they had familiarity was the hit and run system, which in Arabic is called *karr-o-farr* and which means attack and run, and that is the only way the Arabs fought. They attacked the enemy and then they run, before the later had time to recover from the surprise.... And in this case it was the hope of the Mekkan military leaders, that this would be also the strategy, with which they would be able to conquer the city of Medina ...But it was for the presence of a foreigner, who was Salman the Persian, who worked out a strategy of his own, and his counter strategy foiled the Mekkan strategy...

He was knowledgable of the siege operations in warfare between the Persian and the East Roman Empire in their long-lasting and historical wars against each other, and he had the ability to make his own scientific conclusions and observations from it...

This trench warfare was a new and unfamiliar strategy for the Arabs, but the Prophet Mohammad recognized immediately its significance and ordered its application...[251]

Furthermore, Muhammad Husayn Haikal (1888–1956), an Egyptian historian, writer and Minister of Education writes:

Salman el Farsi had more knowledge of the techniques of warfare than anyone else in the Arabic Peninsula. It was he who advised the digging of a trench around Medina and the fortification of the buildings within. Upon this, under the orders of the Prophet, the Muslims hurried to implement this advice....[252]

Another point we have to investigate here concerning this historical episode is how a man who was a non-Arab (and therefore is looked on by Arabs suspiciously) and a former freed slave no less, can have so close access to the Prophet himself and the commander-in-chief of the defending armies, in the first place. Furthermore, how he might propose something to the commander-in-chief and the Prophet that was recognized as being of great strategic importance, and have it accepted and implemented right away. Freed slaves were still regarded as slaves, and their social status was, at the most, that of a servant or a foot soldier.

Another historical note is, when the trench was dug, one of the followers of the Prophet, who was from Mekkah, said, "Salman is one of
us, he is a muhajir, he is an immigrant."

Hearing this, one of them, who was from Medina, said, "No he is
one of us, he is an Ansar."

After long discussions, the Prophet arrived and put an end to this
discussion, by declaring, "He, Salman, is neither a muhajir nor an
Ansar. He is one of the people of my house. He is one of us."

This was regarded as a great honour, to be elevated and to belong
to the household of the Prophet himself. It is said that practically
nobody, in the entire history of Islam, has ever been elevated and honoured by the prophet as much as Rouzbeh called Salman Farsi.

Additionally, the Islamic historian Al Bukhari reports that
the Prophet's favourite wife, Aisha, said that the Prophet spends
so many hours with Salman Farsi discussing details of religious
issues, that Salman many times had to sleep overnight in the
Prophet's house.

Furthermore, we have the documentation of Muhammad al-
Tabari, who in his "The history of al-Tabari writes:

> Salman's pension was 5,000 dirhams a year, and he
> was appointed over 30,000 men...[253]

> The Prophet said, "God has ordered me to love four
> people." The Prophet was asked "Who are they, tell
> us their names." He said, "Ali is one of them" He
> said that three times, "and Abu Dharr and Al Miqdad
> and Salman. God has ordered me to love them, and
> told me that he loves them."[254]

The question is what did Salman do to merit such honour and
friendship from the Prophet. The answer to this important question
is probably that Salman, and only he, had knowledge of certain things

that were important to the Prophet Mohammad, and the Prophet knew it.

We have seen previously, that matters of religion were not common and public knowledge for people from other religious groups. Also, we know from the Koran that the Prophet was not capable of reading and writing. It is clearly mentioned in Sura 7:157 which says:

> Those who follow the messenger, the Prophet, who can neither read nor write, whom they will find described in the Torah and the Gospel which are with them...

The fact that the Prophet was unable to read and write was, in itself, nothing unusual or negative, for only a certain group of scribes and record holders were, in the Arabic Peninsula, taught the art of writing and reading. Therefore, how did the Prophet gain detailed knowledge concerning the traditions and the world view of the existing monotheistic religions. In those times, apart from the fact that no means of mass communication existed, all religious books were handwritten and strictly guarded by only the members of that particular religious community. These sacred and handwritten documents were not accessible to the general public or the members of other faiths, which were, at the same time, the members of other communities. In general, the members of the different communities, such as the Jewish and Christian groups, and also the pagan worshipping Arabs, were rather hostile and reserved to each other, and were hiding their way of life and their faith from each other. Therefore, the knowledge of the religious details of the other communities was extremely limited.

All this point to a close friendship between the Prophet Mohammad and Salman Farsi from the time when Salman was still working for his Jewish master. It is obvious that Salman shared many experiences and knowledge of the various religions he had accumulated in his lifetime with the man who would later became the Prophet Mohammad.

There were probably other sources where the Prophet could have gained some limited knowledge about the world of the monotheistic religions. It is said that Mohamed has visited on, several occasions, Damascus where he would stay overnight at the house of a Jewish carpenter. Another possible source could be a Persian by the name of Jabr, who lived in Makkah.

Another point, which could be of a fundamental importance, not only to the relationship between Salman and the Prophet, but to the general worldview of the Islamic faith towards the world of Christianity in general, is the fact that, in the Islamic terminology, Jesus Christ is regarded as a Prophet and a Messenger of God, the same as the Prophet Mohammad himself. In general, in the Islamic scriptures, Jesus Christ is mentioned always as Isa (Jesus) the son of Mary. Whereas, in the Christian ideology, Jesus Christ is not a Messenger of God, but believed to be the son of God. He is not a messenger but a part of the Holy Trinity—The Father, The Son, and The Holy Ghost. This means that, if Jesus Christ was the son of the creator God, then he too was a God.

The Quran states that, "Isa was created from the act of God's will." Clearly the Quran compares this miraculous creation of Jesus Christ with the creation of Adam by his act of will. In any place when Jesus is mentioned, he is referred to as the son of Mary, but *not* the son of God. In the Quran sura 5 (Al Ma-ida) ayat 46–47 it says clearly the following:

> And in their footsteps We send Isa the son of Maryam, confirming the law that had come before him. We send him the Gospel; therein was guidance and light

In using the phrase *we send* in the Quran, it is evident, that Jesus was send by God as a messenger—rather than being a God himself.

In order to investigate this ideological difference, we have to look in to the historical beginnings of the Christian religion. It was the Roman Emperor Constantine the Great (272–337 AD) who declared the Christian religion to be the official religion of the Roman Empire. Having constituted the Christian religion as the only religion of the Roman Empire, it was necessary to eliminate the different ideological beliefs of that religion, and to create one uniform religious dogma.

For this reason, in 325 AD, the Emperor called for a council of Christian bishops and religious leaders to convene in Nicaea (a modern-day suburb of Istanbul). At the Council of Nicaea, the different ideological directions of the Christian faith were investigated, united, and brought into one main religious belief. It was here too that the Bible was compiled in its final form.

At the council of Nicaea there were two main Christian ideological camps, which were at odds with each other. One camp comprised the majority of the delegates and believed that Jesus Christ was the son of God and was a God himself insofar as he was part of the Holy trinity: The Father, The Son, and the Holy Spirit. The second camp was lead by a man named Arius (250–336 AD), a Libyan by descent who later became the Bishop of Nicomedia. This group were of the opinion that Jesus Christ was not equal to the creator God himself, but was subordinate to him. This ideology was later called Arianism after its leader, and the centre of this belief was Alexandria in Egypt, as Arius later became the presbyter of the Christian church in Alexandria.

Subsequently the Arianists were declared to be heretics, and the direction of their belief was rejected by the council of Nicaea. The Arianists were later ousted from Alexandria and went to Assyria, where they survived for some time in monastic enclaves in Damascus, until they were ideologically extinct and forgotten some centuries later. It can be said that the Islamic view of the nature of Jesus Christ is close to Arianism, for the Quran does not mentioning Jesus as being the son of God the Father, but only Jesus (Isa) the son of Mary. On the subject of Arianism, *The Catholic Encyclopedia* writes:

> Not, therefore, to Egypt and its mystical teach-
> ings, but to Syria, ...should we look for the home

of an aberration, which had its finally triumphed, would have anticipated Islam, reducing the Eternal Son to the rank of a Prophet, and thus undoing the Christian revelation....

Interestingly this ideological direction, concerning the Islamic view of Jesus Christ seems to have originated in Syria, where Salman Farsi was, for ten years, living in a Christian Monastery as a monk. Therefore, it is logical to assume that Salman had been exposed to the ideas of Arianism during that time and would probably have introduced these point of views to the Prophet Mohammad and from there, ultimately, into the Quran.

Logically if the Prophet Mohammad should have received his information concerning Jesus Christ from other independent sources, he would have been exposed to the official Catholic ideological doctrine of the "Holy Trinity" where Jesus is the son of God and a God himself, which was and is still valid today.

8.1 SALMAN FARSI AND THE STORY OF THE BIBLICAL JOSEPH

An episode which has come to us from the Holy Jewish scriptures, the Torah, is the story of "Joseph and the twelve sons of the Patriarch Jacob." This story can be called a key factor in the life of this former Zoroastrian priest Salman Farsi, and the key to the enigma of all his future actions and motivations.

Salman had come across the story of Joseph in the Old Testament, when he was living as a Christian Monk in a Monastery in Damascus, and later heard this story again in the household of his master, the Jewish landowner. The story of Jacob, the grandson of the Prophet Abraham and his son Joseph, as depicted originally in the Torah, is as follows:

According to the Torah, Jacob was the son of Isaac and Rebekah, and the grandson of the Prophet Abraham. Jacob had, by various woman, twelve sons, who later were known to be the fathers of the twelve tribes of Israel. The name of the twelve sons of Jacob were: Reuben, Simeon, Levi, Judah, Dan, Naphtali, Gad, Asher, Issachar, Zebulun, Joseph, and Benjamin. Jacob had also a daughter by the name of Dinah.

In the Torah, the book of Genesis informs us that Joseph was the eleventh son of Jacob and the first born of his mother Rachel. He was sold into slavery by his brothers who were jealous of him because his father Jacob (who is also called Israel) loved him more than his other sons. After he was sold as a slave to Egypt, and following various events there, he rose later in his life to become the most power-ful man in the Egyptian Pharaonic Empire after the Pharaoh himself.

A detail of the story is that Joseph, after having been sold into slavery to Egypt, came to become a servant in the house of Potiphar, the Captain of the guards of the Pharaoh. After some time, Joseph was promoted by Potiphar, to become the head administrator of his household. Potiphar's wife, Zulaykah, who was older than Joseph, started to develop a desire for him and tried to convince Joseph to have an affair with her. Although Zulaykah was very persistent, Joseph refused to touch her, fearing to sinning against God, and because of his loyalty to his master Potiphar. After days of struggle, she grabbed him by his cloak, but he escaped from her by leaving behind his garment. Angered by his refusal, Zulaykah took his garment and falsely accused Joseph, to her husband, of trying to rape her, upon which Joseph was arrested and put into prison.[255]

In prison, Joseph met the Pharaoh's chief cupbearer and chief baker, both of whom had offended the Pharaoh. One day, both of these men had dreams, and they asked Joseph to help them interpreting the meaning of their dreams. The chief cupbearer dreamt he was holding a vine of grapes in his hand and he brought them to the Pharaoh and put them in his cup. The chief baker had three baskets of bread which he was carrying for the Pharaoh, but some birds came and ate all the bread. The interpretation of these dreams by Joseph was that within three days the chief cupbearer would be re-instated with honours, but the chief baker would be executed. That is exactly what happened to both of them. Upon this, Joseph asked the cupbearer to mention his fate to the Pharaoh himself and try to secure his release from the prison. After the cupbearer's release, he forgot about Joseph's request and Joseph had to stay and suffer another two more years in prison.

One day the Pharaoh himself had two dreams, which were very disturbing to him. He dreamt that seven thin cows rose out of the river and attacked and ate seven fat cows, and of seven lean ears of grain which devoured seven fat ears. Hereupon the Pharaoh immediately called his wise men and asked them to interpret these dreams, but at this point the chief cupbearer remembering Joseph's plea and spoke to the Pharaoh about Joseph and his skills.

At the Pharaoh's orders, Joseph was immediately called and his interpretation of Pharaoh's dreams were that in the coming period his empire would, after having passed seven years of abundance of food, would be followed by seven years of famine and hunger. Joseph recommended that the Pharaoh immediately store all surplus grain, during the years of abundance and keep them for the next seven years of famine and hunger.

The Pharaoh acknowledged that Joseph's advice to store all grain possible during the years of abundance was very wise and decided to follow it. The story continues, that Joseph, before having reached the age of thirty years, had been released from the prison by the Pharaoh and put in charge of overseeing the Pharaohs program to store grain for the years of famine and hunger. And so it happened that, after the passing of the seven fat years, the seven famine and hunger years came and they were so severe that from all around the Middle East people flocked to Egypt, in order not to live in starvation.

In Egypt itself, poverty struck the land population and, less the priestly class themselves, all the others sold their properties just in order to buy grain seed from Joseph. Joseph also decreed a regulation that, by harvesting seed on government property, twenty percent of all crops harvested will belong to the Pharaoh. This tradition of one fifth of the produce of everything harvested going to the Pharaoh continued down to the days of Moses himself. This is clearly marked in the book of Genesis (47:20–31).

In the second year of the famous famine, at a time when Joseph had reached a very high position in the Pharaonic government, Joseph's half brothers were sent to Egypt by their father, Jacob. When they came to Egypt and they stood before the minister of the Pharaoh, they did not recognize him to be their half-brother Joseph. Joseph, however, recognized them, and did not receive them kindly, and spoke to them not in Hebrew, but in the Egyptian language using an interpreter.

Finally Joseph revealed himself to his half-brothers and explained to them his real life story. At a later date, his father Jacob, in order to see his son Joseph, came in the next voyage to Egypt, and after having seen his son, died in Egypt. Joseph brought him back and buried him in the land of his ancestors, in the Tombs of the Patriarchs. Joseph herewith redeemed himself and showed himself worthy of his father and triumphed in front of his brothers.

The story ends with Joseph being able to save his brothers and his entire family, and his clan. He had been sold into slavery by them as an innocent man and had to suffer without having committed any crimes, becoming a slave and powerless in a foreign land, abandoned and all alone among strangers. It was only the power of his mind and his knowledge of the world that enabled him, in the end, to save and to redeem himself. Fate had determined his destiny and, in the end, he was vindicated and triumphed in front of his people, by all to be seen.

We see here, very clearly, that Salman Farsi must have identified himself with Joseph. He had heard about this story, which is written in the Torah, in the house of his Jewish master. It is clear that there exists great parallels between the destiny of Salman Farsi and those of the mythological Joseph. In the imagination of Salman, the fate of Joseph was his own fate, and the way Joseph went to reinvent himself and to save himself through the power of his mind and his knowledge only, was the way he, Salman Farsi, had to act. He had to imitate Joseph and to do the same thing he did. Clearly, Joseph was his hero, the man he admired.

We will see later that, at the end of his life, just as Joseph had redeemed himself in front of his own people, also Salman would return to Persia in order—he imagined—to redeem himself in front of his countryman and his father.

At this point, if we want to assess the degree of influence that Salman Farsi had on the mind of the Prophet, and get a clear indication as to the extent of Mohammad's knowledge of the monotheistic religions and their scriptures that depended on Salman, we have to look more closely at the personal opinion that the Prophet of Islam had towards the biblical Joseph.

The Prophet Mohammad, after having met Salman, starts to become a great admirer of Joseph and his father Jacob [in Arabic: Yusuf and Yaqub]. In a hadith (historical episode) narrated by one of the Prophet's companions, Abu Huraira, it says clearly:

> Some people asked the Prophet, "Who is the most honorable amongst the people?" He replied, "The most honorable among them is the one who is the most Allah-fearing."

"Oh Prophet, we don't ask about this." Then the Prophet answered, "Then the most honorable person is Joseph, Allah's Prophet."[256]

This is a hadith, meaning an episode in the life of the Prophet that has been collected and published by Muhammad al-Bukhari.[257] Subsequent to this high assessment of the Biblical Joseph by the Prophet Mohammad—a clear proof of Salman Farsi's influence on him—a vast quantity of information about the episode's surrounding the biblical Joseph and his fate has been entered into the Quran.

We know that a whole Sura in the Quran is dedicated to Joseph (Sura 12:4–18). The name of Joseph's father Yaqub (Jacob) is also mentioned sixteen times in the Quran, for example in Sura 19:49 and then Sura 21:72–73 and then Sura 38:45–47 and again in Sura 12:8–9. The biblical Joseph and his father Jacob are mentioned in the Quran more often than any preislamic personality altogether. Most importantly, further to this, the Quran mentions a detailed and long account of the personal relationship of the biblical Joseph and the woman Zulaykah, who is the wife of Potiphar the captain of the Pharaoh's guard, whose name in the Quran is mentioned as Azeez.

In the Judaic religion, the personality of Joseph and his father Jacob have an important symbolic and mythological significance. Namely the twelve tribes of Israel are been born as the twelve sons of Jacob, and the twelve tribes of Israel start their existence from this moment on. The twelve tribes of the Hebraic people are the twelve sons of Jacob, and Joseph is one of them. Some historians are of the opinion that this story had been added later to the Hebraic scriptures, in order to emphasize the unity of the Jewish people and their descent from the same roots.

In contrast to the Jewish tradition, for the Islamic religion the personalities of the biblical Jacob and his son Joseph are without any significance. More so and especially the story of the personal and intimate relationship between Joseph and the woman Zulaykah are completely without any meaning. There is no logical reason for this story to be marked in the Quran. Asked who is the most God fearing, the Prophet ignores the giants of monotheism, namely personalities as Noah, Abraham, Moses, Jesus, Maria, or the Apostles of Christianity as for example Paulus or Petrus, these being important and religious personalities, whose actions were most significant for the Hebraic and Christian faith, whereas the personality of Joseph is secondary or nearly irrelevant for the great monotheistic religions.

If we ask what might be the reason that the Prophet of Islam thought that the biblical Joseph is the most god fearing of all monotheistic personalities, it would be reasonable and logical to conclude that:

1. Abraham, Moses, Jesus and Maria were not the heroes of Salman Farsi, but Joseph was.

2. The Prophet was probably strongly under the influence of Salman Farsi; therefore, as the Biblical Joseph was Salman's hero, he had mentioned Joseph to him continuously. Very probably Mohammad's only source of information, or maybe the main source of information, about the world and personalities of the great religions of the time Judaism and Christianity plus Zoroastrianism came from the narration of Salman Farsi only. It is evident here that Salman Farsi had wrongly exaggerated the importance of the biblical Joseph in his continuous conversations with the Prophet.

3. The person or persons who have written the Quran must also have looked upon Joseph and his father Jacob as great heroes, for these two persons are represented more than reasonably justified in the Quran. No other pre-Islamic religious personality is mentioned so often in the Quran as Jacob and his son Joseph, or Yaqub and Yusuf. Which reasonably points to the fact that

either the Quran was written by Salman himself, and if not, then he had great influence in its writing.

4. If the narration mentioned above, collected by Mohammad al-Bukhari—probably the most reliable Islamic chronicler of the events surrounding the Prophet and his time—are not correct, and the Prophet did not give the importance to these two personalities in the Quran as it is mentioned there now, then in this case, we have to assume that the Quran contains passages not authorized by the Prophet and that those passages have been add at a later date without the Prophet's knowledge or consent.

Returning to Salman Farsi as the Zoroastrian priest, we see here some Zoroastrian influence in the Quran. It is known that there are various influences in the Quran that can be traced to the Zoroastrian faith. We mention here only a few of them:

> By the sun and his noonday brightness
> By the moon when she follows him
> By the day revealing his glory
> By the night when it enshrouded him

Quran 91:1–15

———

> By the sun, adoring it, and which is forever
> Spreading the grace of God over the earth
> Cleansing the earth and the waters
> If there were no sun, devils would destroy life.

Avesta, Sun Yasht

The Prophet mentions that the Archangel Gabriel appeared to him and advised him that believers should pray five times a day after ablutions. This practise was introduced by Zarathustra for his followers more than two thousand years before, and this was known to Salman as an ex-Zoroastrian priest.

Regarding the elhams[258] the Prophet received—the message of the Archangel *Gabriel* [in Arabic: *Jabraihl*] to the Prophet on all the important questions and decisions—we have to mention here an interesting detail. In his book *The Making of a Prophet*[259] Doctor Hushang M. Payan says that, soon after the death of Prophet, the extremist Islamic sect of the Nusairis were of the belief that Salman was, in reality, the Archangel Gabriel who inspired the Prophet with his continuous advise and revelations. Concerning the Nusairis sect, these are the ancestors of the Islamic group today called The Alawites, who live in Syria.[260] This sect was called the Nusairis until September 1920, when the French forces occupied Syria after the end of the First World War and instituted the policy of referring to this sect by their new name.

A further indication of the involvement of Salman Farsi in the events surrounding the creation of the Quran can be found in the field of linguistics. The Australian historian and linguist Arthur Jeffery, in his important book *The Foreign Vocabulary of the Quran* comes to the conclusion, that a significant amount of words in the Quran have been taken from the Hebrew, Greek, Latin, Ge'ez (Ethiopian) Armenian, but the great majority from the Persian language. He counts in total 318 words of foreign origin in the Quran, which according to him, are mostly from the Persian or the ancient Pahlawy language. According to Jeffery:

> ... but the language which would have been known in Arabia in pre-Islamic times, the language with which Mohammad may have come in contact on a daily basis, was Pahlawy, the official language of the Sassanian empire.

...but not only along the Mesopotamian area was the Persian influence felt. It was a Persian general and the Persian influence, that overthrew and pushed aside the Abyssinians from southern Arabia during Mohammad's lifetime, and there is even a suspicion of Persian influence on personal basis in Mecca itself. How far Persian cultural influence penetrated the Arabian peninsula, we have little means to know...

... there are many cases, where there can be little doubt that we are dealing with a large amount of words borrowed from the Iranian languages...[261]

8.2 THE RETURN OF SALMAN FARSI WITH THE ARAB ARMIES TO IRAN

Previously it was assumed that the attack of the Islamic invaders into the Sassanian Empire had started 634 AD, and we know that the first attempt failed and the invaders were driven back. Professor Parvaneh Pourshariati, in *Decline and fall of the Sassanian Empire*, indicates that the first attempt of the Arabs to conquer Persia was, in fact, not 634 AD but six years earlier in 628 AD. If this is true, then considering that the Prophet Mohammed died on June 8, 632 AD, it would mean that it was under the leadership of the Prophet himself that the orders to invade Persia had been given—the same Prophet whose close advisor was none other than the Zoroastrian priest Salman Farsi. Which again probably would mean that Salman was advising the Prophet to invade Iran as soon as possible, for he knew of the domestic situation and the quarrel in the Iranian ruling Dynastic Family and of the betrayal of its army commander General Shahrbaraz. It was known to Salman that the Iranian leadership was in a crisis and that this weak moment of the

Persian Empire should be taken advantage of as soon as possible. It is known that Mohammad wrote a letter to King Khosrow II, inviting him to accept his new religion.

If we look at the political situation, we see that it would have been much easier and much more fruitful for the Arabs to invade the eastern part of the Byzantine Empire, the territories north of Damascus and north of Palestine. This territory once called Cappadocia (modern-day Anatolia) was geographically much easier to reach, for the distance was much shorter, and the cities and the population were much richer. From ancient times, Greeks, Romans and Byzantine nobleman had populated and lived there. This was a rich and prosperous area, containing a lot of wealth, especially in the cities along the coastline of the eastern Mediterranean. It is true that a half-hearted attempt was made to invade that area in 629 AD, and that this invasion was repelled by emperor Heraclius's brother Theodores. Only much later part of Anatolia was conquered by the Arabs, but this was very unconvincing. The whole idea of the invasion of Anatolia was abandoned for the moment, although the Prophet himself, who had travelled north to Damascus on several occasions, was familiar and knew the terrain and the geography of that area very well from personal experience.

It was more than eight hundred years later, on May 29, 1453, that Constantinople and all of Anatolia was conquered by the mongol Muslim's Sultan Mehmet II. This were not Arabs, but Turk-Mongols, who came from central Asia and had converted to Islam in Persia in earlier centuries. The Byzantine Empire fell in 1453, but the Persian empire fell in 644 more than eight hundred years earlier. This although it would have been, for the Arabs, much easier to invade and pursue what was closer to them, and closer to Europe, namely the Byzantine Empire.

And so the leadership was pushed to invade the Persian Empire, which lay much further away in the east. This was unknown territory to the leadership, for the Prophet himself, and later the Caliph Umar. The territory of the Persian Empire was on the other side of two great rivers, the Euphrates and the Tigris, which had to be crossed, and in case of bridges being destroyed, crossing would have been a very difficult task. Then after having entered the Persian Empire, the attack would mean crossing deserts and finally the Zagros Mountains and from there to the gates of the central Asian steppes to Bukhara and Samarkand—all uncharted territory for people from a small city in the Arabian Peninsula; hostile and unknown, unless you had with you somebody who knew that area very well, a man with great knowledge in that country and their culture, a man who had great influence on the decision makers and leaders of the new founded Islamic movement, and somebody who knew the internal problems of the Persian Empire very well. Who else could that man have been, if not Salman Farsi himself? We will see later that the Zoroastrian priest Salman Farsi was strongly recommending an invasion of the Sassanian Empire, his homeland, by the Arabs, first with the Prophet himself and then with the Caliph Umar.

Concerning the return of Salman Farsi to Iran, we have historical evidence from the chronicles and books of Muhammad ibn Jarir al-Tabari (839–923 AD). In *The History of al-Tabari Volume 13*[262] he reports to us that Salman Farsi was an adviser to Sa'd ibn Abi Waqqas, the commander-in-chief of the Islamic Armies, send by the Caliph Umar to subdue the Persian Sassanian Armies. Al-Tabari writes that, in several written orders from the Caliph Umar in Medina to the Commander in chief Abi Waqqas, the Caliph Umar clearly advises the General to send Salman to negotiate with Iranian authorities and army commanders. Furthermore, Salman is send to the Iranian side of the front to act as an scout or investigator and informer for Abi Waqqas.

After the first invasion against the Persians failed, Salman was put in charge of the second invasion, which was under the military command of Sa'd ibn Abi Waqqas. Probably to supervise personally the attack on Persia and to assist the commanding general. This second attack, with Salman Farsi present, was a great success for the invading Arabs, who won the famous battle at Qadisiyah in 642 AD—or earlier in 637 AD --according to Pourshariati.

We have seen that, in connection to the Arab invasion of the Sassanian Empire, the Arabs contacted local governors and provincial ruling families before their main attack to the country started, and made a separate peace treaty with them, and in so doing weakening the position of the Sassanian rulers of the Empire. This fact is also illustrated clearly in Parvaneh Pourshariati's book. As previously mentioned, two powerful regional powers and families, the one on the western part of the Persian Empire, the Kuste Adurpadaghan, and the other on the northeastern part of the empire, the Kuste Khwarasan, made their separate agreement with the Arabs, breaking the united front of the Persians. How were the Arab invaders savvy enough to discern which of the provincial governors and local ruling families were important and likely to cooperate with the enemy were it not for an insider like Salman himself.

In regards to the second Arab attack, Muhammad al-Tabari writes the following :

> Then the Muslim army turned to the Persian front. In order to confront the Persian King, at one point the Arab armies were located on the opposite bank of the great river Tigris. The commander of the army, Sa'd ibn Abi Waqqas, ordered the entire army to jump into the rushing river. Many people were afraid and started to pull back and wanted to turn back. Sa'd ibn Abi Waqqas who was standing with Salman Farsi at his side, started to pray in saying "may Allah grant us victory and defeat the armies of the enemy." Still without great effect on the soldiers at this point Salman Farsi declared with a very loud voice, "...all people, Islam will generate good fortune by Allah, crossing rivers has become as easy as crossing deserts for Muslims. By HIM in whose hand lays Salman's Soul, may the soldiers emerge

from the water in the same numbers in which they entered it..." At this point Sa'd ibn Abi Waqqas and Salman Farsi plunged themselves into the river Tigris. It is reported that the river was covered with horses and man. The horses swam and when they tired, the river floor seemed to rise up miraculously and support them until they regained their breath. To some it seemed that the horses rode effortlessly on the waves. They emerged on the other bank of the river, as Salman Farsi had prayed, having lost nothing from their equipment and no-one having been drowned. ...

They went on to take the Persian capital. Salma Farsi acted as the spokesman of the invaders, and said to the conquered Persians, I have the same origin as you. I shall be compassionate towards you.[263]

This above story happened in the year 637 AD, or the sixteenth year of the Hijjra according to the Islamic calendar. It is, therefore, historically confirmed that Salman was in Iran with the Arab-Islamic Armies. Furthermore, he was appointed as an ambassador for the Caliph Umar to negotiate with the Persian nobles and army chiefs, who were still in power. We can, therefore, say that Salman had left Iran circa 588 AD as an twenty-year-old young man and returned to Iran in October 636 AD (or January of 637 AD) with the Arab–Islamic armies, at which time he was approximately sixty-eight years old.

Just as the biblical Joseph had, in the end, redeemed himself before his father, Salman was also thinking probably to redeem himself in front of his father, particularly if Salman was his father's only child. The biblical Joseph, after injustice had been done to him, was chosen by destiny, or by god, to save his family and his people; Salman Farsi likened himself to the biblical Joseph and looked upon himself as being chosen by destiny to liberate and to save his people. He was thinking that he was redeeming himself in front of his own countryman.

Returning to the events of the Islamic–Arab invasion of Iran, we have seen above that the first Islamic invasion was under the command of Khalid ibn al-Walid. He invaded at the beginning the lands formerly known as the Lakhmid kingdom, and after that his army attacked Persia, this attack was repelled by the Persians, and the Arab army was mostly destroyed.

Upon this happening, a second army was send by the Arabs under Sa'd ibn Abi Waqqas, with Salman Farsi as an adviser to the commander of the army. That is the above episode mentioned by Muhammad al-Tabari, and in this case the invading Islamists were victorious, and a vast part of the country fell to the invaders. Probably the knowledge of the country and the people by the Zoroastrian priest Salman Farsi had a decisive influence in the Arab conquest of Persia. Unfortunately, it is not known if Salman Farsi, after having returned to Iran with the Arab Armies, contacted or visited his family, or enquired whether his father was still alive, or even traveled to his hometown.

Maybe, after approximately 440 years in power, the Sassanian Dynasty, and with them the Zoroastrian priesthood establishment, had shown signs of wearing out, degeneration and corruption. Probably the powerful hereditary Zoroastrian priesthood clan was connected too closely to the Sassanian Regime. They had become a burden for the Persian people and were holding up further progress in the society. The general public was, therefore, looking at the priesthood clan as their oppressors, without considering that, in any religion, there are people who take advantage of the religion or the system, and in so doing damaging that creed.

It is known that priesthood in the Zoroastrian society were hereditary, and Salman's father before him, logically, must have been himself a Zoroastrian Priest, probably in the rank of an Athravan. In ancient times the Athravans were the keepers of fires, or ceremonial fires in fire temples, and these were chosen mostly from the middle-rank landowners. The historian Herodotus notes that:

> The magi were one of the six Median groups, a tribe
> that specialized in hereditary priesthood duties, and
> who assumed the duties of the Athravan...

Whether Salman's father was indeed an hereditary priest himself is undocumented. Nevertheless, logic and circumstantial evidence points us to that direction. Salman could not have become a Zoroastrian priest were his father not a priest himself before him.

It is no wonder that Salman Farsi is revered by Arab Muslims, who call him *Hazrate Salman Farsi* [The Saint Salman Farsi], and at the same time, is considered to be a great traitor by the Persian nationalists and by all Zoroastrians. However one views him, he played a decisive part in the events of that time period and has an important place in history. Interestingly, according to K.E. Eduljee,[264] the tomb of Salman Farsi in the city of Al-Mada'in (once called Ctesiphon, the winter residence of the former Sassanian Emperor Khosrow II) has been bombed, damaged, and desecrated in February 2006. Furthermore, according to the website www.al-islam.org, the Salman al-Farsi mosque in the city of Medina was been bombed and damaged in the 1920s. His memory has been marked in history as a man who betrayed his homeland and the religion of his ancestors.

8.3 THE INVASION OF THE PERSIAN EMPIRE BY THE MUSLIM ARABS AND THE END OF ZOROASTRIANISM AS A STATE RELIGION

Later during the third invasion, in the year 644 AD, the Islamic invaders succeeded in conquering the whole country, and subsequently the last Sassanian king Yazdegerd III died 651 AD.

It is said that the city of Rhages (modern day Shahr-e-Ray) was one of the most ancient Persian cities, from well before the time of the Achaemenids. Rhages was one of the cities that did not surrender or co-operate in any way with the Arab invaders. Ancient Rhages was, before the Achaemenid period, one of the great spiritual centres of Zoroastrianism. After the invasion of Persia by Alexander of Macedonia, and his subsequent death in Babylon on June 10, 323 BC, one of his generals and successors decided to run the Persian territories from the city of Rhages as their capital. This city, which became for a short time the centre of the Greek administration of Persia, and whose name the Greeks changed to Europos, was governed in the style of a Greek city-state.

After the fall of Rhages to the Arabs, this city was completely destroyed on the orders of the Caliph Umar.

The famous Zarathustra expert and historian R.C. Zaehner in *The Dawn and Twilight of Zoroastrianism* wrote:

> The only place in the Avesta, which is been brought into connection with Zarathustra is Rhages, which is described as Zoroastrian. It is then rather more than possible that Zarathustra was a native of Rhages in Media, and that he fled from there to Chorasmia, where he finally found a patron in king Vishtaspa...[265]

With respect to the decisive battle of al-Qadisiyyah, Parvaneh Pourshariati mentions that there was widespread difference of opinion between the King Yazdegerd III, the last King of the Sassanian dynasty (a young boy at the time) and general Rostam Farrokhzad. The King, of course was too young and inexperienced to lead his own army. The tragedy had started when King Khavadh II ordered all the princes of the Sassanian clan executed. This dramatic situation in the empire at the beginning of the Arab invasion only further destabilized things. This act was not only a great crime, but much worse, a great mistake for which the Iranian Nation had to pay the price.

It is important to know that the Caliph Umar had given explicit orders to target, first and foremost, the enemy leadership and the generals. This strategy proved to be very effective. The Persians lost the battle of al-Qadisiyyah, and all the leading nobles and most of the generals were killed, their commander-in-chief general Rostam Farrokhzad included. The Caliph Umar knew that the Persian army commanders would have probably used the same strategy; therefore, he never participated in any war personally, and lived in Medina, in a safe distance from all hostilities.

Here we have to mention the name of another figure of some importance to the history of the Sassanian Empire. Jalinus Fahmi was a nobleman from Armenia, which at that time, was a part of the greater Sassanian empire, and was an officer of the Imperial guard, during the reign of King Khosrow II. Later, when the counsel of the nobles gave the orders to arrest and to imprison the old king, Jalinus, who was involved in this events, was promoted and made the commander of the guard, in charge of the imprisonment of the old king. He was promoted again at the battle of al-Qadisiyyah, when the new king, Yazdegerd III, made him a general and gave him the command of the troops of the right centre flank under the supreme commander Sepahbod Rostam Farrokhzad, who entered the battle of al-Qadisiyyah with an army of 60,000 men against the Islamic invaders.

After the death of the commander-in-chief, Rostam Farrokhzad— and most of the other army commanders—and the dispersement of the Iranian front, and the subsequent withdrawal of some of the other commanders, General Jalinus Fahmi took command of all the remaining soldiers of the Sassanian army. He gained control of the one remaining bridge over the river Euphrates, secured the bridge-head, and succeeded in getting the grand majority of his man over the bridge safely. He was waiting to cross the bridge—at the end of all his troops—but he was killed by an Arab arrow before reaching the bridge himself.[266]

Another noteworthy person was Sepahbod Hormozan,[267] the dynastic and hereditary ruler of Elam (modern-day Khuzestan). He was a member of the seven houses of ancient and wealthy feudal and provincial independent local rulers of Persia,[268] a provincial king in his own rights.

Being an army commander and general himself, he was in charge of the right flank of the Persian army, under the command of the commander-in-chief, Sepahbod Rostam Farrokhzad when they confronted the Arab Islamists Army at the battle of al-Qadisiyyah. The Persians lost this battle, and general Hormozan's army dispersed, but his personal whereabouts became unknown, as the Arabs had targeted to kill him personally. Many of his forces were killed at this battle, but he managed to escape to his own home province of Ahvaz-Khuzestan region, from where he conducted an attack and run strategy against the Arabs in the style of today's guerrilla warfare. For some period of time, Hormozan's isolated and guerrilla-style warfare had an initial success against the Arabs, and their local commander, Utbah ibn Ghazwan, had to ask for reinforcement, from his commander-in-chief, Sa'd ibn Abi Waqqas. Ultimately Hormozan's resistance could not be successful, for it was not in support of a coordinated front, but represented only an isolated resistance. It is said that, in the end, he voluntarily surrendered and stated to the Arab army commander who arrested him that he had an important message for the Caliph, which he had to give him personally. Thereupon, he was sent to Medina to face the Caliph Umar in person.

In Medina, in the fall of 642 AD, he succeeded in convincing the Caliph that he came voluntarily and wanted to see him personally because he wanted to convert to Islam. The caliph was impressed, pardoned him, and appointed him as his adviser in matters of administration and taxes. At a later date he was employed by the Islamic administration and was paid a monthly pension until his death. Several fiscal and administrational decisions and laws, for which the Caliph Umar is famous, were the work of this man. Whether Sepahbod Hormozan ever met or had any contact with Salman Farsi in Medina is not known.

In any case, Caliph Umar was assassinated on November 644 by a Persian. Various historians see this assassination as a conspiracy by the Persians against Caliph Umar, but there is no convincing proof for that, and this assassination could have been an isolated incident. The murder was a captive Persian Zoroastrian soldier by the name of Piruz Nahavandi , sold into slavery by the Arabs, who had persued and attacked the Caliph on a personal basis. Shortly after this event, under the pretext that Sepahbod Hormozan was among the conspirators behind this assassination, he was murdered by one of Umar's sons.

Notwithstanding the continuous demise and tragedy of Zoroastrianism in the Iranian mainland, the salience of the hope for its eventual re-establishment in the region remained pervasive amongst the Zoroastrian community in Iran. Zoroastrians still hoped that a miracle would happen and the old glorious times of the Sassanian world would be restored. This notion is best exemplified in the well-known ninth century Pahlavi (Middle Persian) Text titled *Abar Madan i Shâh Vahrâm Varzâvand* [*On the Coming of the Victorious King Vahrâm*]. The text bewails the Arab conquest of the region and highlights the then popular myth of the return to Iran of the quasi-messianic figure Shâh Vahrâm—a mythological King saviour—and his reestablishment of the Zoroastrianism as the state religion in Iran[269] and, with it, the rule of the ancient order. In reality, it was believed that, one day, one of the ancient Persian Kings would return to Iran and return the country to their ancient civilization.

A translation of a selection of a text from a document dating to the tenth century is as follows:

> When will a page arrive from the land of the Hindus,
> announcing the coming of the King Vahrâm from
> the lineage of the Kavis? As he shall come with

1,000 elephants ahead, he shall stand ahead of them holding the embellished coat-of-arms in the style of the Sassanian kings. The [Zoroastrian] believers shall then march their army ahead ... [An interpreter] will be sent to the land of the Hindus and described what we have seen and endured by the hand of the Arabs. [...] Upon one group they have caused religious affliction, and have murdered our king and under them, they have adopted the demonic religion, they eat bread like a dog! They have usurped the kingship from the Sassanians, neither by art nor by virtue, but via abhorrence and deceit. They have conquered and forcefully took and enslaved from the people their women, ...destroyed our perfumed gardens ... May we throw down Mosques and set up sacred fires! May we cleanse the world from wicked idols. May these demonic creatures be annihilated from the world!

Jean de Chardin (1643–1713), the seventeenth century French emissary to the Safavid dynasty, who arrived 1666 to Isfahan, and lived there for several years, underlines the prevalence of this myth amongst the Zoroastrians in Isfahan, and that they hoped that one day an ancient mythological King would return and their religion would once again be established as the dominant religion of the ancient Persian Empire.

After the Arab conquest, Zoroastrianism was strongly suppressed, and Zoroastrian communities shrunk and soon withdrew into ghettoes. It was mainly the Zoroastrian priesthood who preserved the middle Persian writings, which explains the loss of a great amount of secular literature due to the Arab invasion. In these latter secular writings, the heritage and the culture of the Sassanian era was preserved. This was a powerful force in the making of the Persian Islamic culture, which was based on the earlier Sassanian–Zoroastrian world.

The last remnants of the Zoroastrian–Sassanian culture in Persia was in the northeastern part of the empire. It seems certain that the small states of central Asia, were too part of the ancient Iranian world, and their role in bringing the Iranian cultural influence to China and to the southern part of the later Russian empire will always be remembered.

---

228. Richard Nelson Frye, *The Heritage of Persia The pre-Islamic History of one of the world's great civilizations* (New York: World Publishing company, 1963)

229. Gustav Rothstein, *Die Dynastie der Lahmiden in al-Hira. Ein Versuch zur arabisch-persischen Geschichte zur Zeit der Sasaniden* (Berlin: Reuther & Reichard, 1899)

230. Herodian, *The Parthian War of Caracalla* (Herodian 4.10.4 to 5)

231. Cassius Dio 79.1

232. The name of that catalogue, which still exists today, is Al-fihrist

233. Alfred Joshua Butler, *The Arab Conquest of Egypt and the Last Thirty Years of the Roman Dominion* (Oxford: Clarendon, 1902)

234. Satraps were provincial lords and local ruling families, who were ruling a part of the country on behalf of the King.

235. Clive Foss "The Persians in Asia Minor and the End of Antiquity", in: *English Historical Review* 1975, pp. 721–747

236. Virasp Mehta, *Causes of the Downfall of the Sassanian Empire* (Palo Alto, 2007)

237. Walter E. Kaegi, *Heraclius: Emperor of Byzantium* (Cambridge University Press, 2003)

238. René Grousset, *The Empire of the Steppes a History of Central Asia* (Rutgers, 1970), p. 179

239. Arthur Koestler, *The Thirteenth Tribe: The Khazar Empire and Its Heritage* (G S G & Associates Pub, 1976)

240. Abu Ja'far Muhammad ibn Jarir al-Tabari, *Tarikh al-Rusul wa al-Muluk* pp. 1045-1060

241. Parvaneh Pourshariati, *The Decline and Fall of the Sassanian Empire: the Sasanian-Parthian confederacy and the Arab conquest of Iran* (I.B. Tauris in association with the Iran Heritage Foundation, 2008)

242. Arthur Christiansen, *L'Iran Sous Les Sassanides* (Copenhagen:Ejnar Munksgaard, 1944)

243. Parvaneh Pourshariati, *The Decline and Fall of the Sassanian Empire: the Sasanian-Parthian confederacy and the Arab conquest of Iran* (I.B. Tauris in association with the Iran Heritage Foundation, 2008)

244. RA.A. Razwy, *Salman El-Farsi: Salman the Persian: friend of Muhammad, the messenger of Allah: a short story of his life* (Qum: Ansariyan Publications – p.o.box- nr.37185 Qum, Islamic rep. of Iran), p. 29

245. Ben Abrahamson and Josef Katz, "The Persian conquest of Jerusalem in 614 AD compared with Islamic conquest of 638 AD. Its Messianic nature and the role of the Jewish Exilarch." http://www.eretzyisroel.org/~jkatz/index.html

246. Louis Massignon, "Salman Pak et les prémices spirituelles de l'Islam Iranien", in: *Société des études iraniennes*, 7 (1934)

247. A.A. Razwy, *Salman El-Farsi: Salman the Persian: friend of Muhammad, the messenger of Allah: a short story of his life* (Qum: Ansariyan Publications – p.o.box- nr.37185 Qum, Islamic rep. of Iran)

248. The celebrated Danish historian Arthur Christiansen has written extensively on the subject, and so has professor Ehsan Yarshater from the Columbia University.

249. In this connection, see further in Arthur Christensen, *Le Regne du Roi Kavadh I, et le Communisme Mazdakite* (Copenhagen, 1925).

250. Also Dr. Modi, *Two Visions of the History of Mazdak* (Bombay, 1930).

251. John Glubb, *The Life and Times of Mohammad* (New York, Stein and Day Publishers, 1970)

252. Muhammad Husayn Haykal, *The Life of Muhammad* (Cairo, 1933)

253. Ella Landau trans., Ehsan Yarshater ed., *The History of Al Tabari* Volume 39 (Albany: State University of New York Press, 1998), p 66

254. Ibid., p.99

255. Torah – Book of Genesis 39:1–20.

256. Abu Huraira (603–681 AD) was a companion of the prophet Mohammad, and for three years he went on all travels and journeys with the Prophet. This episode has been related by him, and is most accurate. Abu Huraira is probably the most quoted chronicler of Islam by the Sunni faith.

257. Muhammad al-Bukhari (810–870 AD) was a Persian Sunni historian of the Islamic faith, and his chronicles are regarded as being among the most accurate in the Islamic history. Two of his important Books are *Sahih al Bukhari* and *Al adab al Mufrad*.

258. Elham—messages from God the Prophet had received concerning important questions of the Islamic faith.

259. Hushang M. Payan, *The Making of a Prophet:Muhammad and his Creations* (Word Association Publishers, 2010)

260. This sect formerly known as Nusairis were founded by Abu Shu'ayb Muhammad ibn Nusayr (d.ca. 863 AD) who is reported to have been a member of the circles of the last three Imams of the Prophet's line.

261. Arthur Jeffery, *The Foreign Vocabulary in the Quran* (Oriental Institute, 1938), Introduction pp. 10-16

262. Gauthier H.A. Junyboll trans., *History of al Tabari* (State University of New York Press, 1989), pp. 16, 18, 21, 63, 65

263. Abu Ja'far Muhammad ibn Jarir al-Tabari, *History of al-Tabari*, Vol. 13

264. K.E. Eduljee, http://www.heritageinstitute.com/zoroastrianism/

265. R.C. Zaehner, *The Dawn and Twilight of Zoroastrianism* (London: Phoenix Press, 1961), 33

266. Parvaneh Pourshariat, *Decline and fall of the Sasanian Empire* (I.B.Tauris Publishers, 2008), pp. 157, 216, 225

267. Clifford Edmund Bosworth, "Sepahbod Hormozan" in: *Encyclopedia Iranica* (New York, 2007)

268. *History of al-Tabari*, Vols. 31–34

269. Various editions of this text have been analyzed by Mary Boyce (*Middle Persian Literature*) and F. de Blois (*Persian Literature: a Bio-Bibliographical Survey*) wherein he highlights the text as a poem rhyming consistently in ân.

9. ZOROASTRIANISM TODAY AND A SHORT LOOK AT THE EVENTS IN PERSIA AFTER 1800 AD

If we look at the Zoroastrian community today, we see that the relatively small group of believers, who are the descendants of the ancient Persians, who did not covert to Islam and did not mix with other communities, are scattered all over the world, their number estimated at about 120,000 people. From these, about ten to twenty thousand live in Iran, and the rest in western Europe, North America, Australia and the Far East. The largest community of Zoroastrians live in India with a group of approximately 60,000 people. They are known in India as Parsis, meaning Persians.

At the beginning of the British rule in India, in the 1770s, the Zoroastrian community in India was mainly concentrated in the state of Gujarat. At this stage of history, the Zoroastrian community had no political or financial significance and were living as self-sufficient farmers. It was to this rural area that most of the refugees had immigrated after the Islamic conquest of Iran, as this area, the western

Gujarat was, in fact, en-route to the Iranian border of Balutchistan and western Afghanistan, then being a part of greater Persia. After the British Empire solidified its domination over the Indian subcontinent, it was their policy to align themselves with minorities, and give them power and authority over the masses of the population, in this case the Hindus and the Indian Muslim.

Their policy was to support the minorities, for the minorities would then always be loyal to the British, who would then protect them against the local Hindu or Muslim majority. Accordingly, we see by the 1840s, the Parsis moving from the countryside in Gujarat to the major urban centres and receiving the help and the special assistance of the British colonial authorities. Parsi businessmen gradually received permits and licences from the colonial administration, which would be impossible to obtain for Hindu or Muslims. Here we have to mention the name of a prominent British policymaker in the British India Administration, Thomas Babington Macaulay (1800–59), the first Baron Macaulay. Having held the office of the Paymaster General and the Secretary of War between 1839 and 1848 in England, Macaulay was sent to India as the Secretary to the Board of Control of the India Administration. He also served on the Supreme Council of India, and in both positions, he made important and far-reaching policy decisions for the future of British India. Firstly, he supported the replacement of the Persian Language, which was the official administrative language of India for centuries, with English from 1848 onward. Concerning the internal policy towards the Indian population, he stated the following:

> We British must at present do our best to form a new
> class who may be interpreters between us and the
> millions whom we govern, a class of persons, Indian
> in blood and colour, but English in taste, in opinion,
> in morals, and in intellect, whose absolute loyalty to
> us must be out of question.[270]

The Parsis, in many ways, were foremost in forming such a class. By the 1830s, as Britain began to strengthen its hold in India, the Parsis—who were one of the strongest advocates of westernization and supporters of assimilation with British culture—were able to take advantage of the new situation. The Parsis were among the first Indians to travel to Europe (or perhaps better to say, who were *permitted* by the British to travel to Europe). At that time of the British rule in India, the Indian population needed a special permit to leave the country, *especially* if they intended to travel to Europe or England. Indigenous people of the colonies were not permitted to travel to the UK, and if so, an English person had to sponsor, and act as a guarantor for the Indian person. For Parsis, this regulation would not apply. By the 1880s, a considerable number of Parsis travelled to Europe; they studied in British universities and later, most importantly, occupied top level positions in the Indian industrial and business community. It is significant to mention here the degree of Parsis loyalty and dependency on the British colonial administration, which was evident in the fact that only Parsis were permitted to join the ranks of the British intelligence community. For example, persons in charge of the internal Iranian affairs in the Indian administration were mostly Parsis.

In the 1920s and 1930s, Parsis coming from India to Iran did not identify themselves with Iranians nor with Iranian Zoroastrians. They had no loyalties to the old country which they claimed descent from, nor to their Iranian coreligionists; rather they regarded themselves to be on a higher level. On the other hand, the Iranian rulers of the 1850s, the Turkic Qajar Dynasty, were very ineffective against the secret cooperation and agreements between the British Empire and Czarist Russia, whose aim was to weaken and dominate the Persian Empire. Britain was strongly focused on the protection and the preservation of their important dominion, India. For this reason, the British Empire, in a series of secret and semi-secret agreements with the Russian Empire, established spheres of influences that effectively divided Persia into two halves. Three highly disadvantageous agreements between Persia and Russia, were forced on Iran, resulting in loss of a vast territory, loss of control of tariff rates, and Iran's complete dependence on primary commodities from Britain and Russia.

For example Baluchistan, a province of Persian Empire since antiquity, was cut off from Persia and annexed to the greater Indian colony in 1876. This one-sided political move by the British Empire was done without the consent of the Iranian Government at the time. Sir Frederic John Goldsmid and Sir Oliver St John in *Eastern Persia: An Account of the Journeys of the Persian Boundary Commission 1870-71-72* show the degree to which they viewed Iranians and Iranian authorities with askance and held them in contempt.

> The Qajar Shahs of Iran were not in a position to counter the British action in this case, as the Persian local and provincial tribal leaders in their struggle against the central government of Iran, this mainly in the eastern and central part of Persia received funds and arms from the British India administration. This was to encourage semi-autonomous rulers in Iran to rebel and show their independence against the central Persian government. This policy of divide and rule by the Indian Office had succeeded in destabilizing and weakening the authority of the Persian central government.

It was not until 1927, under the rule of Reza Shah Pahlavi, that the power of the tribal leaders and provincial ruling families were neutralized, and the country was united again under the central government. The Province of Herat, which was form antiquity the hearth land of Khorasan, the eastern province of Iran, was forcibly separated from Iran by the British. So creating as buffer zone between the Russian Empire and India, this being the newly created country of Afghanistan.[271]

Until the death of the Persian Emperor Nader Shah Afshar on June 20, 1747, Afghanistan was a part of greater Persian Empire. Nader Shah Afshar, invaded India from the north, and in the famous battle of Karnal on February 13, 1739, defeated the Indian armies of the Mughal Emperor Mohammad Shah. Subsequently, Nader Shah dismantled and destroyed the military infrastructure of the Mughal Emperors and decentralized the Indian administration in order to be able to govern the country easier. In the end, he concluded that his presence was needed in the motherland Persia itself, and he returned to Persia, leaving a power vacuum and the Indian central Government in a state of Anarchy. The organization, which started the British domination of India—the famous East Indian Trading company— was already present and active at that time in India, as it had received, from the Mughal Empire's administration, initial trading rights in the year 1617. If the central Mughal Imperial government was still strong and functional, it would have been impossible for the British to start an attempt to dominate the whole country. Historians are united in the understanding that, without the invasion and the destruction of the Mughal Empire's central power in India by the Persian Nader Shah Afshar, the British dominance of the Indian Subcontinent would probably not have been possible.

Nader Shah Afshar was murdered in 1747 by one of his servants; at the day of his death two of his generals and the commanders of his main two cavalry regiments, one of them being Karim Khan Zand and the other Ahmad Khan Durrani, arrived moments too late to avert the murder of the King with whom they had an appointment. Confronted with the new situation, after lengthy discussions of who should succeed the Shah, they agreed between them, to divide the country among themselves. Karim Khan Zand (1705–1779), who was from Azerbaijan, born in the city of Malayer, and being of Kurdish background, took the western part of the Persian Empire. Ahmad Durrani (1722–1773) who was born in Herat, at that time the capital of the Persian province of Khorasan, being of Pashtun origin, took the eastern part—Nader Shah always had great sympathy for Ahmad Durrani, for both of them were from the province of Khorasan. Shortly after that Ahmad Durrani first declared himself to be the ruler of Khorasan, calling himself the Emir of Khorasan. Later (1757) he was named by his troops to be the king of a new country, namely Afghanistan, which until that date, was an eastern province of Greater Persia. The city of Herat, where Shah Abbas, one of Iran's greatest kings was born, is now in Afghanistan.

One of the famous ancient ruling provincial families of the ancient Persian Empire, namely the house of Suren-Pahlaw, being one of the ancient Zoroastrian family clans, ruled as Satraps or Provincial rulers the province of Sistan–Baluchestan. Their ruling domain included what it today western Afghanistan with Kandahar, Helmand Province, Sistan and Baluchestan from approximately 200 BC until well into the thirteenth century Islamic Period. This means the same family clan ruled that area for a approximately 1,500 years. It was one of the members of this house, Sepahbod Rostam Surena, who defeated an Imperial Roman Army under the command of the Consul Marcus Licinius Crassus (115–53 BC) at the battle of Carrhae in 53 BC.

We see that, after the British Domination of India took shape, British Policymakers, believing India to be vulnerable to an overland invasion from Russia, planned the creation of Afghanistan, which had to include the eastern provinces of Persia. Therefore, when the Persian Shah Mohammad from the Qajar Dynasty (ruled 1834–1848) the father of Nasser al Din Shah, marched with his army to Herat, in 1837, to reassert the old Iranian claim over that city, the British intervened, and Mohammad Shah had to back down. Later his son, Nasser al Din Shah (ruled 1848–1896) did not accept that Iran's claim to its ancient city of Heart had lapsed; therefore, in October 1856 Iranian troops again entered the city of Herat and raised the Iranian flag over the citadel. A few month after this event, the British authorities in Bombay decided to invade Iran from the south, and dispatched forty-five ships with an army of 6,000 men. The invasion troops landed in the south of the country and seized the Iranian port of Bandar Bushehr and started to push inland. The Shah had no choice but to give in, and in 1857, at the Treaty of Paris, Persia had to accepted the British conditions concerning the creation of the new country of Afghanistan.

After the discovery of oil reserves in the region around the Persian gulf, and the growing dependency of the world economy on fossil fuel, the fate of that geographical region was sealed, for all the major world powers were now trying to establish a foothold in that region. The political action plan by the western world powers was to dominate that region by creating smaller and weaker political entities that were dependent on the colonial or western powers for survival. Then by signing one-sided economic agreements with the newly established rulers of that country, those regimes could be kept in power against the will of the general populations of said countries if they suspect that their regimes are betraying the interest of their own nations. A small, corrupt elite will always be ready to betray its own country's interest for personal gain.

Religion is strongly promoted by the foreign powers, but Nationalism is dangerous and must be avoided. This Political action system was initially developed and perfected by the Roman Empire, calling it *Divide et Impera* [divide and conquer]. The British colonial administration used the same system as the Roman Empire, only perfecting it and applying it on a grander scale. Concerning Iran, it was the British Empire, who for the sake of India, the Jewel in their Crown, initially brokered secret agreements with the Russian Empire, and later, for the sake of the Iranian oil reserves, had to systematically destabilize and cut Iran down to size.

But returning to the future of Zoroastrianism, the population of the region of the Central Asian steppes is Muslim, but for some time, travellers and historians have noticed in the myths, legends and some ritual practices, certain elements that have a clear Zoroastrian origin. In recent times several small and previously hidden communities from Tajikistan have contacted the Zoroastrian community in Bombay

India, and have asked to be recognized as Zoroastrian communities. Their argument is that, although having been forced to accept Islam under duress from ancient times, they and their ancestors remained privately faithful to their ancient religion, which was Zoroastrianism. The Parsi community in India has rejected these claims, fearing that millions of Iranian Muslims might make that claim as well. This, on the other hand, does not prevent new groups of people, in the framework of recent revival of Zoroastrianism, especially in Central Asian post-Soviet Republics, from deriving political legitimacy through referring to themselves as Zoroastrian. Moreover, some Kurdish communities in western European countries and some Muslim Iranians living abroad have started to define themselves as Zoroastrians. The German Professor at the University of Bergen, in Norway, Michael Strausberg, has further investigated this phenomenon in a recent article.[272]

It is no secret that, during the colonial times that saw the British dominance of the Indian sub-continent and major parts of the Middle East, the loyalties of the Indian Zoroastrian Community was not with Persia, the country of their ancestors, but with the rulers of the British Empire. Members of the Indian Zoroastrian community were in the forefront, acting again the interests of the country of their so-called forefathers, which was Iran. As an example, Sir Shapoor Reporter, who was born 1922 in Iran and who at one time held an Iranian citizenship, played a crucial role in the subduing and discrediting of the democratically elected Persian government and the 1953 coup d'état in Iran by the British Government. As an agent for the British secret service MI6, Sir Shapoor Reporter, together with Ann Lambton (1912–2008), the famous Iran specialists and most importantly Mr. Robert Charles Zaehner (1913–1974) the foremost expert in Zoroastrianism, played a crucial role in 1953 of overthrowing the government of the legitimate Prime Minister of Iran Dr. Mohammad Mossadegh, who wanted to nationalize the Iranian Oil industry. It is known that, in a letter, Sir Winston Churchill wrote to the then President Harry Truman, saying

"…They want to take away our Oil…" Ann Lambton and R.C. Zaehner reportedly advised the British Government not to negotiate in any circumstances with Dr. Mossadegh, or any other member of the legitimate Persian government. Stephen Kinzer, in his book *All the Shah's Men*, mentions that the then acting British Prime Minister, Sir Winston Churchill had commented in this regard "…I am strongly against any further dismantling of the British Empire." Meaning that Persia was still a part of the British Empire.

The Zoroastrian Sir Shapoor Reporter was born in Iran and was an Iranian citizen, and yet he acted against the interests and aspirations of Iranians. His father, Ardeshir Reporter, was also an important British intelligence officer in Iran. It is said that, in 1919 and 1920, Ardeshir Reporter travelled throughout Persia for the British to find a suitable candidate as the future ruler of Iran, who would be later imposed by the British government on the Persian people. It was he who chose and introduced General Reza Khan—who at that time was the Commander of the Military Garrison of the city of Qazvin but later become Reza Shah Pahlavi—to the British Envoy to Iran General Sir Edmund Ironside in early 1921.[273] His son Sir Shapoor Reporter was later the Chief of the Iran Desk at the Secret British Intelligence Service in London, and the liaison officer of that office to the Shah of Iran, Mohammad Reza Pahlavi.

On a personal note, I had personaly the privilege of meeting Sir Shapoor Reporter in the summer of 1982 in the south of France in Cannes, where a group of prominent Iranians and *Zarthoshtis* [Persian: Zoroastrians] known and close to Sir Shapoor were assembled. At the end of the meeting, I asked him:

"Sir Shapoor, now that Iran has reached this phase in its history, with the coming to power of the Islamist there, if you look back, would you have done something differently in the past. After all the British Empire has fallen and is now finished—"

"The British Empire has not fallen," Sir Shapoor said, "and will never be finished."

Furthermore, we have to mention here an interesting footnote to history regarding the last Shah of Iran, Mohammad Reza Pahlavi. The man of confidence of Mohammad Reza Pahlavi, General Hossein Fardoust, who later was accused of having betrayed the Shah and cooperated and helped his enemies, writes an interesting detail in his memoir, one worth mentioning here. Hossein Fardoust, the son of a minor officer and a childhood friend of the late Shah, was sent together with the crown prince Mohammad Reza Pahlavi as a young boy to Switzerland to a boarding school. Later they visited together the Iranian Military academy, and as a friend, Fardoust enjoyed the Shah's full confidence. After the events of 1979 and the fall and death of Mohammad Reza Pahlavi, it was rumoured that Fardoust had instructions from those powers, who wanted the Pahlavi's to leave Iranian politics, to act against his friend.

In any case, after his death on May 18, 1987, a book was published in Iran *under his name*, in which "General H. Fardoust" was very critical of the late Shah's regime. In this book, humiliating Fardoust's old friend, the "author" claimed that Iran had been run by the Freemasons, Jews, and Bahais. But some time later *another* book was published, in India, which appears to be the real memoirs of the old general smuggled out of the country and published abroad.[274] In this book, contrary to the other book printed in the Islamic republic of Iran under his name, General Fardoust speaks of the Shah with words of respect and admiration, as a man who did what he could for his country to the best of his personal and psychological abilities, and who believed in what he was doing. Two details from this book published in India are noteworthy here to be mentioned. The one being, according to General Fardoust, that Shah Mohammad Reza Pahlavi had one day said to General Fardoust in confidence that, "… the Islamic religion is not the religion of our people… this religion is alien to the people of the Iranian Nation, … the real religion of Iran was that of Zarathustra."

The second noteworthy detail is that, during the Second World War, when the Germans had invaded Russia, Mohammad Reza

Pahlavi had a small shortwave radio and was secretly listening to the German Radio broadcast at night. In his bedroom cupboard, behind his underwear on the wall he had hidden a map of Russia, where he was, at night, following the advances of the German Army and pinning coloured pins on the map. This was after the father of the then prince, the old Reza Shah was forced out of the country by the British for being a German sympathizer. One day, the British intelligence Service representative in Teheran called General Fardoust and told him to inform the Prince that, "if he continues his interest in German military advancements in Russia, we will not let him become the next Shah of Iran."

10. ZOROASTRIAN PERSIA AND ITS RELIGIOUS-STRATEGICAL GOALS

If we look carefully at the history of the ancient Middle East and the eastern Mediterranean region, from the events which started around at the beginning of history itself, until at least the emergence of the Islamic religion, and beyond, we see that, from the beginning, the geopolitical strategy of the Persian rulers were always the same. One of the political constellations, which constantly repeated itself, from the time of the early Zoroastrian period of the Iranian history, was the close relation between the Persians and the Hebrews, two of the ancient people of the Middle East. There are various reasons for this, one being that they always shared common enemies. It is known that geography ultimately determines the course of history and politics. As the geography never changes, therefore logically, the history of a particular region has to repeat itself constantly. Therefore, in order to investigate the geopolitical situation in the Middle East from ancient times, we have to look again at some historical events.

From ancient times, the Iranian and Jewish communities were confronted with the question of whether there was, in reality, any genuine and cordial cooperation or assistance by the Zoroastrian Persian rulers—for example the Achaemenid and the Sassanian rulers—towards the Jews, and if so, what was the reason for it. A person can assist or help another person for emotional or personal reasons, but an Empire always has strategic and political considerations to follow. Therefore the fact that, for example, Cyrus the Great of the Achaemenid Dynasty sends back the Jews to Jerusalem, after having conquered Babylon in 538 BC and builds them the new temple and helps them to re-establish Judea—this has to be explained probably from a Persian strategic perspective. Looking at history, at latest from the time of the emergence of the Greek city states, and particularly after the beginnings of the Roman Republic, circa 700 BC and onwards, there were always rivalries and hostilities and continuous war between the rulers of greater Persia and the powers in the west. At this period of time, the Egyptian-Pharaonic Empire had been in decline, and was not a major player in the region any more. The Persians had conquered Egypt in 525 BC under Cambyses II.

The Persian–Achaemenid policy towards religions in the various regions of their Empire was, in general, not dogmatic (they have to believe in our gods) but rather pragmatic and manipulative (we have to act, with them, as if we believe in the same things as they do, in order to gain their loyalty). At no time did the Achaemenids (or even at a later date the Parthian and then the Sassanian Dynasty rulers up until 644 AD) try to convert people under their rule to become Zoroastrians, not even in the heartland of the Empire. Whereas the Christian rulers of the later Byzantine Empire and their Islamic successors, the Ottoman rulers, always tried to pressure the people under their control to convert to the religion they had at the time. History is full of examples of Byzantine–Christian rulers putting pressure on the Jews to convert to Christianity; Emperor Justinian (482–565 AD) is famous for his fanaticism in converting minorities to Christianity, even ordered the Jews to alter and change their Religious practises and rituals in Synagogues in order to conform to Christianity. Therefore, from the Byzantine point of view, the region of ancient Judea and Samaria with the city of Jerusalem was too close, geopolitically, to the power centre of Byzanz (modern-day Istanbul) to be left in the hand of non-believers. Their religion, at all times, had to be the same as the one of the central rulers, to ensure their loyalty. Geopolitically, the backyard of the Empire can not be in the hand of non-believers, it has to be secured.

Contrary to this, the ideological worldview at the power centres of the various Persian Zoroastrian Empires was completely different. The focal point of the big powers of that time, approximately after 700 BC, was the eastern Mediterranean counties. The Greeks and then later the Roman republic were looking to the east. In a time when the western and northern European regions were considered places where the Romans had to still introduce their civilization, all the culture and the riches seemed to be concentrated in the eastern shore of the Mediterranean. Because the agricultural products of the Nile delta in Egypt was later essential for survival of the city of Rome, Julius Caesar had to invade Egypt in 47 BC, to secure Rome's bread supply. Then there were, of course, the rich cities of Damascus, Jerusalem, Byzantium, countries like Judea, Samaria, Syria, Phoenicia and others, with an abundance of gold, olive oil, exotic fruits—it is there that the goods coming from east Asia, such as silk and spices were traded.

On the contrary, the Parthian Zoroastrian rulers in the east, the other big power and the competitors of the Romans, were looking to the west. They had the same aspirations, the Mediterranean shores and Egypt were the gates to the western world, which they wanted to conquer and dominate. This clearly shows that the centre of the ancient western world was indeed the eastern shores of the Mediterranean. The Romans were looking to the east, whereas the Persians were looking to the west.

What happened later is well known in history; starting from the time of Emperor Caligula, the relationship between the Roman Empire and the Jews deteriorated rapidly, culminating in the first Roman–Jewish war in 66–73 AD. In this war, first Vespasian and then Emperor Titus Flavius (39–81 AD)—an experienced army commander at the head of the the fifth, tenth and fifteenth Roman Legion, with a total of 60,000 professional Roman soldiers—devastated Judea and destroyed the second temple. After approximately 40,000 Jewish deaths and an additional group of people committing suicide, this war ended, with a large segment of the Jewish population leaving the country.

Here we come to the second Roman–Jewish war. In the year 130 AD, Emperor Hadrian visited Jerusalem and started with some massive anti-Jewish decrees. Firstly, he abolished the traditional circumcision which he called barbaric, then he forbid the Torah, which had to be collected and destroyed, then, to make things even worse, he built, on the site of the ancient second temple, which had been destroyed sixty-four years earlier by Vespasian and Titus, a temple dedicated to the Roman God Jupiter. Furthermore, Jews were not allowed to live or enter the city of Jerusalem. This hostility of Rome against the Jews continued for years. It was at this time that the Jewish population started a massive emigration, the majority of Jewish emigrants going to the Parthian Empire, for most of the other regions of the ancient world were under the dominance of the Roman Empire.

Some prior Jewish presence has been documented in Persia from well before the Achaemenid Period circa 650 BC. In 2004, a Jewish cemetery was discovered in a settlement close to the Mount Damavand—the sacred mountain of ancient Iran since the times of Zarathustra and before. Archaeologist have dated this cemetery to approximately 1000 BC. Furthermore, it is said that the invasion of Babylon by king Cyrus the Great in 538 BC was assisted and influence by the Persian Jewish Community, showing that there existed a Jewish community in Iran from before the Achaemenid times. We have here the documentation of the Greek historian Cassius Dio (150–235 AD), a Roman historian, who wrote in the Greek Language. Cassius Dio worked for twenty-two years, collecting documentation and evidence on his gigantic 80-volume *Historia Romana* which covered 1,400 years of Roman history up to the year 229 AD. As of now, the beginning of the twenty-first century, only fragments of some 36 of his books are surviving and are known to us.

Though Romans were, from their beginnings, very cordial and close to the Greek people and their culture—for example Emperor Hadrian was a great admirer of the Greeks and their culture (Cassius Dio called him a great Philhellene)—such was decidedly not the case with the Jews, for whom Rome harboured nothing but hostilities which ultimately led to war. Whereas, with the rulers of the Persian Empire, it was exactly the opposite; the Persians were, from the beginning, hostile to the Greek city-states, but always cordial and close to the Jews. There are several possible reasons for this, the first being the strategic location in the west and on the Mediterranean cost of Judea and Samaria for the Persians in the east. It is no coincidence that both times that the Persians conquered and held Egypt, occurred just years after either the Persians re-establishing or renewing the Jewish state and the city of Jerusalem. Once Cyrus the Great conquered Babylon in 538 BC and sent the Jews back to their homeland and helped to reinforce the Jewish nation, it allowed his son Cambyses II to conquer Egypt in 525 BC, which the Persians held for 192 years.

The second time the Persians conquered Egypt was in the year 619 AD, a mere five years after Sassanian King Khosrow II sent a great Persian Army led by the General Shahrbaraz to defeated the Byzantine army, take Jerusalem, and re-established the Jewish state. This made it possible for the second conquest of Egypt by the Persians, which gave them, a foothold on the eastern Mediterranean. Strategically the Persians always needed an established Jewish state in Judea and Samaria as their allies to be active in the eastern Mediterranean region.

10.1 THE FUTURE OF ZOROASTRIANISM AND SOME HISTORICAL EXAMPLES CONCERNING RELIGION IN THE FUTURE OF HUMANKIND

Returning back to history, we have seen that rulers, dictators and revolutionaries have continuously tried to abolish or discontinue a religion, alternatively they try to convince people that the God they believe in does not exist or, as in Nietzsche's case, simply assert that "God is dead."

All these actions taken in history by various known leader have ended in failure. There are several cases in history to demonstrate this fact, from which we will chose one notable—the French Revolution of 1789.

In 1789 the people of France revolted against the nobility and the king, in what was later called the French Revolution. The most serious damages and dangerous consequences of this uprising was felt by the French Catholic church. Until that time, the French church and clerical establishment owned vast estates, from which they received a substantial yearly income, and they were, in reality, competing with the French aristocracy. Cardinals, the so-called princes of the church, competed in power with the authority of the King of France himself, and it was no secret that, at times, the power of the cardinals of France, who acted also as Prime Ministers, was higher than that of the King. This was the case with Cardinal Richelieu and Cardinal Mazarin. We remember the book of Alexandre Dumas, *The Three Musketeers*, in which the three Musketeers fight to defend the Queen and King against the intrigues of the famous and all powerful Cardinal Richelieu.

Therefore, one of the great requests of the French Bourgeoisie (the newly forming French middle class), who subsequent to the French revolution came to power, was to abolish and to destroy the power and the wealth of the Catholic Church in France. Historically the de-Christianisation of France during the French revolution is a conventional description for the results of a number of separate policies which were enacted by several revolutionary governments who came to power in Paris between 1789 and 1801. The goal of this campaign, conducted by the French revolutionary governments, was nothing less than the total destruction of the Catholic religious practice and ultimately the discontinuation of the Christian religion in the French society itself.

It is, of course, a long debated discussion by historians as to whether this movement had a *popular* backing or was something which was forced upon the people by those intellectuals and revolutionaries who, at that moment, were in power. In any case, the largest landowner in the country, the French Catholic church, controlled properties which provided them with gigantic sums and revenues from its tenants—mostly peasants and workers. Since the church in France kept the registry of births, deaths and marriages, was the only institution that provided primary and secondary school education for the citizenry, and ran all the hospitals in France, its influence on the general public was unrivalled, even by the King or the government of France itself.

A group of members of the convention (the new assembly which was now the master of the country) around one of the more outspoken and active members of the powerful Committee of Public Safety (namely a certain Maximilien Robespierre) started to propose, and then push through, certain extreme and radical measures against not only the Catholic church, but the Christian religion in general. These new laws and regulations, which were proposed and enacted step-by-step, mostly by Robespierre and his group, resulted in wide-ranging legislations, which was going to change the course of the French society, as never before. These new laws had the following effect:

1. The implementation of a new calendar, to replace the Christian one. The calendar, which was adopted in 1793 and used for the next twelve years, abandoned the seven day week and replaced it with a ten day week, and had declared the year 1792, the year King Louis XVI was taken into custody, as the year 1. The name

of days and months were changed. If we look at coins of the Napoleonic era when Napoleon was the emperor, and France was an empire, we see on the coins written year 10 or year 12 or year 13.

2. The dispossession, deportation and brutal martyrdom of thousands of clergy. Christians being denied freedom of speech, freedom of the press, and freedom of thought if it contravened the secular humanist ideology of the revolution.

3. The criminalization of all religious education.

4. The elimination of all Christian symbols from the public sphere, including removing the word 'saint' from street names and destroying or defacing churches and religious monuments.

5. The replacing of Christian holidays and symbols with civic and revolutionary cults like the 'Cult of Reason' and 'Cult of the Supreme Being' (the new gods). A statue to the Goddess Reason was even erected and worshiped in Notre Dame Cathedral on 10 November 1793.

6. The "convention" passed a law, enacted on October 21, 1793, which saw all lands and property of the Church seized by the government and all statues and places of worship (churches and cathedrals) stripped of everything which reminded them of Christianity. All crosses, bells were destroyed, and all persons who harboured priests and clerical people and helped them were faced the death penalty.

7. Maximilien Robespierre declared that God and the Catholic church had been cancelled and abolished, and in its place he put a new god whose name was the Goddess of Reason.

8. On November 10, 1793, Robespierre held a big formal ceremony in the famous cathedral of Notre Dame (the most famous
cathedral of France) in which he dedicated this cathedral to
the Goddess of Reason calling the Cathedral of Notre Dame
by its new name *Le Temple del la Raison* [The Temple of the
Goddess Reason].

9. On May 7, 1794, the Committee of Public Safety, which controlled France, decreed worship of a Supreme Being, but this
was not the God of the Bible, who enters into personal relationships with men, rather a Deist god. Eighteenth-century Deism
taught that God created the universe but did not interfere in its
operation. According to the Deists, their god could be discovered through natural law and his existence was an inspiration to
moral behaviour.

Maximilien Robespierre—who was in reality a great idealist and
said to be incorruptible and honest—insisted that he was strongly
opposed to atheism, for he believed that the people need religion,
but his idea was to create a new religion, which would be carried by
two strong pillars namely, human virtue on one side, and the laws of
nature on the other side. The new religion would be called The Cult
of the Supreme Being, and its god would be the Goddess of Reason,
which meant logical and reasonable thinking.

Not only were thousands of priests executed by the guillotine or
deported to the colonies, but in the year 1799, the situation for the
Catholic church worsened after the French army led by the general
Louis-Alexandre Berthier captured Rome and imprisoned Pope Pius
VI, who would later die in captivity in August 1799 in the city of
Valence in France. Robespierre himself was initially a member of the
Committee for Public Safety, the de fact ruling body of the French
nation. Later on, he became the chairman of the same committee,
which could basically arrest and execute any individual at any time.

On May 3, 1794, Maximilien Robespierre was elected as the new President of the national convention, the most powerful position of revolutionary France at the time. On May 7, 1794, Robespierre had the convention pass a decree which officially abolished the Christian religion and establish, in its place, a new God, namely the Goddess of Reason (Dieu de la raison) and a new religion for the French nation. Napoleon Bonaparte, who at that time, was just an artillery general, is famous of having said, "If I have to believe in something at all, I prefer to believe in the sun, after all, all life on this earth depends on her."

"Reason is God," said the leaders of the French Revolution. But people are so unreasonable that the revolutionary leader, Maximilien Robespierre, soon realized that reason makes a weak God. He became afraid that, without belief in some powerful being like the old Christian God, morals would collapse. Strong nations need strong virtues. The idea for this new religion came from a man who was, in reality, the chief ideologue and the brain behind the French revolution, a man by the name of Jean Jacques Rousseau. In his famous book *Le Contract Social* [The Social Contract], Rousseau, who was born in the French part of Switzerland, was of the opinion that the highest authority to rule any society is reasonable thinking and that two valuable things have to be considered in the human societies in the future. On the one hand it is sincerity, honesty and general virtue; and on the other, the eternal laws of nature itself. In June 1794, Robespierre organized a festival of the Supreme Being. At that festival it was proclaimed, with Robespierre's own words.

> Citizens, the day forever fortunate has arrived, which the French people have consecrated to the Supreme Being. Never has the world, which he created offered to him a spectacle so worthy of his notice. He has seen reigning on the earth tyranny, crime, and imposture. He sees at this moment a whole nation, grappling with all the oppressions

of the human race, suspend the course of its heroic labours to elevate its thoughts and vows toward the great Being, who has given it the mission it has undertaken and the strength to accomplish it.... Is it not he whose immortal hand, engraving on the heart of man the code of justice and equality, has written there the death sentence of tyrants? Is it not he who, from the beginning of time, decreed for all the ages and for all peoples liberty, good faith, and justice?

Ultimately, Maximilien Robespierre—lawyer, intellectual, patriot, and perhaps one of the greatest extremists of the French revolution—was himself executed on the guillotine. It is useless to say that the end of this story is like the ending to any other story which tries to fight with a popular religion. The still very powerful Monsieur Maximilien Robespierre, who on June 8, 1794, was leading a vast, popular procession through Paris, for the victory, greater glory and inauguration of his new faith, was arrested, condemned to death and subsequently executed on July 28, 1794. He met his fate at the same Guillotine that had killed so many aristocrats and clergy men before him on his personal orders.

France's famous Premier Republic, born of blood in 1789, came to an end in 1804 when Napoleon named himself Emperor and established the first French Empire. That French Empire subsequently ended on June 18, 1815, when the great Napoleon lost the battle of Waterloo to English and German forces. Following the defeat of Napoleon at Waterloo, the Allies restored the Bourbon Dynasty, who had ruled France until the revolution, to the French throne, and with it, of course, they restored the Catholic religion, the Churchs, and the seven days week, and the Christian calendar and so on, but that again is another story.

The idealistic escapades of the French Revolution, and the abolition of the Catholic Church in France, are now long forgotten, as if nothing had have happened at all. The name of Maximilien Robespierre, a man who, for a short period of time, had dictatorial authority in revolutionary France, is nothing more now than a minor footnote in the history of the French Revolution. But this episode in history, teaches us an important lesson: Religion is an integral part of the human psyche, and deeply rooted in the human nature.

We are not speaking about all humankind perhaps, but the great majority of the general public. If some individuals in the beginning of the twenty-first century say, "I don't believe in God any more," then we have to reply with Martin Heidegger's words: "The old Gods have lost their power, and their credibility, we are expecting the new God… who will come and rule for the next few thousand years humankind…"

It has, by now, become clear that religion can never been abolished from a society—*any* religion from *any* society. A religion can only be replaced by another religion. A new religion in a society has to take the place of an old religion. This is the lesson that history has thought us, and there are no exceptions. It would be a great mistake to believe that humankind, having arrived now at this stage of their technological development, can ignore values that have been valid since the beginning of civilization.

According to the first man in human history, who can be called a Prophet, the path to a harmonious and balanced live for humankind does not depend on education or intelligence of that individual alone, neither power nor wealth, but lies simply in the knowledge and the distinction between the Good and the Evil, in the mechanics of the human existence, and the following of the path of morality. Zarathustra is the man whose view and religion endures the millennia after him, if not directly, then in the form of other religions. It was Zarathustra who stood at the beginnings of morality and ethics as a social principle for humankind in the western world. Even if his name is now mainly forgotten by the general public in the western civilization, his genius will endure time as long as humanity exis ts.

10.2 ZOROASTRIANISM AND ITS RELATIONSHIP TO SOME IMPORTANT PHILOSOPHICAL CATEGORIES OF MODERN TIMES

Considering the Zoroastrian ideology, and monotheism in general, to be a philosophical category in itself, we have to make, at this point, a short excursion into the world of some relevant philosophical schools of thought, which have in the past affected the monotheistic point of view.

It is said that Plato was of the opinion that "If at all, the only thing in the galaxy and this world which might be immortal and absolute is Mathematics, therefore if God exist, he must be a mathematician." Unfortunately today, even this statement of Plato is looked upon by scientists as a romanticized idea and discarded as unreliable. The latest notion of mathematics as absolute has been challenged by various individuals in the scientific community as being just an abstract system invented by human mind, pointing out that other similar systems could exist parallel to mathematics known by humans, which could fulfill the same purpose. As we know there are, in the world of science, several very important and unanswered questions on which the top elite of the world intelligentsia are working. Among these fundamental questions for humanity, at this stage of its development, are question like: *What is human consciousness, and how deep are its roots?* –and– *How did life begin on this planet?* But probably the deepest mystery of all is this: *Why does the universe appear to follow mathematical laws?*

According to the theory of the Big Bang, all matter and all energy, space and time were created during the primeval explosion. All in one instant, in the one millionth of a second, instantly everything began unfolding according to a mathematical plan. Here comes the great question: *but where did the mathematics for that great event come from?* Was mathematics there before the Big Bang? What are the origins of numbers and their relationship to the facts they seem to obey?

The ancient Greek mathematician Pythagoras declared that numbers were the basic elements of the universe. Since then, all scientists have embraced a kind of mathematical creationism which suggests that God, if he exists, is a great mathematician, and he has declared, "Let there be *numbers*" before he could say, "Let there be light." Plato proposed that numbers and mathematical laws are eternal ideas and that they exist outside of time and space in a realm beyond the reach and intellect of human kind. According to mathematician and professor at the University of New Mexico, USA, Reuben Hersh "ideal entities, independent of human consciousness violate the empiricism of modern science" –and that– "…while science is anchored in observations of the physical world, mathematics is more of a human creation, like literature, religion."[275]

We have seen that the source of mathematics lies not just in the brain, but in the human body, and the physical world. For example, people favour number systems based on the number ten, just because they have ten fingers and ten toes. We hold out vague hopes that the mystery of mathematics might one day be solved if humans ever encounter an alien civilization. If mathematics is indeed universal and eternal, the scientists believe that an alien race would understand the concepts and the formulas of abstract mathematics.

The fundamental question here is this: *Why is there something, rather than nothing at all?* Why, for example, should we assume that nothingness is more natural than *somethingness*, or why should there be somethingness rather than nothingness? Indeed we could ask why is it that we think that there is something rather than nothing? The total energy of the known universe might be actually zero, if we believe in the strange bookkeeping of Albert Einstein's General Theory of Relativity. Even space and time themselves might be some kind of holographic illusion. Modern scientists and cosmologists differentiate three kinds of nothingness. First is what many have recognized as the nothingness of the ancient Greek mathematicians, which is the empty space, but we know now that every empty space is filled with vibrating electromagnetic fields and energy and other virtual particles.

The second nothingness can be thought of without even considering space and time; scientists are now proposing a new theory which suggests that whole universes, like little bubbles of space-time could pop into existence like bubbles in boiling water, and disappear again.

Thirdly there is even a deeper nothingness in which even the laws of mathematics and physics could be absent. Where do the laws of mathematics come from? Are they born with the universe? Or is the universe born according to the laws of mathematics? In effect, which came first the universe or mathematics? This theoretical reflection could be extended indefinitely if we enter the field of the theory of quantum principles and the quantum randomness in the universe.

If nothingness is our past, then nothingness could also be our future. As the scientists point out, the universe is being driven by dark energy—that is to say the negative pressure of nothing—and therefore the universe is expanding faster and faster. One day in the future, the galaxies known to us will become completely invisible to us, then all the energy, information and our knowledge of the galaxies will be sucked out of the known cosmos and be lost for us forever, provided that humankind should still exist at that time. The universe will revert to nothingness. From nothing to nothing. We see here that, no matter how far science, mathematics and human mind drives us forward, we always reach a limit where we have to say, this is the frontier of science and knowledge, and therefore, from *here*, starts the world of philosophy and maybe religion. God will never be excluded from the human scientific calculations, no matter how far we advance into the mysteries of the universe, as there always will be unanswered questions, which will confront the human mind.

The teachings of the great Charles Darwin and his monumental work *On The Origins of the Species*, first printed 1859, tells us that all living species, included ourselves, evolved and developed from initially one kind of primitive and simple living cell, which appeared on our planet approximately five hundred million years ago. This is of course a *theory*, but it is the latest belief in the world of scientific knowledge about life on our planet. The discussion in the academic world is now over the question of how this simple living cell evolved or came to be in the first place. Some scientists are now trying to create life itself, and start a simple living cell in the laboratory from chemical components; others are talking about the possibility of this first primitive live form to have reached the earth inside a meteorite which came from outer space, possibly from the planet Mars.

As for the point of view of the monotheists, or the creationists, their ideology is not based on recent scientific discoveries, but its effect on the human society has proven to be very constructive and beneficiary. We have seen that in times of wars, or the confrontation of different cultures, religions bond people and groups together in a way that no scientific discovery or other ideology can. This hold true even for people who are non-believers or atheist, for they are integrated and moved by the enthusiasm and the power of religious beliefs, as it suggests loyalty and gives people an identity.

Should the human mind develop to a higher stage and become more intelligent, and should the human race reach a new scientific level where the old god and his religion should lose its power, should the circumstances of the society changes to a point, where the old religion loses its credibility, then a new religion has to emerge again from the human mind itself, which will take the place of the old religion. No religion can be abolished or deleted from the society, unless a new religion can take its place. This is an important lesson, which history teaches us.

In his recent book, the New York University Philosophy professor Thomas Nagel is distancing himself from the Charles Darwin scholars, and declaring why "the Neo-Darwinian conception of nature is almost certainly false."[276] Thomas Nagel extends his ideas about consciousness into a sweeping critique of the modern scientific worldview, which he calls " ... a heroic triumph of ideological theory over common sense..." His thesis is that consciousness is not just a incidental feature of life on earth, but a important and fundamental aspect of the Universe. Instead of a random evolution, Nagel sees the unfolding of a "cosmic predisposition", furthermore, the depiction of a universe, gradually waking up through the emergence of a universal consciousness...

Returning to Zoroastrianism, and to clarify and to strengthen its religious and ideological base and worldview, and furthermore, to understand what is the position of religion in general in the modern world, we have to enter here into some detail into the latest development in world philosophy.

Modern thinkers today, such as the German professor of Philosophy Markus Gabriel, at the University of Bonn[277] and also the professor of philosophy Thomas Nagel of the New York University[278] think basically that, "... the world we think exists, doesn't exist at all, ... even if we would find a world formula for all the questions regarding our existence and our being that would in reality only constitute as segment of the reality... The universe, as known by us, is only a part of a total but not the total itself..." Thomas Nagel is himself critical of the new Darwinist school, with its *emergence of consciousness theory*. Also the newly emerging school of Intelligent Design (simply called ID), which propagates the unity of science and the creativity theory of the monotheistic religions, has been rejected by the new philosophical movement around Thomas Nagel, Gabriel Marcus and others.

What is obvious here is the fact that a lot of factors and values, on which we rely in our daily existence, are in reality absolutely dependent on our consciousness and are non-existent in the real universe. Humankind's worldview of the reality in our existence is absolutely wrong, as it is based on the assumption that there is a reality upon which humans could look to from *outside*, as an object. We humans are, at all times, looking to the reality of this world, or the fact of our existence, necessarily from a certain point of view, which is from our point of view. That means that every person watching the reality is tied to one certain perspective. According to Nagel, "The look to the reality from nowhere is unreachable to us humans, therefore any scientific worldview of the reality by humans must be geometrically distorted." In considering this new outlook into the realities of our existence, we can therefore say that existence is always relative, and it is not identical with what we conceive as the truth. For example, imagination also exists as a reality.

For us, our imaginations are also realities, and therefore many things perceived by us as facts and realities exist only in our imagination, and are therefore dependent on our consciousness. In our thinking categories, we are always asking for a meaning or a raison d'etre, but the universe does not asks for any purpose or meaning. The universe is a cold and meaningless space, devoid of purpose, and it is only following its own mathematical laws, at least that's what we have formulated in our mind. This changes fundamentally when we, as humans, ask for our position in this endless and meaningless space. The nature of being a human is not explicable without the question of purpose and meaning, the raison d'etre becomes imperative. The reason for this is simply the fact that human beings know that they exists, and know that, for them, the reality exists only because and through their consciousness. We are sub consciously constantly aware of the time and space limitation of our existence, and this reflects in our subjective evaluation of the reality in which we live.

If we look at the natural sciences and its advances in history, these paradigms do fail necessarily because of the human mind, as the human mind is constantly searching for a meaning or a purpose. If we discard the existence of the human mind and look at the universe, we see that the question of meaning and purpose becomes non-existent. The great question of our time is *how did the human mind develop a consciousness and the ability to investigate through his mind and consciousness his own mind and consciousness.* We could say that the historical category of philosophy was, from the beginning of its existence, an investigation of the human mind, consciousness and human spirit through his own mind and consciousness. Meaning that, in effect, philosophy is nothing more than the human mind investigating itself, as all realities perceived by us are formed in our mind only.

Furthermore, we have to mention here specifically the human spirit, as it is more vast and complex than the simple human thinking or the human mind. The human spirit includes factors not enveloped in our thinking, such as emotions, creative imaginations and phantasies, and most importantly, the abstract spheres of our archaic and hidden sub-conscious drives and urges, which originate from our pre-archaic and animalistic origins. The ultimate consequence of the modern philosophical category is, in essence, the knowledge that the human mind does not recognize that it is, at all times, investigating itself. We are unable to view the realities of the universe from the point of view of nowhere, any kind of human thinking and investigation of the realities of this world is, in reality, the investigation *of* our own mind *through* our own mind. Any real objectivity, therefore, is ultimately unachievable for the human mind.

As human beings, we are part of a living species whose existence has a beginning and an end, and we are, in our sub-consciousness, always aware of the limitation of our existence. Therefore, all human logic is based on the question *where does our existence come from and where does it go to*. In other words, we are constantly looking for a logical reason for things to exist or not to exist. It seems that time therefore exists only for things which have a beginning and an end. In contrast, however, to our existence, the universe seems to be timeless, in a state of continuous change but still constant. It is the human mind which is determining a beginning and an end for the universe, all according to our own logic. The question of God's existence is, therefore, not only closely tied to the human mind and consciousness itself but has, furthermore, an additional important psychological factor, which is independent of the conscious mind, and is biologically pre-determined and unique to humankind. As for example, the urge to believe in God is, for some humans, a psychological–biological necessity, which is unrelated to the degree of intelligence or education or the ability of logical and reasonable thinking of that individual. Many highly intelligent and educated persons—some scientists among them—are firm believers in the existence of a supreme creator God, whereas we can see that relatively average and uneducated individuals profess to be atheists. The urge to believe in God, for some humans, is independent of their mind or consciousness, but is directly rooted in their biological nature.

Having seen that the limitation of our *Weltanschauung* [German, meaning *world view*] is dependable or restricted to our perspective of the reality in which we necessarily exist, we can return to the world which is dependent on our mind. That is necessarily the reality in which we live, and here we can return to the ideal world order, which must be desirable to all humankind. This ideal world order—which would satisfy humanity whose desire it would be to live in a balanced and healthy environment—would point necessarily to the balanced and moral worldview, presented by Zarathustra at the beginnings of history to humankind.

As we have seen in the moral teachings of Zarathustra and his outlook for the future of humanity, apart from the fact that, philosophically speaking, the birthplace of this ideology again was also the human mind itself—Zarathustra's mind—this worldview encompasses the humans as well as the animal and natural world as a total unity. The existence of humanity set in an environment of a world where animals and nature and humans are coexisting in a balanced harmony must be the ultimate goal of humanity. This ultimate goal for humanity is envisaged by the worldview Zarathustra presented to humankind. Should an ideal world order be sought by humanity in the future, one which is realistic, based on ethical principles, and encompasses all aspects of nature and the environment, including us the humans, then the Zoroastrian worldview is an ideal candidate to be chosen.

A philosophical category which became very fashionable in the period shortly after the Second World War in the intellectual circles of western European capitals was the school of existentialism. In the years after the second world war, mainly in France, it was, in some intellectual circles, fashionable to be an existentialist. After the very tragic and unprecedented events of the Second World War had ended, the general public in Europe, but also to some extent in the western world, after having recovered from the tragedy and the shock of the war, asked themselves a very important question. Namely, how could these unprecedented atrocities and systematic killings happen? What had happened to the ancient values and moral principles we all believed in? What about the ground rules of western civilization, which had previously bound all the nations of the western world to each other? And finally we come here to the main question: where was God when millions of people, innocent and uninvolved in the war activities, were murdered systematically? The tragic and historical events of the Holocaust, only known to the world public after the end of the war, was a first in history. Atrocities had been committed by all parties involved in the hostilities because that was the nature of war. After the end of the war, the general intelligentsia in Europe came to the conclusion that those moral and religious values in which they had believed—if they previously really existed at all—were not valid any more, and, in fact, that they had been proven to be wrong. The old traditional moral and religious values, once the pillars of bourgeois society in the western world, had lost all their credibility. Additionally, the spread of communism across eastern Europe and China had endangered the moral and traditional values existing since antiquity in the western civilization. The world intelligentsia was a witness to the fact that those powers, namely the Marxist, who believed that God never existed and felt that *religion is the narcotics for the masses* (Karl Marx: *Religion ist Opium für das Volk*) were actually winning country after country to their cause. This general collapse of the old traditional and moral religious values in western Europe shortly after the end of the Second World War had created an ideological void, which not only needed a philosophical explanation, but had to be filled ideologically.

Therefore, as a reaction to this moral bankruptcy, new intellectual personalities emerged after the war in the western European capitals, who not only propagated their new ideology, but also lived according to it. The new philosophy emerging after the end of the second world war in western Europe was *existentialism*. One of the intellectuals, probably the most prolific proponent of the new existentialism was the French philosopher Jean-Paul Sartre (1905–1980). Sartre was one of the key figures in the philosophy of existentialism and one of the leading figures in the French Marxist and anti-colonialist movement in post-war era (1948 and after) France. Sartre being a playwright, novelist, screenwriter, political activist, literary critic and a philosopher, was awarded the Nobel Prize for literature in 1964, which he declined. He was, in fact, the first Nobel Prize Laureate to voluntary decline the prize, and he had also previously refused the Légion d'Honneur in 1945. Coming here finally, to essence of existentialism, Sartre was on the opinion that:

> All previous traditional religious and ethical guidelines for humanity have been proven to be wrong and they have lost their credibility.

These were all theories, which had been invented by the powerful rulers and those who previously were believed to be prophets and patriarchs by humanity. Therefore, in the absence of any creator God, we can say with Jean-Paul Sartre's own words that:

> Humanity as a whole are condemned to be free, only responsible to itself…[279]

This means, in essence, that in the absence of any higher authority, meaning God, individuals could be held responsible for their own deeds and ultimately the actions of all humanity. Previously, individuals could have referred their actions to have been done in the name of divine orders or commandments, but in this case (in the absence of a creator God) humankind is ultimately responsible personally for anything they do in their existence. The absolute freedom of humans, who have broken the chains of thousands of years of traditions and the belief in divine rules and commandments, makes them absolutely responsible for any action taken by them in their existence. The ultimate and the only authority to which humankind must answer is from now on their own personal conscience. Again with Jean-Paul Sartre's own words:

> We are left alone and abandoned without excuse…
> The concept of authenticity and individuality
> by human kind has to be earned, but it cannot
> be learned.[280]

The authentic guidelines in the life of humanity is experience not knowledge. Death, for humanity, is an act and the final point when we as beings on this world cease to live for ourselves; we permanently become an object that exists only for those surviving in the outside world.[281] As such, that death emphasizes or magnifies the burden of our free and individual existence.

The main worldview of existentialism could be perhaps called the principle of existence precedes essence, which Sartre mentions in his book *Existentialism and Humanism*. This means that human beings—through their own consciousness—create their own values, and so determine a personal meaning to their life. And also, as he says: "… man first of all exists—then encounters himself—surges up in the world—and only defines himself afterwards." This has been also mentioned similarly by Martin Heidegger.[282] Jean-Paul Sartre did, in reality, take a great deal of inspiration from the academic world of past known philosophers, and it is clear that Sartre's main inspiration was Karl Marx, and he openly declared himself to be ideologically a communist, although he never joined the communist party in France. Additionally, he took ideas from man who founded the categories of the *phenom-enologist epistemology*, Franz Adler. Franz Adler, one of the chroniclers of the existentialistic school, explains this ideology this way:

> Man chooses and makes himself by acting. Any action implies the judgement that he is right under the same circumstances not only for the actor but also for everybody else in similar circumstances.[283]

In reality, Jean-Paul Sartre and his wife (the two were never legally married), Simone de Beauvoir—a great intellectual in her own rights, a professor of philosophy, and the founder of the feminist movement of the mid-twentieth century—were celebrated in the public eye of Western Europe as famous and prominent public intellectuals during their lifetimes.[284] The real academic thinkers and founders of this philosophical category were less known by the general public. These were man like Soren Kierkegaard (1813–1855) the Danish philoso-pher, who is been regarded as the first existential thinker and maybe the founder of this category. Then we have the German psychoanalyst and philosopher Professor Karl Jaspers (1883–1969) of the University of Basel. Karl Jaspers, bases his thoughts on previous thinkers such as Kierkegaard, and Nietzsche but also Martin Heidegger, whom he knew personally. Jaspers writes:

> Beginning with modern science and the empiricism (meaning scientific method) we clearly question reality, we confront and approach borders that an empirical (scientific) method simply can not tran-scend. It is at this decisive point that the individual faces a choice: namely to sink into despair and res-ignation, or to take a leap of faith forward into the —*Transcendence*. In making this decisive leap, indi-viduals confront their own limitless freedom.[285]

Karl Jaspers calls this freedom *Existence,* and suggests that the individual can experience his personal boundless free existence. At the end of his life, Jaspers wrote extensively on the threat to human freedom posed by modern science and modern political and economical institutions, a subject that worried him. Before ending our excursion into the world of existential thought, we have to mention here the great Russian writer Feodor Dostoyevsky (1821–1881). In his masterwork, the *Brothers Karamazov*, Dostoyevsky mentions that "…if God would not exist, then everything would be permitted." The only way to the salvation of the human soul is the existence of a higher being, namely God. Furthermore, in his novel *Notes from the Underground,* he portrays a man, who is unable to fit into the society, and is unhappy with the identities he has created for himself. This, for the protagonist, represented an existential crisis that called into question all values created or believed by the society.

As already mentioned, the surge of the existential philosophy in the 1950s and 1960s was a reaction to the tragic events of the Second World War, but these events are now being mostly forgotten by the new generation. We have seen now, instead, the emergence of religious fundamentalism, which is a sign that every generation, again and again, has to make their own experiences, and that history, therefore, will have to continue to repeat itself. In terms of Zoroastrian teachings and its worldview, the events of the first half of the twentieth century in Europe, the trauma of two world wars, and also the rise and fall of world communism, have shown one fundamental point very clearly. Namely the fact that, in the workings of the world—i.e. human nature and its consciousness—evil is an independent force in and of itself, one which must be combatted at all times.

For those individuals outside the Zoroastrian faith, but who have a knowledge of its ideology, the notion of evil that fights with the forces of goodness and truth is just an archaic and theoretical myth, which can not be taken seriously anymore. The world of science believes that every person acts according to the situation in which they find themselves, and the theory of "Freedom of choice for humanity" is in reality just an ideal, which belongs to the vocabulary of naïve idealists.

The truth is, unfortunately, much more tragic and unfavourable for humankind. We know, for example, that humankind is the only species on the planet that kills and destroys for pure pleasure. No animal is known to science kills for the pleasure of killing. Animals only attack when hungry, when threatened, when defending their territory on which their survival depends, or to establish their supremacy in the group—which is also a matter of survival—but never purely for the pleasure of killing or destroying. It is true that, apparently, dolphins play with other sea animals until they are dead, but their aim is not to kill that other animal, but rather just to play, therefore, dolphins are probably not aware of the consequences of their actions. This is different with humans, we have many examples in history when, in wars or conquests, men of power have ordered, without any strategic or political reason or benefit to them, the destruction, torture, and killing of vast groups of humans. In many cases, not only were these killings without benefit to them, but often at that scale were technically a difficult, time consuming, and/or costly task. Apart from the real and tragic events of the Holocaust, which has no precedent in human history, other mass killings happened in the Second World War, which had no strategic or military or any other benefit to the power committing it.

An earlier example: In September of 1220, the Mongol conqueror Genghis Khan and his armies approached the cities of Marv and Balkh in Bactria, in what was then northwestern Iran. These two cities decided to surrender to the Mongols. The city of Balkh was one of the oldest and most historically important cities in the ancient world; the Aryan tribes entering the Iranian Plateau from the north, settled in this city circa 2000 BC, and according to historians, Zarathustra's religion started to expand from this area. Although the two cities had surrendered and were cooperating, Genghis Khan ordered the killing of all the inhabitants and the total destruction of both cities. After hundreds of thousands of humans, old young and child had been massacred and the two cities destroyed completely, the huge Mongol army proceeded to the southwest to the heartland of Iran.

A few days later, Genghis Khan received a report to the effect that when the soldiers were killing the people, some woman and children, had pretended to be dead and had mixed themselves among the other corpses in order to escape the slaughter. Genghis Khan immediately ordered his army to stop their advance to the southwest and to return to the destroyed cities in the north. There he ordered the soldiers to decapitate every corpse and to build a gruesome pyramid of severed heads. This story sounds very unrealistic and made up, but unfortunately it is true and historically documented. This and other such details can be found in the book of the American historian and diplomat Jeremiah Curtin entitles *The Mongol: a History*.[286] It shows that this act had no benefit whatsoever either strategically or politically for Genghis Khan, on the contrary, it delayed his advance. The only explanation is that an uncontrollable urge, coming from his subconsciousness, forced this decision on him. There are many similar examples in history

Then we have the case, where some humans enjoy the senseless and purposeless killing of animals. Traditionally, hunting was a challenge between animal and human, where the animals had a realistic chance of at least escaping, as the humans were hunting with bow and arrow. The killing of animals by humans was only for the purpose of eating meat or when humans were threatened by animals. We have now a systematic killing of animals with long range firearms and binoculars, where the animal is not even aware that his life will end in a few seconds. A famous and celebrated man in his time was Buffalo Bill (William Cody, 1846–1917) who had made a name for himself in the old West of the United States by indiscriminately killing and exterminating North American buffalo (bison more accurately) whose killing had served no purpose whatsoever. American natives of that region dependet mostly on this animal for there survival. This big and powerful animal existed only in some parts of the USA. The big pride of Buffalo Bill was that he, sitting on his horse with his rifle at one time had killed exactly 4,280 animals in short period of time. People later intervened and stopped him, just in time, as there were only a handful buffalo left in the old west. Now, more than one and a half centuries later, the bison population is still only a small fraction of what it was before.

When we analyze these events, we necessarily come to the conclusion that evil, under whatever name we want to call it, is an independent phenomenon in and of itself, whose existence, at least in the human mind, has not yet been investigated empirically (scientifically). To discard the evil and sadistically motivated behaviour of humans as just another case of psycho-pathological deviation, is not a satisfactory explanation. The empirical (scientific) cause of sadism or evil behaviour in mass murderers for example has usually been explained as having a psycho-pathological base, or some experiences made in early infancy by that individual—forgetting that many other humans have the same psychological problems, or had the same experience in infancy, but did not act in the same way or did not commit those crimes. Maybe one day, science will come to the conclusion that the reason for the evil behaviour of some humans, lies beyond the realm of simple psychological factors. These are urges coming from deep in the sub-consciousness of that individual, and powers unknown and uncontrollable by these persons themselves involved. These are currents deep in the sub-consciousness of humankind, which derives probably from the pre-archaic (prehistoric) and animalistic period of the human race. As a conclusion, therefore, we can say that this analysis of our true being conforms to the Zoroastrian world view, in which evil is an independent force in itself, which must be combatted at all times.

Here finally we come to the last and most important philosophical category, which is that of *historical and dialectical materialism*. The knowledge of this philosophical category is of the greatest importance for all of those who believe in a society whose ethical rules of conduct are derived from—or at least inspired by—divine origin. As all the present monotheistic religions can trace their roots to the teachings of the Prophet Zarathustra, it can be said that the general adversary of all monotheistic religions, without exception, from Zarathustra until today, could be called historical and dialectical materialism. Therefore, for all people who are concerned with the theistic (theism: belief in an supernatural being, or belief in God) perspective of seeing the existence of humankind in the future, it is imperative to enter more in detail into the mechanics of this important philosophical category. It is herewith important, if you will, to enter into the heart of darkness.

Firstly we have to understand that dialectical and historical materialism classifies all religions and other moral values derived from a creator God, into the category of idealism—meaning that they belong purely to the world of ideas—dependant only on our mind and consciousness with no real basis in the natural world. Speaking about the philosophical school of dialectical materialism, we have to mention that, this is a strand of philosophical disciplines which was initially founded and developed by George Friedrich Wilhelm Hegel (1770–1831) the famous German philosopher and Professor at the University of Berlin, who was the teacher of Karl Marx. At a later date, this idea was further developed, and it was Friedrich Engels, who referred to it for the first time, with the name historical materialism, in his book *Dialectics of Nature.*[287] This philosophical school is the methodological approach to looking at the economics, history, and society of human kind, from the materialistic point of view.

Historical materialism starts from a fundamental reality of human existence, namely that in order for human beings to survive and continue their existence from one generation to the next, it is necessary for them to produce and to again reproduce the material requirements of their daily life. In so doing, not adapting passively to nature itself, but acting actively against the laws of nature. In order to achieve this first and important step in order to carry out production, people have to enter into very definite and hierarchical social relationships with each other. This again means that human beings collectively work on nature, but do not do the same work. There is a division of labour in which people not only do different jobs, but some people actually live from the work of other people, by owning the means of production itself. This philosophy is the backbone of all scientific atheism. Dialectical and historical materialism is the philosophical discipline which constitutes the backbone of all of those trying to prove the impossibility of a supernatural being or a supernatural consciousness who created or caused to exist the present world or the reality in which we are living and humankind itself and the other species. Boiled down to its essence it is this:

Thesis Against Antithesis Is Equal To Synthesis

This essentially means that all realities in the material world are the result of various forces which are constantly fighting and balancing off each other. Things we see or know are the synthesis (or the result) of several forces in the real world, which have collided with each other, or are colliding constantly and in so doing create a new realities, which is called the synthesis. Historical materialism represents the laws of dialectical materialism extended to the world of the human society and human history.

At this point we can enter this discussion, by saying that, for those who regard the Zoroastrian religion as a dualistic ideology, it could be argued that basically his system of seeing the realities of this world is of a dialectical nature. From this point of view, the basic ideology of the Zoroastrian worldview or Weltanschauung is essentially based on a dialectical principle. Namely the reality in which we are living is a synthesis of the collision of the forces of good and evil, which we have, ourselves, helped to create with our actions. This, of course, is a simplified version of dialectic, but it shows that the Zoroastrian ideology views the reality of the world in a constant struggle of opposed forces, therefore the reality is not static but dynamic and in constant change.

After having mentioned various times the Zoroastrian notion of good and evil, which forms an essential part of Zarathustra's world-view, we have to investigate here the true meaning of these words from the philosophical as well as from the psycho-pathological point of view. What is the meaning of the notion of good versus evil; do they really exist outside of the human mind, or are they pure emotional invention of our consciousness, which we project into the real world?

When it comes to define the reality, in essence, what the materialistic ideology believes, and in particular historical materialism points out, is that we have to make a clear distinction and a big line between those words or values or factors in our worldview which are existent in the real world and those which are non-existent. Those things, deemed to be *materia*, meaning words or values or things deemed to be real and existent in the real world and in nature, are those things which are absolutely independent of our mind or our consciousness. But in contrary, those matters or values which are dependant of our mind, consequently exist *only* in the human mind, created by us and therefore dependent on us, and hence they do not exist in reality but only in our mind.

Those values, words, factors which are dependent on the human mind and dependent on our consciousness do not really exist in the real world, and they have been made up, invented, imagined by the human mind itself. In philosophical terms, they belong to the category of idealism. Dyads such as beautiful/ugly, good/bad, just/unjust, faithful/unfaithful are all value-dependent on the human consciousness, and therefore non-existent in the real, material, and natural world.

It is my assertion that evil, the way Zarathustra saw it, is an independent force in itself and not dependant on the human mind and consciousness; it is a natural force, which is real and existent in the dogmatic-materialistic sense. In the contrary, nature has laws and regulations and facts of its own, which are, to a certain extent, known or unknown to us. Even if those laws or facts of nature are unknown to us, they still are a part of the natural, material world and they do exist in reality, as they are existing independently from our consciousness or our mind. There exist two type of material, the objective materia and the subjective materia. The objective materia are things which exist independently from our mind, things we can touch or see; and the subjective materia are things which exist independently from our mind, but we cannot see or touch them. Subjective materia, are those things which can not be seen or touched, but still exists, as for example hunger, thirst, the urges to do evil or good, and of course the sexual drive, which are in many cases uncontrollable by us, and unrelated and independent from our conscious mind. For example, in nature and in the material world, the important human values like trust, mistrust and fairness, God, equality and justice-do not exist, these are purely inventions of our mind. The fundamental law of nature is the daily struggle for survival for all living species, included us humans, and those values (as justice, fairness, God, the soul, and specifically love) are not existent in real nature.

The fundamental argument of historical materialism is the following: we humans, in the course of our history and development, in order to create for ourselves a better quality of life, have created in our mind a certain system, this system is called *civilization*, which includes creations and inventions or ideas or values as equality, justice, fairness, goodness, evil, love, beauty, the soul and afterlife, reincarnation, the immortality of the soul, day of judgment, the idea of the sacred and of the profane. Therefore, in the materialistic worldview, factors and phenomena such as god and religion are thought to be inventions, or ideals created by our mind; therefore, these belong in the classification of idealism.

In Marxist terms, God and religion are invented by the rulers of society and therefore serve as a great ally of the ruling economic class and the oppressors. Feudal landowners—and above them the nobility and ultimately the king himself—who are living off the work of the peasant and working class, have practically invented or at least are strongly relying on the existence of a higher being, namely God.

This in order to appease and calm the lower classes—the peasant and the working class people—and to make them believe that the cause of their misery is not class inequality, but can rather be traced to the divine order of the world, atop which sits a creator God. Basically the worker and the farmer of the lower classes are forced to believe that their destiny was decided by God, and cannot be changed by humans.

What the founders of the historical and dialectal materialism and the great philosophers of materialism in general did not consider, was the fundamental truth that the existence of God and the general human attachments and the human need for religion and religiosity cannot be attributed alone to economic factors or to the struggle of economics classes in history, like for example, peasant against landlord, worker against factory owner and so on.

The latest scientific discoveries show that the human need for God and religion is not an economical, but a psychological and anatomical need. This means that the vast majority of human beings anatomically-psychologically need—and will always need—a higher being, namely God, and the religion which goes with it. The mind and the nature of the majority of the members of the human society will always need the existence of a higher being. This, of course, on the condition that this religion and its regulations are fitting to the environment and the circumstances those humans are living in.

According to historical materialism, if we analyze the history of philosophy, then we come to the conclusion that, generally speaking, the whole history of philosophy is the history of the struggle and the development of two mutually opposed schools of philosophy, namely, idealism and materialism. All philosophical currents and schools are manifestations of these two fundamental schools. Again, according to the historical materialism, all philosophical theories have been created by men belonging to a definite and certain social class. Meaning, for example, a financially well-to-do person's outlook of the realities in which he exists and his worldview, would be different from the worldview of a member of the oppressed worker or farmer class. All philosophical doctrines express the needs of a definite social class and reflect the historical stage in men's comprehension of nature.

We can also say that the Zoroastrian worldview was a reflection of the circumstances in which the Prophet himself lived and in which his consciousness was formed—namely the era of economic harmony. As we do not see any signs of class struggle in the Gathas, the emphasis of the Zoroastrian ideology is on the moral and ethical behaviour of each person with regards to the deeds of each human individually. For Zarathustra, the beginning and ongoing condition of the harmonious existence of all humankind lies in the recognition, by all individuals, in the difference between the forces of good and the forces of evil as independent natural forces and principles, which are uncontrollable by the individual himself. In essence, the recognition that good and evil are factors in the human mind, which are beyond his control, and that the individual has simply to chose the right path, which is the path of *the good*. This seemed, to Zarathustra, to be far more fundamental than, for example, simply the struggle of economic classes in the society.

Whereas the social origins of idealism and materialism lie in a social structure marked by class contradictions and class struggle. The earliest idealism was the product of the ignorance and superstition of savage and primitive man. Then, with the development of the productive forces and the ensuing development of scientific knowledge, it stands to reason that idealism should decline and be replaced by materialism. And yet, from ancient times to the present, idealism has *not* declined, rather, on the contrary, it has developed and carried on a struggle for supremacy with materialism from which neither has emerged the victor. The reason lies in the division of society into classes. For the philosophies and ideology of the left, it is clear, in its own interest, that the oppressing class must develop and reinforce its idealist doctrines. On the other hand, the oppressed classes, likewise in their own interest, must develop and reinforce their materialist doctrines.

Both idealism and materialism are weapons in the class struggle, and the struggle between idealism and materialism cannot disappear so long as different economical classes continue to exist in the society. The oppressors are using the idealistic philosophy as their ideological weapon against the oppressed classes in the society, and for the oppressed classes their weapon and their ideological philosophy is the materialistic worldview. The materialist left believe that idealism, in the process of its historical development, represents the ideology of the ruling classes (landowners and capitalists) and serves solely their purposes; whereas materialism is the worldview of the revolutionary class (the working class, the proletariat, the peasants, soldiers, etc.). Consequently, the history of the struggle between idealism and materialism in philosophy reflects the struggle of interests between the ruling class and the revolutionary class.

Wherein lies the basic difference between idealism and materialism? It lies in the opposite answers given by the two to the fundamental question in philosophy, that of the relationship between spirit and matter (that of the relationship between consciousness and existence). Idealism considers spirit (consciousness, the mind, concepts, the subject) as the source of all that exists on earth, and matter (nature and society, the object) as secondary and subordinate. Materialism on the other side, recognizes the independent existence of matter as detached from spirit and considers spirit as secondary and subordinate to matter. The Zoroastrian worldview believes that the good and the evil are an independent factor from the human mind, independent of his consciousness. This would make these two independent forces a part of the *material* world. This would mean that the Zoroastrian worldview would be philosophically a part of materialism and not idealism. Idealism sees matter as the product of the spirit, but materialism sees the notion of spirit as idealism and therefore as non-existent. Zarathustra's ideology is based on the assumption that the good and evil forces are existing independently in this world, meaning independently of the human mind, and real in time and space.

The recognition that matter exists independently and apart from consciousness and the human mind, in the external world, is the foundation of materialism. Man created this foundation through practice, obliged to submit to natural forces. Capable of using only simple tools, primitive man could not explain the surrounding phenomena and hence sought help from spirits, or the supernatural world. This is the origin of religion and idealism. But in the long-range process of production, man came into contact with surrounding nature, acted upon nature, changed nature, and created things to eat, to live in, and to use, and adapted nature to the interests of man and caused man to believe that matter has an objective existence.

In the beginning, man acted passively to the forces of nature, and he adapted to them like all living species. At a certain point in history, man learned how to actively address the forces of nature, he was no longer simply adapting himself to them passively. This was the moment our species separated themselves from other living and started the long journey to became humans. It was at this moment that the consciousness of mankind started to investigate itself vis-a-vis its relationship to its environment. By actively setting its will against nature, mankind entered into history, for he *created* history. All other living species adapt passively to natural forces; they have no history. Interestingly also some primitive human tribes and races (in the Amazon basin, and in Africa) who are still adapting to the forces of nature passively, have not entered into history, or they did not create history.[288]

Materialism believes that the history of science furnishes man with proof of the material nature of the world and of the fact that mankind is governed by laws; this helps mankind to see the futility of the illusions of religion and idealism and to arrive at materialist conclusions. In short, the history of humankind's practice comprises the history of his struggle with nature, which is the history of science.

Under the heading of *the object of philosophy*, we must still solve another problem, namely the problem of the unity of dialectics, logic and epistemology [the study of scientific knowledge]. According to Friedrich Engels, the materialist dialectics is the only scientific epistemology, and it is also the only scientific logic. Materialist dialectics studies the origin and development of our knowledge of the outside world. It studies the transition from not knowing to knowing, and from incomplete knowledge to more complete knowledge; it studies how the laws of the development of nature and society are daily reflected more profoundly and more extensively in the mind of humanity. This is precisely the unity of materialist dialectics with epistemology

The first fundamental principle of dialectical materialism lies in its view of matter. This principle of the unity of the world has already been explained above in discussing matter. The second fundamental principle of dialectical materialism lies in its theory of movement (or theory of development). This means the recognition that movement is the form of the existence of matter, an inherent attribute of matter, a manifestation of the multiplicity of matter. This is the principle of the development of the world. The combination of the principle of the development of the world with the principle of the unity of the world, set forth above, constitutes the whole of the world view of dialectical materialism. The world is nothing else but the material world in a process of unlimited and constant movement and development.

Dialectical materialism's theory of movement is in opposition, first of all, with philosophical idealism and with the theological concepts of religion. The German idealist philosopher Hegel held that the present world results from the development of the so-called *world idea*. In China, the philosophy of the *I Ching* [*Book of Changes*] and the metaphysics of the Sung and Ming all put forward idealist views of the development of the universe. Christianity and the monotheists says that God created the world, Buddhism attribute the movement and development of all the myriad phenomena *(Wan Wu)* of the universe to spiritual forces. All of these doctrines which think about movement apart and not connected to matter, are fundamentally incompatible with dialectical materialism.

Dialectical materialism considers rest—or equilibrium—as merely one element of movement, one particular circumstance of movement. A sentence popular with the metaphysical thinkers of ancient China is, "Heaven does not change and the Ways also does not change." This corresponds to a theory of the immobility of the universe. In their view, the basic nature of the universe, and of society, was eternally unchanging. The reason why they adopted this attitude is to be found primarily in their class limitations. If the feudal landlord class had recognized that the basic nature of the universe and of society is subject to movement and development—and especially to change—then most certainly they would have been pronouncing, in theory, a death sentence on their own class. The philosophies of all reactionary forces (reactionary forces = the oppressing class, or the members of the oppressing establishment)[289] are theories of immobilism. The world intellectuals, revolutionary classes, and the world of science have all perceived the principle of movement and the development of the world, and consequently advocate transforming the society into a better and better world for future generations of humankind.

What we have just discussed is the theory of the movement of the world, or the principle of the development of the world in accordance with dialectical materialism, and its extension to the society and history, which is called historical materialism. We have also investigated the possible relationship of the Zoroastrian worldview with the philosophical category of dialectical thinking.

---

270. T.B.Macaulay, Minute Recorded in the General Department, 2 February. L. Zastoupil and M. Moir "The Great Indian Educational Debate: Documents relating to the Orientalist–Anglicist Controversy 1781–1843" (London: Curzon Press, 1835), p. 171

271. Sir Frederic John Goldsmid and Sir Oliver St John, *Eastern Persia: An Account of the Journeys of the Persian Boundary Commission 1870-71-72* (London: McMillan and Co., 1876)

272. Michael Strausberg, *Zarathustra and Zoroastrianism* (Sheffield: Equinox Publishing Ltd., 2008), p. 7

273. Cyrus Ghani, *Iran and the Rise of Reza Shah* (London: I.B.Tauris Publishers, 1998)

274. Ali Akbar Dareini trans., *The fall and the rise of the Pahlawy Dynasty: Memoirs of the former General Hossein Fardust* (Delhi: Motilal Banarsidass publishers, 1996)

275. Reuben Hersh, *What Is Mathematics Really* (Oxford University Press, 1997)

276. Thomas Nagel, *Mind and Cosmos* (Oxford University Press, 2012)

277. Marcus Gabriel, *Warum es die Welt nicht gibt* (Berlin: Ullstein Verlag, 2013)

278. Thomas Nagel, "What Is It Like to Be a Bat?", *The Philosophical Review*, Vol. 83, No. 4 (Oct. 1974), pp. 435-450.

279. Jean-Paul Sartre (tr. Philip Mairet), *Existentialism and Humanism* (London, Methuen, 1948), p. 27.

280. Jean Paul Sartre, *Being and Nothingness* (New York: Philosophical Library, 1956), p. 246

281. Gordon Haim, *Dictionary of Existentialism* (Santa Barbara: Greenwood Press, 1999), p. 105

282. Martin Heidegger, *Being and Time*, trans. by John Macquarrie & Edward Robinson (London: SCM Press, 1962)

283. Franz Adler, "The social thoughts of J.P.Sartre" *American Journal of Sociology* 55 (3)

284. Further Philosophical Essays by Jean Paul Sartre include "The transcendence of the Ego" (1936), "The critique of dialectical reason" (1960), and "Truth and existence" (1989)

285. Karl Jaspers, *Philosophy*, trans. E. B. Ashton, (Chicago: Chicago University Press, 1969–1971)

286. Jeremiah Curtin, *The Mongols: a History* (Boston: Da Capo Press, 2007)

287. Friedrich Engels, *The Dialectics of Nature* (1883).

288. Friedrich Engels, *Historical Materialism*

289. The reactionary forces are, according to Marxism, those landowners or capitalists or members of the old class who are afraid of changes in the social structure of the society.

11. FRIEDRICH NIETZSCHE AND HIS BOOK *THUS SPOKE ZARATHUSTRA*

Here we have to mention the German philosopher Friedrich Wilhelm Nietzsche (1844–1900), who in the year 1893, wrote maybe his most important and well known work, *Also sprach Zarathustra* [*Thus Spoke Zarathustra*]. Firstly we have to mention here the fact that the real name of the prophet is written with the sibilant 'sh', namely *Zarathushtra*, but Nietzsche's way to write it, Zarathustra, unfortunately entered the vocabulary of the European languages after his book. Furthermore, it is not clear for what reason Nietzsche had the idea to chose the name of Zarathustra as the name for the hero of his book. In fact, Zarathustra and his philosophy had nothing in common with the worldview of this nineteenth-century German philosopher. In one of his later works, *Ecce Homo* (1889) he himself explains the following:

> The first in history was Zarathustra, who was able to see the fight of good and evil, which is the actual wheel in the gear of things...

Nietzsche had recognized that Zarathustra saw, in the workings of the world, a clear sign that evil was an independent force in itself that must be combatted at all times. Maybe this clear understanding of the nature of things by Zarathustra induced Friedrich Nietzsche to use his name as the protagonist in his Book. In contrast to Zarathustra, Friedrich Nietzsche strongly opposed any excessive overemphasis on morality. In his work *Der Wille zur Macht*, Nietzsche says:

> "The Idealist is in reality a hidden coward, who flees from reality…"

Concerning Zarathustra himself, Friedrich Nietzsche writes:

> "The invention of Morality by Zarathustra was the greatest Philosophical error in human history…"

After his death, in Nietzsche's papers, they found the name of Zarathustra for the first time in his unpublished notes, namely the "Nachgelassene Fragmente" of 1870–1871; these notes were written more than twelve years before he wrote the first part of his *Also sprach Zarathustra*. In these notes, he speaks of Zarathustra with great admiration, to the point of showing an open and implicit sympathy for the dominance of Zoroastrianism in Greece, "… Had Dariush the Great, the Persian Emperor, succeeded in conquering Greece…". Again in his posthumously published work of the same period[290] he refers to the story of Heraclitus' studies under Zarathustra (KSA 1/806). The name Zarathustra first appeared in *Die frohliche Wissenschaft* [*The Gay Science*].[291] In this work Nietzsche included the first section of the Prologue from *Also sprach Zarathustra*, that is, Zarathustra prays before the sun; this section appeared in the published text, as the first part of the book the following year.

The first reasonable question we have to ask is *why did Nietzsche used the original old Persian name of Zarathustra instead of the more familiar Greek name of Zoroaster?* At the time of Nietzsche, the historical investigations into the life and time of Zarathustra was limited to a few historical researchers. Consequently, the name of Zarathustra was known only to some experts of the ancient Indo-Iranian languages. Therefore Nietzsche, owing to his philological expertise, was also familiar with that ancient Aryan Name. It is evident from his notes that Nietzsche, in general, admired the Persians of antiquity, and he regarded the Zoroastrian cyclical conception of eternity positively, which somehow resembled his own conception of cyclical time. In one of his notes dated from 1884 he writes:

> ...I must pay tribute to Zarathustra, a Persian (einem Perser). Persians were the first who thought history in its full entirety ... (KSA 11/53).

It is clear that Nietzsche, by adopting the original name of Zarathustra for communicating his own philosophy, at the same time pays homage to the historical Zarathustra. Nevertheless, he does it, paradoxically, by setting his own ontological immoralism against the ontological moralism of the ancient Aryan Prophet. The second Zarathustra radically challenges the proto-historic ontological stance of the *original* Prophet Zarathustra. In his writing *Ecce Homo*, Nietzsche himself explains why he chose the name of Zarathustra as the principal personality for his prophetic work:

> I have not been asked, as I should have been, what the name of Zarathustra means in my mouth, the mouth of the first immoralist. For what constitutes the tremendous historical uniqueness of that Persian, is just the opposite of this. Zarathustra was the first to consider the fight of good and evil, the very wheel in the machinery of things. The transposition of morality into the metaphysical realm, as a force,

> cause, and end in itself, is his work. But this question itself is at the bottom of its own answer. Zarathustra created this most calamitous error, which is morality, consequently, he must also be the first to recognize it... To speak the truth and to shoot well with arrows, which was an ancient Persian virtue.... Am I understood? ... The self overcoming of morality, out of truthfulness, the self-overcoming of the moralist, into his opposite—into *me*—that is what the name of Zarathustra means in my mouth.

The original Prophet Zarathustra stands at the dawn of human spiritual history as one of its founding figures and greatest thinkers. It was he, who was one of the initiators of the historical beginnings with his teachings, which interpreted the "history of Being" in moralistic terms. According to Zarathustra, the "history of Being" first began and was continually dominated by the struggle between the fundamental elements of good and evil. These were represented in two divine figures, namely Ahura Mazda the God of Good and light and truth—and Ahriman the representative of the evil forces. This primordial interpretation of the general condition of humankind and the "Being" in general, with its promise of the final victory of the Good over the Evil, has given from the beginning of history a meaning, a direction, and a *telos* (ultimate object or goal) to the world and to the existence of humankind.

The moralistic interpretation of *presence* or *being there* [German: Dasein], according to Nietzsche, has been the core of all metaphysical philosophies and religious beliefs until recent history. Therefore the onset of modernity, and the attitude of the modern human beings towards life and being, have thrown this persistent ancient historical interpretation into deep crisis, in which reality on one side, and perceived morality on the other, are diverging and fighting each other. Just like his namesake, Nietzsche's Zarathustra goes to the mountains to meditate when he is thirty years old. He remains on the mountains for ten years, but then, after ten years, he descends to convey his message to humankind. However, in contrary to the moralistic interpretation of Being thought by the real Zarathustra, Nietzsche's Zarathustra appears at the end of the spiritual history of humanity and teaches his ontological immoralism.

In Nietzsche's book, Zarathustra begins his prophetic mission by announcing the most tragic news for all humankind: the death of God. The crucial, fundamental and logical implication of the death of God is the impossibility of a moralistic interpretation of Being and the denial of the historical and eschatological expectations based on it, i.e. the final victory of Good over Evil. Without the eternally stable foundation of Being, as determined by the supernatural destiny, Being and human life also lose direction and its meaning; in other words humanity is in danger of being lost in the turmoil of nihilistic attitudes toward itself and the whole world as such. Therefore, as a result, Friedrich Nietzsche's view of the coming era in history is full of apprehension because he witnesses the appearance of nihilism on the world horizon. It is with great anxiety and disgust that Nietzsche regards the descent of man from his historically and ontologically privileged position in Being, as a "Being in the presence of God", addressed by His words, degenerating and becoming morally subhuman, sinking to the person of the last man.

According to the Zarathustra of Friedrich Nietzsche, it is for this reason that humankind, in order to overcome the terrible darkness of the nihilistic prospects caused by the absence of God, and the extinguishing of "His light" (the divine Light of guidance), must transcend from *Man* to *Over Man* [German: Ubermensch] through the forces of will and a consciously chosen objective. It is for this reason that Nietzsche teaches humankind how to replace God and give meaning to the world and their own lives, by voluntarily and courageously accepting responsibility for being the world as it is, in its full temporality and natural presence. This wold and existence being devoid of any metaphysical or eternal element. For this reason he must discard the old and the false conception by the humankind of Being, which in essence, contains the belief in the metaphysical, changeless or eternal ideals, principles of godliness. Therefore this eternal concept of morality must be replaced now with the concept of "Becoming" as opposed to "Being".

This second prophet Zarathustra appears at a time, when modern civilization is faced with a dangerous moral crisis caused by the dawn of nihilism in the modern world era. Nietzsche therefore tries to persuade the Europeans to abandon their Christian morality and their Greco-Judaic world views, for he views them to be historically responsible for this dangerous new development in European civilization. Nietzsche tries to convince the members of the western world to partake in a post-metaphysical history, founded on self-sustaining free human will. He says that man must overcome his past human history as a metaphysical being and become, instead, an Ubermensch. The Ubermensch is a human being who has been redeemed of his illusory, metaphysically afflicted history, a history full of superstition, ignorance falsehood and human miseries. All of which is, according to Nietzsche, embodied in Christianity.

In terms of the style in which Nietzsche's book *Also sprach Zarathustra* is written, it is interesting to note that he, in fact, tried to imitate the style in which the old and new testament has been compiled. This style maybe called the Messianic, or Prophetic style. This book is both a uniquely poetical and philosophical work, created with a grand prophetic intonation, which imitates in part the aphoristic and parabolic style of the Bible. In fact, Nietzsche's *Also sprach Zarathustra* is a book like no other, and Nietzsche himself looked upon his Zarathustra as a prophetic and evangelistic book—and an antidote for Christian Evangelism meant to redeem humankind from its false and sinister effects. This book attempts to overcome the unwise and obsessive rationalism of the classical and modern western traditions of thought. This is including likewise the Christian irrationalism by replacing them both with more courageous and therefore deeply founded wisdom based on a more realistic and critical ontology. Here Nietzsche tries, with his poetical and philosophical insight, to put forward a wisdom which attempts to undermine all superstitions and illusions of antique, medieval and modern fabrication. This book begins by reminding us of the real and historical Zarathustra, the prominent initiator of ethical and spiritual history, and of his most fundamental error, namely the heightening of a most necessary element of human history—morality—to the level of the ontological foundation of Being.

12. THEISM VERSUS ATHEISM OR A SHORT HISTORY OF GOD IN HUMAN CONSCIOUSNESS

The old God has lost its power. We are awaiting the new one.

—Martin Heidegger

Taking into consideration the scientific discoveries of the last two centuries, and considering the teachings of giants of science and philosophy, men like Isaac Newton, Charles Darwin, Sigmund Freud, Georg Friedrich Wilhelm Hegel, Karl Marx and Friedrich Engels and not to forget Albert Einstein and others, we are now in a position to be able to look at the existence of God, as a general creator of everything we know included ourselves, from the perspective of a third person, and as an investigator or as a scientist. At this point we are not trying to dispute or make a judgement about the general existence of a creator God, but we are just asking here some hypothetical and logical questions.

Looking from the monotheistic point of view, where the human and his creation is the centre point of any worldview, we could say that, form our point of view, this ideology is reasonable, balanced, harmonious, legitimate and highly justified. Therefore, if logically humans really created the gods they believed in, at any given stage of their intellectual development, then these gods and their creation had to be balanced, harmonious and legitimate to the mind of those who created them.

At that certain stage of the human development, when humans were still at the beginning of their intellectual development, for example at the beginning of the stone age, an advanced and sophisticated abstract or highly intellectual deity, God or religion, would have been undoubtedly not accepted by the humans and would have failed. That means the humans of that period in time would have rejected it, as their own intellectual capabilities were not up to that standard. We will see that, by the same token, divinities could not be ahead of their time, it also should not be behind in the development of human intellectual capabilities. There comes a time when gods will lose their power over the humans, or as Almut Hintze puts it, "they are not any more worthy of worship." This will always happen, when the scientific and the intellectual capabilities of the human mind has advanced much further, then the mind of those humans who previously had created, or discovered, the same god.

We will see later in this chapter that several times man in history have presented a new god, a new religion, a new creator or simply a new and revolutionary idea, without success—they were rejected, they failed and often the bringer of the new idea was eliminated and persecuted with his followers. However, years later, the same god or religion is accepted and venerated by the masses. There are several examples of this kind of events in history. For example, a man like Akhenaten, the Egyptian pharaoh, who tried to introduce a new religion to the people of Egypt, which was, as historians call it, some sort of monotheism. As the public was not yet ready for this religion, which had come before the mind of the public was ready for it, Akhenaten failed, as we have seen that in previous chapters. The German philosopher Martin Heidegger, who before his death had a interesting discussion about this subject with Rudolf Augstein, founder, owner and editor of the German news magazine *Der Spiegel*, was on the opinion that:

> *Der alte Gott hat seine Glaubwurdigkeit verloren... wir mussen den neuen Gott herbeidenken"* [the old god has lost its credibility, we are expecting the new God – or– we have to prepare his coming or his appearance in our mind]

He declares furthermore:

> ...historically seen, there are events which happen in human history approximately every two thousand years, namely the coming of a new age, and with it the coming of a new God...We are now at that moment in history...

It was Martin Heidegger's wish that this interview should only be published after his death. Therefore, shortly after his death, the German Newsmagazine *Der Spiegel* published this famous interview in the issue of May 31, 1976. As for us, the famous proverb says, "Once the people are ready, then the master will appear." But let us here, in a nutshell, look at the beginning of the history of humankind and their gods.

12.1 THE BEGINNING

If we look at the beginning of the human history, we see that once humans gained self consciousness, or we could say, once our consciousness had formed and developed to a stage where we could look at the world objectively, we entered into our new existence of being humans. Speaking again in terms of the doctrines of the historical materialism, as Friedrich Engels says:

> Once the human race stopped adapting themselves passively to the forces of nature, but acted actively against it, that was the moment when our race separated from the world of animals and started to be humans.

We entered into the development of a distinct new species and race, who would start the long and dramatic journey which would ultimately lead us to the point of our development as humans. This was the start of humanity, as we know it now. At the point of humans not acting purely on instincts as animals do, but rather acting upon logical reflections, as small as that might have been initially, that was the moment of the beginning of humankind and its self-consciousness. After this initial fundamental step, after the humans realized in their mind the basic realities of their existence—time, space, struggle for survival, strong, weak, the fact that they were alone, abandoned, and helpless against the cruel forces of nature—they realized that there was a beginning and an end for them, they recognized their mortality, the fact of death. Ultimately and logically they must have asked themselves the most important and most logical questions of all: *Who are we, and where are we coming from? Is death really the end, and what is the purpose of our existence?* And maybe the key question: *Who made us?*

Interestingly, when humans started to act actively against the forces of nature, instead of adapting themselves passively to them, that was also the moment humankind made, and entered into, history. In comparison to this, many human tribes and groups in Africa and or the Amazon region were, until recently, living in a state of passive adaptation to the forces of nature, therefore, according to historical materialism, they did not make or had not entered into history.

Animals act on instincts, and as far as we know, they do not realize the beginning and the end of their existence; therefore, all of their endeavours are focused on their daily struggle for survival, and the reproduction of the future generations of their own species. But we humans are confronted from the beginning with questions, which are still open and unanswered for us. For example, *what is the purpose of our existence?* Obviously, the prehistoric humans on this planet, existing in small groups, geographically separated and dispersed from each other, and of different races and living under completely different circumstances, must have entered the stage of becoming humans at different times. Therefore, it is logical for us to assume that this specific and precise moment of human development when they started to act actively against the forces of nature versus adapting themselves passively to the same forces, all humans, wherever they lived on this planet, and independently from each other, came to the same logical conclusion, namely:

> An unknown higher power—who is, unlike us, immortal—has created us. We are subjected to and under its power, who and what it is, we do not know. We must try and gain its favours, in order to master our struggle for survival.

Concerning the scientific chronology of the human development, we know now that humanlike creatures, or the pre-human race, lived for approximately 3.4 million years in the stone age, but the so-called *modern* humans were living on this planet, according to science, for only about 100,000 years, before entering, what we call the early bronze age. It must have been probably at the beginning, or early stone age, that humans started to ask themselves those or similar questions, and all of them came probably simultaneously to the same conclusion. It is interesting to realize, that at one specific moment in human history, all humans on this planet believed in the same god.

That moment was the moment of the first realization in our newly developed consciousness, that we are impotent versus the forces of greater nature, that we are different from all other living species, and that only a higher supernatural power can help us. All humans, wherever they were, at the realization of this first fundamental fact, they perceived the supernatural power in the same way. They recognized, that he was existent, all powerful, but unreachable and unknown to us. That was the very short but historical moment, when all humans believed in the same God.

Once humans started to act actively against the forces of nature and subsequently developed the beginning of what we can call a consciousness, they immediately looked upon nature and the animal world as an separate object, meaning from an objective point of view. Humanity and the general nature had separated. The mind of humankind was looking upon the nature as a matter, or as an object. This moment in human history, is when our race lost its initial innocence and perceived, necessarily, the existence of a higher being who logically must have created us; let us call this being the god of the first generation.

12.2 THE GOD OF THE FIRST GENERATION

Obviously, as humans were living in different geographical areas, different circumstances and different natural environments, their imagination and ideas in the creation of their god was different from each other. Every group of humans created, in their minds, a different type of creator or god, who was reflected by the environment in which they were living. It is therefore evident that the gods of the various societies were a product of the circumstances in which those particular tribes, clans, or society lived in—historical materialism suggests that *everything* is a product of the circumstances. After the first moment of realization, in which humans recognized the necessity and the logic of a creator, every society chose a creator, which was suitable to its needs and fitting to their environment, circumstances they lived in and surroundings. Generally these first gods were associated with natural phenomena such as thunder, lightning and other furies or expressions of the natural forces. Strong manifestation of natural and environmental events were understood as messages from of gods, being angry and unsatisfied with their subjects. We see that, during long periods of dry weather when the food supply was in danger, the people of South and Central American pre-Columbian world would sacrifice humans to the angry deities in order to make the gods more favourable. In the Aztec empire in Mexico, for example, to appease the gods, not to send dry weather and famine, young children were sacrificed by way of priests, who would split open their chests and pulling their still-beating hearts, holding them to the sun in the sky and saying prayers. This was done atop structures similar to pyramid, which still exists today, and can be visited by tourists.

But this is not unique to the pre-Columbian America, all over the ancient world of the Middle East and the Mediterranean civilizations, animal sacrifices to the gods, in order to appease them, were common. It is known that when Hulagu Khan, the grandson of Genghis Khan and the conqueror of the Middle East, died on February 8, 1265 AD and was buried on an island on the lake Urmia in southern Azerbaijan, live humans were sacrificed on his grave by the Mongols, to appease their gods.[292]

In the world of the Nordic tribes—for example in Germany or the Scandinavian world—we see that the god named Wotan in Germanic [Old Saxon: Woe den] [Nordic/Scandinavian: Odin] was a major pagan deity in the continental Germanic, Nordic and Anglo-Saxon world, in the pre-Christian times. These gods were associated with the fury and anger and other manifestations of the natural forces like thunder, lightning and storms. The God Wotan had a wife, Freja, who had several sons, among whom the most famous was Thor, also a Nordic pagan deity in his own rights.

The Lombard historian, Paul the Deacon, who died in southern Italy in the 760s AD in his work *Historia Langobardorum* relates to us that:

> I myself being proud to belong to the tribe of the Longobards, who emigrated from southern Scandinavia to northern Italy in to a province now called Lombardia, ... Wotan is been adored as a god by all the peoples of Germania, and Wotan's wife Freya has given victory to the Longobards in their fight against the Vandals.

However, Wotan represented an older cult of proto-Germanic hunter-gatherers, his association with being a wanderer and having shamanic qualities. This might, on the contrary, mean that the Wotan cult was taken over by newer sedentary cults. Probably, the existence of this pagan deity, dates back to the late Stone Age in northern Europa.[293] Last but not least, we have to mention here the German composer Richard Wagner, who in his famous opera cycle *Der Ring des Nibelungen* deals with the deities of the ancient Germanic pantheon and whose operas play all in the pre-Christian mythological world with Wotan mentioned several times, as the main deity. In Richard Wagner's Opera cycle Wotan, who was the father of the Nordic gods, had a daughter by the name of Brunhilde, and Siegfried was her lover. Brunhilde commits suicide when she hears that Siegfried had betrayed her with Gudrun, and that Siegfried had died.

In other parts of the world, for example in the Arabian peninsula, a *black stone* [in Arabic, *hajar al aswad*] was regarded as sacred and worshipped as a deity—in reality it was a meteorite fallen from the sky. It had to be, at a later date, incorporated into a corner of the Kaaba in Mecca, as the belief in this stone was too widespread and too strong by the pre-Islamic population, to be ignored or prohibited by the founders of Islamic religion. This stone is still revered today, the same as it was in the time before the founding of Islam. All Islamic pilgrims must visit Mecca the holy city once in a lifetime, kiss or at least touch the holy stone with their hands even today. This being a remnant of archaic deities still revered today. One important fact, which connects all the societies of antiquity, is that nearly all of them, as a sign or seat of their ancient gods, worshipped in one way or another mountains. This was not only a manifestations of the natural forces and as deities and gods, but also connected them as their own identity as people or as a nation. We see that, from prehistoric times, mountains have been worshiped or given divine status, and these beliefs were so strong and so deeply anchored in the human minds that subsequent and later religions and gods, no matter how strong and powerful they were, could not eradicate these beliefs. These prehistoric relics in our subconsciousness mind have still a very strong validity and presence. Here some examples:

- In Greece, where the mythological gods were involved in a sacred war with their parents, the Titans, they fought this war on the sacred mountain of Olympus. Afterwards, Zeus, the father of all the Greek gods, reigned from there. Mountain Olympus, which was the seat and home of all the ancient Greek deities, is still today regarded as an national symbol by all Greeks.

- In the Roman Empire, the god of fire, Vulcan, had his seat on Mount Vesuvius. When the god of fire was angry, he used to spit fire into the air. The words Vulcan and Volcano are related. This was the same mountain that destroyed Pompey years later, but the mountain was still worshiped and feared by the Roman masses.

- The Armenians worshiped Mount Ararat in antiquity, and it is today still regarded as their symbol of national identity and unity.

- In Japan we have Mount Fuji, which together with two other mountains—Tate and Haiku—were sacred since pre-historic times. Mount Fuji is the symbol of greater harmony and purity, and it was forbidden for woman to climb it until the end of the Meiji Period (1868–1912). The Japanese still regard Mount Fuji to be the symbol of the Japanese nation.

- In Australia, the famous Ayers Rock is called Uluru by the Australian aboriginal tribe of Anangu who have worshiped this rock since the beginning of their history as being the seat of their God.

- The Navajo, a native tribe in the United States, had five mountains sacred to them. The four mountains were the boundaries of their homeland. Their god had told them never to travel beyond these mountain boundaries as she, their creator god, would not be able to protect them if they did. Thus the boundaries of their habitat was clearly defined for them by their gods. Those mountains were: Sisnaajini to the east [Blanca Peak in Colorado], Tsoodzil to the south [Mount Taylor in New Mexico], Dook'o'oosliid to the west [San Francisco Peaks in Arizona], and mount Dibe Nitsaa to the north [Hesperus Mountain in Colorado]. It is interesting to note, that their god was a female deity, and the fifth and the last mountain was the seat of their goddess, and the centre of their world.

- We have also in Africa the sacred Mountain of Kilimanjaro; this mountain is still worshipped as being divine by the people of Tanzania.

- Then there is the Mount Damavand, an extinct ancient Volcano in Iran. This mountain was venerated since the beginning of history in one way or another by the Persian people, especially under the Sassanian dynasty. According to ancient myth, the fire spitting dragon Azi Dahaka is imprisoned and chained in a cave within the mountain, there to remain until the end of time. It is noteworthy that, on the slopes of Mount Damavand, in prehistoric times, there was an extensive forest, which contained mostly fruit trees and all kind of food, especially milk and honey in great abundance. That big forest garden, in old Persian was called Baghe Perdous [Garden of Perdous]. It was said, from ancient times, that he who was an honest and honourable person, would live in the next existence in Perdous, as in that place a person could live without working and in peace forever. It is believed that the word Perdous in reality has been transformed into Paradise. The expression Baghe Perdous is still in use in the Persian (Farsi) language today.

Prof. Jenny Rose mentions in her book *Zoroastrianism: A Guide for the Perplexed* that "...the Greek Author Xenophon, who fought as a Greek mercenary in ancient Persia against the armies of the Achaemenid King Artaxerxes II, later after having returned to Greece, in his memoirs calls the Persian Gardens, where trees of every kind give life and prosperity "Paradaisos". By the time of the new Testaments book of Revelations, the concept of Paradise with the tree of life in its centre had already become associated with humanities restoration of the Garden of Eden.

Last but not least we would like to mention here, the five sacred mountains in ancient china. The Chinese Emperors throughout the ages made pilgrimages to those mountains, which s ceremonies and rituals were extensive, and were a part of ancient China's rituals honouring the gods.

Interestingly all nations of the ancient world have gone in their early history through more or less the same period of worshipping deities, who were connected to some kind of manifestation and phenomena of natural forces. These were all nature-based gods or religions[294] here we will call them the gods of the second generation.

12.3 THE GODS OF THE THIRD GENERATION

After having surpassed this period in human history, rulers realized that, with the power of the sword alone, the control of the population would not be complete. Institutionalized religions with priests were emerging in the society as the basis for worldly and political dominance and social structures. We see here a new class of people emerging in society and gaining considerable power, at least in some nations, namely the priestly class. New national and personal gods emerge in each nation, completely separately from each other, and if these nations compete or make war with each other, so do their gods. By this stage in history, the new gods have human characteristics, for example, they are married or have partners, change them from time to time, have children, they create things and they destroy things. They have, each one of them, their own personal domain, their field of action or their territory, where they rule, and they even compete or even fight with each other. The only difference between them and the humans who worship them is that they are immortal and have power over life and death. Therefore, in many cases, the rulers associate themselves with these gods, or even claim descent from them. In order to emphasize to their subjects that their power over their nation was granted by God and can thus only be taken away by God.

Two very clear example of these new national gods exist in the Egyptian Pharaonic Empire and Greece and the Hellenistic cultural world. What we know today as Greek mythology, was the belief and worship of the people in the ancient Hellenistic society and civilization in a number of personal gods. Most important of all the Hellenistic gods was Zeus, who was called the Father of Gods and Man; he ruled the Olympians of Mount Olympus—meaning the other gods—as a father rules the family. He was married to Hera, the Queen of the Gods, and also considered the Goddess of Marriage, Woman, and Childbirth. Zeus had with his wife Hera—and with a number of other Goddesses—several children who were among the most famous gods of the Greek mythology. Among the children of Zeus are Aphrodite, Athena, Apollo, Artemis, Hermes, and Dionysus. Then there were other gods, for example, Hades the King of the Underworld and the God of the Death; and Poseidon, the elder brother of Zeus and the god of the sea. We also have Kronos the God of Time, and Okeanos the God of the Great Oceans.

At a later period in history, the Roman Empire had a very similar pantheon, only with different names. The Romans had, for each Greek deity, a counterpart with a Latin name, for example Zeus the Godfather, became Jupiter with the same functions; Poseidon became Neptune; Artemis, the Greek virgin Goddess of the Hunt, became Diana; the Greek God of Love, Aphrodite, became Venus; Hades the God of the Underworld and Death became Pluto.

We have seen in previous chapters that the word Deu, devin, devain, diva, divina, deus, theos [all of which all mean God] is of very ancient Indo-Germanic provenience, and was used in archaic and pre-historic times in Europe as well as in central Asia. Therefore many important name of ancient gods in the western cultural World can be associated with the word Deus. P.O. Skjaervo the linguist at Harvard University, in his Book *Introduction into Zoroastrianism* associates Zeus to Theos/Deus and, among others, Deu-pater to Jupiter.

Concerning the divine beings and the gods of the Egyptian Pharaonic world, the Egyptian religion has a long history, which reaches into the dark pre-historical period. As Egypt, in the beginning of its history consisted of several smaller independent regions, each one of them had their own gods, and after the re-unification of those smaller nations into one empire ruled by the Pharaohs, all those regional gods were taken over. A vast array of different forms of symbolism related to animals living in the Egyptian environment and fauna was later embraced and incorporated by the ancient Egyptians into their pantheon. Most Egyptian deities are symbolized and return constantly in the form or in the themes of various regional animals as symbols for gods. For example, the cobra goddess, symbolizing the goddess Wadjet, was worn on Egyptian crowns, from the beginning of the Pharaonic times until the end of Egyptian history and the conquest of Egypt by the Roman Empire. Among the important gods of the ancient Egyptian religion, maybe the most senior was Amun and later Amun-Ra, the creator god, he was the hidden one. Other gods included Osiris, the God-judge and Ruler in the Afterlife; Sekhmet the lion-headed God of Destruction and War; Seth the God of Chaos, and so on.

Unlike the Roman Imperial cultural world, where humans were humans and gods were gods—although many Roman emperors were deified, at no time did any Roman Emperor pretended that either of his parents were actual gods—in Egypt, formal religious practice was centred on the Pharaoh himself, who was regarded as an immortal being. More than that, the pharaohs themselves were perceived to be descendent from the gods, and they acted as the link between the gods and their people, as intermediaries. The Pharaoh was obligated to sustain the gods through rituals and offerings, so that they in turn could maintain order in the greater universe. In the world of the Egyptian Pharaonic religion, gods did mix with humans to produce children, who became later kings and rulers. Historically, a number of Egyptian pharaohs declared their father to be a deity and, in so doing, pretended to be of divine and immortal origin.

In contrast to this, at no time in the Iranian history did any king or ruler believe, declare or pretend to be of divine origin or to be related to divinities. There was never a case in ancient Iranian history where a ruler had deified either himself or another person. We see here that Zarathustra had introduced his only creator god Ahura Mazdâ [meaning the great Lord] to the Iranian nation at a time when the civilizations of the eastern Mediterranean—Rome, Greece, Phoenicia,

Assyria, and Egypt—were still worshipping a variety of polytheistic deities.

Amun and later Amun-Ra was the creator god of the Egyptian Pantheon and possibly equivalent to the Greek Zeus and the Imperial Roman Jupiter, but these were one of the several gods worshiped in those nations. As in Egyptian prayers of the pharaonic period always the name of the deity was mentioned at the end of any prayer; therefore, this custom of saying Amen [Amun] after the prayers in the Christian tradition, could have been taken over from ancient Egypt, first by the Hebraic religious tradition and, from them, into Christianity.

We know that, according to the ancient Egyptian religion, every person after death had to face Osiris, the god of the underworld. He would asked them ten questions, and only if those questions were answered in the negative could that person could pass to the underworld for his or her journey to the after life. These procedures of the final judgment were known as the Weighing of the Heart. These ten questions and ten rules were followed by the ancient Egyptian society since the late antiquity and the beginning of the Pharaonic era. These ten rules were markedly identical to what the Mythological Moses, at least thousand years later, announced to be the Ten Commandments, given to him by God on Mount Sinai.

Furthermore, the name Moses, [Hebrew: Moshe] is not a word or name of Hebrew origin, but is likely an ancient Egyptian name. According to Sigmund Freud, Moses was called previously Tuthmoses, a common ancient Egyptian name, which he later shortened to Moses. Concerning the ten rules for the afterlife and its similarities to the ten commandments of Moses, this is a known detail from the ancient Egyptian religious history.[295]

Clearly, since the beginning of humans living together, there have been rules regulating any community. This was—and remains—a technical necessity, for no community can function without rules. The first condition of any humans living together, is the acceptance of basic ground rules, followed by everyone. Even in the world of animals, these accepted rules exist, and are rigorously enforced. For example, we know that elephants, who spend their lives as part of a herds, always have a leader. It is not the most powerful or the strongest male, but rather the most experienced and oldest female, who is the highest in the hierarchy. Then we have the wolves, who form wolf packs, and live via strict rules and hierarchy. And of course many other animal species live in communities with exact defined rules of behaviour. Interestingly, in the animal kingdom, the highest punishment for a member acting against the rules of their community is expulsion from the community—which almost always results in the death of that animal.

Here a new word has entered our vocabulary—*hierarchy*. From the very beginning of human community, as in the animal world, the necessity of rules and order was always the precondition of any harmonious co-existence between the members of that group or society. And soon enough the members of that group come to the conclusion that no order can exist without hierarchy. History is full of social and political ideologies suggesting that freedom and equality can be achieved without hierarchy. Those ideologies and the communities who have tried them have, without exception, failed. All of them came to the conclusion that order and hierarchy are not only tightly connected, but that the former is impossible without the latter.

Returning to the personal gods of antiquity, we can say that these types of personal gods and divinities who ruled in ancient Egypt, Greece, Rome, India and other civilizations of the world, could be called the gods of the third generation.

And, consequently, the creator gods of the three big present monotheistic religions—Judaism, Christianity and Islam—could be called the gods of the fourth generation.

13. ZOROASTRIAN HOLY SCRIPTURES AND OTHER RELATED DOCUMENTS

13.1 THE GATHAS, THE MOST HOLY SCRIPTURES

The Gathas are a document believed to have been written by the Prophet Zarathustra himself. They are the most sacred texts which exists in the Zoroastrian religion. The Gathas [Iranian: Gahan] comprise approximately 6,000 words or 1,300 lines or 238 verses or 17 hymns. The word *gatha* (which exists also in Sanskrit) is variously rendered as hymn, poem, or psalm. Zarathustra's Gathas are short verse texts, cast largely in the form of utterances addressed by him to Ahura Mazdâ the creator; and they convey, through inspired poetry, visions of God and his purposes, and prophecies of things to come. They are full of passionate feeling and conviction, with meaning densely packed into subtle and allusive words; and in form they belong, it seems, to an ancient and learned tradition of religious poetry composed by priestly seers, seeking through study and meditation to reach direct communion with the divine. However, they are the only examples of this tradition to survive in Iran; and this literary isolation, together with their great antiquity, means that they contain many words of unknown or uncertain meaning and have baffling complexities of grammar and syntax. All this, added to their depth and originality of thought, makes them extraordinarily difficult to translate.

Only a few of the verses can be understood by themselves in a wholly unambiguous way, but keys to their interpretation are provided by the Younger Avesta and the Pahlavi Zand (see below), which set out, clearly, doctrines often only alluded to in the Gathas. Linguistically the Rigveda, being composed in a closely related sister language of comparable antiquity, provides great help. The living tradition of the faith, especially in worship, is also an invaluable aid. The Avesta has two sections, the Older Avesta and the Younger Avesta. The Older Avestan texts, which include the Gathas and the Yasna Haptanghaiti are authentic and are believed to have been written by Zarathustra himself. These Older Avestan texts deal mostly with abstract philosophical ideas. The Younger Avestan texts, on the other hand, have been written hundreds of years later, by priests, and are mainly concerned with questions of rituals and religious law and regulations.

The texts, in which the Gathas (Old Avestan texts) have been written, presumably by Zarathustra himself, are compiled in a language which, even at the time of the Prophet himself, was antiquated and not used anymore. It is believed that Zarathustra used the old language to emphasize the legitimacy of his doctrine and his message to humankind, this according to Martin Haug, (1827–1876) the German Professor of Sanskrit, University of Munich—and later in India as a Professor of Sanskrit from 1859–1866.[296]

The main source for the teachings of Zarathustra is the compilation of holy works called the Avesta, a name which probably means The Injunction (of Zarathustra). The Avesta is composed in two stages of an otherwise unrecorded Eastern Iranian language: Gathic Avestan

(GAv.), which in its forms is close to the language of the Indian
Rigveda (which is generally assigned to the second millennium BC),
and Younger Avestan (YAv.). Gathic Avestan takes its name from the
chief texts to survive in this dialect, i.e. the seventeen Gathas composed by the prophet himself. Although only this part of the Avesta is
directly attributable to Zarathustra, traditionally the whole Avesta is
held to be inspired by his teachings; and many Younger Avestan texts
are presented as if directly revealed to him by God.

Therefore, we can say that the language in which Zarathustra has
written the Gathas is, in reality, reflecting a consciousness which was,
even in the Prophet's lifetime, pre-Zoroastrian. In other words, he was
thinking in terms of an era which existed before his lifetime, and he
probably regarded that era to be the ideal time of the human society.

Concerning the various languages used by the Iranians from the
beginning of their history, it is known that, in order to enter into the
proper soul and the way of thinking of a nation and their civilization,
you have to speak their language. Karl Marx says, "Die Sprache ist das
Bewusstsein" [the language is the consciousness]. To understand the
various periods, and with that the documents written in that period,
of the Iranian history, we have to give here, very briefly, a short
explanation about the languages used by the Iranian people during
their history.

The first major civilization in the territory that is now Iran was
that of the Elamites, who may have settled in southeastern Iran
as early as 3000 BC. Later, when Zarathustra lived, the Iranians
left very few records of writing, and when, in the eighth century
BC, Zoroastrianism reached the western part of the Iranian homeland, which is to say the lands of the the Medes and the Parthians,
the system of writing encountered for this period—cuneiform and
alphabetic Aramaic—were unsuitable for recording accurately the
Indo-European language. The collection of holy texts, which was in
the otherwise unknown east Iranian language called Avestan, therefore, remained in oral transmission for more than a thousand years,

until probably in the fifth century AD. Later, the forty-four character Avestan Alphabet evolved to record the texts. The Gathas, having been strictly memorized, were well preserved, but much detail, handed down in a more fluid transmission, suffered textual corruption to a great extend. Professor P.O. Skjaervo writes in this connection the following:

> The oldest known Iranian languages are Old and Young Avestan and Old Persian. These languages permits us to reconstruct proto-Iranian as a Branch of Indo-Iranian, an eastern branch of the Indo-European languages. Proto-Indo-Iranian (the parent language of Iranian and Indic or Indo-Aryan) may have been spoken in the area south and southeast of the Aral sea in the third millennium BC. It split into Iranian and Indo-Aryan sometime around 2000 BC.

Regarding the Avestan as a language P.O. Skjaervo writes:

> While both history and linguistics indicate that old Persian was the language spoken in the modern Fars provinces in southern Iran, the language of the Avesta must have belonged to the tribes from north eastern Iran.... The Avesta contains a few geographical names, all belonging to northeastern Iran... Only once is a possible western name mentioned, namely Rhaga, if this is modern Rey, south of Teheran, which in antiquity was regarded as the centre of the Median Magi.... The Old Avestan texts comprise the Gathas and the Yasna Haptanghaiti, both of which are contained in the section of the Avesta called the Yasna, as well as various fragments scattered throughout the Yasna.[297]

Concerning the Videvdad or Vendidad, or the prayers for the healing of body and soul, the name of Vendidad comes from the Avestan and is a compendium of the words of Vi – Daevo – Datha and means approximately as "Given against the Daevas", the Daevas being the Demons in this case. The Vendidad is basically a recounting of various manifestations of the Demons and the evil spirits, and prayers to counter them. The Vendidad includes all of the nineteenth Nask (Prayers) of the Denkard, the only Nask which has survived in its entirety from ancient times, meaning well before the Sassanian era. The Videvdad or the Vendidad is a ancient group of texts, which are included in the greater collection of writings of the Avesta, and these codes and prayers are mainly for the ecclesiastical use. The Vendidad is widely considered to be a link to the ancient oral traditions, which was, at a later time, written down as a book of laws for the Zoroastrian community. The compilation of these scriptures of the Vendidad date substantially from the time of before the Median and Persian Empires circa 800 BC. The Vendidad consists of 22 prayers or chapters as follows:

The first chapter is a dualistic creation myth, this is then followed by a general description of the great flood and the destructive winter which followed it, comparable to various other ancient mythologies.

The second chapter recounts the legends of the great Jamshid [Avestan: Yima].

The nineteenth chapter is the story of the temptation of the prophet Zarathustra by the destructive spirit Angra Mainyu [Middle Persian: Ahriman] who urged him to turn toward him and to turn away from the good religion; Zarathustra turns instead to Ahura Mazdâ.

The remaining chapters are a compendium of various rules and regulations, which concern "how to confront the evil spirits and Demons and the evil Eye." In some detail we can classify the various chapters as follows:

- General hygiene: Chapters 3, 5–8, 16, 17, & 19

- Cleansing procedures: Chapters 9 & 10

- Diseases and their origins and the prayers against it: Chapters 7, 10, 11, 13, & 20–22

- The mourning of the death or deceased loved ones: Chapter 12

- The towers of silence, or general funeral practices: Chapter 6

- The remuneration of deeds after death: Chapter 19

- The sanctity and the invocation of Fire (Attar), the Earth (Zam), the Water (Apas), and the light of the Stars: Chapters 3, 6, 8, & 21

- The dignity of wealth and the necessity of charity: Chapter 4

- Marriages and its ceremonies, the necessity of physical effort: Chapters 4 & 15

- Statutes on unacceptable social behaviour, the dishonesty of breaching a contract, violence and assault: Chapters 4 & 15

- On the worthiness of priests and the respect due to them: Chapter 18

- The general praise of the bull, the cow, the dog, the otter, the sraosha bird, and the haoma tree: Chapters 6, 13–15, & 21

These texts have been discussed extensively by Karl Friedrich Geldner in 1877, and also R.C. Zaehner mentions them in detail.[298] Concerning the word Visperad, it is an amalgamation of two Avestan words: *vispe* and *ratavo* with an misunderstandable signification, but in general *vispe ratavo* is translated as "prayer to all the Lords/Masters/ Patrons." The Visperad is a particular Zoroastrian ceremonial or religious handbook, and is a collection within the greater Avestan compendium of scriptures. Maybe we could call it a Zoroastrian Liturgical Manual. The Visperad itself contains various texts of the Yasna compendium, including the *Yasna Haptanghaiti* and the *Ahuna Vairya* further the *Airyaman ishya*, and the Gathas itself. These are all reflected in the Visperad (13, 16, 18, 21, 23, & 24). The Visperad is only performed in the time between sunrise and the noon, on the six gahambar days of the week, during the Havan Gah ceremony.

The translation of the Visperad has been initially the work of the German Professor Karl Friedrich Geldner, and also of Christian Bartholomae, and is mentioned also in writings by Mary Boyce and also Strausberg.

The Avesta is a prayer book, and what can be called the books of daily worship of the Zoroastrian faith. These are, in general a wide selection of the content of the Gathas and the Vendidad and Visperad and were written first in the Pahlavi language and then in Farsi—the language spoken in Iran today. The Avesta is a collection of texts which contains probably all the content of the Gathas and the Vendidad and Visperad together, and can be called, therefore, the Zoroastrian Bible.

The oldest part of the ancient Iranian religion is known from the Avesta, the holy book of the Zoroastrians, this is a collection of writings of different dates and various content that was orally transmitted for several thousand years, before being finally written down probably around 500 AD. The text of the language are in two forms, the old Avesta and the young Avesta. The language of the old Avesta is the language spoken probably in central Asia around 2000–1500 BC. The language of the young Avesta was spoken in Iran around 1000–500 BC. There are strong linguistic and cultural similarities between the texts of the Avesta and those of the Indian Rigveda. As we have seen in previous chapters, we know that the similarities are assumed to reflect the common beliefs of proto-Indo-Iranian times, and the differences to reflect the independent evolution, that occurred after the pre-historic split of the two cultures. From the beginning of the Achaemenian Dynasty, we have the Zoroastrian religion and the rules of the Avesta firmly established in the Persian Empire, as we have seen above, the inscriptions of king Darius are dating from 521 BC.

Under the Sassanian Dynasty, a canon of Avestan texts was established, grouped into twenty-one nasks (books); and it was this massive collection of holy texts which was, at last, committed to writing in the fifth or sixth century AD. This Great Avesta contained all the texts already described, and much else, including the life and legends of the prophet, expositions of doctrine, apocalyptic works, and books of law, cosmogony, and scholastic science.

13.2 THE MOST SIGNIFICANT PRAYER, OR THE AHUNA VAIRYA

Zarathustra also composed, for the believers, a short version of the prayer which, as Mary Boyce says, is basically to the Zoroastrian believer, what the Lord's Prayer is to the Christian community. This prayer is called the Ahuna Vairya, which later was shortened and called Ahunvar. This is the first prayer a Zoroastrian child learns, and it may be uttered, if needed in place of all other forms of worship or supplication. It is naturally in the ancient Gathic dialect, which was spoken by the Prophet himself. In later periods, there has been much discussion among scholars about the exact meaning of these venerable lines. The following version represents a conflation of recent renderings:

> He, Ahura Mazdâ is as much the desired Master, as
> the Judge, according to Asha. He is the doer of the

acts of good purpose, of life. To Ahura Mazdâ is the
Kingdom whom they have established as a pastor for
the poor.[†]

———

† Poor has, in this context, the meaning of a humble
and devout person.

There is one more Gathic prayer, which was probably composed
by Zarathustra's earlier disciples. Unlike the Ahunvar, it is traditionally not attributed to the Prophet himself. This prayer is called the
Airyema ishyo and this prayer invokes Airyaman, who with Fire will
cleanse the world at Frashokereti and this prayer says:

> May longed for Airyaman come to the help of the
> man and woman of Zarathustra, and to the help of
> their good intention. The conscience which deserves
> the desirable recompense, for I asked the longed for
> reward for righteousness, which Ahura Mazdâ will
> measure out.

This prayer is still uttered daily in Zoroastrian acts of worship, and
at every marriage ceremony.

THE GATHIC PORTION
OF THE YASNA

The Gathas were piously preserved by being made part of the liturgy
of the Yasna (Y.), the Act of Worship, which was solemnized daily.
They were arranged formally in five groups, according to their
five metres, and were set before and after the Yasna Haptanghaiti
(YHapt.), the Worship of the Seven Sections. This, also in Gathic
Avestan, appears to be made up of what are in essence even more

ancient texts, composed to accompany the traditional offerings to fire and water, and revised in the light of Zarathustra's teachings. So in Zoroastrian worship the Gathas, as the greatest of mantras (inspired holy utterances) guard the central rituals of the faith with their sacred power. Before and after them the four great prayers are recited, brief but very holy utterances which are constantly being said. They were later assembled into the 72-chapter *Yasna* [In English: *Worship*; German: *Gebet*]. These writings are the main part and the hearth piece of the liturgical collection of texts within the greater collection of the Avesta, the so-called Zoroastrian bible. The 17 hymns are known by their chapter numbers in the Yasna and are divided into five major sections.

THE YOUNGER AVESTAN PORTIONS OF THE YASNA

The Yasna liturgy was extended over the centuries and finally grew to have seventy-two sections. These, almost all in Younger Avestan language, are of varying age and content. The Gathic texts were kept at the heart of the liturgy, being now protected in their turn by the Younger Avestan additions. These are the sequential chapters of the Gathas:

- Ahunavaiti Gatha (Yasna 28–34)

- Ushtavaiti Gatha (Yasna 43–46)

- Spentamainyush Gatha (Yasna 47–50)

- Vohukhshathra Gatha (Yasna 51)

- Vahishtoishti Gatha (Yasna 53)

The sequential order of the Gathas is structurally interrupted by the Yasna Haptanghaiti—these famous seven chapters of the Yasna run 35–41. Linguistically these are as old as the other gathas, but are written in prose. Additionally there are two other minor hymns, which are the Yasna 42 and 52. The language in which the Gathas have been written, which is the Old Avestan or Gathic, is a part of the old Iranian language group, which in itself is related and is a sub-group of the Indo-European languages. Other than that, the Gathas are in an otherwise unknown language. Unfortunately, our dependency on Vedic Sanskrit is a significant weakness in the translation or deciphering of the Gathas, as the two languages, initially from the same origin, had developed independently at a later period in history. During the Sassanian period, translations and commentaries (the Zand) have been used to interpret the Gathas, but later, during the third century AD, the Avestan language was completely extinct. Some important scholars (James Darmesteter for one) have advised not to use the Zand to complete the missing parts of the Gathas, but no other possibilities exist up to this date. The Middle Persian translation seldom offers an useful point of start for a exact knowledge of the Gathas, but an intensive comparison of its content and its single lines with the Gathic original normally reveals the train of the thought of the translator. This certainly shows us the Gatha's interpretation of the Sassanian period, which is closer to the original, than the translations of our time.

There are, at this time, four monumental translations of the Gathas which have to be mentioned. The first one is the work of James Darmesteter, his version of the translation[299] which is based on the Middle Persian commentaries and translations. The second one is Christian Bartholomae[300] then Helmut Humbach[301] and the fourth is that of Stanley Isler.[302] These last three are using the Vedic approach. The importance of the Gathas to the religion and the teachings of Zarathustra cannot be overstated. They are the heart of the scriptures and the main inspiration for Zoroastrianism. The Gathas are also quite enigmatic and obscure. According to Helmut Humbach:

Zarathustra did not compose the Gathas to teach
people, but to invoke and glorify Ahura Mazdâ in
a predominantly psalmodic way, very far from any
dogmatic systematizing.[303]

The Gathas are also filled with wordplay and deliberate ambigui-
ties, for example as an incredible sophistication of the Gathas we have
to see professor Martin Schwartz's analysis of the parallel clusters of
lexical, semantic, and phonic data which occurs in concentric rings.
According to Mary Boyce:

>...their poetic form is very ancient one, which has
>been traced back, through the Norse Parallels to
>the Indo-European times. It seems to have been
>linked with a mantic tradition, that is, to have been
>cultivated by priestly seers who sought to express
>in lofty words their apprehension of the divine. It
>is marked by subtleties of allusion, and great rich-
>ness of complexity of style. Such poetry can only
>have been fully understood the learned, and since
>Zarathustra believed, that he had been entrusted by
>God with a message for all mankind, he must also
>have preached again and again in plain words to
>ordinary people...[304]

This connection to the Nordic Parallel, and the Nordic Mythology
which Mary Boyce mentions here, is also a documentation for
Zarathustra's Aryan background. The problem that faces the translation of the Gathas are very significant, as we are dealing here with
a language which was old or not used any more even in the time of
the prophet Zarathustra himself. The Gathas have been written by the
Prophet in this language probably to emphasize its legitimacy of antiquity. In any case, historians are united in believing that the language of

the Gathas has been extinct, or partly forgotten, even during the time of the Prophet himself.

THE CONTENT OF THE GATHA HYMNS

Looking at the meaning of the Gatha hymns, we see here that some of these verses are directly addressed to the creator Ahura Mazdâ; these verses allude directly to the divine essence of the Truth (Asha) the good spirited mind (Vohu Manah) and the spirit of righteousness. Some other verses are addressed directly to the general public; in these the Prophet pleads and recommends the people to live according to the orders of the creator Ahura Mazdâ, and he pleads to Ahura Mazdâ on their behalf. In some other verses, there is some autobiographical data about the prophet himself, but in general, we see here the efforts of Zarathustra to promote his mission of the Truth (Asha).

Some verses describe the Prophet's first attempt to propagate the teachings of Ahura Mazdâ, and his following rejection by the people. These rejections bring him to a point where he doubts about his mission and asks for assistance from Ahura Mazdâ. The various hymns appear to have been composed at different periods in the life of the prophet, and a certain conviction and earnestness is apparent in the verses, whereas in the earlier part of the hymns, the prophet expresses his doubt about his personal suitability for his mission, but until the end of the hymns, he is always deeply convinced that his message is correct. As the Gathas have been written over time, there is no systematic arrangements of the texts or of its content or its doctrine, and so aspects of the Zoroastrian philosophy are scattered randomly over the entire collection of the Gathas. Here some selected excerpts from the Gathas from the translation of Helmut Humbach and Ichaporia.

ZARATHUSTRA SPEAKS TO HIS BELIEVERS AND FOLLOWERS:

Truth is best, of all that is good. As desired, what is being desired is truth for him who represents the best truth (24.17)

The person who is pure in heart towards me, I for my part assign to him the best things in my command, through Good Thought, but harm to him who schemes to harm us. O Mazdâ, thereby gratifying your will by the Truth. Such is the discrimination made by my intellect and thought.

ZARATHUSTRA ASKS AHURA MAZDÂ FOR GUIDANCE:

Where and which part of land shall I go to succeed. They keep me away from the family and the tribe. The community that I wish to join does not gratify me, nor do the deceitful tyrants of the lands. How shall I gratify you, O Mazdâ Ahura (46.1).

ZARATHUSTRA ASKS MAZDÂ FOR BLESSINGS:

I approach you with good thought, O Mazdâ Ahura, so that you may grant me the blessings of two existences, physically and mentally, the material and that of thought, the blessing emanating from Truth, with which one can put you support in comfort (28.2).

I ask you, O Ahura, about the punishment for the evil-doer, who delegates power to the deceitful one and who does not find a livelihood without injury to the cattle and man of undeceiving herdsman.

Grant us a share of it both this material existence, and the spiritual one, that share of it through which we may come and be in Your shelter and that of Truth, for all time... (41.6)

With these entreaties, O Mazdâ Ahura, may we not anger you, nor Truth or Best Thought, we who are standing at the offering of praises to you. You are the swiftest bringer of invigorations, and you hold the power over benefits.

Let good rulers assume rule over us, with actions of Good Insight, O right mindedness. Let not bad rulers assume rule over us. The best insight, which purifies progeny for mankind, let it also be applied to the cow. Her You breed for us for food. (48.5)

ZARATHUSTRA TO THE FOLLOWERS OF DRUJ (DRUJ, DRUGH -THE LIE):

Exceptional and brilliant things instead of weeping will be the reward for the person who comes to the truthful one. But a long period of darkness, foul food, and the word woe to such an existence your religious view will, O deceitful ones, of your own actions. (31.20)

RHETORICAL QUESTIONS POSED BY ZARATHUSTRA TO THE CREATOR AHURA MAZDÂ:

> This I ask you, O Ahura, tell me truly, Of what kind is the first stage of Best Existence? The desired on who implements it so that we may enjoy benefit, that one indeed, holy through truth, watching with His spirit the outcome left for all, is the healer of existence, our ally, you O Mazdâ. (44.2)

> This I ask you, O Ahura, tell me truly, Who, by procreation, is the prime father of Truth? Who created the course of the sun and the stars? Through whom does the moon wax and wane? These very things and others I wish to know, O Mazdâ (44.3)

Although unclear in some parts, the principal message and meaning of the Gathas seem to be evident. The struggle between good and evil: the humans of the truth (Ashavans) who worship Ahura Mazdâ, in their fight and fundamental struggle against the humans of the lie (Drughvands) who are the followers of the Daevas [Monster; in modern Farsi: Dive]. The goodwill of Ahura Mazdâ, the importance of Asha. The need of the support of those people who raise and live from livestock, fighting those who live from looting and destroying the work and the labours of others. The expectation for future reward for living according to good deeds, the partnership and friendship with Ahura Mazdâ. The necessity of offerings, fire ritual and Mantra. We have here clearly a vague impression of the society in which Zarathustra and his people were living.

Maybe it is appropriate to mention at this point, again, Christian Bartholomae (1855–1925), the German historian at the University of Heidelberg, who devoted the main part of his life to Iranian linguistics, His main work and aim was the integration of the old Iranian language into the framework of Indo-European languages. The progress of Iranian studies around the turn of the century is most clearly enriched and reflected in his main publication on the old Iranian language, which is *Das Altiranische Verbum* (1878) and his masterwork, *Das Altiranisches Worterbuch* (1904, and the supplementary volume of 1906). Bartholomae worked over ten years compiling this lexicography, which has been called by M.J. Dresden "... one of the best and most complete dictionaries ever written of any language." *Das Altiranische Worterbuch* was, for decades, and is still today, the basis for all work on the Avesta and the Avestan language. It is still today one of the important and essential tools of every Iranian scholar, and it is indispensable for any person wanting to investigate the ancient Iranian literature or religious documents. Bartholomae's *Das Altiranisches Worterbuch* is still the only comprehensive dictionary of any Old or Middle Iranian language today.

Here we have to mention the Rigveda, which derives from the Sanskrit *ric* [verse] and *veda* [knowledge] and is an ancient archaic sacred collection of Vedic Sanskrit hymns from the Indian subcontinent. It is counted among the four canonical *sruti* [sacred texts] of Hinduism known as the Vedas. Some of its verses are still recited today at Hindu prayers, putting these among the world's oldest religious texts in continued use today. The Rigveda contains several mythological and poetical accounts of the origin of the world, and various prayers for the daily life. Centuries-old philological and linguistic evidence suggests that the Rigveda was composed in the northwestern region of the Indian subcontinent, between approximately 1700–1100 BC. There are strong linguistic and cultural similarities with the early Iranian Avesta, deriving from the proto-Indo-Iranian-Aryan times, often associated with the early Andronovo Sintashta-Petrovka culture circa 2200–1600 BC.

13.3 DENKARD

The Denkard [in Farsi: Deen Kard], which means "Act of the Religion", is a collection of religious writings, written down shortly after the Islamic conquest of the Sassanian Empire. These papers were written in a time when the Zoroastrian believers started to become persecuted by the Muslim rulers of the country. As a result of that persecution, there was a trend to write down, and preserve the ancient religion's beliefs, rules, and traditions for future generations. Therefore, it can be said, that the Denkard is a general Encyclopedia of the Zoroastrian religion, written down in the beginning of the ninth century AD. Of the nine volumes, some parts are lost, but the surviving part of the third book is a major source of the religion of Zarathustra. Books four, five and six discuss metaphysics, doctrinal history, the history of mankind with the emphasis of the history of the Persian Empire and the people of greater Iran, and specially the fundaments of moral principles. Book seven is partly dedicated to the person of Zarathustra himself, with a biography of the prophet. Books eight and nine are commentaries on the Avesta. These can be called the "Zoroastrian Bible" or the prayerbook of Zoroastrianism. Furthermore, the Avesta, which is the main Zoroastrian scripture, is the only source of our information about the original form of the Denkard, before some part of it were lost, meaning how it was when the complete text existed. Further to this Mary Boyce writes in this regard:

> First, in place of the former fraternity of regional communities, a single Zoroastrian fire temple was created under the direct and authoritarian control of Persia, and together with this went the establish-ment of a single canon of Avestan texts, approved and authorized by Tansar[†] himself. This action is described in a Pahlavi book, the Denkard in

the following words "…His Majesty, the King of Kings, Ardeshir son of Papak, following Tansar as his religious authority, commanded al those scattered teachings, to be brought to court. Tansar set about his business, and selected one tradition, and left the rest out of the canon. And he issued this decree: The interpretation of all the teaching of the Mazdâ-worshipping religion is our responsibility, for now there is no lack of certain knowledge concerning them…."[305]

---

† Tansar was the chief priest of the first Sassanian king, Ardeshir I, who ruled 224–241 AD

13.4 BUNDAHISHN - OR THE ORIGINAL CREATION

A much more important and fundamental work of compilation is the Bundahishn, which is translated as Primal Creation, also called Zand-agahih [Knowledge from the Zand], which survives in two recensions, the Great (or Iranian) Bundahishn and a shortened version, the Indian Bundahishn (deriving from a different MS. tradition). One of the two great Zoroastrian compilations, this work probably grew through different redactions, from some time after the Arab conquest down to 1178 AD, when a few additions were made in imperfect Middle Persian. The last important redaction belongs to about the end of the ninth century. The Bundahishn has three main themes: creation, the nature of earthly creatures, and the Kayanians—their lineage and abodes, and the vicissitudes befalling their realm of Eranshahr. The compiler does not name individual sources, but shows an encyclopaedic knowledge of the Zand, and exemplifies excellently the process whereby treatises on chosen themes were created out of the scriptures. Many passages of the Bundahishn evidently derive fairly closely from the Middle Persian translation, for an Avestan syntax underlies them, and one section consists simply of the translation of the first chapter of the Vendidad coinciding (except in small details) with the canonical Zand. Glosses and commentaries provide part of the continuous text, and in these, foreign learning is adduced. According to Mary Boyce:

> There are also a few isolated attempts to bring the work up to date, by the identification of traditional, and even mythical, geographical names with Arabic ones. In the main, however, the absorbing interest of the Bundahishn lies in the antiquity of its material. Here is preserved an ancient, in part pre-Zoroastrian, picture of the world, conceived as saucer-shaped, with its rim one great mountain-range, a central peak thrusting up, star-encircled, to cut off the light of the sun by night; a world girdled by two great rivers, from which all other waters flow; in which yearly the gods fight against demons to end drought and famine, and to bring protection to man. Natural phenomena are speculatively explained; the sprouting of the plants, for example, is ascribed to the mythical Tree of All Seeds growing in the ocean, whose seeds are mingled with water and so scattered annually over all the earth when the god Tishtar brings the rains. Not only is the matter ancient and often poetic, but the manner of presentation, although arid, is of great antiquarian interest; for after the distinctively Zoroastrian account of creation, the speculative learning and legendary history is set out in traditional oral fashion, that is to

say, in schematized mnemonic lists: so many types of animals, so many kinds of liquid, so many names of mountains, so many great battles. This is the learning of ancient Iran, as it must have been evolved and transmitted by generations in the priestly schools.[306]

The Bundahishn survives in two recensions. The one is called the shorter or the lesser Bundahishn, which was found in India and was brought to Europe by Abraham Anquetil-Duperron in 1762. A longer and more complete version, which existed in Iran, was introduced to Europe by T.D. Anklesaria in 1870. The greater Bundahishn is more than twice as long as the shorter version.

---

290. Friedrich Nietzsche, *Philosophy in the Tragic Age of the Greeks,* (Washington: Regnery Gateway, 1962)

291. Friedrich Nietzsche, *Die frohliche Wissenschaft* (fragment nr. 342) published in 1882.

292. Christopher P. Atwood, *The Encyclopaedia of Mongolia and the Mongol Empire* (New York: Facts on File, 2004)

293. Historians, who investigated this pagan religion, particularly concerning Wotan, and have written about them include E.A. Ebbinghaus, Jan de Vries, and Thor Templin.

294. G.F.W. Hegel mentions them as *Naturreligionen* [Natural based religions].

295. Ahmed Osman, *Moses and Akhenaton* (London: Grafton, 1990)

296. Martin Haug, *Die funf Gathas, oder Sammlungen von Liedern und Spruche Zarathustras und seiner Junger* 2 Vols. (Leipzig, 1858–1860)

297. P.O. Skjaervo, *Introduction to Zoroastrianism*—Course notes (Cambridge: Harvard, 2006) http://www.fas.harvard.edu/~iranian/Zoroastrianism/Zoroastrianism1_Intro.pdf

298. R.C. Zaehner, *Dawn and Twilight of Zoroastrianism* (New York: Putnam publishers, 1961), pp. 160 ff

299. James Darmesteter, *The Zend-Avesta* (Oxford: Clarendon, 1883)

300. Christian Bartholomae, *Die Gathas des Avesta* (Strassburg: Trubner,1905)

301. Helmuth Humbach, *The Gathas of Zarathustra: and the other old Avestan Texts* (Heidelberg: C Winter, 1991)

302. Stanley Isler, *The Gaths of Zarathustra* Acta Iranica IV (Leiden: Brill, 1975)

303. Helmuth Humbach *The Gathas of Zarathustra: and the other old Avestan Texts* (Heidelberg: C Winter, 1991) p. 81

304. Mary Boyce, *Zoroastrians: Their Religious Beliefs and Practices* (London: Routledge, 1979), 17

305. Ibid., p. 103

306. Mary Boyce, "Middle Persian Literature", in: *Handbuch der Orientalistik, 1. Abt., IV. Band, 2. Abschn., LFG.1* (Leiden, 1968) pp. 40–41

14. IMAGE COLLECTION

Cover Image. This is the image of the Prophet Zarathustra, imagined by the Renaissance painter Raphael (Rafaele Sanzio da Urbino 1483 --1520 AD). Painted 1509 AD, this painting is called "The school of Athens" and is located in the "Apostolic Palace" in the Vatican. Art historian believe that the face depicting Zarathustra is in reality the portrait of Raphael's patron and friend Count Baldassare Castiglione.

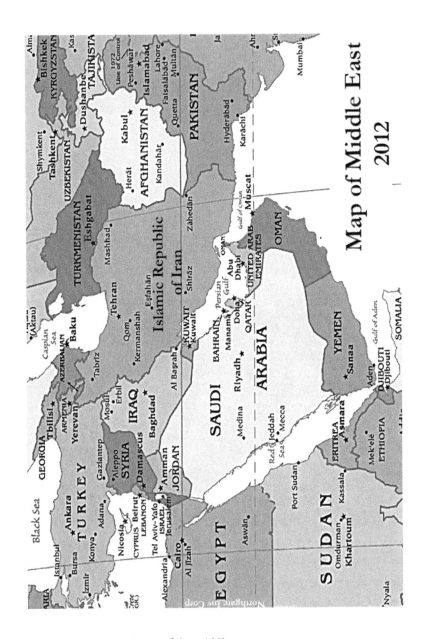

Contemporary general map of the Middle East.

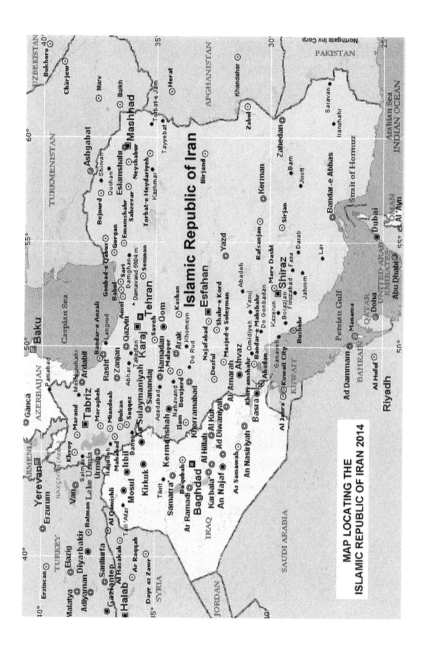

Contemporary map of the Iran of today.

These images show the ruins of the Imperial Palace at Persepolis, the nominal capital of the Achaemanian Empire. Persepolis was burned by the troops of Alexander of Macedonia circa in 329 BC.

This image shows the imaginary portrait of the Hetaira Thais. According to historians, after Alexander declined to give the orders to burn the Palace at Persepolis, the Hetaira Thais, a greek girl who was an entertainer together with a group of musicians, who had followed the troops from Greece, started with the fire to torch the Palace by herself at first. This painting by Sir Joshua Reynolds.

The Zarathustrian religion believes in the purity of the three natural elements, such as water, earth and fire. These elements can not be polluted at any time by death corpses. Therefore after death, human bodies had to be exposed to nature in a remote location. These images show the Zarathustrian funerary locations, called also "The Towers of Silence".

The first two images show the locations of the Zarathustrian cemeteries, which consisted of a large and high tower on the peak of remote mountains, where the corps of the deceased humans were placed after death, to be disposed of there body, except the bones, by animals such as vultures. The bones would be later collected in the central round tract.

The image above shows the interior of these "Towers of Silence", where around the central round tract, the death bodies were placed one next to each other. The closest to the round tract the death children were placed, and than the woman and at the outer end the male bodies. According to Iranian Zarathustrian tradition in the region of the city of Yazd, the bones once collected in the central tract, were mixed with lime and phosphorus, which turned them into dust.

As of today the Iranian Zoroastrian community does not any more follow this tradition since circa 1929 AD.

This image shows the statue of Mithra, who is slaying the bull with a dagger, in a typical Mithraic manner. From the blood of the bull various animals are nurturing, as seen here, the snake, the dog and the scorpion. The hat worn by Mythra in all this statues, is known as the persian hat. This statues were displayed in the Mithraic temples of the Roman Empire.

The image on the following page shows a stone relief carved in the rocks of the mountain at "Taqhe Bostan" in Iran, depicting the investiture of the Sassaninan King Ardeshir I, who ruled 379-383 AD (Ardeshir in greek is Artaxerxes).

These carvings on the mountain rock were done circa 381 AD, and show on the left side a man standing, who by later generations thought to be the image of the prophet Zaratustra himself.

This means the statue of the man standing on the left of the king, was showing how the perception of Zarathustra's image was in the years circa 380 AD by the iranian population. Therefore from this date on, illustrated images of Zarathustra were a copy of this statue, as we can see in the following picture.

Stone relief carved on the mountain rock at "Naqshe Rostam" in southern Iran, showing the transfer of power to the new Sassanian King Ardeshir I, (Ardeshir—known in Europe in his greek spelling Artaxerxes) who ruled 224-241 AD. The King is the person on the center of the picture.

The following image shows the ancient fire temple called Ateshgah at Surakhani which is a suburb of the city of Baku in the republic of Aʒarbaijan. Both words are persian, Ateshgah means in persian "the temple of fire" and Surakhani comes from "Surakh" which is in persian "a hole or a subterranean conduit". As known Aʒarbaijan (which in ancient persian means the land of fire") and particularly its capital city of Baku are the center of natural Gas and Petroleum production today. From prehistory around the city of Baku natural gas and oil was ooʒing from the ground, which once ignited burned in a natural way continuously from prehistorical times. At the location of this fire temple there were seven natural gas exits from the ground, continuously nurturing a fire, which was burning continuously for thousands of years.

From ancient times all travelers and chroniclers, who visited that location, have reported about the seven continuos natural fires.

In 732 AD the Armenian historian Ghevond, who reported the Invasion of the Kha₂ars to Albania (Albania—A₂arbijan of today) in 730 AD, mentioned the seven fires, as the "Atash-Baguan" (Atash is fire in Iranian and Baguan was persian for Baku at the time—but the word Baguan comes from Baga, which again in ancient persian means "God") this meaning the fires of Baku. The German traveler Engelbert Kampfer, who visited this location in 1683 AD also reported of the seven natural fires.

These big natural gas flames were known in antiquity as the famous "The Temple Of The Eternal Fire" of Zoroastrianism, some historians initially believed therefore this place to be the beginning of Zoroastrianism, and the original birthplace of Zarathustra himself. This theory in the meantime has been abandoned. From circa 800 BC. there were fire temples in that location associated with Zoroastrianism, particularly in the Sassanian era (224-652 AD) there are records of ₂oroastrian Fire temples in that location.

Later in the eight century AD this ancient Fire temples were destroyed by the Islamic invaders.

In 1713 AD Indian merchants who lived in that area, started to build the now existing Temple, which was build on top of one of the existing flames (see image from previous page) this indian Merchants being initially of Sikh and also Zoroastrian origin coming from India, the temple structures was terminated 1810. At that date this temple was known locally as the Hindu temple.

The seven fires were burning now inside the temple compound on a permanent basis. It is known, that since antiquity zoroastrian pilgrims were visiting this site, and the temple was still revered among believers. The next two images show the temple and the fires burning in ancient engravings of circa 1890. The first one is an illustration from the Brockhaus and Efron Encyclopedia Dictionary (issue 1890-1907).

In the years 1870 AD the brothers Nobel established there oil company (Branobel, headquarter in St.Petersburg) and started to extract Oil in Azarbaijan on a industrial basis. All natural oil and gas leaks were stopped, and the first Oil was produced in 1875. The seven permanent (eternal) fires, which were burning inside the temple, stopped in 1880, after which zoroastrian pilgrims interpreted this to be a divine punishment, and all pilgrimage ended 1880.

In end October 1888 the russian Zar Alexander lll, who with family and Ministers was inspecting the oil fields in Baku , visited this fire Temple the "Atheshgah". Today this temple in Baku and also the "Atesh Kadeh", an ancient and similar impressive Zoroastrian fire temple in Tiblisi in the Republic of Georgia are a popular tourist destination.

As mentioned in previous chapters, Zoroastrian Priests were called the Magi or Magus by the greeks. We see here in the image above, this detail from a Greek Vase of the fourth century BC. This is how the greeks imagined the Zarathustrian Priest, the Magus, to perform the ceremony in the fire temple. In reality, as fire is a sacred element in Zoroastrianism, priests are obliged to wear a cloth in front of there mouth and nose, in order not to pollute with there breath the sacredness of the flame.

Furthermore the priest has to cover his head, which is a general and ancient rule, all persons in a religious place or ceremony have to cover there head as a principle. He has also to turn his head always to the source of light, and he wears entirely white, as a sign of purity. The image above shows a priest performing a ceremony in circa 1950. The detail from the greek Vase is Vase #3297, side A, Staatliche Antikensammlungen ind Glyphothek, Munchen, Germany, with their permission.

Plate, Sassanian dynasty. Silver-gold plated—showing King Shapur I in battle, circa 269 AD. Museum of the city of Tabriz, Iran.

Following page: A solid golden drinking cup (22 carat gold), five and a half inches in height, recently discovered, Iranian origin of the Achaemanian period. Circa 520 BC. The golden cup shows two women locking in opposite directions, both wearing a crown formed by snakes.

Above: Rython, which is a decorated drinking cup. Sassanian dynasty, silver-gold plated, circa 285 AD.

The royal Palace of the Sassanian Kings in Ctesiphone, which is a city close to the city of Bagdad of today. The Sassanian Kings stayed in Ctesiphone in winter, in the summer they stayed in Ecbatana, the Hamadan of today. The name Ctesiphone is greek, in persian it is Tisfun. The last Sassanian King staying in this palace was Khosrow II (in iranian Khosrow Parviz), who was murdered in 628 AD. This Palace was abandoned by the Sassanian Kings in 632 AD, and was destroyed by the Arab invaders a few years later.

In the years 1922 a colossal statue was discovered in a hidden cave in the Zagross mountains in southern Iran. This cave being near the city of Kazeroun. The colossal statue found in that cave was carved from one piece of Staglamite with the dimentions of 25 feet high (7.3 meters) and shoulders 8 feet wide.

The statue shows the Zarathustrian --Sassanian King Shapur I, who ruled 242--272AD, and who in battle defeated the Imperial roman Armies of Emperors Philip the Arab, Gordian and Emperor Valerian . Shapur the first was probably the greatest King of the Sassanian dynasty, and one of the greatest Rulers of the ancient Persian Empire. He defeated the Imperial Roman Armies three times, Roman Emperor Valerian was captured alive by him in 260 AD.

The city of Bishapur (Bishapur—Shapur's city) and Kaserun was build according to historians by roman prisoners. This ancient city which King Shapur I had build as his capital, was also Roman Emperor Valerian's home until the end of his life. Here excavations have just started in a Grand Temple dedicated to Anahita, where from the ancient Kings palace a underground stairways has been discovered leading to that temple. The Kings palace contained extensive mosaic floors in the Irano-roman style, which are now partly in the Louvre Museum.

After the down fall of the Zarathustrian Sassanian Empire, and the Islamic invasion of Persia (Iranshahr), the islamic-arab invaders destroyed this statue, which was pulled down, his face, feet and arms broken and buried in the floor of the cave, after which the path to the cave was demolished and the caves entrance hidden . Only to be discovered circa 1400 years later. In 1957 the late persian King Mohammad Reza Shah Pahlavy ordered this statue to be reerected and repaired again. Iranian Archaeologists believe, that the tomb of this great King, and further rock inscriptions are hidden somewhere in this extensive cave.

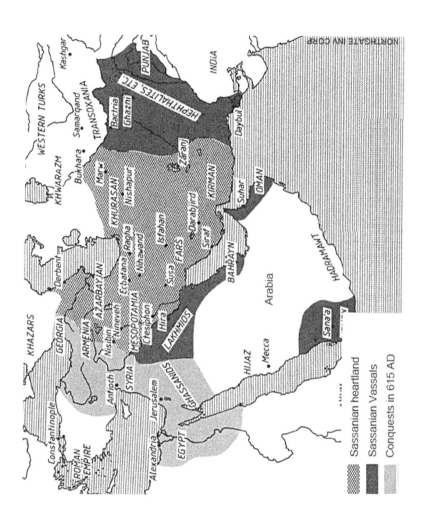

Territories controlled by the Sassanian Dynasty King Khosrow II (iranian Khosrow Parviz) circa 613-627 AD.

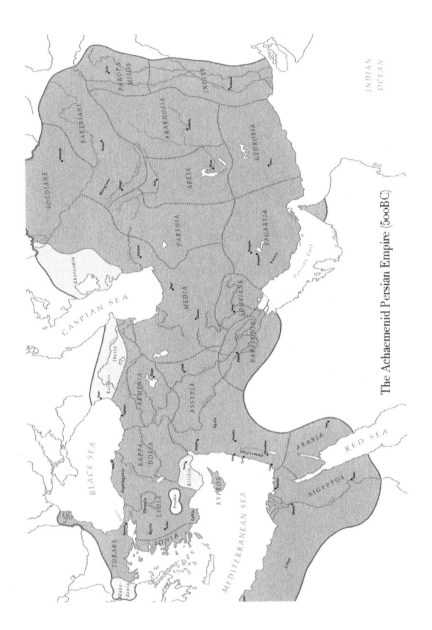

Achaemanian Empire at its greatest extent in circa 525-470 BC.

This image shows the presumed portrait statue of the Parthian General--Sepahbod Rostam Surena-Pahlav. The descendant of an very ancient hereditary local ruling family in the eastern part of the Parthian Empire, his family secured for centuries the south eastern frontiers of the Persian Empire. This ancient family, whose roots go back to the times of the Achaemanian era, meaning before 350 BC, ruled for centuries as Satraps, or local Kings, on a

hereditary basis the region of Sistan, Baluchistan and all the western part of Afghanistan of today .

In the year 53 BC the Roman Consul Marcus Licinius Crassus, who shortly before had crushed the uprising of the Slave Armies of Spartacus, invaded the Parthian Empire from the west with 30 000 roman soldiers. The Parthian King Orodes II, in 54 BC had been saved and reinstated to his Throne before by Surena, who had crushed an uprising in the city of Seleucia, therefore Orodes ll gave now his cavalry to be commanded by General Surena to counter the invading Roman Armies.

In 53 BC the numerically superior Roman Armies were defeated by the cavalry of General Surena in the battle of Carrhae (Haran--in present day Turkey). The Roman historian Plutarch speaks of 20,000 roman soldiers death and 10,000 prisoners. This battle is seen as one of the earliest and most important battles between Rom and the Parthian Empire, and amongst the most crushing defeats in roman history.

Years later during the reign of Roman Emperor Augustus, when the Parthian Kings as a gesture of good will returned the emblems and golden signs of the lost roman legions to the romans, Emperor Augustus ordered this fact to be carved and shown in his breast armor plate, in the statue of "Augustus prima porta".

As for General Rostam Surena, the roman historian Plutarch in his "Life of Crassus" writes about him to be "...honorable...a tall and strong and extremely distinguished man, in birth, wealth, and honor paid to him...".

At the end the destiny of General Rostam Surena was the one of many honorable military man before and after him, the Parthian King Orodes ll fearing the devotion and admiration of his troops to him, had him arrested and executed. His position and his destiny in history is uniquely paralleled to that of the Iranian Hero Rostam, created by the Poet Ferdowsi in his book "Shahnameh". Therefore it is a matter of historical investigation, weather Surena was indeed taken over by the poet Ferdowsi and glorified as the hero in his book.

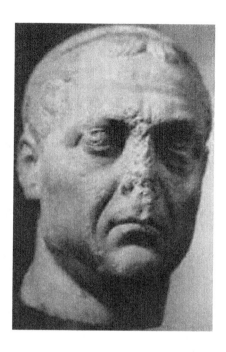

This image shows the statue of the Roman Emperor Valerian, 195-264 AD, whose armies were decisively defeated in Edessa (todays western Syria) by the Persian Army, and who was taken prisoner by the Sassanian King Shapur I in 260 AD. In contrary to the christian chronicler Lactantius's recount, according to recent scholars, Valerian and thousands of roman soldiers, who became prisoners, were living in a relatively good condition in Iran. The Persian King Shapur I used the Roman soldiers in his engineering and development plans for his new Capital city of Bishapur. A Water reservoir and Dam, called in persian "Bande Kaisar" or "Caesar's dam" was a remnant of Roman Engineering. The location of Kaisars dam or Caesars dam and other roman building projects, is today's city of Shushtar. Today's city of Kazerun (Kaisaruniqum) was the place where the Roman soldiers and Emperor Valerian weresettled in southern Iran by the King Shapur l in the years260-264 AD. As of Emperor Valerian, he lived according to Iranian records four more years in relatively good condition in that same city newly build and populated by the roman soldiers and died there in 264 AD.

A.

B.

C.

D.

E.

Image A. Shows a 22 carat gold coin, both sides. Iranian, Aachaemanian dynasty period. Circa 475 BC.

Image B. Shows a coin, both sides. Iranian Parthian period, Ashkanian. King Arsaces I, 247-211 BC. King Arsaces was the founder of the city of Ashkabad, and the founder of the Arsacid dynasty, he was of Scythian descent.

Image C. Shows a 22 carat gold coin of Sassanian King Shapur I, reigned 242-272 AD. The back of the coin shows a Zarathustrian fire altar. He is mentioned many times positively in the Talmud , where he is referred to as King Shabur.

Image D. Shows Sassanian King Hormiẓd I (persian Hormoẓ) he was the son of King Shapur I , and ruled as the King of Armenia from 251-270 AD. Later he became King of the Persian Empire (Iranshahr) from 272-273.

Image E. Gold coin. Shows Sassanian King Bahram I , ruled 273-276 AD, he was the younger brother of King Hormiẓd I.

This image shows the german philosopher Friedrich Nietzsche (1844-1900) close to the end of his life. He was the author of the book "Thus spoke Zarathustra", which in reality was the use of the Prophets name for Nietzsche's own personal philosophy, and had nothing to do with the real Zarathustrian religion. About Zarathustra himself Nietzsche wrote; "...The invention of morality by Zarathustra was the greatest philosophical error in human history...".

15. GENERAL BIBLIOGRAPHY— REFERENCES AND FURTHER READING

RELIGIOUS BACKGROUND IN PRE ZOROASTRIAN TIMES—A SHORT LOOK AT MITHRAISM AND ITS HISTORIC CONSEQUENCES AND THE PHARAOH AKHENATEN

M. Boyce, - "Ātas-zohr and Āb-zohr,"- JRAS, - 1966, pp. 100–18.

Idem, - A History of Zoroastrianism I, - Leiden and Cologne, 1975.

É. Benveniste, - "Hommes et dieux dans l'Avesta," -in Festschrift für W. Eilers, Wiesbaden, -1967, pp. 144–47.

A. Christensen, Les types du premier homme et du premier roi dans l'histoire légendaire des Iraniennes I, Stockholm, 1917; II, Leiden, 1934

T. Burrow, -"The Proto-Indoaryans," JRAS, 1973, pp. 123–40.

E. Benveniste and I. Renou, -Vrtra et Vrθ-ragna, -Paris, 1934.

G. M. Bongard-Levin- and F. A. Grantovskii, -De la Scythie á l'Inde. -E´nigmes de l'histoire de anciens Aryens, tr.- P. Gignoux, -Paris, 1981.

J. Brough, -"Soma and Amanita Muscaria,"- BSOAS 34, -1971, pp. 331–62.

F. Cumont. -Les mystežres de Mithra, - Bruxelles, 1913.

R. N. Dandekar.- Der vedische Mensch, - Heidelberg, -1938.

J. Darmesteter, -E´tudes Iraniennes, -Paris, - 1883.

A. de Jong, -Traditions of the Magi.- Zoroastrianism in Greek and Latin Literature, Leiden, 1997.

J. de Menasce, - "La promotion de Vahrām,"

G. Dumézil. "Les 'trois fonctions' dans le Rgveda et les dieux indiens de Mitani,"

Académie Royale de Belgique. Bulletin de la classe des lettres …, 5e série, 47, 1961, pp. 265–98.

D. S. Flattery and M. Schwartz, - Haoma and Harmaline, - Berkeley, 1989.

I. Gershevitch, -The Avestan Hymn to Mithra, - Cambridge, 1959.

Idem. -"An Iranianist's View of the Soma Controversy," -in P. Gignoux -and A. Tafazzoli, -eds., Mémorial Jean de Menasce, Louvain, 1974, pp. 45–75.

G. Gnoli, - "Ašavan. Contributo allo studio del libro di Ardā Wirāz," in G. Gnoli and A. V.

Rossi, -Iranica, - Naples, 1979, pp. 387–452.

Idem, - Les religions de l'Inde, I, - tr. by L. Jospin, Paris, 1962.

Idem, - The Vision of the Vedic Poets, -The Hague, 1963.

L. H. Gray, - The Foundations of the Iranian Religions, Bombay, 1929.

S. S. Hartman.- Gayōmart, Uppsala, 1953.

V. Henry, - "Esquisse d'une liturgie Indo-Iranienne," in W. Caland and V. Henry.

A. Hillebrandt.- Ritualliteratur, Vedische Opfer und Zauber-, Strassburg, 1897.

G. Hüsing, - Die Iranische Überlieferung und das arische System, - Leipzig, 1909.

THE CULT OF MITHRA AND THE PHARAOH AKHENATEN

Thames & Hudson. pp. 236–240 Wilkinson, Richard H.- (2003). *The Complete Gods and Goddesses of Ancient Egypt.*

M. Lichtheim, - *Ancient Egyptian Literature,* -Vol.1, 1980, p.223

Fleming, Fergus, and Alan Lothian -(1997).- *The Way to Eternity: Egyptian Myth.* -Duncan Baird Publishers. p. 52

Jan Assmann, -*Religion and Cultural Memory: Ten Studies,* Stanford University Press 2005, p.59

Dominic Montserrat -, *Akhenaten: History, Fantasy and Ancient Egypt,* - Routledge 2000, ISBN 0-415-18549-1, - pp.36ff.

Collier, Mark and Manley, Bill. -*How to Read Egyptian Hieroglyphs: 2nd Edition.* Berkeley: University of California Press, 1998, p. 29

Maarten J. Vermaseren—Mithras Geschichte eines Kultes— Stuttgart—W. Kohlhammer 1965.

Hugo Gressmann—Die Orientalischen religionen im Hellenistisch –romischen Zeitalter –-Berlin –de Gruyter –1930.

Paul Thieme—The Arian Gods of the Mittani Treaties—Journal of the American oriental society—Vol. 80 1960 pp. 301–317

Mirko Novak— Mittani Empire and the Question of Absolute Chronology—-Wien 2007.

Anneliese Kammenhuber—Die Arier im Vorderen Orient, ein Mythos?—Wien –1974

Trevor Bryce—The kingdom of the Hittites—Oxford University Press—page 98

ZARATHUSTRA—HIS LIFE IN HISTORY
AND LEGEND—AND HIS MESSAGE.

Khan, Roni K- (1996), -"The Tenets of Zoroastrianism",

Black, Matthew; Rowley, H. H., eds.- (1982), *ePeake's Commentary on the Bibl*, New York:- Nelson, - ISBN 0-415-05147-9

Boyce, Mary - (1984), - *Textual sources for the study of Zoroastrianism*, Manchester: - Manchester Univ.Press-, ISBN 0-226-06930-3

Boyce, Mary -(1987), - *Zoroastrianism: A Shadowy but Powerful Presence in the Judaeo-Christian World*, - London: -William's Trust

Boyce, Mary (1979), -*Zoroastrians: Their Religious Beliefs and Practices*, - London: Routledge, ISBN 0-415-23903-6 (note to catalogue searchers: the spine of this edition misprints the title "Zoroastrians" as "Zoroastians", and this may lead to catalogue errors)

Boyce, Mary -(1975), -*The History of Zoroastrianism* 1, - Leiden: Brill, ISBN 90-04-10474-7, - (repr. 1996)

Boyce, Mary- (1982), -*The History of Zoroastrianism* 2, -Leiden: Brill, ISBN 90-04-06506-7, -(repr. 1997)

Boyce, Mary- (2007), - *Zoroastrians: Their Religious Beliefs and Practices*, - London: -Routledge, -ISBN 978-0-415-23903-5

Boyce, Mary (1983), "Ahura Mazdā"-, *Encyclopaedia Iranica* 1, - New York: Routledge & Kegan Paul pages 684–687

Bulliet, Richard W. - (1979), - *Conversion to Islam in the Medieval Period: An Essay in Quantitative History*, -Cambridge: Harvard UP, ISBN 0-674-17035-0

Carroll, Warren H. -(1985), - *Founding Of Christendom: History Of Christendom* 1, Urbana: Illinois UP, - ISBN 0-931888-21-2, (repr. 2004)

Clark, Peter -(1998), *Zoroastrianism. An Introduction to an Ancient Faith*, - Brighton: Sussex Academic Press, ISBN 1-898723-78-8

Dhalla, Maneckji Nusservanji - (1938), - *History of Zoroastrianism*, New York: OUP

Duchesne-Guillemin, Jacques- (1988), - "Zoroastrianism", - *Encyclopedia Americana* 29, -Danbury: Grolier- pages 813–815

Duchesne-Guillemin, Jacques -(2006), -"Zoroastrianism: Relation to other religions", - *Encyclopædia Britannica* (Online ed.), -retrieved 2006-05-31

Foltz, Richard- (2004), - *Spirituality in the Land of the Noble: How Iran Shaped the World's Religions*, -Oxford:- Oneworld publications, ISBN 1-85168-336-4

Kellens, Jean, - "Avesta", - *Encyclopaedia Iranica* 3, - New York: Routledge and Kegan Paul- pages 35–44.

King, Charles William -(1998) [1887], - *Gnostics and their Remains Ancient and Mediaeval*, -London: Bell & Daldy, ISBN 0-7661-0381-1

Malandra, William W.- (1983), -*An Introduction to Ancient Iranian Religion. Readings from the Avesta and Achaemenid Inscriptions*, -Minneapolis: U. Minnesota Press-, ISBN 0-8166-1114-9

Malandra, William W.- (2005), - "Zoroastrianism: Historical Review", *Encyclopaedia Iranica*, -New York: iranicaonline.org

Moulton, James Hope- (1917), - *The Treasure of the Magi: A Study of Modern Zoroastrianism*, - London: OUP, 1-564-59612-5 (repr. 1997)

Russell, James R.- (1987), -*Zoroastrianism in Armenia- (Harvard Iranian Series)*, Oxford: Harvard University Press, ISBN 0-674-96850-6

Simpson, John A.; Weiner, Edmund S., eds.- (1989)-, "Zoroastrianism", -*Oxford English Dictionary* (2nd ed.), London: Oxford UP, ISBN 0-19-861186-2

Stolze, Franz -(1882), - *Die Achaemenidischen und Sasanidischen Denkmäler und Inschriften von Persepolis, Istakhr, Pasargadae, Shâpûr*, -Berlin: A. Asher

Zaehner, Robert Charles -(1961), - *The Dawn and Twilight of Zoroastrianism*, London: Phoenix Press, ISBN 1-84212-165-0

AHRIMAN OR ANGRA MAINYU—
THE DEVIL—OR THE DESTRUCTIVE SPIRITS

Dhalla, Maneckji Nusservanji - (1938), -*History of Zoroastrianism*, -New York: -OUP p. 392.

Haug, Martin -(1884)-, *Essays on the Sacred Language, Writings and Religion of the Parsis*, London: Trubner,

Jenny Rose-Zoroastrianism—an Introduction-I.B.Tauris

Jenny Rose-Zoroastrianisme—Aguide for the perplexed (Continuum)

Boyce, Mary -(1982)-, *A History of Zoroastrianism. Volume 1: The Early Period.*- Third impression with corrections.- pp. 192–194

Wilson, John- (1843), *The Parsi religion: Unfolded, Refuted and Contrasted with Christianity*, - Bombay: American Mission Press pp. 106ff.

Maneck, Susan Stiles -(1997), - *The Death of Ahriman: Culture, Identity and Theological Change Among the Parsis of India*, -Bombay: K. R. Cama Oriental Institute- pp. 182ff.

Boyce, Mary -(2001), *Zoroastrians: Their Religious Beliefs and Practices*. Routledge. p. 20

Gershevitch, Ilya -(1964)-, "Zoroaster's Own Contribution", *Journal of Near Eastern Studies* 23 (1): 12–38, doi:10.1086/371754 p. 13

Duchesne-Guillemin, Jacques- (1982), -"Ahriman", -*Encyclopaedia Iranica*, 1, New York: Routledge & Kegan Paul, pp. 670–673,

Boyce, Mary -(1990), -*Textual Sources for the Study of Zoroastrianism*. University of Chicago Press. p. 16:

Clark, Peter- (1998), *Zoroastrianism: An Introduction to an Ancient Faith*. Sussex Academic Press. pp. 7–9

Nigosian, Solomon Alexander. -(1993), - *The Zoroastrian Faith: Tradition and Modern Research*. McGill-Queen's Press. p. 2

A SHORT HISTORY OF IRAN

Abrahamian, Ervand- (2008). -*A History of Modern Iran.*- Cambridge University Press. ISBN 0-521-82139-8.

Cambridge University Press (1968–1991).- *Cambridge History of Iran.* (8 vols.). Cambridge: Cambridge University Press. ISBN 0-521-45148-5.

Daniel, Elton L. (2000). -*The History of Iran.*- Westport, Connecticut: Greenwood. ISBN 0-313-36100-2.

Olmstead, Albert T. E. -(1948).- *The History of the Persian Empire: Achaemenid Period.* -Chicago: University of Chicago Press.

Van Gorde, A. Christian. -*Christianity in Persia and the Status of Non-Muslims in Iran*- (Lexington Books; 2010) -329 pages.- Traces the role of Persians in Persia and later Iran since ancient times, with additional discussion of other non-Muslim groups.

Benjamin Walker, - *Persian Pageant: A Cultural History of Iran,* -Arya Press, Calcutta, 1950.

Nasr, Hossein- (1972).- *Sufi Essays.*- Suny press. ISBN 978-0-87395-389-4.

AHURA MAZDÂ—THE CREATOR GOD

Frye, Richard Nelson -(1996), *The heritage of Central Asia from antiquity to the Turkish expansion,* -Markus Wiener Publishers, - ISBN 978-1-55876-111-7

Boyce, Mary (1975), - *History of Zoroastrianism,* - Vol. I, *The early period,* Leiden: Brill

Boyce, Mary (1982), - *History of Zoroastrianism,* - Vol. II, *Under the Achamenians,* Leiden: Brill

Boyce, Mary (1983), - "Ahura Mazdā", -*Encyclopaedia Iranica* 1, -New York: Routledge & Kegan Paul, - pp. 684–687

Maneck, Susan Stiles- (1997), -*The Death of Ahriman: Culture, Identity and Theological Change Among the Parsis of India*, -Bombay: K. R.- Cama Oriental Institute

Sims-Williams, Nicholas -, *Sogdian and other Iranian inscriptions of the Upper Indus*, University of Michigan, - ISBN 978-0-7286-0194-9

Unknown (1999), -*History of civilizations of Central Asia*-, *Volume 3*, - Motilal Banarsidass Publ

King, Karen L.- (2005), - *What is Gnosticism?*, - Harvard University Press, ISBN 978-0-674-01762-7

Nigosian, Solomon (1993), - *The Zoroastrian faith: tradition and modern research*, - McGill-Queen's Press – MQUP-, ISBN 978-0-7735-1144-6

Dhalla, Maneckji Nusservanji- (1938), - *History of Zoroastrianism*, -New York: OUP, ISBN 0-404-12806-8

Boyce, Mary (2001), -"Mithra the King and Varuna the Master", -*Festschrift für Helmut Humbach zum 80.*, - Trier: WWT, pp. 239–257

Humbach, Helmut -(1991), - *The* Gathas *of Zarathustra and the other Old Avestan texts*, - Heidelberg: Winter-, ISBN 3-533-04473-4

Kent, Roland G. -(1945), - "Old Persian Texts", - *Journal of Near Eastern Studies* 4 (4): 228–233, doi:10.1086/370756

Kuiper, Bernardus Franciscus Jacobus- (1983), "Ahura", - *Encyclopaedia Iranica* 1, New York: Routledge & Kegan Paul, pp. 682–683

Kuiper, Bernardus Franciscus Jacobus -(1976), "Ahura Mazdā 'Lord Wisdom'?", -*Indo-Iranian Journal* 18 (1–2): 25–42

Ware, James R.; Kent, Roland G.- (1924), "The Old Persian Cuneiform Inscriptions of Artaxerxes II and Artaxerxes III", - *Transactions and Proceedings of the American Philological Association* (The Johns Hopkins University Press)

AHURA MAZDÂ AND THE ROCK
INSCRIPTIONS IN ANCIENT IRAN

E. Denison Ross, -The Broadway Travellers: Sir Anthony Sherley and his Persian Adventure, -Routledge, 2004, ISBN 0-415-34486-7

Robert Ker Porter, - Travels in Georgia, Persia, Armenia, ancient Babylonia, &c. &c. : during the years 1817, 1818, 1819, and 1820, -volume 2, Longman, 1821

Carsten Niebuhr, -Reisebeschreibung von Arabien und anderen umliegenden Ländern, - 2 volumes, -1774 and 1778

"Old Persian". Ancient Scripts. -Archived from the original on 18 April 2010. Retrieved 2010–04-23.

A. V. Williams Jackson, - The Great Behistun Rock and Some Results of a Re-Examination of the Old Persian Inscriptions on It, - Journal of the American Oriental Society, -vol. 24, - pp. 77-95, 1903

W. King and R. C. Thompson, - The sculptures and inscription of Darius the Great on the Rock of Behistûn in Persia : a new collation of the Persian, Susian and Babylonian texts, - Longmans, 1907

George G. Cameron, -The Old Persian Text of the Bisitun Inscription, Journal of Cuneiform Studies, - vol. 5, no. 2, - pp. 47-54, 1951

W. C. Benedict and Elizabeth von Voigtlander, -Darius' Bisitun Inscription, Babylonian Version, - Lines 1–29, - Journal of Cuneiform Studies, - vol. 10, no. 1, pp. 1–10, 1956

"Iran's Bisotoon Historical Site Registered in World Heritage List".-Payvand.com. 2006-07-13.- Retrieved 2010–04-23.

Intl. experts to reread Bisotun inscriptions, - Tehran Times, -May 27, 2012

Thompson, R. Campbell. -"The Rock of Behistun". *Wonders of the Past*. Edited by Sir J. A. Hammerton.- Vol. II. New York: Wise and Co., 1937. (pp. 760–767) "Behistun". Members.ozemail. com.au. Retrieved 2010–04-23.

Cameron, George G.- "Darius Carved History on Ageless Rock". *National Geographic Magazine.* -Vol. XCVIII, Num.- 6, December 1950. (pp. 825–844)

Louis H. Gray, -Notes on the Old Persian Inscriptions of Behistun, - Journal of the American Oriental Society, - vol. 23, - pp. 56–64, 1902

Thompson, R. Campbell. -"The Rock of Behistun".- *Wonders of the Past.*- Edited by Sir J.

Cameron, George G.- "Darius Carved History on Ageless Rock"-. *National Geographic Magazine.* Vol. XCVIII, Num. 6, December 1950. (pp. 825–844)

Louis H. Gray, - Notes on the Old Persian Inscriptions of Behistun, Journal of the American Oriental Society, -vol. 23, pp. 56–64, 1902

T. Olmstead, - Darius and His Behistun Inscription, -The American Journal of Semitic Languages and Literatures, -vol. 55, no. 4, pp. 392–416, -1938

THE WORLD OF ANIMALS AND ZOROASTRIANISM.

Moazami, Mahnaz - (2005).- Evil animals in the Zoroastrian religion. -History of Religions Avesta. -The various Avestan and Pahlavi texts, including those mentioned in this article, are avail-able in English translations (of variable quality) at -www.avesta.org.- Citations are from this site unless otherwise noted.

Boyce, M. (1975). -A history of Zoroastrianism, -Vol. 1. Leiden: Brill.

Curtis, V. S. -(1993). Persian myths. -Austin:- University of Texas Press.

De Jong, A.- (2002). -Animal sacrifice in ancient Zoroastrianism: A ritual and its interpretations. In A. I. Baumgarten (Ed.),

Sacrifice in religious experience (Studies in the History of Religions 93), (pp. 127-148). Leiden: Brill.

Herodotus, Histories. George Rawlinson's complete English translation is available online.

Foltz, R. C. (2006). Animals in Islamic tradition and Muslim cultures. Oxford: Oneworld.

Foltz, R., & Saadi-nejad, M. (2007). Is Zoroastrianism an ecological religion? Journal for the Study of Religion, Nature, and Culture 1(4), 413-430.

Strabo, Geography. H. L. Jones's complete English translation is available online at http://classics.mit.edu/Strabo/strab.6.html

Hultgård, A.- (2008) - Zoroastrian influences on Judaism, Christianity and Islam. -

M. Stausberg (Ed.), Zarathustra and Zoroastrianism (pp. 101–112). London: Equinox.

Humbach, H.- (1991). The Gathas of Zarathustra and the other Old Avestan texts.Kellens, J.- (2000). Essays on Zarathustra and Zoroastrianism. Costa Mesa: Mazda Publishers.

Macuch, M.- (2003). On the treatment of animals in Zoroastrian law. In A. Van Tangerloo

(Ed.), Iranica Selecta. Studies in honour of Professor Wojtiech Skalimowski on the occasion of his

seventieth birthday (pp. 167-190). Silk Road Studies. Turnhout: Brepols.

Modi, J. J. (1912). -The Persian Mârnâmeh, or the Book for Taking Omens from Snakes.- In

Anthropological Papers, - (Vol. 1, pp. 34-42). Bombay

Vahman, F. -(1986). Ardā Wirāz Nāmag: the Iranian 'Divina Commedia. -London: Curzon.

THE GATHAS

Humbach, Helmut -(2001), - *Gathas: The texts*,

Schlerath, Bernfried (1969), "Der Terminus aw. Gāθā", *Münchener Studien zur Sprachwissenschaft* 25: 99–103

Humbach, Helmut; Ichaporia, Pallan- (1994), - *The Heritage of Zarathustra, A new translation of his Gathas*, -Heidelberg: Winter

Malandra, William (2001), Moulton, James Hope (1906), - "Bartholomae's Lexicon and Translation of the Gathas (Review)", - *The Classical Review* 20 (9): 471–472

Humbach, Helmut (2001), "Gathas: The texts", *Encyclopedia Iranica* (Costa Mesa: Mazda) 10.

Moulton, James Hope (1906), "Bartholomae's Lexicon and Translation of the Gathas (Review)", *The Classical Review* 20 (9): 471–472

Humbach, Helmut; Ichaporia, Pallan (1994), *The Heritage of Zarathustra, A new translation of his Gathas*, Heidelberg: Winter

Malandra, William (2001), "Gathas: Translations", *Encyclopedia Iranica* (Costa Mesa: Mazda)

Bartholomae, Christian (1951), - Taraporewala, Irach Jehangir Sorabji- (trans.), ed., - *Divine Songs of Zarathustra: A Philological Study of the Gathas of Zarathustra, Containing the Text With Literal Translation into English*, - Bombay: K. R. Cama Oriental Institute Bartholomae's translations ("Die Gatha's des Awesta", 1905) were re-translated into English by Taraporewala. The raw texts, sans commentary or introduction, are available online (avesta.org).

Irani, Dinshaw Jamshedji; Tagore, Rabindranath (1924), *The Divine Songs Of Zarathustra*, London: Macmillan Skjærvø, Prods Oktor (1999), - "Avestan Quotations in Old Persian? Literary sources of the Old Persian Inscriptions", - in Shaked, Saul; Netzer, Amnon, - *Irano-Judaica IV*, Jerusalem: Makhon Ben-Zvi (Ben-Zvi Institute), - pp. 1–64

ZURVANISM

Boyce, Mary (1957). -"Some reflections on Zurvanism".- *Bulletin of the School of Oriental and African Studies* -(London: SOAS) 19/2: 304–316.

Duchesne-Guillemin, Jacques (1956).- "Notes on Zurvanism". *Journal of Near Eastern Studies* (Chicago: UCP) 15/2 (2): 108–112. doi:10.1086/371319.

Frye, Richard (1959)-. "Zurvanism Again".- *The Harvard Theological Review* (London: Cambridge) 52/2: 63–73.

Shaki, Mansour (2002). -"Dahri"-. *Encyclopaedia Iranica*. New York: -Mazda Pub. pp. 35–44.

Zaehner, Richard Charles (1940). -"A Zervanite Apocalypse". *Bulletin of the School of Oriental and African Studies* -(London: SOAS) 10/2: 377–398.

Zaehner, Richard Charles (1955).- *Zurvan, a Zoroastrian dilemma* -(Biblo-Moser ed.). Oxford: Clarendon. ISBN 0-8196-0280-9.

Zaehner, Richard Charles (1961).- *The Dawn and Twilight of Zoroastrianism*- (2003 Phoenix ed.). New York: Putnam. ISBN 1-84212-165-0. A section of the book is available online.

Zaehner, Richard Charles- (1975). -*Teachings of the Magi: Compendium of Zoroastrian Beliefs*. -New York: Sheldon. ISBN 0-85969-041-5.

Yasna 30 -translated by Christian Bartholomae. In Taraporewala, Irach (ed.) (1977). *The Divine Songs of Zarathustra*. New York: Ams. ISBN 0-404-12802-5.

The *Selections of 'Zadspram'* -as translated by- Edward William West. In Müller, Friedrich Max (ed.) (1880). *SBE, Vol. 5.* Oxford: OUP.

Denkard 9.30 -as translated by -Edward William West. In Müller, Friedrich Max (ed.) (1892). *SBE, Vol. 37.* Oxford: OUP.

The Kartir Inscription as translated by David Niel MacKenzie.- In *Henning Memorial Volume*. -Lund Humphries. 1970. ISBN 0-85331-255-9

SAOSHIANT—OR THE ZOROASTRIAN MESSIAH.

Boyce, Mary- (1975), *A History of Zoroastrianism, Vol. I-*, Leiden/Köln: Brill,

Mary Boyce -Textual sources for the study of Zoroastrianism- university of chicago press

Dhalla, Maneckji Nusservanji- (1938), *History of Zoroastrianism*, - New York: OUP

THE ZOROASTRIAN PRIEST
ARDA WIRAZ (OR ARDA VIRAF)

Josef Regenstein- Library -1872Jack Finegan—the archaeology of world religions—page 80—isbn-0-41522155-2 "…Alexander of Macedonia was called the –Roman—in Zoroastrian tradition, because he came from the Roman provinces, which later were a part of the eastern Roman empire…"

Kassock, Zeke—2012—The Book of Arda Viraf-transcription and translation—Isbn-978-1477603—406

J.A.Pope-The Arda Viraf Nameh, or the revelation of Arda Viraf-— London 1816

Mary Boyce-—Middle Persian Literature—(page 48—49-)-1968

Ph.Gignoux-la signification du voyage extra—terrestre dans l escha- tology mazdeenne -pages 63-69-Paris—1974

M.Mole-—Les implication historique du prologue du livre de Arda Wiraz-pages 36—44-Paris 1951

J.C. Tavadia—Die Mittelpersische Sprache und Literathur der Zarathustrier—Leipzig—1956 -pages 116

W. Hinz—Dante's persische Vorlaufer –pages 117-126-1971

Kassock, Zeke, - (2012), -The Book Of Arda Viraf: A Pahlavi Student's 2012 Rendition, Transcription And Translation, ISBN 978-1477603406

Dastur Houshangji Jamaspji Asa-Arda Viraf Namak—Bombay— 1872-Govenmt. Central Book Depot—

E.W.West—-Arda Viraf -library university of Chicago—

THE PROPHET MAZDAK—
BABAK E KHORRAMDIN AND MARDAVIJ

Ehsan Yarshater:- "Mazdakism"-. In: Cambridge History of Iran:- The Seleucid, Parthian and Sasanian periods -2. Cambridge 1983-, pp. 991–1024.

G. Gnoli:- "Nuovi studi sul Mazdakismo"-. In: Accademia Nazionale dei Lincei (Hrsg.)-, La Persia e Bisanzio [Atti dei convegni Lincei 201].- Rome 2004, - pp. 439–456.

A. Christensen:- Le règne du roi Kawadh et le communisme Mazdakite.- Kopenhagen 1925.

H. Börm:- Prokop und die Perser. Untersuchungen zu den römisch-sasanidischen Kontakten in der ausgehenden Spätantike-. Stuttgart 2007, p. 230–233.

P. Crone:- "Kavad's heresy and Mazdak's revolt". In: Iran- 29, 1991, - p. 21–42.

H. Gaube:- "'Mazdak: Historical reality or invention?"- In: Studia Iranica 11, 1982, pp. 111–122.

Z. Rubin:- "Mass Movements in Late Antiquity". -In: I. Malkin/Z. Rubinsohn (Hrsg.), Leaders and Masses in the Roman World. Studies in Honor of Zvi Yavetz. Leiden/New York 1995, pp. 187–191.

Shaki Mansour, in his " Cosmogonical and cosmological teachings of Mazdak "Acta Iranica—Leiden—1985 Page 529–543

W. Sundermann: -"Neue Erkenntnisse über die mazdakitische Soziallehre".- In: Das Altertum 34, 3, 1988, pp. 183–188.

Josef Wiesehöfer:- Kawad, Khusro I and the Mazdakites. A new proposal.- In: P. Gignoux u. a. (Hrsg.): Trésors d'Orient. Paris 2009, pp. 391–4

K. E. Eduljee, http://heritageinstitute.com/zoroastrianism/

ZOROASTRIAN ESCHATOLOGY AND WORLDVIEW

Boyce, Mary (1979), - *Zoroastrians: Their Religious Beliefs and Practices*, - London: Routledge & Kegan Paul, pp. 27–29, - ISBN 978-0-415-23902-8 .

Moazami, Mahnaz. -(Winter 2000) -*Millennialism, Eschatology, and Messianic figures in Iranian Tradition*- (Journal of Millennial Studies) Boston University

Boyce, Mary. -(1984) -*Textual Sources for the Study of Zoroastrianism*- (Textual Sources for the Study of Religion). London:Rowman & Littlefield.

Taylor, Richard P.- (2000), *Death and Afterlife: A Cultural Encyclopedia*, ABC-CLIO.

Boyce, Mary. (1975) -*A History of Zoroastrianism, Vol. 1*- (Handbuch der Orientalistik Series).- Leiden: Brill; Repr. 1996 as- *A History of Zoroastrianism: Vol 1, The Early Period*.

Shaul Shaked—Professor at the Hebrew University of Jerusalem, - Comparative Religion, Faculty Member, the following of his work is very important;

The Notions Menog and Getig in the Pahlavi Texts -and Their Relation to Eschatology

Dualism in Transformation: -Varieties of Religion in Sasanian Iran

Ritual Tests or Treasury Documents? Magic Spells and Formulae.

Some notes on Ahremen:- the Eveil Spirit, and His Creation

Two Judaeo-Iranian Contributions: 1-Iranian Functions in the Book of Esther

Specimens of Middle Persian Verse. The Iranian Influence on Judiasm: First Century BC to Second Century AD

THE JEWISH PEOPLE AND THE BABYLONIA CAPTIVITY

Coogan, Michael -(2009). *A Brief Introduction to the Old Testament*.- Oxford:Oxford University Press.

Finkelstein, Israel; Silberman, Neil Asher- (2001).- The Bible Unearthed: Archaeology's New Vision of Ancient Israel and the Origin of Its Sacred Texts. Simon and Schuster. ISBN 978-0-684-86912-4

"Babylonian Ration List: King Jehoiakhin in Exile, 592/1 BC". -*COJS.org*. The Center for Online Judaic Studies. Retrieved 23 August 2013. "Ya'u-kīnu, king of the land of Yahudu"

Dan Cohn-Sherbok, -*The Hebrew Bible*, Continuum International, -1996,

The Oxford History of the Biblical World, - ed. by Michael D Coogan. -Pub. by Oxford University Press, -1999. pg 350

Yehud being the Babylonian -Persian equivalent of the Hebrew Yehuda, or "Judah", and "medinata" the word for province -Rashi to Talmud Bavli, avodah zara p. 9a. Josephus, seder hadoroth year 3338 -malbim to ezekiel 24:1, abarbanel et al. -Second Temple Period (538 B.C.E. to 70 C.E.) Persian Rule.

Thomas, David Winton- (1958). -*Documents from Old Testament Times* (1961 ed.).- Edinburgh and London: Thomas Nelson. p. 84.

Translation from Aḥituv, Shmuel.- *Echoes from the Past*. Jerusalem: -CARTA -Jerusalem, 2008, pg. 70.

Bedford, Peter Ross- (2001). *Temple Restoration in Early Achaemenid Judah*. Leiden: Brill. p. 112 (Cyrus edict section pp. 111–131). ISBN 9789004115095.

Becking, Bob (2006). ""We All Returned as One!": Critical Notes on the Myth of the Mass Return". In Lipschitz, Oded; Oeming, Manfred. *-Judah and the Judeans in the Persian Period.*- Winona Lake, IN: Eisenbrauns. p. 8. ISBN 978-1-57506-104-7.

Grabbe, Lester L.- (2004). *A History of the Jews and Judaism in the Second Temple Period: Yehud - A History of the Persian Province of Judah v. 1.*- T & T Clark. p. 355. ISBN 978-0567089984.

Rainer Albertz, *-Israel in exile: the history and literature of the sixth century BC (page 15 link)*- Society for Biblical Literature, 2003, pp.4–38

THE BABYLONIAN CAPTIVITY
AND CYRUS THE GREAT

Dandamaev, M. A. -(1989).- *A political history of the Achaemenid empire.*- Leiden: Brill. p. 373. ISBN 90-04-09172-6.-

Cardascia, G- (1988)-. "Babylon under Achaemenids"-. Encyclopaedia Iranica. Vol. 3. London: Routledge. ISBN 0-939214-78-4.

Boardman, John, - ed. (1994).- The Cambridge Ancient History IV: Persia, Greece, and the Western Mediterranean, - C. 525-479 B.C.- Cambridge: Cambridge University Press. ISBN 0-521-22804-2.

Cite uses deprecated parameters (help)Chavalas, Mark W.-, ed. (2007).- *The ancient Near East : historical sources in translation*. Malden, MA: Blackwell. ISBN 0-631-23580-9.

Freeman, Charles- (1999). *The Greek Achievement: The Foundation of the Western World*. New York: Viking.- ISBN 0-7139-9224-7.

Fried, Lisbeth S.- (2002).- "Cyrus the Messiah? The Historical Background to Isaiah 45:1".- *Harvard Theological Review* 95 (4).

Ball, Charles James- (1899). *Light from the East: Or the witness of the monuments.* -London: -Eyre and Spottiswoode.

Cannadine, David; Price, Simon -(1987).- *Rituals of royalty : power and ceremonial in traditional societies* -(1. publ. ed.). Cambridge: Cambridge University Press. ISBN 0-521-33513-2

Amelie Kuhrt:- *Ancient Near Eastern History: The Case of Cyrus the Great of Persia.* In: Hugh Godfrey Maturin Williamson:- *Understanding the History of Ancient Israel.* Oxford University Press 2007, ISBN 978-0-19-726401-0, pp. 107–128

Bickermann, Elias J.- (September 1946). "The Edict of Cyrus in Ezra 1". *Journal of Biblical Literature* 65 (3): 249–275. doi:10.2307/3262665.

Dougherty, Raymond Philip- (1929).- *Nabonidus and Belshazzar: A Study of the Closing Events of the Neo-Babylonian Empire.*- New Haven: Yale University Press.

Drews, Robert -(October 1974).- "Sargon, Cyrus, and Mesopotamian Folk History". *Journal of Near Eastern Studie-s* 33 (4): 387–393. doi:10.1086/372377.

Harmatta, J. (1971). -"The Rise of the Old Persian Empire: Cyrus the Grea".- *Acta Antiquo* 19: 3–15.

Lawrence, John M. -(1985). "Cyrus: Messiah, Politician, and General".- *Near East Archaeological Society Bulletin.*- n.s. 25: 5–28.

Lawrence, John M.- (1982). -"Neo-Assyrian and Neo-Babylonian Attitudes Towards Foreigners and Their Religion". -*Near East Archaeological Society Bulletin.* n.s. 19: 27–40.

Mallowan, Max- (1972).- "Cyrus the Great (558–529 BC)". -*Iran* 10: 1–17. doi:10.2307/4300460.

Wiesehöfer, Josef- (1996).- *Ancient Persia : from 550 BC to 650 AD.* -Azizeh Azodi, trans. -London: I. B. Tauris.- ISBN 1-85043-999-0.

GENERAL SHAHRBARAZ.

Walter Kaegi-Byzantium and the decline of Rome-Princeton University Press-1970

Warren Treadgold-A concise history of Byzantium-New York -MacMillan Publishers -2001

Shapur Shahbazi-The Sassanian Dynasty-2005

Parvaneh Pourshariati-Decline and fall of the Sassanian Empire-Tauris Publishers-2008

TO FRIEDRICH NIETZSCHE AND HIS BOOK *THUS SPOKE ZARATHUSTRA*

Pippin, Robert. -"Nietzsche: Thus Spoke Zarathustra".- *Cambridge Texts in the History of Philosophy*, - University of Chicago, - 2006.- ISBN 0-521-60261-0. p. ix.

Nietzsche, Friedrich.- Trans. Kaufmann, Walter. *The Portable Nietzsche*. 1976, page 108-9.

Nietzsche, Friedrich Wilhelm.- "How One Becomes What One Is: -With a Prelude in German Rhymes and an Appendix of Songs". -(Edition) Random House, 1974. p. xii.

C. Guignon, D. Pereboom.- *Existentialism: Basic Writings, 2nd ed.*, Hackett, 2001. pp. 101-113

Gutmann, James. -"The "Tremendous Moment" of Nietzsche's Vision".- *The Journal of Philosophy*, -Vol. 51, No. 25. American Philosophical Association Eastern Division: Papers to be presented at the Fifty-First Annual Meeting, - Goucher College, - December 28–30, 1954. pp. 837-842.

Behler, Ernst, - *Nietzsche in the Twentieth Century* in *The Cambridge Companion to Nietzsche*, Magnus and Higgins (ed), - Cambridge University Press, 1996, pp. 281-319

Shapiro, Gary -(Winter 1980).- "The Rhetoric of Nietzsche's Zarathustra". -*boundary 2* (Duke University Press) 8 (2). Retrieved 26 August 2012.

> "Zarathustra does not want to be worshipped himself, and he will be remembered only by continual dance and play which by its very nature must avoid any centreing of a privileged object or person. Even the notion of eternal recurrence is treated playfully in a number of ambiguous references to the confusion of times. That a play upon the tropes should end with irony makes the fact of play itself unavoidable but it does not leave much standing in the way of straightforward doctrines or teachings-just as the higher men must surrender their desperately gleaned fragments of doctrine for Zarathustra's dances."

THE FUTURE OF RELIGIONS FOR THE HUMAN RACE—THE FRENCH REVOLUTION AND MAXIMILLIAN ROBESPIERRE

Aulard, François Victor Alphonse.- Christianity and the French Revolution; -Translated by Lady Frazer.- New York: -H. Fertig, - 1966.

The French Revolution; a political history, 1789 - 1804; -Translated from the French of the 3d ed., with a pref., notes, and historical summary, by Bernard Miall.- New York:- Russell & Russell, 1965.

"French Revolution."- Modern History Sourcebook. -"Maximillian Robespierre on the Festival of the Supreme Being." -The History Place; -Great Speeches Collection. http://www.historyplace.com/speeches/robespierre.htm

FOR THE PROPHET MANI-MANICHAEISM

Boyce, Mary (2001), *Zoroastrians: their religious beliefs and practices*, - Routledge, p. 111, -"He was Iranian, of noble Parthian blood..."

Taraporewala, I.J.S.-, *Manichaeism*, -Iran Chamber Society, retrieved 08-09-2012

Ball, Warwick (2001), - *Rome in the East: the transformation of an empire*, - Routledge, p. 437, "Manichaeism was a syncretic religion, proclaimed by the Iranian Prophet Mani".

Sundermann, Werner (2009), - "Mani, the founder of the religion of Manicheism in the 3rd century AD", *Iranica* (Sundermann),

"According to the Fehrest, Mani was of Arsacid stock on both his father's and his mother's sides, at least if the readings al-ḥaskāniya (Mani's father) and al-asʿāniya (Mani's mother) are corrected to al-aškāniya and al-ašḡāniya (ed. Flügel, 1862, p. 49, II. 2 and 3) respectively. The forefathers of Mani's father are said to have been from Hamadan and so perhaps of Iranian origin (ed. Flügel, 1862, p. 49, 5–6). The Chinese Compendium, which makes the father a local king, maintains that his mother was from the house Jinsajian, explained by Henning as the Armenian Arsacid family of Kamsarakan (Henning, 1943, p. 52, n. 4 = 1977, II, p. 115). Is that fact, or fiction, or both? The historicity of this tradition is assumed by most, but the possibility that Mani's noble Arsacid background is legendary cannot be ruled out (cf. Scheftelowitz, 1933, pp. 403–4). In any case, it is characteristic that Mani took pride in his origin from time-honored Babel, but never claimed affiliation to the Iranian upper class."

Bausani, Alessandro (2000)-, *Religion in Iran: from Zoroaster to Baha'ullah*, -Bibliotheca Persica Press, p. 80, -"We are now certain that Mani was of Iranian stock on both his father's and his mother's side".

W. Sundermann, "Al-Fehrest, iii. Representation of Manicheism.", *Encyclopaedia Iranica*, 1999.

.Encyclopædia Britannica. Mani (Iranian religious leader) (2011)

Henning, W.B., -The Book of Giants, -BSOAS, Vol. XI, Part 1, 1943, pp. 52–74:

"It is noteworthy that Mani, who was brought up and spent most of his life in a province of the Persian empire, and whose mother belonged to a famous Parthian family, did not make any use of the Iranian mythological tradition. There can no longer be any doubt that the Iranian names of Sām, Narīmān, etc., that appear in the Persian and Sogdian versions of the Book of the Giants, did not figure in the original edition, written by Mani in the Syriac language."

W. Eilers (1983), -"Iran and Mesopotamia" in- E. Yarshater, The Cambridge History of Iran, vol. 3, Cambridge: -Cambridge University Press, p. 500:

"Mani, a Parthian on his mother's side, was born at Ctesiphon in the last decade of the Arsacid era (AD 216). "

Marco Frenschkowski (1993). -"Mani (Iran. Mānī<; gr. Μανιχαῖος < ostaram. Mānī ḥayyā »der lebendige Mani«)". In Bautz, Traugott. *Biographisch-Bibliographisches Kirchenlexikon (BBKL)* (in German) 5. Herzberg: Bautz. cols. 669–80. ISBN 3-88309-043-3.

John M. Robertson, -*Pagan Christs* -(2nd ed. 1911), § 14. The Problem of Manichæus.-

Gustav Flügel, -*Mani, seine Lehre and seine Schriften*, -18f 2 (trans. from the *Fihrist* of Muhammad ben Ishak al Nurrâk, with commentary), pp. 84, 97, 99-100, 102-3.

Asmussen, Jes Peter, - comp., *Manichaean Literature: Representative Texts, Chiefly from Middle Persian and Parthian Writings*, - 1975, Scholars' Facsimiles & Reprints, ISBN 978-0-8201-1141-4.

Alexander Böhlig, - 'Manichäismus' in: *Theologische Realenzyklopädie* -22 (1992), 25–45.

Amin Maalouf, *The Gardens of Light* [Les Jardins de Lumière], translated from French by Dorothy S. Blair, 242 p. (Interlink Publishing Group, New York, 2007). ISBN 1-56656-248-1

THE PROPHET MANI AND
THE TEMPLES AT TAKHTE SOLEYMAN

Mary Boyce, - *Zoroastrianism: Its Antiquity and Constant Vigour*, - Cosa Mesa and New York, 1992.

Arthur Christensen, - *L'Iran sous les Sassanides*, -2nd ed., - Copengagen, 1944, p. 167.

Bernhard Damm, - *Geologie des Zendan-i Suleiman und seiner Umgebung*, *südöstiches Balqash-Gebrige Nordwst Iran*, -Wiesbaden, -1968.

Dietrich Huff, - "Sasanidisch-frühislamische Ruinenplätze im Belqis-Massiv in Azerbeidjan, "- *AMI*, N.S. 7, 1974, pp. 203-13. Idem, -"Takht-i Suleiman: Vorläufiger Bericht über die Ausgrabungen im Jahr 1976, " *AMI*, N.S. 10, 1977,

Rudolf Naumann and Dietrich Huff, -"Takht-i Suleiman, " tr. Farâmarz Najd Sami'i as "Haffârihâ-ye Takht-e Solaymân, " *Bastân-šenâsi wa honar-e Irân*, - nos. 9-10, 1977, pp. 25-61.

Rudolf Naumann, Dietrich Huff, and Rudolf Schnyder, -"Takht-i Suleiman:- Bericht über die Ausgrabungen 1965-1973, "- *Archäologischer Anẓeiger*, 1975, -pp. 109-204.

Abu Dolaf Mes'ar b. Mohallel Yanbu'i, *Resâla*, - tr. Vladimir Minorsky -as *Abu Dulaf Mes'ar b. Muhalhil's Travels in Iran*, Cairo, 1955

Ahámad b. Yaháyâ Balâdhori, -*Ketâb Fotuhá al-boldân*, - ed. Michaël Jan de Goeje, -Leiden, 1866; repr., Leiden, 1968

Abu 'Ali Moháammad Bal'ami, - *Târikh-e Bal'ami*, -ed. Moháammad-Taqi Bahâr, -Tehran, 1962; tr. Hermann Zotenberg as -*Chronique de...Tabari traduite sur la version persane d'Abou-Ali Mohammed Bel'ami*, - 4 vols., - Paris, 1867-74.

"Eine sasanidische Glasbläserwerkstatt auf dem Takht-i Suleiman (Iran), " in Uwe Finkbeiner et at. eds., *Beiträge zur Kulturgeschichte Vorderasiens: Festschrift für Reiner Michael Boehmer*, Mainz, 1995, pp. 259-66. Idem, "Das 'medische' Grabrelief von Deh Now, " *Stud. Iranica* 28/1, 1999, pp. 7-40. Idem, "Takht-i Suleiman: Tempel des sassanidischen Reichsfeuers Atur Gushnasp, " in Deuttsches Archäologisches Institut, *Archäologische Entdeckungen: Die Forschungen des Deutschen Archäologischen Instituts im 20. Jahrhundert* I, Mainz, 2000, pp. 103-9.

Ebn al-Faqih, *-Ketâb al-Boldân*, Leiden, 1885.- Ebn Khordâdbeh, *-Ketâb al-masâlek wa 'l-mamâlek*, -Leiden, 1889.

Kurt Erdmann, - *Das Iranische Feuerheitigtum*, -Leipzig, 1941

Hans Henning von der Osten and Rudolf Naumann, *-Takht-i Suleiman: Vorläufiger Bericht über die Ausgrabungen- 1959*, -Teheraner Forschungen 1, Berlin, 1961.

SALMAN FARSI AS A HISTORICAL PESONALITY

Sayed A.A. Razwy-Salman el Farsi, Friend of Prophet Muhammed- Ansaryian Publications—Qum—Islamic rep. of Iran

Lt. General Sir John Glubb-Al- Bidaya-wan-Nihaya-(in Arabic) by Imam ibn Kathir.

Sir William Muir-The Life of Muhammad.

Tor Andre—Muhammad, the man and his faith—

The Enzyclopedia of Islam

The Enzyclopedia Britannica

D.S.Margoliouth-Mohammad and the rise of Islam.

Sahih al Bukhari—Writings—3—31—189.

Muḥammad 'Alī Mu·addin Sabzawārī, Mohammad Hassan Faghfoory -(translator), Tuhfah-yi 'Abbasi, -University Press of America, 2008.pg 33

Abu Ja'far Muhammad ibn Jarir ibn Rustom al-Tabari.- *Dalail al-Imamah*. p.447.

A Restatement of the History of Islam and Muslims on Al-Islam.org Umar bin al-Khattab, the Second Khalifa of the Muslims

"Salman The Persian - Biography". Experiencefestival.com. Retrieved 2013-01-05.

"Salman al-Farsi (Salman the Persian)". Islamawareness.net. Retrieved 2013-01-05.

"سلمان الفارسي - الصحابة - موسوعة الاسرة المسلمة". Islam.aljayyash. net. Retrieved 2012-12-25.

"Seventh Session, Part 2". Al-islam.org. Retrieved 2013-01-05.

Akramulla Syed- (2010-03-20).- "Salman the Persian details: Early Years in Persia (Iran)". Ezsoftech.com. -Retrieved 2013-01-05.

Sunan Abu Dawood, 27:3752

An-Nawawi, Al-Majmu', (Cairo, Matbacat at-'Tadamun n.d.), 380.

THE ZOROASTRIAN PRIEST SALMAN FARSI AND THE PERSIAN INFLUENCE ON ISLAM.

Fred M. Doner-in his book - " Mohammad and the believers "-Harvard University Press

Patricia Crone-in her book-"Meccan trade and the rise of Islam "-Princeton University Press—1987

Lt. General Sir John Glubb-The life and times of Muhammad-Stein and Day Publishers-1970

Muhammad Husayn Haikal-The life of Muhammad-1933-Cairo

Patricia Crone-in her book –" Slaves on Horses "

Ali Dashti-in his book –" Twenty-three Years, a study of the prophetic career of the Prophet Mohammad "1985-translated by T.R.C.Bagley

Houshang M. Payan-The making of a Prophet-World Association Publishers. Sahih al-Bukhari, 3:31:189

Sayed A.A.Razwy- Salman el Farsi, friend of Prophet Muhammed-Ansariyan Publications-QUM-islamic rep. of Iran.

Modarressi, Hossein- (1993).- "Early Debates on the Integrity of the Qur'an: A Brief Survey". *Studia Islamica* 77: 8

Donner, Fred -(2010).- *Muhammad and the Believers: at the Origins of Islam.* London, England:- Harvard University Press. pp. 153–154.

Zoroastrian Heritage-K. E. Eduljee

Esack, Farid -(2005).- *The Qur'an: A User's Guide.*- Oxford England: Oneworld Publications. pp. 39–41

Leaman, Oliver- (2006).- "Revelation". *The Qur'an: an Encyclopedia.* -New York, NY: Routledge. pp. 540–543

Al Faruqi, Lois Ibsen (1987). -"The Cantillation of the Qur'an". *Asian Music* 19 (1): 3–4.

Leaman, Oliver (2006).- *The Qur'an: an Encyclopedia.* -New York, NY: Routledge. pp. 540–543

Leaman, Oliver (2006).- "Ali". *The Qur'an: an Encyclopedia.*- New York: Routledge. pp. 30–31.

Al-Tabari;- Gautier H. A. Juynboll (translator) (1989). -E. Yarshater, editor-*The History of al-Tabari:- The Conquest of Iraq, Southwestern Persia, and Egypt.* Albany, - NY: State University of New York Press. -pp. 2–6

The Crisis of the Early Caliphate.- Albany, NY: State University of New York Press. pp. 8

Rippin, Andrew -(2009).- *The Blackwell Companion to the Qur'an.*- Chichester, West Sussex: Blackwell Publishing. pp. 166.

Warraq's book -The Origins of the Koran: - Classic Essays on Islam's Holy Book. Book information: Publisher: Prometheus Books (September 1998) ISBN 157392198

Sahih al-Bukhari, 3:31:189

Sunnan Abu Dawud, 27:3752

An-Nawawi, Al-Majmu'-, (Cairo, Matbacat at-'Tadamun n.d.), 380.

Abu Ja'far Muhammad ibn Jarir ibn Rustom al-Tabari.- *Dalail al-Imamah*. p.447.

A Restatement of the History of Islam and Muslims on Al-Islam.-org Umar bin al-Khattab, - the Second Khalifa of the Muslims

M. M. Azami (2003).- *The History of the Qur'anic Text from Revelation to Compilation: A Comparative Study with the Old and New Testaments*. UK Islamic Academy.

Gibson, Dan (2011).- *Qur'anic Geography: A Survey and Evaluation of the Geographical References in the Qur'an with Suggested Solutions for Various Problems and Issues*.- Independent Scholars Press, Canada..

Jane Dammen McAuliffe, -ed. (2006).- *The Cambridge Companion to the Quar'an*.- Cambridge University Press.

Adam J. Silverstein-(2010). *Islamic History: A Very Short Introduction*. Oxford University Press.

Sunnan Abu Dawud, 27

SALMAN FARSI —
THE PROPHET JOSEPH IN THE TORAH

The Torah-Book of Genesis—37-21.22.23.

The Jewish Enzyclopedia.com -Joseph

The Old Testament—Jacob and his sons.

Barry J. Kemp, *Ancient Egypt*, Routledge 2005, p.159

Asante, Molefi K. From Imhotep to Akhenaten: An Introduction to Egyptian Philosophers. Paris: Menaibuc, 2004.

SALMAN FARSI AND THE
PROPHET JOSEPH IN THE QURAN.

The Quran-Sura 12-(Yusuf)-ayat-5-6

The Quran-Sura -12 " " - 11—18

The Quran -Sura -12 " " - 19—22

The Quran -Sura —12 " " -23—24

The Quran-Sura-12 " "-38

Keeler, Annabel (15 June 2009). "Joseph ii. In Qur'anic Exegesis". *Encyclopedia Iranica* XV: 34

Coogan, Michael- (2009). *The Old Testament: A Very Short Introduction.* -Oxford University Press. pp. 70–72.

Wheeler, Brannon- (2002). *-Prophets in the Qur'an.* Continuum.- p. 127.

Bruijn -(2013). -"Yūsuf and Zulaykhā". *Encyclopedia of Islam-; Second Edition*: 1.

Mir, Mustansir -(June 1986).- "The Qur'anic Story of Joseph". *-The Muslim World.* LXXVI (1): 1

al-Tabari, Muhammad ibn Jarir (Translated by by William Brinner) (1987). *-The History of al-Tabari Vol. 2:- Prophets and Patriarchs.* SUNY. p. 148.

Wheeler, Brannon -(2002). *-Prophets in the Quran: An Introduction to the Quran and Muslim Exegesis.*- Continuum. p. 128.

Quran 12:5–6 - and Quran 12:10 - and Quran 12:11–18 - and Quran 12:30 and 12; 19; -22

Sahih al-Bukhari, -4:55:593 Quran 12:8–9

Wheeler, Brannon (2002). *Prophets in the Quran: An Introduction to the Quran and Muslim Exegesis.* Continuum. p. 127.-151

al-Tabari, Muhammad ibn Jarir (Translated by by William Brinner) (1987). *The History of al-Tabari Vol. 2: Prophets and Patriarchs.* SUNY. p. 150.-160

Torah-Genesis, 39:1 - Genesis, 39:1-23

Tottoli, Roberto (2013). "Aziz Misr". *Encyclopaedia of Islam, Three*: 1.

Quran 12:23–24

THE HISTORIAN HERODOTUS

English translations of- *The Histories of Herodotus*- are available in multiple editions as :

The Histories of Herodotus Interlinear English Translation Heinrich Stein (ed.), George Macaulay (Trans.), Handheldclassics.com, 2013. Kindle ed. AISN B00B27G1QW

Aubrey de Sélincourt, originally 1954; revised by John Marincola in 1996. Several editions from Penguin Books available.A. D. Godley 1920; revised 1926. Reprinted 1931, 1946, 1960, 1966, 1975, 1981, 1990, 1996, 1999, 2004. Available in four volumes from Loeb Classical Library, Harvard University Press. ISBN 0-674-99130-3 Printed with Greek on the left and English on the right.

David Grene, Chicago: University of Chicago Press, 1985.

George Rawlinson, translation 1858–1860. Public domain; many editions available, although Everyman Library and Wordsworth Classics editions are the most common ones still in print.

Strassler, Robert B., (ed.), and Purvis, Andrea L. (trans.), *The Landmark Herodotus*, Pantheon, 2007. ISBN 978-0-375-42109-9 with adequate ancillary information.

Robin Waterfield, with an Introduction and Notes by Carolyn Dewald, Oxford World Classics, 1997. ISBN 978-0-19-953566-

AND FOR FURTHER READING

Dewald, Carolyn; Marincola, John, eds. (2006). *The Cambridge companion to Herodotus*. Cambridge: Cambridge University Press. ISBN 0-521-83001-X.

Evans, J.A.S. (1991). *Herodotus, explorer of the past : three essays*. Princeton, NJ: Princeton University Press. ISBN 0-691-06871-2

Bakker, Egbert J.; de Jong, Irene J.F.; van Wees, Hans, eds. (2002). *Brill's companion to Herodotus*. Leiden: E.J. Brill. ISBN 90-04-12060-2.

De Selincourt, Aubrey (1962). *The World of Herodotus*. London: Secker and Warburg.

Evans, J.A.S. (2006). *The beginnings of history : Herodotus and the Persian Wars*. Campbellville, Ont.: Edgar Kent. ISBN 0-88866-652-7.

Evans, J.A.S. (1982). *Herodotus*. Boston: Twayne. ISBN 0-8057-6488-7.

Dewald, Carolyn; Marincola, John, eds. (2006). *The Cambridge companion to Herodotus*. Cambridge: Cambridge University Press. ISBN 0-521-83001-X.

Fornara, Charles W. (1971). *Herodotus: An Interpretative Essay*. Oxford: Clarendon Press.

Thomas, Rosalind (2000). *Herodotus in context : ethnography, science and the art of persuasion*. Cambridge: Cambridge University Press. ISBN 0-521-66259-1.

Flory, Stewart (1987). *The archaic smile of Herodotus*. Detroit: Wayne State University Press. ISBN 0-8143-1827-4.

Giessen, Hans W. Giessen (2010). *Mythos Marathon. Von Herodot über Bréal bis ʒur Gegenwart*. Landau: Verlag Empirische Pädagogik (= Landauer Schriften zur Kommunikations- und Kulturwissenschaft. Band 17). ISBN 978-3-941320-46-8.

Hartog, François (2000). "The Invention of History: The Pre-History of a Concept from Homer to Herodotus". *History and Theory* 39 (3): 384–395. doi:10.1111/0018-2656.00137.

Hartog, François (1988). *The mirror of Herodotus : the representation of the other in the writing of history*. Janet Lloyd, trans. Berkeley: University of California Press. ISBN 0-520-05487-3.

Lateiner, Donald (1989). *The historical method of Herodotus*. Toronto: Toronto University Press. ISBN 0-8020-5793-4. the *liar school of Herodotus*. Amsterdam: Gieben. ISBN 90-5063-088-X.

Selden, Daniel (1999). "Cambyses' Madness, or the Reason of History". *Materiali e discussioni per l'analisi dei testi classici* 42: 33–63.

ALEXANDER AND THE ZOROASTRIAN IRAN

Primary and historical sources

Plutarch (1936). Babbitt, Frank Cole, ed. *On the Fortune of Alexander* IV. Loeb Classical Library. pp. 379–487. Retrieved 26 November 2011.

Plutarch (1919). Perrin, Bernadotte, ed. *Plutarch, Alexander*. Perseus Project. Retrieved 6 December 2011.

Arrian (1976). de Sélincourt, Aubrey, ed. *Anabasis Alexandri (The Campaigns of Alexander)*. Penguin Books. ISBN 0-14-044253-7.

Siculus, Diodorus (1989). "Library of History". CH Oldfather, translator. Perseus Project. Retrieved 14 November 2009. -

Secondary Sources

Curtis, J; Tallis, N; Andre-Salvini, B (2005). *Forgotten empire: the world of ancient Persia*. University of California Press. p. 272. ISBN 0-520-24731-0.

Bose, Partha (2003). *Alexander the Great's Art of Strategy*. Crows Nest, NSW: Allen & Unwin. ISBN 1-74114-113-3

Bosworth, AB (1988). *Conquest and Empire: The Reign of Alexander the Great*. New York: Cambridge University Press.

Cawthorne, Nigel (2004). *Alexander the Great*. Haus. ISBN 1-904341-56-X.

Chamoux, François; Roussel, Michel (2003). *Hellenistic Civilization*. Blackwell.

INCESTUOUS MARRIAGES AND THE BOOK OF VIS AND RAMIN

Julie Scott Meisami-Medieval Persian court poetry—Princeton—1987

Vladimir Minorsky-Vis u Ramin-, - a parthian romance-Bulletin of the school of Oriental and African studies—vol 11—1943—1946-vol 12—1947—1948 pages 20—35—volume 16 –1954—page 91—92

Fakhraddin Gorgani-Vis and Ramin-translated by Dick Davis—Wash. DC.- Mage publishing feb-2008

Alexandre Gvakharia—Georgia IV—Literary contacts with Persia.

George Morrison-Julia Baldick -...History of Persian literature—Persian heritage series—Columbia university press –1972.

THE LAKHMID KINGDOM.

Rothstein, Gustav (1899) (in German), - Die Dynastie der Lakhmiden in al-Hira

Brtitannica Encyclopedia- (http://www.britannica.com/eb/article-9011793

Bosworth, Clifford Edmund, ed. (1999)- The History of Al Tabari, -Volume V: The Sasanids, the Byzantines, the Lakhmids, and Yemen

History Book of- Ibn Khaldoun

Philip De Souza and John France, - War and Peace in ancient and medieval history, - p. 139 Khuzistan Chronical 9

History book of -Ibn al-Athir

History book of-Ibn Hisham

Histoire nestorienne, -Il me Partie, - p. 536, 546

ZOROASTRIANISM TODAY—AND A SHORT LOOK AT THE EVENTS IN PERSIA FROM 1800 AD ONWARDS

John R. Hinnels-" The Zoroastrian Diaspora—Religion and Migration " 4-28-2005

Allan Williams-Manchester University—" Later Zoroastrianism " -- The Enzyclopedia of Asian Philosophy—London—1997

Edward Brown—" A year among the Persians "—1893

Jesse Palsetia—University of Guelph—In his book –" the Parsis of India " –Leiden—2001

Michael Strausberg—University of Bergen –Norway—" Zarathustra and Zoroastrianism " Equinox Publishings -2008

THE PERSIAN INTERVENTION IN YEMEN

Touraj Daryaee—2009- Sasanian Persia The Rise and Fall of and Empire—London- I.B Tauris.

Farrokh Dr. Kaveh- Shadows in Desert Ancient Persia at War- Oxford: Osprey Publishing 2007.

Richard N. Frye- The History of Ancient Iran

Richard N. Frye- The Heritage of Persian.-World Publishing Company, 1963

Richard N Frye- The Reforms of Chosroes Anushirvan (of Immortal Soul)

James Howard-Johnston-State and Society in the Late Antique Iran, the Sassanian Era, -London I.B. Tauris & CO. 2008 page 118-12 9.- Edited by- Vesta Sarkhosh Curtis

Beate and Winter Dignas, Engelbert, - Rome and Persian the Late Antiquity:- Neighbours and Rivals:- Cambridge Univerisity Press 2007.

Mischa Meir, -Justinian, Herrschaft, Reich, und Religion- Munich 2004

Averil Cameron et al- The Cambridge Ancient History- Volume 14, - Cambridge 2000.

THE GEOGRAPHIC LOCATION OF THE CITY
OF CTESIPHONE AND ITS CONSEQUENCES

J Upton, -The Expedition to Ctesiphon 1931–1932, -Bulletin of the Metropolitan Museum of Art, vol. 27, pp. 188–197, -1932

The Torah-Ezra 8:17

Kröger, Jens- (1993), - *Encyclopedia Iranica*, - 6, Costa Mesa: Mazda,

K. Schippmann, - Ktesiphon-Expedition im Winter 1928/29, -Grundzüge der parthischen Geschichte, -Darmstadt, 1980

O. Reuther, -The German Excavations at Ctesiphon, - Antiquity, vol. 3, no. 12, - pp. 434–451, 1929

E.J. Brill's- First Encyclopaedia of Islam- 1913–1936, - Vol. 2 (Brill, 1987), p. 75.

Oates, Joan-, *Babylon*, - Thames and Hudson 1996, 48

E. Meyer, - Seleukia und Ktesiphon, Mitteilungen der Deutschen Orient-Gesellschaft zu Berlin, - vol. 67, pp. 1–26, -1929

G. Gullini and A. Invernizzi, -First to Seventh Preliminary Report of Excavations at Seleucia and Ctesiphon. -Season 1966 -1977, Mesopotamia, vol. 3–4, -5-6-7- 1968–69

M. Streck, - *Die alte Landschaft Babylonien nach den Arabischen Geographen*, 2 vols.- Leiden, 1900–1901.

M. Streck, -"Seleucia und Ktesiphon, "- *Der Alte Orient*, - 16 (1917), 1–64.

A. Invernizzi, -"Ten Years Research in the al-Madain Area, Seleucia and Ctesiphon, " *Sumer*, 32, (1976), - 167–175.

Luise Abramowski, -"Der Bischof von Seleukia-Ktesiphon als Katholikos und Patriarch der Kirche des Ostens, "- in

Dmitrij Bumazhnov u. Hans R. Seeliger (hg), - *Syrien im 1.-7. Jahrhundert nach Christus.- Akten der 1. Tübinger Tagung zum Christlichen Orient (15.-16. Juni 2007)*. (Tübingen, Mohr Siebeck, 2011) (Studien und Texte zu Antike und Christentum / Studies and Texts in Antiquity and Christianity, 62

THE KHAZAR INVASION OF NORTHERN PERSIA AND THE THIRD PERSO-TURKIC WAR OF 627 AD.

Walter E. Kaegi-Heraclius, Emporer of Byzantium-University of Chicago Press.

The Sasanian Empire (224-651 AD), - Touraj Daryaee, - The Oxford Handbook of Iranian History, -Ed. Touraj Daryaee, - (Oxford University Press, 2012), 201.

Parvaneh Pourshariati, - *Decline and Fall of the Sasanian Empire*, - (I.B.Tauris, 2008), 185-186

Movsēs Daskhurants'i: -*The History of the Caucasian Albanians by Movsēs Dasxuranc'i*, tr. C. J. F. Dowsett, - London, 1961.

A.G. Perikhanian, -'Pekhlevijskie papirusy cobranija GMII imeni A.S. Pushkina', *Vestnik Drevnej Istorii*, 77, -1961, pp. 78-93.

Ps.-Sebeos: -*The Armenian History Attributed to Sebeos* I, -*Translation and Notes*, II *Historical Commentary*, tr.- R. W. Thomson and J. Howard-Johnston, with T. Greenwood, Translated Texts for Historians 31, Liverpool, 1999

Moḥammad b. Jarir Ṭabari, - *Ketāb ta'rik al-rosol wa'l-moluk*, - tr. as *The History of al-Ṭabarī*, -General ed.- Ehsan Yar-Shater, V, -*The Sāsānids, the Byzantines, the Lakmids, and Yemen*, -tr. C. E. Bosworth, - Albany, N.Y, 1999.

A. Palmer, in A. Palmer, S. P. Brock, and R. G. Hoyland, - *The Seventh Century in the West-Syrian Chronicles*, - Chronicles to 724 AD-Translated Texts for Historians 15, Liverpool, 1993.

Chronicon Paschale: -*Chronicon Paschale 284-628 AD*, -tr. Michael Whitby and Mary Whitby, Translated Texts for Historians 7, Liverpool, 1989.

Eutychius, *Annals*, -ed. and tr. M. Breydy, as- *Das Annalenwerk des Eutychios von Alexandrien: Ausgewählte Geschichten und Legenden kompiliert von Sa'īd ibn Batrīq um 935 A.D.*, CSCO 471-2, - Scriptores Arabici 44-5, Louvain, 1985.

Georgian Chronicles: -*Rewriting Caucasian History: The Medieval Armenian Adaptation of the Georgian Chronicles: The Original Georgian texts and the Armenian adaptation*, -tr. and comm. Robert W. Thomson, - Oxford, 1996.

O. Hansen, - *Die mittelpersischen Papyri der Papyrussammlung der Staatlichen Museen zu Berlin*, - Abhandlungen der Preuss. Ak. Wiss., -1937, Nr.9, Berlin, 1938.

Khuzistan Chronicle:- tr. Th. Nöldeke, - 'Die von Guidi herausgegebene syrische Chronik übersetzt und commentiert', - *Sitzungsberichte der kais. Ak. Wiss., Phil.-Hist.- Classe* 128.9, Vienna, 1893.

Seert Chronicle:- *Histoire nestorienne (Chronique de Séert)*, - *Seconde partie*, ed. and tr. A. Scher, -P.O. 13.4, Paris, - 1919.

Chisholm, Hugh, ed. (1911).- "Chosroes". *Encyclopædia Britannica* -(11th ed.). Cambridge University Press.

Edward Walford, - translator, -*The Ecclesiastical History of Evagrius: A History of the Church from AD 431 to AD 594*, -1846. Reprinted 2008.- Evolution Publishing, ISBN 978-1-889758-88-6. [1] —- a primary source containing detailed information about the early reign of Khosrau II and his relationship with the Romans.

THE CONQUEST OF JERUSALEM BY THE PERSIANS JULY-17-614 AD

The Persian conquest of Jerusalem in 614 AD compared with Islamic conquest of 638 AD -By Ben Abrahamson and Joseph Katz

G.J. Reinink et.al. -*The Reign of Heraclius: 610–641 crisis and confrontation.*- p.103. [1]

Sharkansky, Ira -(1996).- *Governing Jerusalem: Again on the world's agenda.*- Detroit: Wayne State University Press. p. 63.

A History of the Jewish People, - by Hayim Ben-Sasson (Editor), -Harvard University Press, 1985

Eutychius, ii. 241

Elijah of Nisibis.- *Beweis der Wahrheit des Glaubens*, - translation by Horst, p.108, Colmar, 1886

Antiochus Strategos, - *The Capture of Jerusalem by the Persians in 614 AD*, - F. C. Conybeare, English Historical Review 25 (1910) pp. 502–517.

The Coptic Encyclopedia, Volume 3, (AD:1093a-1097a).- Published in print by Macmillan, reproduced with permission at http://ccdl.libraries.claremont.edu/col/cce.

Pertz, -"Monumenta Germaniae Historica, " i. 286, vi. 25; -compare Joseph ha-Kohen, -"'Emek ha-Baka, " tr. Wiener, p. 5

Sackur, "Sibyllinische Texte, "- p. 146, Halle, 1898, - seems to refer to these occurrences, since about one hundred and twenty years elapsed from the time of the Persian war under Anastasius, in 505, to the victory of Heraclius in 628. It has been suggested that several Jewish apocalypses refers to this expedition of Heraclius against the Jews.

David Lewis. -*God's Crucible: Islam and the Making of Europe*, 570–1215, - publisher Norton, 2008: p69

Katz, Shmuel l. *Battleground- (1974)*, p. 97.-" The Persian conquest of Jerusalem in 614 compared with Islamic conquest of 638 "

THE COUNCIL OF NICAEA 325 AD AND
ARIANISM AS CHRISTIAN HERETICS

Casey, R. P.- 1935. An Early Homily Ascribed to Athanasius of Alexandria. JTS 36: 1–10.

Bibliography Bardy, G. -1930. Fragments attribués à Arius. RHE 26: 253–68.

. 1936. Recherches sur Saint Lucien d'Antioch et son école. Études de théologie historique. Paris.

Gregg, R. C., ed. 1985. Arianism. Historical and Theological Reassessments. Papers from the Ninth International Conference on Patristic Studies September 5–10, 1983, Oxford, England.

Gregg, R. C., and Groh, D. E. 1977. The Centrality of Soteriology in Early Arianism. ATR 59: 260–78.

Groh, D. E. 1986. Review Article: New Directions in Arian Research. ATR 68: 347–55.

Barnes, T. D. 1981. Constantine and Eusebius. Cambridge, MA.

Boulerand, E. 1964. -Les debuts d'Arius. BLE 65: 175–203.

Kannengiesser, C. -1982a. Athanasius of Alexandria Three Orations against the Arians: A Reappraisal.

Holy Scripture and Hellenistic Hermeneutics in Alexandrian Christology: The Arian Crisis. Protocol of the

Colloquy of the Center for Hermeneutical Studies in Hellenistic and Modern Culture 41. Berkeley.

Kelly, J. N. D. 1972. Early Christian Creeds. 3d ed. New York.

Kopecek, T. A. 1979. A History of Neo-Arianism. 2 vols. Patristic Monograph Series 8. Philadelphia.

Lorenz, R. 1979. Arius judaizans? Untersuchungen zur dogmengeschichtlichen Einordnung des Arius. Forschungen zur Kirchen—und Dogmengeschichte 31. Göttingen.

Ricken, F. -1969. Nikaia als Krisis des altchristlichen Platonismus. TP 44: 321–41.

Norderval, Ø. 1985.- Arius Redivivus? Tendenser innenfor Arius-
forskningen. NorTT 86: 79–90.

Opitz, H.-G. 1935a. Athanasius: Werke. Vol. 2. Berlin. - Vol. 3,
Urkunden zur Geschichte des arianischen Streites 318–328.
Berlin.

Schneemelcher, W.- 1954. Zur Chronologie des arianischen Streits.
TZ 79: 394–99.

Stead, G. C. -1976. Rhetorical Method in Athanasius. VC 30: 121–37.
- 1978. The Thalia of Arius and the Testimony of Athanasius.
JTS 39: 20–52.

Tetz, M. 1952–53. Eine arianische Homilie unter dem Namen des
Athanasius von Alexandrien. ZKG 64: 299–307.

Williams, R. 1987. -Arius, Heresy and Tradition. London.

THE EMERGENCE OF THE SASSANIANS DYNASTY—AND SOME PRE-ISLAMIC ZOROASTRIAN PRIEST-KARTIR AND OTHERS.

Boyce, Mary (1975). -"On the Zoroastrian Temple Cult of Fire".
-*Journal of the American Oriental Society* -(Ann Arbor: AOS/
UMich. Press) 95 (3): 454–465. doi:10.2307/599356. JSTOR
599356.

Boyce, Mary (1975). -"Iconoclasm among Zoroastrians". -*Studies for
Morton Smith at sixty*. Leiden: Neusner. pp. 93–111..

Boyce, Mary (1957).- "Some reflections on Zurvanism".- *Bulletin
of the School of Oriental and African Studies* (London: SOAS)
19/2: 304–316

Huyse, Philip- (1998). -"Kerdir and the first Sasanians". -In Nicholas
Sims-Williams (ed.). *Proceedings of the Third European
Conference of Iranian Studies* 1.- Wiesbaden. pp. 109–120.

Sprengling, Martin -(1940).- "Kartir. Founder of Sassanian Zoroastrianism". -*American Journal of Semitic Languages and Literature* 57- (57): 197–228. doi:10.1086/370575.

Gignoux, Philippe- (1991). *Les quatre inscriptions du mage Kird⬚r.-* Leuven: Peeter

ZOROASTRIANISM AND ITS RELATIONSHIP TO SOME IMPORTANT PHILOSOPHICAL CATEGORIES OF MODERN TIMES—EXISTENTIALISM

Marino, Gordon –Basic writings of Existentialism.-modern library-200

Jean Paul Sartre-Existentialism is a Humanism-1946

William Mc Donald -Soren Kierkegaard—

Edward N. Zalta-Stanford Enzyclopedia of Philosophy-Summer 2009—Edition.

Walter Lowrie-Kierkegaards attack upon Christendom-Princeton 1969-pages 37—40

John Macquarrie -Existentialism-New York –1972

The Oxford companion to Philosophy-ed. Ted Honderich—Nwy York—1995—pages-259

Rudiger Safranski-Martin Heidegger, between Good and Evil-Harvard University Press

William J. Richardson—Marin Heidegger, from Phenomenology to thought-1967.

Ernst Breisbach-Introduction to modern existentialism—New York –1962—page—173.

Jean Paul Sartre—Being and Nothingness—Routledge Classics-2003

Karl Jaspers-Philosophical Authobiography-Tudor Publishing co.1957—page—75

Simone de Beauvoir-Force of Circumstance—University of Chicago Press-2004-page 48

THE START OF THE ARAB-PERSIAN HOSTILITIES— SEPAHBOD HORMOZAN—THE CALIPH UMAR AND THE FALL OF THE SASSANIAN EMPIRE.

Parvaneh Pourshariati -" The decline and fall of the Sassanian Empire " I.B. Tauris

Arthur Christianson—"-L Iran sous les sassanides "- Copenhagen 1937 -Teheran 1938

William Muir-" The caliphate its rise, decline and fall, from original sources " Kessinger Publ.

Wilfred Madelung- "The succession to Mohammad- " Cambridge University press-1998

THEISM VERSUS ATHEISM...

Michael Martin-the Cambridge companion of Atheism-Cambridge University Press

Michael Martin-Atheism, -a philosophical justification—1990—

David Hume-1779- -Dialogues concerning natural religion—London.

Richard Dawkins—2006—The God Delusion—Bantam Press

Paul Edwards-Atheism-In Donald M.Borchert—The Enzyclopedia of Philosophy-Mcmillan Publ

Bertrand Russel-1957-Why I am not a Christian, and other essays on religion—Simon -Schuster.

Jean Paul Sartre—1946-Existentialism and Humanism-included in Stephen Priest book by the name of —Jean Paul Sartre, Basic Writings-London –Routledge

HISTORICAL AND DIALECTICAL MATERIALISM, AND THE DIALECTICAL NATURE OF THE ZOROASTRIAN WORLDVIEW

Gustav A. Wetter, Dialectical Materialism: a Historical and Systematic Survey of Philosophy in the Soviet Union. (alternative survey)

Gerald Cohen, Karl Marx's Theory of History: A Defence. (influential analytical Marxist interpretation)

Aronowitz, Stanley, The Crisis in Historical Materialism, -1981

Marx, Karl, Theses on Feuerbach, 1845

Marx, Karl, Economic and Philosophic Manuscripts of 1844, -1844; Published -1932

Marx, Karl, The German Ideology, 1846; 1932

Marx, Karl, Preface to A Contribution to the Critique of Political Economy, 1859

Marx, Karl, Manifesto of the Communist Party, 1848

Marx, Karl, The Grundrisse, (foundations for the study of Capital), 1857

K. Marx, *A Contribution to the Critique of Political Economy*, Progress Publishers, Moscow, 1977, with some notes by R. Rojas.

Karl Marx and Frederick Engels, *Selected Works in One Volume* (London: Lawrence and Wishart, 1968), p. 660.

Marx, Karl, Capital, Vol. 1, 1867- Vols. 2 & 3, 1867 - 1883, (unfinished)

Karl Marx & Martin Nicolaus, Grundrisse: Foundations of the Critique of Political Economy Penguin Classics, 1993, ISBN 0-14-044575-7, pg 265

Frederick Engels. "Socialism: Utopian and Scientific (Introduction - Materialism)". Marxists.org. Retrieved 2011-12-07.

Frederick Engels. "Ludwig Feuerbach and the End of Classical German Philosophy —

Joseph Stalin, Historical and Dialectical Materialism. (classic statement of Stalinist doctrine, emphasizes understanding the roots of class society and the state)

Mao Zedong, (Mao Tse Tung) Four Essays on Philosophy.

Louis B. Boudin, *The Theoretical System of Karl Marx*. Chicago: Charles H. Kerr Publishing Co., 1907, contains an early defense of the materialist conception of history.

Ernest Mandel, *The Place of Marxism in History* (modelled on Lenin's "Three components of Marxism"

"The Part Played by Labor in the Transition From Ape to Man". Marxists.org.

H. B. Acton, The Illusion of the Epoch. (critical account which focusses on incoherencies in the thought of Marx, Engels and Lenin)

Paul Blackledge, Reflections on the Marxist Theory of History (2006)

Franz Jakubowski, - *Ideology and Superstructure*- attempts to provide an alternative to schematic interpretations of historical materialism.

Foster, John Bellamy; Clark, Brett. *Critique of Intelligent Design: Materialism versus Creationism from Antiquity to the Present.* Monthly Review Press. ISBN 978-1583671733. -Helmut Fleischer, Marxism and History. (good reply to false interpretations of Marx's view of history)

Anthony Giddens, A Contemporary Critique of Historical Materialism, 1981

Chris Harman, A People's History of the World (Marxist view of history according to a leader of the International Socialist Tendency)

Z.A. Jordan, The Origins of Dialectical Materialism (good survey)

.Alexander Spirkin; Sergei Syrovatkin (translator) (1990), *Fundamentals of Philosophy.*, Moscow: Progress Publishers, ISBN 5-01-002582-5,

S.H. Rigby, Marxism and History, 1977

G.A. Cohen (1978, 2000), *Karl Marx's Theory of History: A Defence*, Princeton +Oxford.

Ernest Mandel. *The Place of Marxism in History*